MONEY: IN EQUILIBRIUM

The Cambridge Economic Handbooks

General Editors

J. M. Keynes (Lord Keynes)	1922–1936
D. H. Robertson (Sir Dennis Robertson)	1936–1946
C. W. Guillebaud	1946–1956
C. W. Guillebaud Milton Friedman	1956–1966
C. W. Guillebaud	1966–1971
F. H. Hahn	

Money: in equilibrium

Douglas Gale, Reader in Economics in the University of London at the London School of Economics

The right of the University of Cambridge to print and sell all manner of books was granted by Henry VIII in 1534. The University has printed and published continuously since 1584.

Cambridge University Press

Cambridge
New York New Rochelle
Melbourne Sydney

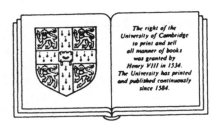

CAMBRIDGE UNIVERSITY PRESS
Cambridge, New York, Melbourne, Madrid, Cape Town, Singapore,
São Paulo, Delhi, Dubai, Tokyo, Mexico City

Cambridge University Press
The Edinburgh Building, Cambridge CB2 8RU, UK

Published in the United States of America by
Cambridge University Press, New York

www.cambridge.org
Information on this title: www.cambridge.org/9780521289009

First published 1982
Reprinted 1986, 1988

A catalogue record for this publication is available from the British Library

Library of Congress Cataloguing in Publication Data

ISBN 978-0-521-24694-6 Hardback
ISBN 978-0-521-28900-9 Paperback

Acknowledgements

My greatest debt is to Frank Hahn. As teacher, friend and editor, he showed me how to write this book. He violently disapproves of the crypto-monetarism he detects in these pages but not, I hope, of the intellectual spirit in which they were written.

I would also like to thank David Webb, for reading the manuscript and many hours of enjoyable conversation about money, and Gilbert McLean, for being such a patient and helpful publisher. Richard Jackman and Chris Pissarides looked at Chapter 4 and made useful comments. Anne de Sayrah and Sue Kirkbride completed the heroic task of typing the manuscript cheerfully and efficiently. They have both earned undying gratitude.

Finally, my wife Susie has been a sympathetic listener and a constant source of practical advice as well as keeping my spirits up while I struggled to finish the manuscript.

To my parents

CONTENTS

Introduction

This book is one of a series of *handbooks* on aspects of economic theory. The use of the term handbook suggests a degree of comprehensiveness and accessibility which the present volume lacks. No attempt has been made to include every recent development in monetary theory and some parts of the book are considerably more difficult than others. Nonetheless the label "handbook" is not entirely undeserved. In the following pages I have selected for investigation what seemed to me to be the central ideas in the development of contemporary monetary theory. The result is a more or less self-contained primer on these ideas. It is presented in the hope that the reader who perseveres will be adequately equipped, technically and conceptually, for anything he encounters in the wider literature which has escaped these pages. In that sense this is a handbook.

The book falls naturally into two parts. The first, which is technically the easier, deals with questions which will be recognized as falling within the traditional field of (macroeconomic) monetary theory, though the treatment is unflaggingly microeconomic. The second is less conventional, dealing with the general equilibrium theory of money in a rather fundamental way. The chapters too are divided in half. As far as possible, issues requiring highly technical or formal arguments are discussed in the second half but the second half is neither a technical appendix to nor a repetition in formal language of the first half. The segregation is designed to allow readers with little formal preparation to read what they can more easily. But those who can cope with formal arguments are encouraged to read everything for there are undoubtedly some ideas that cannot be understood without the use of some formal apparatus or other.

Contents

The neutrality of money is a constant theme in the monetary theory of the last three decades. From the Patinkin controversy in the 1950s to the advent of the rational expectations hypothesis in the 1970s, it has scarcely left the stage. In Chapter 1 I have tried to chart the development of this idea and provide an historical perspective from which to view the state of monetary theory at the start of the nineteen-eighties.

Perhaps the most interesting idea to arise from the debate on the neutrality of money was the hypothesis that the Phillips curve might be the result of a "noisy" monetary policy. In a seminal paper, R. Lucas showed that even when there is no useable trade-off between inflation and unemployment a random monetary policy may give rise to an apparent trade-off because agents confuse changes in absolute prices with changes in relative prices. The ideas in this paper are not easy to grasp and some are rather contentious. Chapter 2 continues the discussion of rational expectations begun in Chapter 1 by examining in greater detail the definition of a rational expectations equilibrium, the phenomenon of information revealed by prices and the question of the efficiency of such equilibria.

Another theme which surfaces from time to time in the literature of the 'sixties and 'seventies is the prejudice against discretionary monetary policy. One argument against discretionary policy is quite explicit in Lucas's critique of econometric policy evaluation. What a government is expected to do will have an impact on the economy just as much as what it actually does. Unless a government follows a systematic policy, which Lucas interprets to mean a policy rule, the private sector's expectations, and hence the impact of the government's policy, are likely to be unpredictable. So far so good, but some economists have argued that any optimal policy ought to be expressible as a rule of some sort and in the models which have been studied this appears to be the case. What, then, is a discretionary policy? I think there is a meaningful distinction to be drawn between a discretionary policy and one based on rules. A discretionary policy is by definition open-ended: it can evolve in ways that a rule, however complicated, cannot. This raises two problems which are explored in Chapter 3. The first is how to make credible commitments when future policy is not yet determined; the second is how to stabilize expectations when policy can evolve in perhaps unpredictable ways.

One of the weaknesses of neo-monetarist theory is that, while accepting the importance of combating inflation and hence of controlling the money supply, it does not provide a convincing account of the costs of inflation. The optimal quantity of money argument, which reduces inflation to a distortion in the cost of holding money, trivializes the problem. There may be many answers to the question why inflation is a bad thing but it seems difficult to provide any in the context of a model which makes the usual assumptions of market-clearing prices, rational expectations and so on. In Chapter 4 I look at the problem of capital market imperfections trying to rationalize *under standard assumptions* the idea that high nominal interest rates may lead to liquidity problems.

The last three chapters of the book constitute an attempt to provide a foundation for a particular theory of monetary equilibrium. Studies of the microfoundations of monetary theory usually concern themselves with the role of money in exchange, transaction costs, information and so forth. The corresponding work in general equilibrium has been largely concerned with a single question: why does money have a positive value? But this is simply part of a larger question, which ought to be answered first, namely, why is there monetary equilibrium at all? Instead of taking for granted a theory of equilibrium in which money and other commodities have market-clearing prices and then asking why the price of money is positive, one really ought to provide a rationale for a particular notion of equilibrium *and* the positive price of money in one fell swoop. Without a sequence of budget constraints there is no point in holding money or any other financial asset. The notion of a sequence of budget constraints is the crucial concept in the study of the efficiency properties of monetary equilibria, as shown in Chapter 5, and also holds the key to the problem of providing a rationale for our concept of monetary equilibrium, which is investigated in Chapters 6 and 7.

Omissions

As was pointed out above, this book makes no pretence to being comprehensive. There are several reasons for not attempting an encyclopaedic treatment. In the first place, monetary economics has developed rather unevenly. Some branches stand comparison, in terms of their rigour and sophistication, with the most advanced parts of economic theory. Others are still struggling to escape from old-fashioned, macroeconomic habits of thought. Furthermore, monetary economics lacks a single "paradigm" which is adequate to describe the disparate phenomena that involve money in an interesting and essential way. Different models and different analytical methods are used to study a wide variety of theoretical problems; but they all have a claim to be included in the corpus of monetary theory. To have written a comprehensive account of this sprawling literature would at best have produced an indigestible *potpourri*. The greater danger, however, was that the attempt to cross too many boundaries would have precluded investigating any one area at the depth required to encourage real understanding. Instead, I have chosen to restrict the scope of the enterprise in the belief that by studying central problems and ideas it is possible to provide an adequate foundation for further reading and research.

As the title suggests, the book deals mainly with what can be described, for lack of a better expression, as the general-equilibrium approach to monetary theory. What I want to denote by this phrase is that part of monetary theory which is characterized by a neo-Walrasian view of the economy and especially that part which uses the assumptions of market-clearing prices and rational expectations. It is important to state at the outset that I am not interested in justifying these assumptions as descriptions of the world. There are many reasons, apart from "realism", for finding this theory interesting and helpful. As ideal economies, general-equilibrium models provide a benchmark against which the performance of actual economies may be judged. Because the general-equilibrium theory is more highly developed than other approaches, it is possible to pose questions in this context which could not be precisely formulated in any other. That general-equilibrium theory has provided substantial insights in economics cannot be doubted. What may be doubted is whether the best strategy is to continue milking general-equilibrium for every last insight or whether it might not be better to strike out in a new direction. But the experience of the last ten years and in particular the explosion of interest in models of rational expectations suggest that general-equilibrium has much to offer.

There is, of course, a view of economic theory which holds that in order for a theory to have any relevance it is necessary for it to be "realistic". I have never understood this argument and it does not appear to be the case that self-consciously "realistic" models add more to our understanding of the world than the admittedly artificial constructions of general-equilibrium theory. Having said that, it must be admitted that the concentration on general-equilibrium theory excludes a number of important problems for which general-equilibrium analysis in this sense is not a suitable tool. In mitigation, I can promise that a volume on *Money: in Disequilibrium* will appear eventually. A number of the omissions are sufficiently important to merit an immediate explanation, however.

First there is the virtual absence of any reference to "Keynesian" problems. For many people, Keynes and money are inseparable in the sense that one cannot be understood without the other. Also, there has been a great deal of work on disequilibrium theory in the past ten years and much of this work has a Keynesian flavour. It might well be thought essential to include this material in a book on money. I admit that a serious discussion of, say, the "right" monetary policy to follow at this juncture, would be pretty meaningless without a reference to Keynesian economics. And some people will certainly jump to the conclusion that any discussion of monetary matters is meaningless without reference to Keynes. The error lies not only in failing to take account of the manifold functions of economic theory, some of which have nothing to do with economic policy, but also in the extremely primitive, implicit view of how theory works. A good theory is one that helps us think about the world. It need not (and probably will not) be a true "picture" of the world. Keynesian theory has a certain claim to realism but it is often muddled, *ad hoc* and partial. As long as this is the case, sensible theorists will have recourse to "unrealistic" general-equilibrium models about which they can think clearly. The task of transposing their insights into the policy arena is fraught with difficulties but it is worth doing and is certainly better than beginning and ending in muddle.

A second notable absence is that of firms. This reflects nothing more sinister than the lack of a convenient theory of the firm in economies with incomplete markets. When markets are not complete there is no agreement about what firms should do. More precisely, different shareholders will want the firm to choose different production plans. This conflict of objectives resolves itself into a rather messy game-theoretic problem to which there are no obvious solutions. Grossman and Hart have developed an elaborate "competitive" theory for a sequence economy. To have incorporated this theory of the firm would have made the analysis contained in Chapters 5, 6 and 7 much more complicated without corresponding increases in understanding. This would be the result partly of notational over-kill and partly of the need to deal with two types of assets. But the main difficulty would arise from trying to deal with the complexities of the shareholders' decision-making problem and develop a theory of how agents arrive at equilibrium trades. The material in Chapter 7 deals with the game-theoretic foundations of the theory of monetary equilibrium. Tackling two different game theory problems at the same time is just too difficult so in the end I stuck to pure exchange.

The final omission that must be explained is the almost total neglect of banks and banking. This is partly explained by the fact that many of the functions of the banking world do not make sense in general equilibrium models of the sort studied in this book. For example, borrowing and lending scarcely requires intermediation in a world in which markets are perfect, expectations are rational, and uncertainty is represented by states of nature. But by excluding the banking sector general equilibrium models are somewhat impoverished. The money supply must be represented by a stock of fiat money. Monetary policy must be represented, if at all, by exogenous changes in this stock. The role of money in the credit markets becomes fairly trivial: it is simply a form of wealth like any other durable good. This is not to say that the questions which can be asked and answered in a non-banking model are less interesting or important than those which might be posed if banks were included in the model. On the contrary, one of the objectives of this book is to show that a number of fundamental questions can be discussed in a conceptually very simple model. Nonetheless, a number of important issues have been left out and I have come lately to the view that some of these issues, which involve banks in an essential way, might usefully be analysed using general equilibrium techniques. One such is the question of how the money supply is controlled. The neo-monetarist literature which relies heavily on helicopters to alter the money supply, implicitly assumes that the means of controlling the money supply do not matter. Clearly such an assumption ought to be investigated but, for better or worse, it has not been in the pages that follow. Some of the issues discussed in Chapter 4 give a hint of the importance of taking seriously the role of financial institutions in a monetary economy. The development of a proper theory of banking seems to me to be one of the top priorities for future research in monetary economics.

CHAPTER 1

The neutrality of money

After the war monetary policy was rather discredited as a means of controlling the economy. The intellectual impetus behind this change of attitude came from Keynes's *The General Theory of Employment, Interest and Money*, published a decade earlier. The slogan of the vulgar-Keynesians, that "money doesn't matter", had various, more sophisticated analogues. These took precise shape in arguments about the existence of a liquidity-trap but the general suspicion of monetary policy may have arisen equally from doubts about the stability of the demand-for-money function, a doubt which seems closer to Keynes's own position than Modigliani's famous formulation.[1] In any case, interest in monetary theory declined.

The resurgence of inflation in the early 'fifties was followed by increased interest in monetary policy as a tool for controlling it. Milton Friedman in particular argued strongly in favour of giving the quantity of money an important role in any explanation of inflationary processes.[2] But the main theoretical activity of the 'fifties centred around a remarkable project which had little direct relevance to the practical problems facing policy-makers. The publication of Patinkin's *Money, Interest and Prices* was the culmination of several years' research and controversy by a number of authors. It represented an attempt to integrate monetary theory and value theory but it can also be understood as an attempt to clarify the Keynesian critique of classical monetary theory and, by so doing, to evaluate Keynes's own contribution.

In retrospect, it seems clear that Patinkin's world was not Keynes's world.[3] Patinkin's criticism of classical monetary theory focussed on what he called "the classical dichotomy". The dichotomy consisted of the belief that demands and supplies depended only on relative prices, so that an equiproportional change in all money prices would leave demands and supplies unchanged, and that the role of the quantity of money and velocity of circulation was restricted to the determination of the general price level.[4]

Implicit in the first part of the dichotomy is the assumption that real money balances do not influence the demand for and supply of other commodities. The assumption is unacceptable because the quantity theory implicit in the second part of the dichotomy relies on the real balance effect of an increase in the quantity of money to explain the resulting change in the price level.[5] Patinkin's resolution of this problem consisted of making demands and supplies depend on *real* balances as well as relative prices.[6] In his model there could be a real balance effect whose function was to explain the adjustment of the price level in response to changes in the quantity of money but an equiproportional change in all prices and the quantity of money would leave real magnitudes unchanged. Much of Patinkin's analysis is aimed at discovering the conditions under which an equiproportional change in prices and money balances would have no effect on real magnitudes. Patinkin seemed to feel that this *homogeneity property* defines the boundary between the classical and "Keynesian" cases. Whatever the relevance of this analysis to the Keynesian theory—and many would now question it—the analysis of the homogeneity property (or the *neutrality of money* as it is also called) is nonetheless important because of the continuing strength of monetarist attitudes in theoretical debates. For this reason alone it is worth outlining the main conclusions of the Patinkin controversy.

Let us begin with what every undergraduate knows. A consumer faces a vector of prices p and must decide how to spend his money income w on goods so as to maximize his utility. His *budget set*, the set of all possible consumption bundles he could purchase at prices p with income w, is denoted by $\beta(p, w)$ and it is defined by putting

$$\beta(p, w) := \{x \geq 0 \mid p.x \leq w\}^7$$

for each ordered pair (p, w). The familiar homogeneity property of the consumer's demand function can be expressed as follows: if p and w change in the same proportion, from (p, w) to $(\lambda p, \lambda w)$, say, where $\lambda > 0$, then the budget set is unchanged and since preferences are independent of prices and income, demand will also be unchanged. But although prices and income are expressed in terms of money, money itself has not yet made an appearance. The homogeneity property described above really applies to a situation in which the consumer has an endowment e of goods, so that his income $w = p.e$ automatically increases by a factor of λ when all prices do so. In that case the budget set can be written as $\beta(p) \equiv \beta(p, p.e)$ and the "neutrality" of money is reduced to the obvious fact that only relative prices matter. "Money" is reduced to being a fictional unit of account.

To give money a more substantial role, suppose the consumer has a debt (or credit) denominated in terms of money, that is, he has promised to deliver a certain number of units of money (or someone else has promised to deliver a certain number of units to him). Let d denote the number of units to be delivered (negative if he is to receive money). Then the consumer's wealth is $w = p.e - d$ and his budget set is $\beta(p, p.e - d)$. The homogeneity property breaks down here, for though an equiproportionate change in p and d will leave the budget set unchanged, the pre-existing commitments to deliver money are fixed, i.e. d does not change, so an increase in the price level alone will have a real effect, reducing the real income of creditors and raising that of debtors. Because a change in the price level increases the real income of some consumers at the expense of others the result is known as a *distribution effect*. If there are pre-existing commitments to deliver money a general change in prices will inevitably change the welfare of individual consumers. It may be, however, that the distribution effects cancel out, so that relative prices remain unchanged in equilibrium.

Suppose, for example, that there are m *consumers* indexed by $i = 1, \ldots, m$ and each consumer has an endowment $e_i \in \mathbb{R}^l_+$ of consumption goods.[8] Under certain assumptions about the consumers' preferences it is possible to represent the behaviour of each consumer by a *demand function* $f_i(p, w_i)$ where p denotes the ruling price system and w_i is the i-th consumer's wealth.[9] The i-th consumer is assumed to have a commitment to deliver d_i units of money (where by convention a negative value indicates that he is a creditor). Then his income w_i is equal to $(p.e_i - d_i)$ when the price system p obtains. An *equilibrium price system* is one at which demand equals supply, that is

$$\sum_{i=1}^{m} f_i(p, p.e_i - d_i) = \sum_{i=1}^{m} e_i .$$

By the usual argument f_i is homogeneous of degree zero in prices and income, i.e. $f_i(p, w_i) = f_i(\lambda p, \lambda w_i)$ for any $\lambda > 0$, but this does not imply that $f_i(p, p.e_i - d_i)$ is homogeneous of degree zero in prices. Under two special conditions it can be shown that the aggregate demand function $f \equiv \sum_{i=1}^{m} f_i$ is homogeneous of degree zero in prices. First, it must be assumed that every debt is balanced by a credit and *vice versa*, that is, $\sum_{i=1}^{m} d_i = 0$. Second, it must be assumed that demand functions have the special form

$$f_i(p, w_i) \equiv w_i f_i(p, 1) \equiv w_i \phi(p, 1) .$$

In other words, all consumers have identical, linear Engel curves which pass through the origin.[10] If these two conditions are satisfied, then the aggregate demand function can be re-written

$$\sum_{i=1}^{m} f_i(p, p.e_i - d_i) = \sum_{i=1}^{m} (p.e_i - d_i) f_i(p, 1)$$

$$= \phi(p, 1) \sum_{i=1}^{m} (p.e_i - d_i)$$

$$= \phi(p, 1) \sum_{i=1}^{m} p.e_i$$

$$= \phi\left(p, \sum_i p.e_i\right),$$

which is homogeneous of degree zero in prices because the common demand function $\phi(p, w)$ is homogeneous of degree zero in prices and income. It follows immediately that if the two conditions are satisfied and p is an equilibrium price system then so is λp for any $\lambda > 0$. Now in this example money has a role to play since debts must be discharged by delivering money; but since there is no final demand for money its function remains largely notional. Another way of expressing this is by saying that all the money is *inside money*. Inside money consists of debt instruments issued by individuals to individuals and, in equilibrium, the net value of inside money is zero. There is no way for the government to influence this process without issuing its own debt instrument, which would be *outside money* since it comes from outside the private sector and therefore is not balanced by a corresponding debit in the private sector's accounts.[11] In short, inside money is neutral if the assumption of linear Engel curves holds. On the one hand, the market-clearing prices are independent of the distribution of inside money among consumers, i.e. the market clearing condition $\phi(p, \sum_i p.e_i) = \sum_i e_i$ does not involve d_i ($i = 1, \ldots, m$). On the other hand, the equilibrium condition is homogeneous of degree zero in prices. For precisely this reason the price level is indeterminate and, in particular, there is no sense in which the supply of money can be used to control the general level of prices, neutrally or otherwise. The introduction of outside money remedies this defect. Suppose that each consumer has an endowment of fiat money, say, pound notes, and denote the quantity of money held by the i-th consumer by $\bar{m}_i > 0$. His demand function will now be denoted by $\hat{f}_i = (f_i^0, f_i)$ where $f_i^0(p, w_i)$ is his demand for money at prices p and income w_i. An equilibrium price system is a vector p such that

$$\sum_{i=1}^{m} \hat{f}_i(p, w_i) = \sum_{i=1}^{m} (\bar{m}_i, e_i)$$

where the i-th consumer's wealth $w_i = p.e_i - d_i + \bar{m}_i$. It is assumed as before that $\sum_i d_i = 0$ and $\hat{f}_i(p, w_i) \equiv w_i \hat{f}_i(p, 1) \equiv w_i \hat{\phi}(p, 1)$, from which it easily follows that

$$\sum_{i=1}^{m} \hat{f}_i(p, w_i) = \hat{\phi}\left(p, \sum_{i=1}^{m} w_i\right)$$

so the equilibrium condition becomes

$$\hat{\phi}\left(p, \sum_{i=1}^{m} p.e_i + \bar{m}_i\right) = \sum_{i=1}^{m} (\bar{m}_i, e_i).$$

In a slightly simpler notation, putting $e = \sum_i e_i$ and $\bar{m} = \sum_i \bar{m}_i$ the market clearing condition is $\hat{\phi}(p, p.e + \bar{m}) = (\bar{m}, e)$. This equation cannot be homogeneous of degree zero in p alone unless $\bar{m} = 0$ and cannot be homogeneous of degree zero in $(p, \bar{m})$ since $\bar{m}$ appears on the right-hand side. Now ϕ^0 is homogeneous of degree one in (p, w) and ϕ is homogeneous of degree zero in (p, w). Then if $(p, \bar{m})$ satisfies the equilibrium condition so does $(\lambda p, \lambda \bar{m})$ for any $\lambda > 0$. Money is neutral in the sense that a change in the total stock of outside money need not change relative prices. On the other hand, for a fixed stock of outside money $\bar{m}$ the general price level is determinate since the equation $\hat{\phi}(p, p.e + \bar{m}) = (\bar{m}, e)$ is not homogeneous in p alone. This is Patinkin's resolution of the "paradox" involved in the classical dichotomy. By adding a demand for nominal balances ϕ^0 he makes the price level determinate through the action of the real balance effect.[12] By making the demand for outside money homogeneous in prices and income he preserves the classical homogeneity property: an increase in the quantity of money $(\bar{m})$ and an equiproportionate change in all prices (p) will preserve equilibrium.[13]

Two questions arise. First, whence comes the demand for money balances and why should it be homogeneous of degree one in prices and incomes? Second, how does the monetary authority engineer a change in the money supply? To answer the first question, suppose that money is an asset which is held as a means of transferring wealth from one time-period to the next. To make the point as simply as possible, suppose that a consumer lives two periods and has an endowment $e > 0$ of goods in the first period but nothing in the second. Then in order to have any expenditure in the second period of his life a consumer must hold some money at the end of the first. The consumer's utility is denoted by $u(x_1, x_2)$, where $x_1 \geq 0$ is the first period consumption and $x_2 \geq 0$ is second period consumption. Suppose that q is a vector of prices in the second period and m is the quantity of money held at the end of the first. If first period consumption is denoted by x then let $v(x, m, q)$ denote the maximum utility that can be achieved over two periods when first period consumption is x, second period prices are q and the consumer has m units of money to spend in the second period. Then[14]

$$v(x, m, q) = \sup_{\substack{x' \geqslant 0 \\ q \cdot x' \leqslant m}} u(x, x').$$

The consumer does not know the exact value of q in the first period; he does have some probabilistic notion, however, and his expectations may depend on the current price system p. For any pair (x, m) and price vector p let

$$v^*(x, m, p) = E[v(x, m, \hat{q}) | p]$$

denote the expected utility derived from (x, m) when p is observed.[15] Here v^* can be interpreted as an indirect utility function in which consumption and money balances both appear. Prices also appear because it is real balances which yield utility and the real value of m is conditioned on p. In order for the demand function $\hat{\phi}$ to have the properties ascribed to it above, namely for ϕ to be homogeneous of degree zero in prices and income and ϕ^0 to be homogeneous of degree one, it is clearly sufficient for v^* to be homogeneous of degree zero in m and p. To see this, note that since individuals have identical linear Engel curves there is essentially one individual with no debts and an endowment $e = \sum_i e_i$ of goods and $\bar{m} = \sum_i \bar{m}_i$ of money. Suppose that at prices p this representative individual chooses (x, m) as the ordered pair which maximizes the value of v^* subject to the wealth constraint $p \cdot x + m \leq w$. Obviously $(x, \lambda m)$ is feasible at prices λp and income λw for any $\lambda > 0$ and, to see that it is optimal, note that if (x', m') satisfies the same constraint and $v^*(x', m', \lambda p) > v^*(x, \lambda m, \lambda p)$ then $(x', m'/\lambda)$ satisfies the budget constraint at (p, w) and $v^*(x', m'/\lambda, p) > v^*(x, m, p)$ by the homogeneity of v^*, a contradiction.[16]

The question now is, under what conditions will v^* be homogeneous of degree zero in (m, p)? A sufficient condition is that the relationship between p and the distribution of $\hat{q}$ should be homogeneous in an appropriate sense. Recall that, by definition

$$v^*(x, m, p) = E[v(x, m, \hat{q}) \mid p]$$

Suppose that $E[v(x, m, \hat{q}) \mid \lambda p] = E[v(x, m, \lambda\hat{q} \mid p]$ for any $\lambda > 0$ and each (x, m). Then it follows easily that

$$\begin{aligned} v^*(x, \lambda m, \lambda p) &= E[v(x, \lambda m, \hat{q}) \mid \lambda p] \\ &= E[v(x, \lambda m, \lambda\hat{q}) \mid p] \\ &= E[v(x, m, \hat{q}) \mid p] = v^*(x, m, p) \end{aligned}$$

since v is homogeneous of degree zero. If the consumer has a point expectation, that is, if he believes with certainty that $\hat{q} = q(p)$, then this condition is equivalent to saying that expectations are *unit elastic*, i.e. $q(\lambda p) = \lambda q(p)$.[17] It is implicit in the argument given above that all consumers have the same expectations, which is not much more restrictive than the assumption already made that consumers have identical preferences.

The list of assumptions made so far is quite restrictive:

(a) consumers have identical, linear Engel curves which pass through the origin;
(b) consumers have identical, "homogeneous" expectations;
(c) outside money is the only net financial asset of the private sector ($\sum_i d_i = 0$);
(d) and, of course, prices are completely flexible.[18]

Even so, the neutrality of money which can be obtained under these conditions is of a peculiar kind. If the price system p and the money holdings $\bar{m}_i$ of each consumer are multiplied by the same positive scalar λ then the equilibrium conditions are preserved. But what sort of monetary policy will lead to an increase of the same proportion in each consumer's endowment of money? The monetary authorities might simply distribute money in proportion to consumers' initial holdings but this is not a very persuasive description of monetary policy. In practice, the monetary authorities are more likely to use open market operations or work through financial intermediaries in some other way. In either case, it is not clear that an increase in the money stock can come about without the real side of the economy being affected. One way to allow for a monetary policy would be to introduce bonds and allow the monetary authorities to trade in them. This would make possible a primitive open market operation and at the same time explain how agents might come to have pre-existing commitments in terms of money (i.e. debts or credits).

For the sake of illustration, suppose that, by the sort of construction used above, one has obtained an indirect utility function in which the amount of bonds held by the consumer at the end of his first period appears as an argument. If the i-th consumer chooses to consume x_i and to hold m_i (resp. b_i) units of money (resp. bonds) then his utility is $v^*(x_i, m_i, b_i, p, r)$ when the commodity price system is p and the price of bonds is r. A bond is a promise to pay different amounts of money at various dates and in various states of nature. In the very special case of a bond which pays one unit of money next period regardless of the state of nature, bonds and money are indistinguishable *as assets* and hence in this context should trade at the same price: $r = 1$. In general, this need not be so.

Suppose that prices today change from p to λp. Under the assumption of homogeneous expectations the random variable of expected future prices $\hat{q}$ is replaced by $\lambda\hat{q}$. In order to have the same configuration of returns to bond-holding in real terms it would be necessary and sufficient to hold λb_i bonds in place of b_i. By an argument already used above, this would be the optimal response in these circumstances.[19] Hence v^* is homogeneous of degree zero in m_i, b_i and p. In order to increase the money supply the monetary authorities would have to buy bonds and "sell" money in exchange. This operation raises two problems. First, the individual's budget constraint is

$$p.x_i + rb_i + m_i \leq w_i = p.e_i + \bar{m}_i - d_i$$

or, aggregating to get the representative individual's constraint,

$$p.x + rb + m \leq p.e + \bar{m}.$$

Now unless $\bar{m} = 0$ the consumer cannot afford $(x, \lambda b, \lambda m)$ at the prices $(\lambda p, r)$ if $\lambda > 1$ and this means that unless initial money balances can somehow be increased independently of the open market operation, the homogeneity argument breaks down and money is not neutral. Second, suppose that the private sector is a net supplier of bonds to the monetary authorities ($b < 0$) and the monetary authorities embark on an open market operation to expand the money supply. The increase in the money supply is

$$\Delta\bar{m} = (\lambda - 1)\bar{m} = r(1 - \lambda)b \quad \text{(quantity of money issued equals value of bonds demanded)}$$

which is consistent with the market clearing conditions. If $b \geq 0$, on the other hand, a neutral increase in the money supply is impossible since

$$0 < \Delta m = (\lambda - 1)\bar{m} = r(1 - \lambda)b \leq 0 .$$

Thus it is not possible, in general, to use open market operations neutrally as long as there is outside money, or more generally government debt, already in the system. And in any case, neutrality applies to changes in the *scale* of the government open market operation, not to the *introduction* of the open market operation.[20]

Even if there were no open market operation, an expansion in initial money stocks ($\bar{m}_i$) would be neutral only if bonds could be increased in proportion (from b_i to λb_i for all $i = 1, \ldots, m$) and there were no government stocks already in the system. Thus, neutrality, even in the weak sense applying to an unexplained increase in $\bar{m}_i$ requires extra assumptions:

(e) there are no government stocks already in the system;
(f) bonds are homogeneous, i.e. their characteristics are unaltered by the change in scale of issue from b_i to λb_i.

The moral of this exercise is that even under the most restrictive assumptions required to ensure that homogeneity properties hold, the "neutrality of money" refers to exogenous increases in initial money balances, not to increases *via* open market operations, etc. Neutrality is thus restricted to the realm of "helicopter economics". Since the control of the money supply envisaged in these stories is very much like those thought experiments in which the reader is invited to imagine a change in the unit of measurement, it is hardly surprising that money is neutral. The real case arising from these examples against the quantity theory of money lies not in the heroic assumptions required to make demand functions homogeneous but rather in their failure to accommodate open market operations and the like in a neutral way. Quantity theorists have struggled long and hard to force the demand-for-money function into a form consistent with their theory, but the supply side has been relatively neglected. The reason may be that once the fictional helicopter is abandoned it becomes impossible to conceive of a neutral increase in the money supply, regardless of the assumptions made about the demand for money. If this be true, it would seem to cut the ground from under the quantity theory in a much more decisive way than theoretical arguments about the homogeneity of demand have done.

The conclusion of the Patinkin controversy appeared to be that the "classical dichotomy" in its extreme form had to be abandoned and the neutrality of money could be retained only at the expense of highly restrictive assumptions like (a)–(f). These assumptions are not "necessary" in the strict sense of that word but it is hard to see what economically meaningful weaker ones might replace them.[21] In addition, these assumptions were sufficient for neutrality only if changes in the money supply took the form of autonomous increases in initial money balances rather than open market operations, changes in reserve ratios and so on. This characterization of neutrality, however restrictive, may seem a pale imitation of the Keynesian critique but it backed classical monetary economics—which is to say the modern quantity theory—into a corner from which it appeared difficult for them to escape. It was not long, however, before the focus of the debate had been shifted to an entirely different aspect of the problem. The reorientation which followed was much more favourable to the classical view.

In a now celebrated paper,[22] Archibald and Lipsey pointed out that while the Patinkin analysis, with amendments, might be correct in the short run, more precisely, if one looked only at the effects in the first period following a change in the money supply, it was not the correct analysis of the long run effects. Briefly, they argued that in the long run the income effects of the change in the price level must disappear and hence the economy could regain its original, long run equilibrium. However money balances were redistributed by monetary policy they would be "reshuffled" and end up in the same hands as before. In view of the extremely simple technical apparatus used by the authors their discussion was surprisingly accurate in places. Their claims could not be true in general and sufficient conditions have never been given except for simple examples. An example of the type studied by Archibald and Lipsey is sufficient to indicate both the main points made by them and their limitations.

Consider an economy in which all individuals have identical preferences. There are two types of goods, one a homogeneous consumption good and the other a perfectly durable asset like gold. An individual's security depends on the stock of gold he holds, so his utility is a function of consumption and his share of the gold stock. Each individual lives for one period and then expires, to be replaced by an identical offspring who inherits his share of the gold. As a result of this assumption, in any time period, an individual is interested in maximizing the utility of his current consumption and his stock of gold, subject to his budget constraint.[23] An individual's wealth consists of his inherited stock plus an endowment of the consumption good. To keep matters very simple it is assumed that there are only two consumers at any one time, that each consumer has an endowment of one unit of consumption good and that, by convention, there is one unit of gold. At date t, an individual has a stock m_{t-1} of gold so if the price of consumption in terms of gold is p_t his wealth is $m_{t-1} + p_t = w_t$. He must choose a level of consumption x_t and gold m_t subject to the budget constraint

$$p_t x_t + m_t \leq p_t . 1 + m_{t-1}$$

and he chooses (x_t, m_t) to maximize $u(x_t, m_t)$. At date $(t + 1)$ his "son" inherits the gold and so has an endowment $(1, m_t)$ and wealth $w_{t+1} = p_{t+1} . 1 + m_t$. The dynamics of this system can be sketched out very easily using an Edgeworth Box Diagram.

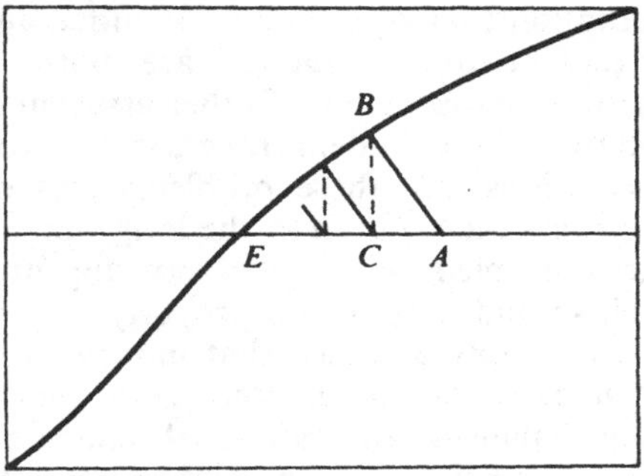

Figure 1.1

The endowment point must lie somewhere along the horizontal line since the consumption endowment is constant but the stocks may vary from period to period. The diagonal line is the set of Pareto-efficient points. Suppose that at some date the endowment point is A (above). The equilibrium that period must lie on the efficient locus somewhere to the northwest, say at B. Since the successors of this pair of consumers inherit their fathers' stocks, the endowment point next period must lie directly below B on the endowment line at C. Continuing the argument in this way it is clear that the process must converge to the unique stationary equilibrium at E.[24] A stationary equilibrium can be defined as a point in the Edgeworth Box at which no trade occurs, or equivalently, at which the distribution of gold is the same from period to period. The stationary equilibria are precisely the points of intersection of the endowment line with the efficiency curve. Under the usual continuity assumptions there is always at least one such.[25]

The fanciful story about the gold incorporates in a rudimentary way the relevant facts about a monetary economy.

In this case, the model illustrates the main points of the critique of Patinkin:

> there is a unique stationary equilibrium which is determined solely by tastes and endowments of goods and not by the distribution of real balances; after any disturbance in the distribution of real money balances between the two individuals, the system returns to the long run stationary equilibrium.

There is no need to make assumptions about Engel curves, nor to assume that individuals have identical tastes. On the other hand, the implicit assumption that equilibrium is unique and the restriction of the argument to two goods are both unacceptable. Furthermore, there is no discussion of other assets and the peculiar generational structure of the model is necessary to avoid the thorny problem of expectations. All these problems cast doubt on the validity of the classical theory even in the long run.

There is another problem which does not appear in the "gold model" but which should appear in a properly specified monetary model. Even if it is simply assumed that money enters the utility function, it is *real* balances that matter. Thus, when m_t is interpreted as money balances an individual chooses (x_t, m_t) to maximize $u(x_t, m_t/p_t)$ subject to the budget constraint

$$p_t x_t + m_t \leq p_t . 1 + m_{t-1} .$$

If the utility function is smooth, an interior maximum can be characterized by the condition that the marginal rate of substitution of consumption for real balances be unity. To describe an equilibrium by means of an Edgeworth Box Diagram draw the endowment line as before and draw the locus of points for one

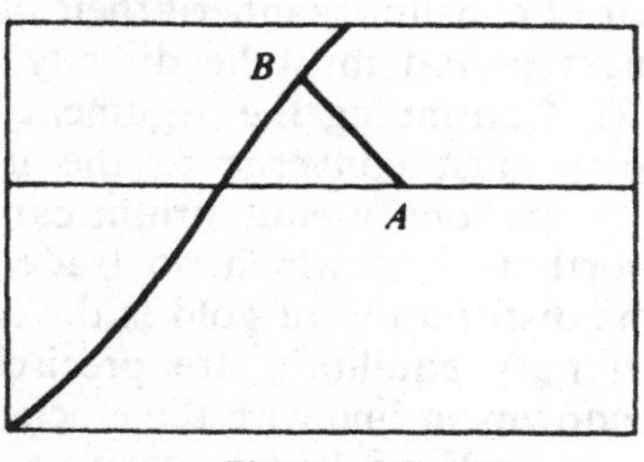

Figure 1.2

individual along which his marginal rate of substitution is unity. If the initial endowment point is *A* the equilibrium is found by tracing out a line with slope minus one through *A* until it intersects the expansion path at *B*, say. The stock of real balances in the economy is $1/p_t$, the length of the Box. Since p_t is determined endogenously the length of the box changes from period to period. Thus, if *C* represents the distribution of consumption and real balances at the beginning of period $(t + 1)$ when the price is p_t, it will be shifted, either towards or further from *E*, if p_{t+1} is different from p_t. The simple argument used to establish convergence above does not work even in this unrealistically simple case.[26]

Despite its inadequacies as a general analysis, the Archibald-Lipsey view has had a powerful effect on the outlook of subsequent writers. The reason, I think, is that their picture of the world is an intuitively appealing one for many economists, however shaky the supporting analysis. In the absence of convincing dynamic theories the theorist, *faute de mieux*, opts for general-equilibrium analysis. In the short run, stocks of assets are given but in the long run, their distribution is determined endogenously. How is the general-equilibrium theorist to explain this long run distribution except in terms of the economy's given needs, preferences, resources and technology? It is this predilection for equilibrium modes of thought, together with a tendency to regard short run phenomena as "merely" transitory, which explains the great influence of Archibald-Lipsey critique. The naive picture of an economy with a unique, long run equilibrium to which it automatically returns after every disturbance is not to be believed. The more serious point is that after an initial disturbance to money holdings, the "real forces" in the economy take over, redistributing assets of all sorts. This much seems incontrovertible. If the economy is determinate, to the extent of having a finite number of long run equilibria, then the capacity of the monetary authorities to control the economy is limited. How limited depends on the importance one attaches to equilibrium and the long run, i.e. on one's preconceptions about the world. Even so the argument is not watertight. To believe that monetary policy is neutral in the long run one must assume that the system will settle down to *some* equilibrium after an initial disturbance. One must also assume that monetary policy consists of an initial disturbance followed by an infinite period of non-intervention. The first of these assumptions is just the professional failing of the equilibrium theorist. Without it, he can say very little. In any case, if the object is to *control* the system it is not clear what can be said unless the economy does settle down. The second assumption is less acceptable. But these weaknesses are not peculiar to classical monetary theory; they are symptoms of a general way of thinking about economic problems, *viz.* general-equilibrium theory. Even if one finds the Archibald-Lipsey case unconvincing as a description of the world it may still be of interest as a theoretical reference point just because it is the "canonical" way of looking at things within the intellectual framework of general-equilibrium analysis.

These ideas can be made more precise by distinguishing two versions of the Archibald-Lipsey story. These will be called Invariance Principles since they assert, in different ways, the invariance of real quantities with respect to changes in the money stock, in the long run. First, the *Strong Invariance Principle* asserts that *there is a unique, long run equilibrium, in which the distribution of real balances is determinate and to which the economy returns after any disturbance.* In their original article, Archibald and Lipsey examined a model in which the strong version might hold, though their analysis was incomplete. Second, the *Weak Invariance Principle* asserts that *the set of long run equilibria is determinate, i.e. at most finite, and the distribution of real money balances is endogenous to the system in long run equilibrium.* The first part of this principle depends only on regularity properties of the model and the second part is more or less a matter of definition. For example, in the trivial example discussed above, "equilibrium" requires that the distribution of real money balances should be unchanged from period to period, i.e.

$$\frac{m_t}{p_t} = \frac{m_{t+1}}{p_{t+1}},$$

and that relative prices should be unchanged too, i.e.

$$p_t = p_{t+1}.$$

This provides an "extra" equation to determine m_t. In any case, there is no given "initial" distribution of money in the long run.

The strong version is unlikely to hold for any except the most special cases and therefore hardly deserves to be called a "principle". The weak version does hold except for special cases and therefore is a "principle", that is, it is a property of equilibrium models in general rather than a statement about the world.

The relevance of the Weak Invariance Principle depends very much on whether one finds general-equilibrium habits of thought congenial. It is clear that many economists do and such deeply engrained habits probably reflect the usefulness of equilibrium as an organizing principle as much as they reflect prejudice or laziness. Similarly, the relevance of the long run equilibrium depends on one's estimate of the possibility of exploiting temporary trade-offs. The short run does not last for ever and the long run never arrives. The truth lies somewhere in between but empirical evidence is unlikely to settle the question. Economists who emphasize the properties of long run equilibrium to the exclusion of all else are really declaring their lack of faith in our ability to master the economy's dynamics sufficiently well to improve its performance in the short run; just as those who favour short run analysis are declaring the opposite. Behind the apparently scientific appeal to facts in support of rival theories lies a clash of world-views.

In retrospect, this episode seems not to have provided very substantial theoretical results. The concern with homogeneity properties and stationary equilibria lasted longer than theoretical difficulty or practical importance would have warranted in the nineteen-seventies. Much more interesting than the "thinness" of the results is the implicit struggle between long and short run views of the world, between those who regard the government as being "in control" and those who regard it as merely postponing the day of reckoning. As so often happens, nothing was finally settled. Theorists still assume homogeneity properties when the fancy strikes them or study temporary equilibria without enquiring into what will happen in the next period or the one after that. This is largely what one would expect. The lasting effect of these debates has been to encourage a consensus that the classical-anticlassical question is one of long run *versus* short run, without indicating which is correct.

The odd thing about this stage in the development of monetary thought is that, although the conclusion was well spelled out at the time, it seemed necessary to repeat the argument in the nineteen-sixties. Despite the relative simplicity of the points made they had to be rediscovered in a different context. The second debate, discussed in the next section, reinforces the impression that the real issue in the nineteen-fifties was more fundamental than either the Patinkin controversy or the Archibald-Lipsey critique would indicate. The homogeneity debate was merely a sympton of a deeper division.

Before passing on another topic should be mentioned and that is the re-emergence in the 'fifties of a serious interest in the quantity theory of money and prices. Largely as a result of the efforts of Milton Friedman and his co-workers, a revised version of the quantity theory became the object of considerable study.[28] The theory was cast in the form of a model of money-demand (supply was assumed to be exogenous) and in its most general form seemed to incorporate many features of the Keynesian theory—the speculative and precautionary motives for holding money, for example—as well as the traditional account of transactions demand, now dressed up in inventory-theoretic clothes. The difference, as Friedman stressed and was to continue to stress, lay not in the general framework but in particular empirical "facts", such as the alleged, low interest-elasticity of demand for money. Compared with the accounts of classical writers such as Thornton and Ricardo or neoclassical writers such as Fisher there were theoretical innovations. The essential feature of money was taken to be its asset-role as a temporary resting place for purchasing power rather than as a medium of exchange.[29] The demand for money is determined by the same factors used in any theory of portfolio selection, rather than by appeals to institutional rigidities and technical constraints. The homogeneity of the quantity equation with respect to the price level and income has an analogue in the homogeneity properties of the demand for money. The constancy of the velocity of money, which appears now as the demand for money per unit of nominal income, is an empirical "fact" and is not explained by theory. Income appears as an argument in the demand for money because it is a proxy for wealth, on which the demand for every asset depends. More precisely, income is the interest on wealth and wealth the capitalized value of a stream of income.[30]

There is a superficial attractiveness about this scheme. By placing the emphasis on wealth and on money as an asset, the demand for which is a function of prices and wealth, like any other commodity, the theory of demand for money is made to look like a version of static demand theory. Quantity theorists often treat it as such in their writings. Needless to say, none of this is very well worked out. The trouble is that the various parts of the new quantity theory do not fit together very well. If wealth is simply the capitalized value of an income stream then wealth must be sensitive to the level of interest rates. If demand for money is a stable function of wealth, the interest-elasticity of demand should not be low. If, on the other hand, it is income itself (i.e. not as a proxy for wealth) that determines demand for money then what is the point of emphasizing wealth? The point, I take it, is to avoid thinking very seriously about time and to get away from Keynesian preoccupations with income as an important explanatory variable. Perhaps the best way to reconcile low interest elasticity of demand with the assumption that demand is a function of wealth is to interpret the independent variable "income" as permanent income. Then the interest rate appearing in the demand function acts as a relative price, i.e. as the opportunity cost of holding money, but does not have any explicit influence on permanent income. Unfortunately, all that this stratagem accomplishes is to banish the interest rate's effect on permanent income to some other part of the model. To put it another way, if the object is to establish a stable relationship between the quantity of money and nominal income, not permanent income, it is not enough simply to make demand for money a stable function of permanent income; one has to show that the relationship between nominal and permanent income is "stable".

The intuition behind the quantity theory is perhaps more interesting than the attempts to make it precise. Suppose the demand for money were a function of permanent income alone. An increase in cash balances over and above the desired amount would lead to an increase of expenditure almost as great, since permanent income would not be much affected by current changes in cash balances. Here the emphasis on a wealth concept (permanent income) seems natural and provides an intuitive explanation for the strength of the short-run, real balance effect. It collides, however, with that other tenet of monetarist thought, the belief that consumption is a function of permanent income.[31] The instability of the multiplier is explained by referring to the fact that, under the permanent income hypothesis, an increase in income, over and above the permanent level, is largely saved in the short-run. Now, individuals will not plan to hold larger than desired cash balances, so the increase in cash balances referred to above must be unintended. But an unexpected increase will only come about as a result of a change in income. More precisely, the increase in cash balances *counts* as income. Increases in income have different effects depending on whether we are considering the consumption function or the demand-for-money function.[32]

The homogeneity properties assumed by the quantity theory are far from obvious, as Patinkin found out. The Archibald-Lipsey solution, if it works, is available only in the long-run. The quantity theory seems to assume that the long-run is here and now, but not in the usual sense of this phrase.[33] The distribution effects disappear instantaneously. This would be the case if individuals rented rather than owned their cash balances, but then what would happen to the real balance effect? If there were a perfect capital market and the rate of interest were zero, cash balances would be a negligible part of total wealth, but in that case why would money be needed as an asset? In any case, the capital market is imperfect and the rate of interest is not zero. Perhaps the quantity theory is intended to be taken as an account of what happens in the long-run. The empirical applications of the theory can then only be explained by the assumption that the long run is very short indeed.[34]

Notes

1. See J. M. Keynes, *The General Theory of Employment, Interest and Money*, London: Macmillan, 1936, pp. 171–3 and F. Modigliani, "Liquidity Preference and the Theory of Interest and Money", *Econometrica*, **12** (1944), pp. 45–88.

2. See, for example, M. Friedman, *A Program for Monetary Stability*, New York: Fordham, 1960 or "Price, Income and Monetary Changes in Three Wartime Periods", *American Economic Review*, Proceedings, **42** (1952), 612–25.

3. This point is made explicitly by F. Hahn in his contribution to G. Harcourt (ed.), *The Microfoundation of Macroeconomics*, London: Macmillan, 1978.

4. In its crudest form let p_h be the price, in terms of some abstract unit of account, of good $h = 1, \ldots, l$, let $p = (p_1, \ldots, p_l)$, let $f_h(p)$ be the market excess demand for good h and let $f_0(p)$ be the market demand for money. Equilibrium in the goods market requires $f_h(p) = 0$ $(h = 1, \ldots, l)$ and in the money market requires $f_0(p) = M$ where M is the given money supply. Since only relative prices affect the demand for goods the equilibrium condition for the goods market only determines relative prices. The general level of prices is determined by the money demand equation $f_0(p) = M$.

5. An increase in real balances over and above their equilibrium level causes individuals to spend part of their balances, thus pushing up the price level and reducing the real quantity of money. A decrease in the price level, which *ipso facto* increases real balances, therefore leads to a compensating increase in the price level. A similar argument shows that the "real balance effect" leads to a compensating reduction in the price level when the price level initially rises above its equilibrium level. If a change in the money supply changes the equilibrium price level the same sorts of arguments can be used to explain the movement of prices to the new equilibrium level. But all these arguments rely on the assumption that a change in real balances changes the demand for goods *directly*. This is incompatible with the formulation in the preceding note.

6. In the notation of note 4 above, Patinkin wrote $f_h(p, M) = 0$ for $h = 0, 1, \ldots, l$, where $f_0(p, M)$ is now interpreted as the market *excess* demand for money. The functions f_h are homogeneous of degree zero in (p, M) but not in p alone.

7. The symbol ":=" indicates equality by definition; the expression on the left-hand side is defined by the one on the right. The symbol "." indicates the inner product of two vectors. For example,

$$x \cdot y := \sum_{h=1}^{l} x_h y_h .$$

8. A consumer is formally defined by his *consumption set*, which is the set of consumption bundles that are feasible for him, his *utility function*, representing his preferences over consumption bundles, and an *endowment* of goods which constitute his initial resources. Here, his consumption set consists of all non-negative bundles (denoted by $\mathbb{R}^l_+$ if there are l commodities), his utility function is a continuous, real-valued function u_i defined on all of $\mathbb{R}^l_+$ and his endowment is contained in $\mathbb{R}^l_+$.

9. u_i is said to be *strictly quasi-concave* if $u_i(x) = u_i(x')$ and $x \neq x'$ implies that $u_i(tx + (1 - t)x') > u_i(x)$ for all $0 < t < 1$, where x and x' belong to $\mathbb{R}^l_+$, of course. If u_i is strictly quasi-concave, if every good has a positive price and the consumer's income is not negative, there is a unique consumption bundle which maximizes utility subject to the constraints $p.x_i \leq w_i$ and $x_i \in R^l_+$. This unique bundle is denoted by $f_i(p, w_i)$.

10. A consumer's Engel curve shows how the consumer's expenditure on each good changes as income changes (prices being held constant). If the Engel curve is linear and passes through the origin, it means he spends a constant fraction of income on each good regardless of the level income (prices being held constant).

11. In other words, the individuals who hold government debt regard it as being a credit even though the debt is in a sense the debt of taxpayers like themselves. Much has been made of this point by J. Gurley and E. Shaw, *Money in a Theory of Finance*, Washington: Brookings Institution, 1960.

12. Equilibrium is said to be *determinate* if there is a finite number of equilibria. This means that each equilibrium is locally unique. This is in contrast to the continuum of equilibrium price levels in the absence of a demand for money equation.

13. The phrasing is quite deliberate here. When equilibrium is not unique it might be that a change in the quantity of money would lead to a new set of relative prices. An equiproportionate change in all nominal prices is only one possibility and without saying something about the dynamics of the system there is no reason to think this possibility is distinguished.

14. Assuming still that u is continuous, v is well defined if the second period price of every good is positive and m is not negative.

15. v^* may not be well defined. One sufficient condition for v^* to be well defined at (x, m, p) is for v to be bounded, i.e. for some large number $\bar{V}$

$$P[-V \leq v(x, m, \hat{q}) \leq V|p] = 1$$

where $P[.|p]$ denotes probability conditional on p. The notation $E[.|p]$ denotes expectation conditional on p; i.e. the mathematical expectation with respect to the conditional probability distribution. Formally, for each p let $\psi(p)$ denote the probability measure which describes the distribution of the random variable q. Then

$$E[v(x, m, \hat{q})|p] \equiv \int v(x, m, \hat{q})\psi(p)(d\hat{q}).$$

For this to be meaningful $v(x, m, .)$ must be measurable in the appropriate sense. This is certainly true if v is continuous.

16. Formally, the argument is that $p.x + m \leq w$ implies that $\lambda p.x + \lambda m \leq \lambda w$ so $(x, \lambda m)$ is feasible at $(\lambda p, \lambda w)$ if $\lambda > 0$ and, furthermore, if $\lambda p.x' + m' \leq \lambda w$ then $p.x' + m/\lambda \leq w$. But this means $v^*(x', m'/\lambda, p) \leq v^*(x, m, p)$ so by the assumed homogeneity properties of v^*, $v^*(x', m', \lambda p) \leq v^*(x, \lambda m, \lambda p)$ and $(x, \lambda m)$ is seen to be optimal at $(\lambda p, \lambda w)$ too.

17. Since expectations are represented by a function ψ that associates a probability measure $\psi(p)$ (the distribution of $\hat{q}$) with each current price system p, it should be possible to characterize homogeneity of expectations in terms of ψ. If A is a subset of $\mathbb{R}^l_+$, let $\lambda A = \{x \in \mathbb{R}^l | (x/\lambda) \in A\}$ for any positive λ. Then expectations are *homogeneous* if for any measurable A, $\psi(p)[A] = \psi(\lambda p)[\lambda A]$ for any $\lambda > 0$. This implies that $E[v(x, m, \hat{q})|\lambda p] = E[v(x, m, \lambda\hat{q})|p]$ where these expressions are defined.

18. One might add that there is assumed to be no "money illusion". Consumers only care about consumption.

19. Suppose the value of the bond next period is a random variable $\hat{r}$. Then second period wealth is $m_i + \hat{r}b_i$. If second period prices are $\hat{q}$ and first period consumption is x_i then utility is $v(x_i, m_i + \hat{r}b_i, \hat{q})$. Since $v(x_i, m_i + \hat{r}b_i, \hat{q}) = v(x_i, \lambda m_i + \hat{r}\lambda b_i, \lambda\hat{q})$, if expectations are homogeneous it is easy to see that $v^*(x_i, m_i, b_i, p) = v^*(x_i, \lambda m_i, \lambda b_i, \lambda p)$.

20. Suppose there were no debt already in the system. If the government decides to supply money after initially settling in an equilibrium in which it supplied nothing, it would have to accept inside money in exchange. The new equilibrium would be different in real terms from one in which no money was supplied.

21. Necessary and sufficient conditions for homogeneity properties of demand functions are studied in a paper by P. Kalman and R. Dusansky, "Illusion-free Demand Behaviour in a Monetary Economy: The General Conditions" in *Some Aspects of the Foundations of General Equilibrium Theory*, New York: Springer-Verlag, 1978, pp. 49–60.

22. G. Archibald and R. Lipsey, "Monetary and Value Theory: a Critique of Lange and Patinkin", *Review of Economic Studies*, **26** (1958), pp. 1–22.

23. A formal description of this economy requires a specification of the consumption set, utility function and endowment of each type of individual in each period. The consumption set is taken to be the set of non-negative pairs (x_i, m_i), where x_i is consumption and m_i the share of the gold stock, for consumer $i = 1, \ldots, m$. Each consumer has a utility function $u_i(x_i, m_i)$ defined on $\mathbb{R}^2_+$ and an endowment $(1, \bar{m}_i)$ where $\bar{m}_i$ is the money holding of a consumer of type i in the previous period. Formally, then, the economy consists of a sequence $\{(i, t): i = 1, \ldots, m, t = 0, 1, \ldots, \textit{ad inf.}\}$ of agents, each one described by a pair like (u_i, e_i), together with the initial money holdings $(\bar{m}_i)$ of agents at date 0.

24. Uniqueness and stability are not assured, however. The diagram below illustrates the possibility of the existence of two equilibria, one stable (A), the other unstable (B).

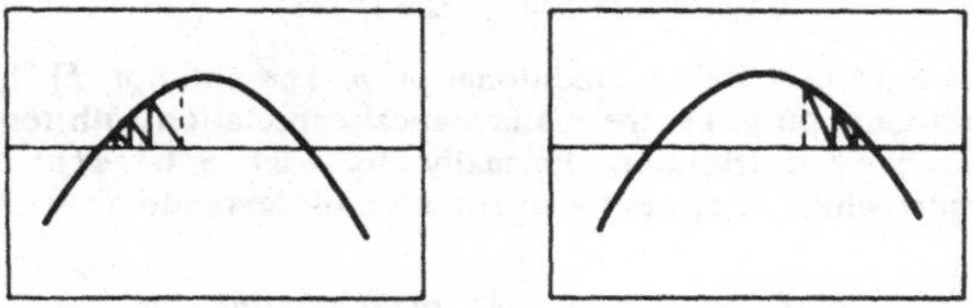

(A) (B)

25. A *stationary equilibrium* is an m-tuple $\{(x_1, m_1), \ldots (x_m, m_m)\}$ and a price p such that $\sum_{i=1}^{m} (x_i, m_i) = (m, 1)$ and for each i the pair (x_i, m_i) is maximal in the budget set

$$\{(x, m) \geq 0 \,|\, p.x + m \leq p.1 + m_i\}.$$

A stationary equilibrium exists if, for example, u_i is continuous, strictly quasi-concave and increasing in each argument. Weaker conditions will also suffice.

26. The typical consumer maximizes $u(x, m/p)$ subject to $p.x + m = p.1 + \bar{m}$. The first order condition for a maximum is $\partial u/\partial x = \partial u/\partial(m/p)$, i.e. the marginal rate of substitution is minus one. The consumer moves from his endowment $(1, \bar{m}/p_t)$ of consumption and real balances to the optimal bundle $(x, m/p_t)$ at which this first order condition is satisfied. His successor, however, begins with the endowment $(1, m/p_{t+1})$ which is not vertically above or below $(x, m/p_t)$, as in the gold case, unless $p_t = p_{t+1}$. A sufficient condition for $p_t = p_{t+1}$ is *identical, linear Engel curves through the origin.*

27. Formally, an economy with overlapping generations is a double sequence $\{(i, t): i = 1, \ldots, m, t = 0, 1, \ldots, ad.\ inf.\}$ of consumers. (i, t) is defined by a consumption set $\mathbb{R}^l_+ \times \mathbb{R}^l_+$, a utility function u_i on $\mathbb{R}^l_+ \times \mathbb{R}^l_+$ and a (first period) endowment, $e_i(s_t) \in \mathbb{R}_+$, of goods if s_t is observed.

28. M. Friedman (ed.), *Studies in the Quantity Theory of Money*, Chicago: Chicago University Press, 1956.

29. But compare the discussion of the optimum quantity of money below.

30. This is only strictly true if capital markets are perfect.

31. M. Friedman, *A Theory of the Consumption Function*, Princeton: Princeton University Press, 1957.

32. Suppose that an individual receives a constant income Y^p in each period but that there are also random additions (positive or negative) to his money holdings, say ε_t. Then his actual income is $Y_t = Y^p + \varepsilon_t$. Suppose $\{\varepsilon_t\}$ are independently normally distributed with mean zero and variance σ. The consumer has a desired stock of money $\bar{M}$, say. Suppose that M_{t-1}, his money holdings at the end of $(t - 1)$, happen to equal M. According to the consumption function theory, C_t is proportional to Y^p. But the demand for money theory and the real balance effect in particular require that all of ε_t be spent. In fact, there seem to be two consumption functions: $C_t = \alpha Y^p$ and $C_t = \alpha Y^p + \varepsilon_t$.

33. The long-run is a planning period and in this sense is in the present. But what Monetarists seem to have in mind is that long-run equilibrium, in which agents do not plan to make any changes, is quickly attainable.

34. M. Mussa, "Tariffs and the Balance of Payments: A Monetary Approach" in H. Johnson and J. Frenkel (eds.), *The Monetary Approach to the Balance of Payments*, London, Allen and Unwin, 1977, especially p. 193.

CHAPTER 1: PART 2

The neutrality of money

Monetary theory in the nineteen-sixties

Monetary policy had begun the postwar period rather discredited and found somewhat greater favour in the early 'fifties when inflation led economists to re-examine traditional remedies. In the early 'sixties it occupied a rather ambivalent position. The conventional wisdom appears to have been that a little inflation is at worst the inevitable consequence of growth and at best a means of stimulating it. The theoretical support for this view, such as it was, came from the recently discovered *Phillips curve*, a negative relationship between the rate of unemployment and the rate of change of money wages.[1] As reformulated by Lipsey,[2] the Phillips curve is a negative relationship between the rate of unemployment and the rate of price inflation, thus incorporating a "cost push" theory of inflation. But there were other rationalizations. For example, if wages and prices are rigid downwards, inflation acts as a lubricant which makes relative price changes easier and hence improves the allocative efficiency of the price mechanism.[3]

If one accepts the existence of a trade off between inflation and unemployment, the implications for monetary policy depend very much on one's preconceptions about the relationship between the change in the quantity of money and the rate of change of prices. If one believes that an increase in the money supply is, or could be, responsible for inflation, the Phillips curve seems to suggest that modest monetary expansion is good for growth. If one believes that monetary policy is like a string—"you can pull on it but you can't push it"—then the Phillips curve suggests that monetary policy, being a tool for the suppression of inflation, might safely be neglected or merely allowed to accommodate inflation.

The backlash against this view started in the late 'sixties. Independently, Friedman and Phelps attacked the heart of the new view,[4] arguing that in the long run there is no trade-off between unemployment and inflation. The argument was based on the claim, which may have been deducible from more primitive assumptions, that only unanticipated price changes could alter the real magnitudes in the economic system. This is an appeal to homogeneity: a completely anticipated change in the price level which leaves relative prices unchanged is assumed to have no affect on real magnitudes.[5] There is no explicit model underlying this proposition; it is treated as a general principle of equilibrium analysis. Taking the claim for granted, one can then ask what will happen if the monetary authorities adopt a policy of steady but modest inflation. It is assumed that monetary expansion is either a prerequisite for this inflation or else is used to promote it. Either way, the result is to make real wages lower than they would otherwise have been or were expected to be. A cut in real wages, or a growth rate of real wages which is lower than the growth rate of productivity, reduces unemployment and stimulates growth.[6] (Why it should stimulate *growth* is not so clear. Keynesian anxieties about aggregate demand are neglected, as is the dependence of investment on expected, rather than current, real wages.) However, modest inflation consistently pursued by the monetary authorities cannot be "unexpected" forever. Sooner or later the workers must wake up to the fact that they are being cheated of part of their wages by inflation. When they do, they will take steps to prevent it by anticipating inflation in their wage claims. Since fully anticipated inflation has no real effects by hypothesis, the monetary authorities are back where they started.[7] In order to have a continuing effect on growth and unemployment, it will be necessary for them to increase the rate of monetary expansion continually, i.e. to provoke runaway inflation.

This argument proved appealing. Whether because of equilibrium habits of thought, antipathy to government intervention or whatever, many economists were satisfied that the Phillips curve was vertical in the long run, even though it had not yet been rigorously analysed, even in the short run. Although it naturally attracted most of the attention, this was not the crux of Friedman's argument. The essential point was that expectations are part of the structure of the economy and they depend on what individuals expect the government to do. Because individuals do learn about government policies, a change in government policy will, in the long run, change expectations and *ipso facto* the structure of the economy. The realization that the Phillips curve is not independent of government policy, indeed cannot be independent as long as the curve depends on the mechanism of expectation formation, has a wider importance than this particular debate may have suggested.

It means that the reaction of expectations to changes in policy has to be taken seriously. Whether the long run Phillips curve is vertical or horizontal is of less importance than the fact that it cannot be treated as a structural *datum* by the government. The fact remains that the analysis which served as a vehicle for this insight was extremely vague. The arguments of Phelps and Friedman were unsupported by formal models and it was not even very clear what sort of economy was envisaged, though one imagined that if it were ever formalized it would have perfect competition, market-clearing prices and so forth.

A crucial part of Friedman's argument about the Phillips curve was the assumption that expectations are formed intelligently, in the sense that individuals eventually "catch on" to what the government is doing and adjust their behaviour accordingly. This does not mean that expectations are "rational" in any sense. Indeed the first empirical work was based on the *adaptive expectations hypothesis.*[8] What is required for Friedman's argument is that the monetary authorities cannot fool all of the people all of the time.

Friedman did not provide a precise model to support his argument and in particular there was no precise account of expectations formation. No one has a clear idea of how expectations are formed and though some may have hunches about how information is digested in special cases, it is very hard to write this down in the form of an equation. This gap occurs at a rather crucial point in the story, so to cover their embarrassment some economists have resorted to an "equilibrium" assumption. Instead of trying to model the process of deciding what information is needed, gathering it, updating probabilities etc. the theorist looks at the extreme case where information is used as efficiently as possible. More precisely, an individual's information set[9] is simply given and it is assumed that in equilibrium no further benefit remains to be derived from it. The result is that expectations are formed as intelligently as possible. For example, consumers, producers and government may be assumed to know the correct, structural model of the economy and observe all the exogenous and pre-determined variables. This is a special case of what is known as the "rational expectations hypothesis" (REH).

It is important to understand the theoretical status of the REH. It is best to think of it as a kind of equilibrium condition. When producers and consumers have rational expectations they have no incentive to make different or better use of the information they have. The converse is not true: taking into account the cost of information there will in general be an incentive to stop short of acquiring rational expectations. Now this sort of process would be extremely hard to model in detail. The REH is a shortcut to a *closed* and *consistent* model of expectation formation.[10] There are several possible justifications for this strategy. It might be that the REH works as an "as if" story: the assumption is not actually believed to be true but it allows us to get correct answers to certain questions from the model. In other words, it generates the right data. Or the REH might be taken as a "benchmark" which tells us what happens if individuals are not "fooled" by the government. It isolates phenomena which cannot be ascribed to mistakes. As a limiting case of Friedman's theory it serves as a theoretical testing ground for certain questions, such as whether the theory is consistent or is only valid if unacceptable assumptions are imposed. Finally, the REH is not a single hypothesis but a family of hypotheses. By changing the specification of the information set, i.e. the set of variables individuals can observe, one can change the expectations conditional on each state of the economy. The REH is therefore not entirely inflexible as a model of expectation formation.

It is easy to make fun of the naiveté of the REH. Critics have seized upon the implication that individuals are perfect forecasters and paraded it around in triumph, as if the REH were thereby proved to be useless. But the usefulness of a research strategy lies in its ability to generate interesting problems and insights. Economics is full of cases where extreme assumptions were used to provide deep insights. In any case, it turns out that the REH is much less crucial than is generally supposed to the debate about the efficacy of monetary policy.

In the early nineteen-seventies Sargent and Wallace, under the influence of the work of R. Lucas, began investigating the effects of monetary policy when the REH is valid.[11] They argued that if individuals have rational expectations, if they have the same information as the monetary authorities and if they know the government's policy rule then monetary policy will have no real effects at all. This proposition, which has come to be known as the Lucas-Sargent Proposition (LSP) comes in many forms but is best illustrated by a very simple example.

Let

y_t = logarithm of real income
e_t = logarithm of real expenditure
p_t = logarithm of the price level
m_t = logarithm of money demand
$\bar{m}_t$ = logarithm of money supply

all measured at the beginning of period t. Let ${}_{t-1}p_t$ denote the logarithm of the price level in period t which is expected to rule, at the end of period $(t-1)$. In other words, at the end of period $(t-1)$ individuals expect the random variable p_t to have the value ${}_{t-1}p_t$. The structure of the economy is given by two equations. First, there is a *supply function*[12]

$$y_t = k_t + \alpha(p_t - {}_{t-1}p_t) + u_t^1$$

where k_t is the logarithm of normal productive capacity and u_t^1 is an error term. Second, the demand side is given by the *quantity equation*:[13]

$$m_t = p_t + \beta e_t + u_t^2$$

where u_t^2 is an error term. It is assumed that:

> u_t^1, u_t^2 are serially independent, mutually uncorrelated random variables with zero mean, and $\alpha, \beta > 0$.

The government's monetary policy is represented by a money supply function:

$$\bar{m}_t = \sum_{i=1}^{\infty} (a_i u_{t-i}^1 + b_i u_{t-i}^2).$$

The model has two *equilibrium conditions* which require that the goods and money markets, respectively, clear:

$$y_t = e_t$$

$$\bar{m}_t = m_t.$$

In order to complete the specification of the model it is only necessary to say how expectations are formed. The *information set* of individuals at the end of period $(t-1)$ is the set of all variables they have observed up to and including period $(t-1)$. It is denoted by Φ_{t-1} and is defined by putting

$$\Phi_{t-1} = \{(p_{t-i}, \bar{m}_{t-i}, y_{t-i}, u_{t-i}^1, u_{t-i}^2) : i = 1, 2, \ldots\}.$$

That is, Φ_{t-1} contains all variables determined prior to period t. Note that k_t is treated as a non-stochastic variable known to all consumers and producers.

The *rational expectations hypothesis* in this context amounts to the assumption that the value of a variable x_t which is expected at $(t-1)$ is simply the mathematical expectation of x_t conditional on Φ_{t-1}, that is,

$${}_{t-1}x_t = E[x_t \mid \Phi_{t-1}].$$ [14]

In particular, ${}_{t-1}p_t = E[p_t|\Phi_{t-1}]$. When the information set is known and there is no risk of confusion, $E[x_t|\Phi_{t-1}]$ is written $\underset{t-1}{E}\, x_t$.

Proposition *The distribution of y_t is independent of the coefficients $(a_i, b_i)_{i=1}^{\infty}$ if the REH is satisfied.*

Proof From the quantity equation and the equilibrium conditions

$$\begin{aligned} p_t &= m_t - \beta e_t - u_t^2 \\ &= \bar{m}_t - \beta y_t - u_t^2 . \end{aligned}$$

Then, using the REH,

$$\begin{aligned} {}_{t-1}p_t &= \underset{t-1}{E}\, p_t \\ &= \underset{t-1}{E}\, [\bar{m}_t - \beta y_t - u_t^2] \\ &= \bar{m}_t - \beta \underset{t-1}{E}\, y_t \\ &= \bar{m}_t - \beta k_t \end{aligned}$$

[Recall that $\bar{m}_t$ is a function of variables in Φ_{t-1}, so $\underset{t-1}{E}\, \bar{m}_t = \bar{m}_t$, and that

$$\underset{t-1}{E}\, {}_{t-1}p_t = \underset{t-1}{E}\, \underset{t-1}{E}\, p_t = \underset{t-1}{E}\, p_t$$

so

$$\begin{aligned} \underset{t-1}{E}\, y_t &= \underset{t-1}{E}\, [k_t + \alpha(p_t - {}_{t-1}p_t) + u_t^1] \\ &= k_t + \alpha\left(\underset{t-1}{E}\, p_t - \underset{t-1}{E}\, p_t\right) \\ &= k_t] . \end{aligned}$$

Then

$$\begin{aligned} p_t - {}_{t-1}p_t &= m_t - \beta e_t - u_t^2 - \underset{t-1}{E}\, p_t \\ &= \bar{m}_t - \beta y_t - u_t^2 - \bar{m}_t + \beta k_t \\ &= \beta k_t - \beta y_t - u_t^2 . \end{aligned}$$

Hence $y_t = k_t + \alpha(\beta k_t - \beta y_t - u_t^2) + u_t^1$. Solving for y_t yields:

$$y_t = k_t + \left(\frac{1}{1 + \alpha\beta}\right)(u_t^1 - \alpha u_t^2)$$

and since this is independent of (a_i, b_i) the proposition is proved. □

This simple example leaves out of account a number of things which are normally important in the determination of macroeconomic equilibrium, for example the rate of interest and money wages. It is quite easy, however, to extend the model to include these variables and, in particular, the proposition is true of log-linear versions of the IS-LM model. The crucial assumptions of the model appear to be the homogeneity of the money demand function, the corresponding dependence of real income on the *unanticipated* inflation term $(p_t - {}_{t-1}p_t)$ and the assumption that Φ_{t-1} contains all variables which are determined before period t. The most pressing question is: how robust is the result? Does it depend on using a small, linear model? Does it depend on the assumption that consumers and producers have perfect econometric skills and full information? Are unacceptable micro-economic (i.e. behavioural) assumptions built into the macro-relations? The result is special but not as special as the example might suggest.

Knowing the true model

The argument of the preceding paragraphs is stated in terms of "true" coefficients of a "correct" structural model and of "true" probability distributions of error terms. But there is nothing in the argument that requires the "true" parameters to be used. Suppose that instead of using the objective probability distributions, the objective coefficients etc. both government and private individuals used the same subjective model, estimates of coefficients etc. Then both government and private individuals will have the same subjective probability distribution for y_t and this subjective distribution will be the same for each choice of the coefficients $\{(a_i, b_i)_{i=1}^{\infty}\}$ of the policy function. Of course, it may no longer be true that the "objective" probability distribution of y_t is independent of the government's policy but the objective distribution is irrelevant since neither government nor private individuals know it. Since a subjective probability distribution is in some sense a best estimate of whatever the true distribution might be, it would be irrational for the government to take into account the possibility that their policy might have an objective effect when this is not reflected in the subjective distribution. To put it another way, it would be inconsistent for the government to conjecture that its policy would have a real effect (on the distribution of y_t) and at the same time have a subjective model and subjective probability distributions (of u_t^1 and u_t^2) which indicated that it had no effect. A similar argument applies to private individuals. If the monetary policy is believed to have no effect, however, it clearly cannot be exploited in any useful way, whether it has an objective effect or not.

It is worthwhile emphasizing this interpretation because one of the points often made against the REH and more generally against the sort of assumptions made by the economists who use it is that they presuppose an incredible econometric ability. Individuals, according to this critique, are assumed to possess an ability not found even among the most talented and resourceful quarterly model builders. They observe the data with perfect accuracy, make no errors in specifying a complete model of the economy, somehow manage to calculate the true values of coefficients and so on. Now it is true that economists who adopt the REH often write as if this were the case, mainly one supposes to avoid lengthy circumlocutions. But as was pointed out above there is no necessity of treating these statements as descriptions of the world. They may be treated as an "as if" story or they may be used as an experimental benchmark to say something about the limits of government policy in the long run. Either interpretation may be more useful than the literalist interpretation. However, even if neither of these alternatives is acceptable to the literalist critic, his criticism may still be unfounded.

All that has been required for the LSP to hold is that individuals should do as well as the government at forecasting, precisely that they should use the same structural model, have the same estimates of coefficients and the same subjective probability distributions of the error terms u_t^1 and u_t^2.[15] This may be asking a lot but it is much less than asking that individuals be able to discover the true structure of the economy they live in. In particular, it is not required that individuals have a complete model, i.e. one that describes every aspect of the economy. It is only required that they have a model as complete as that of the policy-makers. And this may be quite simple, simpler at any rate than the large, quarterly, forecasting models.

Similar arguments can be deployed against other criticisms of the REH. For example, it has been claimed[16] that the REH assumes that individuals can forecast better than any econometrician can since it is well known that the forecasting errors of even the best econometric models tended to be strongly serially correlated. Now this argument is slightly nonsensical because to the extent that there is serial correlation the estimates could be improved, assuming that what one wants is an unbiased estimate. And in fact much of the forecaster's "art" consists of his ability to make just this kind of adjustment. The REH ascribes the same ability to consumers and producers. But even if it were not possible to eliminate this serial correlation of forecasting errors the Lucas-Sargent proposition in its "subjective" form continues to hold as long as government, producers and consumers are prone to making the same mistakes, i.e. have the same structural model, the same information set, the same subjective probability distributions of u_t^1, u_t^2 *and* estimate the coefficients α, β in the same way. If there is any massaging of the data to get rid of serial correlation of forecasting errors, it is done in the same way by all parties.

Full information

One of the most attractive features of the REH is that it generates a whole family of hypotheses about expectation formation, one for each specification of the information set Φ_{t-1}. In a more sophisticated model Φ_{t-1} would be determined endogenously. Even if individuals have unbounded rationality, they will not find it optimal to obtain full information if there are costs of gathering information. Each individual would choose Φ_{t-1} to maximize his utility subject to the appropriate constraints. Because of the difficulty of describing this process it is necessary to adopt the shortcut of assuming that the cost of observing a particular random variable is either zero or infinite. Equivalently, Φ_{t-1} is given. This sort of strategy is frequently used in economic theory. For example, models of economies with incomplete markets may treat the market structure as a datum[17] even though by introducing transaction costs explicitly it is possible to have the set of operating markets determined endogenously, as the result of maximizing behaviour. The rationale for this sort of assumption is that if the costs themselves are not exorbitant, as long as the set of markets which are open is correct, ignoring the transaction costs may not, for certain purposes, bias the analytical results. And so with information costs. From the point of view of expectation formation what matters is Φ_{t-1}, not the cost of observing the variables in Φ_{t-1}, although the latter determines the former. Assuming that Φ_{t-1} has been correctly specified, by taking it as given the only lapse from rigour lies in ignoring the costs of observing Φ_{t-1}.

But this raises the question of whether Φ_{t-1} has been correctly specified. In establishing the proposition it was assumed that Φ_{t-1} included all variables determined before period t and in particular the exogenous variables $\{(u^1_{t-i}, u^2_{t-i}): i = 1, 2, \ldots\}$. It seems implausible that producers and consumers would all find it worthwhile or even possible to meet the cost of acquiring so much information. However, a quick glance at the proof shows that it is in no way necessary that Φ_{t-1} be large in order for the LSP to hold. All that is necessary is that $\bar{m}_t = \underset{t-1}{E}\, \bar{m}_t = E[\bar{m}_t \mid \Phi_{t-1}]$. Make the same assumptions about the model as before but assume that Φ_{t-1} is arbitrary. For this assumption to be sensible all the variables in Φ_{t-1} must be determined before period t but formally it makes no difference. Now, under the REH,

$$\underset{t-1}{E}\, p_t = \underset{t-1}{E}\, \bar{m}_t - \beta k_t$$

so

$$p_t - {}_{t-1}p_t = \bar{m}_t - \underset{t-1}{E}\, \bar{m}_t - \beta y_t + \beta k_t - u_t^2$$

and

$$y_t = (1 + \alpha\beta) - \alpha\beta y_t + \alpha\left(\bar{m}_t - \underset{t-1}{E}\, \bar{m}_t\right) - \alpha u_t^2 + u_t^1$$

or, solving for y_t:

$$y_t = k_t + \frac{\alpha}{1 + \alpha\beta}\left(\bar{m}_t - \underset{t-1}{E}\, \bar{m}_t\right) + \frac{1}{1 + \alpha\beta}(u_t^1 - \alpha u_t^2).$$

The distribution of y_t is independent of the policy function if $(\bar{m}_t - \underset{t-1}{E}\, \bar{m}_t)$ is. This is certainly true if $\bar{m}_t$ is a function of variables in Φ_{t-1}. More precisely, suppose that $\Phi_{t-1} \supset \{(a_i, b_i): i = 1, 2, \ldots\}$ and define a policy function to be *admissible* if $a_i = 0$ (resp. $b_i = 0$) if $u^1_{t-1} \notin \Phi_{t-1}$ (resp. $u^2_{t-i} \notin \Phi_{t-1}$). Then the LSP can be restated as saying that the probability distribution of y_t is independent of the parameters of all admissible policy functions. The interpretation of this fact is clear: as long as consumers and producers have the same information set as the government and know the policy function, the LSP holds independently of the particular specification of Φ_{t-1}.

This extension of the proposition is important, for one often hears it said that the REH requires that agents have full information and this is neither plausible nor "rational" in view of the costs of acquiring such information. This interpretation of the REH is now seen to be unnecessary for the LSP and, in any case, seems unnecessarily restrictive.

Linear models

Another feature of the proposition as presented above is that it assumes a log-linear model of the economy. One consequence of this assumption is that the REH can be stated in terms of a relationship between a point expectation ${}_{t-1}p_t$ and the mathematical expectation of the random variable $\underset{t-1}{E}\, p_t$. More precisely, in the supply equation it is only the difference $(p_t - \underset{t-1}{E}\, p_t)$ which affects y_t. In the quantity equation the usual homogeneity properties ensure that changes in money supply only affect the expected value of the price level. Thus, as long as ${}_{t-1}p_t$ fully reflects these changes—which is what the form of the REH adopted here implies—the money supply does not affect the difference $(p_t - {}_{t-1}p_t)$. As long as these homogeneity properties are retained any other form of linearity can be dispensed with. The really restrictive assumption is that individuals have point expectations. If this is dropped a different form of the REH is required. Instead of dealing with probability distributions one defines states of nature and associates equilibrium price levels with each. Individuals are assumed to know the correct price level for each state of nature,[18] which implies a prodigious computational ability though not much information. However, they may differ in the subjective probabilities they assign to each state. With this reformulation homogeneity is again enough to establish the Lucas–Sargent proposition. To make these ideas really precise requires an extensive formal model and one such is discussed in the sequel. For the moment it is enough to realize that, apart from the homogeneity properties mentioned above, linearity is inessential and that if point expectations are to be abandoned a different framework is required.

Homogeneity revisited

To assume homogeneity is to assume a great deal, as we discovered earlier. And although the conditions are impossibly difficult to satisfy in general, they are rarely discussed by authors wishing to take advantage of homogeneity. However, under certain forms of the REH homogeneity becomes much more plausible. Suppose it were assumed either that the economy began as a sort of *tabula rasa* with no pre-existing commitments of any kind or else that, although the history of the economy stretches back to the infinite past, any individual begins life at a finite point in time with no pre-existing commitments.[19] Individuals will possess the usual homogeneity properties at the moment they are born, where homogeneity is with respect to equiproportional changes in all prices, current and future, in all states of nature. At any point it is permissible to cut the sequence and ask what would happen if there were a change in policy. But if the REH is to be satisfied one must then go back and ask what pre-existing commitments would have been if the change in policy had been anticipated. By "anticipation" one need not mean that the policy change is correctly foreseen, only that agents react in a homogeneous way. Thus, under the REH there are effectively no pre-existing commitments when a policy changes. Unfortunately, this does not mean that homogeneity is assured. In an economy with long-lived securities a state-dependent policy[20] may affect the real trading opportunities of individuals even if the policy is perfectly foreseen.

Suppose we were dealing with a sequence economy, that is, an economy in which trading takes place at successive dates because of the incompleteness of the set of markets at any given date. Suppose the dates are indexed $t = 0, 1, \ldots$ and that at each date t there is a set $\mathscr{F}_t$ representing the information structure (common to all individuals) on the set Ω of states of nature. The elements of $\mathscr{F}_t$ are called *events* and an ordered pair (t, E) such that $E \in \mathscr{F}_t$ is called a *date-event pair*. For simplicity it will be assumed that $\mathscr{F}_t$ is a collection of subsets of Ω which forms a partition. It is also assumed that $\mathscr{F}_{t+1}$ is a refinement of $\mathscr{F}_t$.[21] If $u = (t, E)$ and $v = (t + 1, E')$ are date-event pairs such that $E' \subset E$ then u is the (unique) *predecessor* of v and v is a *successor* of u.

In this simple economy there are various goods: money (which functions as an asset), other assets denominated in money (e.g. Treasury bills) and physical goods. The economy possesses an equilibrium of plans, prices and price expectations, that is, agents "know" the prices which will rule in each date-event pair (although they may disagree about subjective probabilities attached to the events) and accordingly plan once for all how much to trade in each date-event pair in order to maximize utility subject to the usual budget constraints.[22] Expectations are correct in the sense that the prices expected in any date-event pair are market clearing prices, *given* the expectations about prices at later date-event pairs and the planned trades at previous date-event pairs. A *monetary policy* is just a plan, that is, a function from date-event pairs to trades in assets (including money, of course). The policy is state-dependent but it is given once for all at $t=0$. The equilibrium described is clearly characterized by rational expectations. It might be thought, therefore, that in the absence of pre-existing commitments the equilibrium would be invariant to the choice of policy. The usual homogeneity arguments are not sufficient, however, even for very simple policies.

Consider the following suggestion of F. Hahn.[23] An individual holds one unit of money at the end of the date-event pair u. If N_u denotes the set of successors of u then at the next date, for any v in N_u, that unit of money can be transformed into $(p_v^h)^{-1}$ units of good h, where p_v^h is of course the price of good h in the date-event pair v. A unit of money at the end of u may be thought of as a bundle of commodities, *viz.* so many units of h at each v in N_u. Since money is not valued for its own sake but for what it will buy it is these alternative bundles which represent the real value of money. And the real demand for money and goods will not be invariant in general to non-homogeneous changes in these bundles.[24] Now if the monetary authorities, by pursuing a state-dependent monetary policy, can change the ratios $p_v^h/p_{v'}^h$ $(v, v' \in N_u)$ they will have changed the real characteristics of the bundle corresponding to a unit of money. In other words, the real exchange possibilities[25] among the date-event pairs have changed.

Now this argument is not entirely watertight. There has been no very clear statement of what constitutes a monetary policy, nor of how the price level is controlled. One possibility is that the money is distributed as transfer payments, for example, dropped from a helicopter. Now if the transfer payments are proportional to money holdings they will exactly compensate the change in prices. If not, they constitute a redistribution of wealth which is equivalent to taking goods from one individual and giving them to another. To describe this as a pure monetary policy is like calling a change in government expenditure a change in monetary policy just because the purchases are paid for with money. In any case, this is not the way a central bank implements its monetary policy. The usual vehicle for change in money supply is an open market operation, that is, the sale or purchase of government securities (bonds) in exchange for newly printed money. Suppose, under the conditions of the example above, the monetary authorities were to regulate the price level using open market operations. These open market operations cannot be carried out until it is known in which cell of N_u the true state of nature lies. Otherwise the policy would be independent of the date-event pairs in N_u. Suppose that at the second date, once $v \in N_u$ has been observed, the authorities offer to buy or sell bonds in exchange for money. This will have the effect of altering the money supply at the *end* of that date-event pair, which under the usual homogeneity (and uniqueness) assumption, will alter the price level in all successor date-event pairs, i.e. all w in N_v, but *not* in v. Implicitly it is assumed that one transaction per period is allowed here so an open market operation at one date may increase the stock of money held but does not have an effect on commodity prices through the real balance effect until the subsequent date.[26] The one period rates of return $(p_v^h)^{-1}$ considered by Hahn will be unchanged. His analysis seems deficient in this respect.

The argument sketched above is not entirely persuasive because it does not consider the possible effect of changes in expectations about prices in N_v on prices ruling at v. A precise analysis would proceed as follows.[27] At v, imagine that the government orders a monetary policy be adopted which would increase end-of-period holdings by $\mu\%$. Suppose that in all date-event pairs following v (but not including v) the prices of commodities and financial securities are now $\mu\%$ higher. In v, the prices of all securities denominated in money fall to $(1 + (.01)\mu)^{-1}$ of their previous level and the quantity of such assets demanded or supplied increases to $(1 + (.01)\mu)$ times its previous level. It is easy to check that with these changes equilibrium is preserved with a higher money stock *provided* there are no commitments denominated in money existing at v and payable after v. Money, being perfectly liquid, does not fall into this category but a long-dated security purchased at u would. Thus, the Hahn argument would be valid if applied to long-dated securities but not to money.

One other point to note is that neutrality at v requires that the supply of securities increase along with the demand for them. Suppose that the government purchases Treasury Bills in exchange for money. The supply will be *ipso facto* smaller, not larger, and this in itself is a source of non-neutrality.[28] If the government were to purchase one period bonds issued by the private sector no such problem would arise. But as long as there are any government securities outstanding the question of the adjustment of their supply is a source of difficulties for the "neutralist" argument. Also excluded from the model are securities consisting of money and commodities for delivery at various dates, since it will not be possible in general to adjust quantities of one without changing quantities of the other.[29]

It has been shown then that even with the more sophisticated form of the REH, neutrality may not be possible if long-dated securities denominated in money or money and goods have been sold before the proposed monetary intervention. This is not quite a precise statement of the result: if there exist combinations of securities (held in u) which entail no commitment to receive or supply money after $v \in N_u$ then neutrality may still be achieved in spite of the existence of long-dated securities denominated in money. But this calls for a rather far-fetched coincidence. In spite of that qualification, one is entitled to conclude that the traditional source of non-neutrality (*viz.* the real balance effect) is ruled out by the REH but that an open market operation will have real effects (will be non-neutral) if individuals make commitments, *before* the operation, to deliver or receive money *after* the operation. That is all there is to it.

The degree of liquidity of an economy, that is, the extent to which individuals are committed to making payments fixed in terms of money, may turn out to be a key factor in determining the extent to which monetary policy has real effects. For it is clear that while pre-existing commitments to make payments in money will normally preclude homogeneity, there are no pre-existing commitments in the long run and the set of securities itself is endogenous. The authorities were discovered to possess a real leverage on the economy because they could alter the set of "real" securities which could be traded. But this leverage will be reduced or in extreme cases eliminated if individuals find it profitable to invent new securities which replace the old ones or which make the economy more liquid. Likewise, if individuals simply choose to hold shorter dated securities the economy will be more "liquid" in this sense and the authorities' ability to influence the economy may be reduced, although it could not be denied that by driving individuals into the shorter end of the market the authorities have already had a real effect. Even if the set of available securities is unchanged it may be argued that the state-dependent effect of monetary policy is limited and that typically the authorities are concerned with unconditional expansion or contraction where the distribution effects are all important. In that case, it may be argued that the less liquid the economy is, i.e. the more long term commitments there are, the more impact a monetary policy may have. The neutralist line may then rest on the short-livedness of the impact of monetary policy resulting from the degree of liquidity in the economy.

These highly speculative remarks all apply to a once for all change in monetary policy. If monetary policy has short term effects then a policy which operates continuously will have real effects even in the long term. How far this critique can be pushed and whether it provides a basis for an effective monetary policy are questions which require fuller discussion, though both belong so clearly to the realm of pure theory that the reader may despair of obtaining practical insights from this approach.

Sticky prices

Another source of non-neutrality is sticky prices when agents make long term commitments to sell goods for money on fixed terms. By altering the value of money in a state-dependent way the authorities can alter the real terms of trade in spite of the REH. An example of this phenomenon has been provided by S. Fischer,[30] using a version of the linear macromodel introduced above.

Suppose that labour is hired at the end of period $(t-1)$ and produces goods which are available for sale at the beginning of period t. Wages are set when labour is hired at the end of $(t-1)$ and paid at the beginning of t when goods are produced. Let ${}_{t-1}w_t$ denote the logarithm of the nominal wage paid in t and set in $(t-1)$. The supply of goods depends on the real wage, whose logarithm is $({}_{t-1}w_t - p_t)$ if p_t is the logarithm of the price level in t. Precisely,

$$y_t = k_t + \alpha(p_t - {}_{t-1}w_t) + u_t^1$$

where $\alpha > 0$, k_t is some measure of normal capacity and y_t is the logarithm of real output. If the nominal wage is set to maintain the value of the real wage (which without loss of generality is assumed to equal unity) then ${}_{t-1}w_t = {}_{t-1}p_t$, where as before ${}_{t-1}p_t$ denotes the point expectation at the end of $(t-1)$ of the price level in t.[31] Of course, the value of the real wage is only maintained in an expected sense. There is no "catching up" for past losses nor, evidently, any risk aversion on the part of workers. If this assumption is accepted then under the REH

$$\begin{aligned} y_t &= k_t + \alpha(p_t - {}_{t-1}p_t) + u_t^1 \\ &= k_t + \alpha\left(p_t - \underset{t-1}{E}\, p_t\right) + u_t^1, \end{aligned}$$

the same supply function as used in the previous example. Thus, making the rest of the assumptions used before, the LSP will hold.

Now suppose that wage contracts are not renewed every period. For the sake of illustration, suppose that contracts last for two periods and that half of them are renewed at each date. Let $_{t-i}w_t$ $(i = 1, 2)$ denote the nominal wage set in period $(t - i)$ and paid in period t. A *contract* can be identified with an ordered pair $({}_{t-1}w_t, {}_{t-1}w_{t+1})$ which signifies that, at the end of date $(t - 1)$, workers and employers agree to exchange labour for money at the rate of 1 unit of labour for $_{t-1}w_t$ (resp. $_{t-1}w_{t+1}$) units of money in date t (resp. $(t + 1)$). Note that the contract in general specifies *different* nominal wages at each date. The amount of labour actually traded at these rates is left to be determined at the respective dates. If the nominal wage is set to maintain the value of the real wage then

$$_{t-i}w_t = {}_{t-i}p_t \qquad (i = 1, 2)$$

where $_{t-i}p_t$ is the expected value of p_t at the end of $(t - i)$. At date t half the firms will be paying a real wage $\exp\{{}_{t-1}p_t - p_t\}$ and half will be paying $\exp\{{}_{t-2}p_t - p_t\}$. The supply function will therefore be:

$$y_t = k_t + (\alpha/2)\left(\sum_{i=1}^{2} p_t - {}_{t-i}p_t\right) + u_t^1.$$ [32]

Suppose the error terms u_t^j are generated by the first-order autoregressive scheme:

$$u_t^j = \rho_j u_{t-1}^j + \varepsilon_t^j \qquad (j = 1, 2)$$

with $|\rho_j| < 1$ and ε_t^1, ε_t^2 are serially independent, mutually uncorrelated random variables with zero mean. The rest of the model is the same as before.

Proposition *The distribution of y_t is not independent of the parameters $\{(a_i, b_i)\}$ of the policy rule even if the REH is satisfied.*[33]

The "optimal" policy requires the authorities to compensate for nominal disturbances and reinforce real ones.

The effectiveness of monetary policy turns on the fact that some individuals set a nominal price for period t before they observe the error terms (u_{t-1}^1, u_{t-1}^2). The error terms can be thought of as date-event pairs. Then at date t the firms and workers who made a contract at the end of $(t - 2)$ are constrained to have the same nominal wage in every date-event pair whereas the monetary authorities can make their policy depend on (u_{t-1}^1, u_{t-1}^2) and hence change the real wage according to the date-event pair. The correspondence between this interpretation of the Fischer example and the Hahn example is obvious.

The costs of inflation

The Lucas–Sargent proposition, taken literally, claims that changes in the quantity of money will only change the general price level, leaving real magnitudes unchanged. The question which arises immediately is why anyone should care, in that case, how monetary policy is conducted or, slightly more remotely, why such a fuss is made about inflation. If inflation is "always and everywhere a purely monetary phenomenon", that is, if inflation is caused by changes in the quantity of money, and changes in the quantity of money have no real effects, then neither can inflation. The alleged costs which it imposes on the community must clearly be illusory. To the first question, the short answer is that monetary policy matters when it is unpredictable. There are two blades to the monetarist scissors. It is argued, on the one hand, that perfectly anticipated changes in the money supply have no effect and, on the other, that in order to have some impact on the economy, the monetary authorities must "fool" the private sector and so will be led to follow destabilizing policies, always trying to do the unexpected. These are large claims which will be examined more closely later. The second question, about the costs of inflation, can be dealt with here.

There is a well-developed, traditional theory which is doubly relevant because it explains, in terms which are acceptable to the purest monetarist, both why inflation is costly and why monetary policy is not neutral. It represents the closest thing there is to an *internal* inconsistency in the neutralist argument. Briefly, there is a cost to holding real money balances, namely the real rate of interest forgone plus the rate of inflation. An increase in the rate of inflation by raising the cost of holding cash balances may be expected to reduce the level of real balances. There is a consequent loss of consumer surplus as well as a possible change in the real rate of interest. In this way the rate of change of the money supply can have a real effect even when the level of the money supply does not.

The argument can be made precise using a simple model of a pure exchange economy with overlapping generations. There is a doubly infinite sequence of dates labelled $t = \ldots, -1, 0, 1, \ldots,$ *ad. inf.* At each date, a new generation is born, which lives for two periods. There are n-types of agents labelled $i = 1, \ldots, n$ in each generation. The i-th type of agent has an endowment e_i of goods in the first period of his life and none at the second. Formally, e_i is a non-negative vector in $\mathbb{R}^l$ if there are l commodities at each date. The i-th type of agent chooses a consumption bundle x_i^0 (resp. x_i^1) in the first (resp. second) period of his life to maximize his utility

$u_i(x_i)$ where $x_i = (x_i^0, x_i^1)$. Formally, u_i is a real-valued function defined on the set of non-negative consumption plans $\mathbb{R}^l_+ \times \mathbb{R}^l_+$.

At each date t there are two generations in existence, the *older generation*, which was born at $t - 1$ and the *younger generation*, born at t. The economy is stationary in the sense that the characteristics of the agents (their preferences and endowments) do not vary from generation to generation. In a stationary equilibrium, agents of the same type choose the same consumption plan x_i in each generation and relative prices are the same at each date. Consider an economy which is growing at a steady rate, for example, one in which there are λ^t individuals of each type in the generation born at date t, where $\lambda > 1$ is the "growth factor". At date t there will be λ times as many individuals of each type in the younger generation as there are in the older generation. A stationary allocation of commodities for this economy is a n-tuple $\{x_i\}_{i=1}^n$ of consumption plans, one for each type of agent. The allocation is attainable if and only if

$$\sum_{i=1}^{n} (x_i^1 + \lambda x_i^0) = \lambda \sum_{i=1}^{n} e_i \,.$$

The equation simply says that total goods consumed are equal to the total endowment at each date, but the consumption of young agents as well as their endowments are multiplied by λ because there are λ times as many of them. An attainable and stationary allocation $\{x_i\}$ is called efficient if there is no other stationary and attainable allocation $\{\hat{x}_i\}$ which makes everyone better off, i.e. $u_i(\hat{x}_i) > u_i(x_i)$ for all i.

Although there is no storage and no production, goods can be transferred between generations and apparently made to increase. If every agent, in his first period, gives up one unit of consumption to the older generation, he will receive λ units of consumption in the second period because of the growth of population. It's just like having a linear production process where each unit of input today produces λ units of output tomorrow. Efficiency requires that the marginal rate of substitution between consumption today and consumption tomorrow should equal this "marginal rate of transformation" λ. Whether it does so in equilibrium depends on the rate of inflation.

Each generation has an endowment of goods in the first period but none in the second. There is no storage so in order to provide themselves with consumption at the second date, these individuals exchange part of their endowment for money at the first date. At each date there is a transfer of goods from the younger generation to the older generation and a transfer of money in the opposite direction. Let p^t denote the vector of money prices of goods at date t and let m_i^t denote the money balances held by the i-th type of agent at date t. It is also assumed that in the second period of their lives, agents receive lump sum payments in the form of money. Let π_i^t denote the "pension" received by the i-th type of agent at date $(t + 1)$, i.e. by an agent born at t. In the sequel, I am only concerned with equilibria in which prices increase at a steady rate $(\mu - 1)$. In that case, it is expected that $p^t = \mu^t p$, $m_i^t = \mu^t m_i$ and $\pi_i^t = \mu^t \pi_i$, where p, m_i and π_i are the corresponding values for the generation born at date 0. Clearly, it is sufficient to analyse the behaviour of the economy at a single date, say date 0, since every other date is the same, up to a scalar multiple. At date 0, an older agent of type i has a cash balance $\mu^{-1} m_i$ carried forward from his first period (the factor μ^{-1} takes account of the change in the price level) and receives a pension of $\mu^{-1}\pi_i$ units of money. There are λ^{-1} agents of each type in the older generation so the total supply of money is $(\lambda\mu)^{-1} \sum_{i=1}^{n} (m_i + \pi_i)$. Each agent of type i in generation 0 wants to hold m_i units of money and since there is one agent of each type, total demand is $\sum_{i=1}^{n} m_i$. An attainable, stationary allocation of cash balances is a n-tuple $\{m_i\}_{i=1}^{n}$ of non-negative numbers such that

$$\sum_{i=1}^{n} (m_i + \pi_i) = \lambda\mu \sum_{i=1}^{n} m_i .$$

Alternatively, this equation can be thought of as defining the rate of inflation μ.

A stationary equilibrium consists of a price vector p, an inflation factor μ and an attainable, stationary allocation of commodities $\{x_i\}$ and money balances $\{m_i\}$ such that, for every $i = 1, \ldots, n$, the ordered pair (x_i, m_i) maximizes $u_i(x_i)$ subject to the budget constraints

$$p.x_i^0 + m_i \leq p.e_i$$
$$p.x_i^1 \leq m_i + \pi_i .$$

If (x_i, m_i) solves this problem, then at date t an agent of the i-th type (who faces prices $\mu^t p$ and $\mu^{t+1} p$ and will receive a pension $\mu^t \pi_i$) will maximize his utility subject to analogous constraints by choosing $(x_i, \mu^t m_i)$.

A stationary equilibrium is efficient if $\mu\lambda = 1$ *and* $m_i > 0$ *for* $i = 1, \ldots, n$.

I shall only give a sketch of the proof since the details are easy to fill in. Since $m_i > 0$, x_i maximizes $u_i(x_i)$ subject to $p.x_i^0 + \mu p.x^1 \leq p.e_i + \pi_i$. If there exists an attainable, stationary allocation $\{\bar{x}_i\}$ which everyone prefers then

$$p.\bar{x}_i^0 + \mu p.\bar{x}_i^1 > p{\cdot}e_i + \pi_i \qquad (i = 1, \ldots, n)$$

and

$$\lambda \sum_{i=1}^{n} \bar{x}_i^0 + \sum_{i=1}^{n} x_i^1 = \lambda \sum_{i=1}^{n} e_i .$$

This last equation implies that $\sum p.\bar{x}_i^0 + \mu \sum p.x_i^1 = \sum p.e_i$ since $\mu\lambda = 1$. But $\mu\lambda = 1$ implies $\sum \pi_i = 0$ so summing the inequality implies that $\sum p.\bar{x}_i^0 + \mu \sum p.\bar{x}_i^1 > \sum p.e_i$, a contradiction. This completes the proof of the proposition. Under slightly stronger assumptions the converse can also be proved.

> *If $(p, \mu, \{x_i\}, \{m_i\})$ is an efficient stationary equilibrium such that $(x_i, m_i) > 0$, for every i, and if the utility function u_i is strictly increasing and continuously differentiable and $x_i \gg 0$ for every i, then $\lambda\mu = 1$.*

Let a_i be the gradient vector of u_i at $x_i . a_i(\bar{x}_i - x_i) > 0$ if and only if $u_i(x_i + t(\bar{x}_i - x_i)) > u_i(x_i)$ for sufficiently small $t > 0$. Since $m_i > 0$ it follows as before that x_i maximizes $u_i(x_i)$ subject to $p.x_i^0 + p.x_i^1 \leq p.e_i + \pi_i$. Therefore it maximizes $a_i . x_i$ subject to the same constraint and $x_i \gg 0$ implies a_i is proportional to $(p, \mu p)$. If $\mu\lambda \neq 1$ there exist arbitrarily small vectors z_i, for $i = 1, \ldots, n$, such that

$$(p, \mu p) . z_i > 0$$

$$\lambda \sum z_i^0 + \sum z_i^1 = 0 .$$

Then $\{x_i + z_i\}$ is attainable and preferred to $\{x_i\}$ by everyone. This contradicts the assumed efficiency of $\{x_i\}$ and completes the proof of the proposition.

The model is very simple but it makes the crucial point. Efficiency requires deflation ($\mu < 1$), not inflation, in a growing economy. Because of the growth of population a central planner can transform consumption today into consumption tomorrow at the rate of one for λ. The rate of inflation (deflation) must take this into account. To ensure that the marginal rate of substitution between dates equals the marginal rate of transformation, the rate of exchange between consumption today and consumption tomorrow must be one for λ, for each commodity.

In this story money is the only asset. If agents wish to consume in both periods of their lives they have to hold money. When alternative assets are available the story is different but the results retain a family resemblance. Capital goods can be introduced by providing each agent with a neoclassical production function. Using consumption goods as an input an agent produces consumption goods as an output in the next period. The cost of holding money balances from one period to the next is now the rate of inflation *plus* the marginal product of capital forgone. Consumers will not hold money unless there is deflation, that is, unless the cost of holding money is actually zero. To avoid this outcome one can assume that the holding of money balances yields non-pecuniary benefits, i.e. put real balances in the utility function. This is not a very good way to proceed but it suffices for the purpose of illustration. The sources of inefficiency are increased now. As before, there may be permanent inefficiency as the relative price of consumption today in terms of consumption tomorrow is at the wrong level. There is another inefficiency, this one resulting from too little money in the system. If real balances appear in the utility function, then an increase in real balances, *caet. par.*, makes everyone better off. But the cost to society of increasing real balances is zero. It is only necessary to lower the price level, for example. This argument, which often goes under the heading of the Optimum Quantity of Money,[34] can be analysed in a rather different framework. Money is not the only asset in the economy; there is usually an alternative such as a deposit account which is almost as safe and bears a positive rate of interest. For the sake of concreteness suppose the alternative is a riskless bond. One measure of the opportunity cost of holding money is the interest forgone. A rational agent will only hold money if, at the margin, there is some real benefit which balances the opportunity cost. This benefit is usually identified with the convenience of holding money rather than, say, having to make more frequent trips to the bank. The important point is that holding money does increase welfare and at the margin the benefit of the last unit (as measured by the interest forgone in order to hold it) is positive. From this it follows that a monetary equilibrium is inefficient because the marginal benefit of holding cash balances is greater than the marginal cost. A reduction in *all* prices, present and future, would increase the real quantity of money at no extra cost.[35] There have been various proposals for remedying the inefficiency: a steady decline in prices would reduce the nominal interest rate on bonds to zero, thus reducing the gap between the return on money and bonds to zero; the payment of interest on cash balances would have the same effect.[36] These proposals will only work under very special conditions. In particular, it must be assumed that the divergence between the rate of return on bonds and money is the only source of inefficiency. Otherwise the theory of Second Best warns us that eliminating the divergence may make things worse rather than better. Among other things, it would have to be assumed that there was a complete set of Arrow securities, a perfect capital market and so forth. The following example gives an idea of the sort of world in which the theory of the Optimum Quantity of Money would be valid.

Suppose that time is divided into days and that on each day consumers have an endowment of a homogeneous consumption good. The consumption good is perishable and there are no forward markets so the only way that consumers can alter their stream of consumption is to trade the consumption good daily for some asset. Assume that there are two types of asset, money and a bond. The bond is defined as a promise to pay one unit of money to the bearer one month after the day the bond was issued. A consumer who sells bonds is selling promises to deliver money. The market for bonds is open only once a month, say on the first day of the month. Thus anyone who wants to buy or sell the consumption good in between must be willing to hold money. Suppose that the price of consumption goods at each date is foreseen with certainty so that at the beginning of the month every consumer can make his optimal, i.e. utility maximizing, plan for trading in money, bonds and consumption.[37] Now consider an individual making this decision at the beginning of the month. Suppose that the rate of interest is positive (the price of a bond is less than unity). Then a rational individual will not plan to hold a positive amount of money on every day of the month since by planning to hold slightly lower cash balances at every date and putting the money into bonds, he could start the next month with more money and have the same consumption stream in the interim.[38] The representative individual will thus plan to hold no money on some day of the month. Efficiency requires that the marginal rate of substitution between any pair of goods should be the same for each consumer, assuming that consumers have smooth preferences and consume a positive amount on each day. This condition will not be satisfied. A consumer who has positive cash balances from the first to the t-th day of the month faces an exchange ratio of p_1/p_t, where p_t is the price of consumption on the t-th day, between consumption on day 1 and consumption on day t. Similarly, a consumer who has positive cash balances from day t to the first of next month faces an exchange ratio of p_t/p_{32} between the t-th day and the first of next month. But the exchange ratio between the first of this month and the first of the next is p_1/q_1p_{32}, where q_1 is the price of bonds on day 1. Clearly, the two consumers must have different marginal rates of substitution between consumption at some pair of dates.[39] This inefficiency would be removed if $q_1 = 1$, in which case there would be no cost of holding cash balances and consumers would not be effectively constrained in their ability to trade between different dates.[40]

The crucial characteristic of this model is that, given perfect foresight and no uncertainty, when the nominal rate of interest is zero the model collapses to what is essentially an Arrow–Debreu economy with complete markets. Just as in the economy in which inflation was used as a tax, so too here money is lightly grafted on to an otherwise smoothly functioning economy and leads to inefficiency because it allows a slight but rectifiable divergence between actual prices and efficiency prices. Money is more than a veil but it only requires the right monetary policy to convert it once more into a veil.

The examples that I have been considering suggest two sources of inefficiency which result from inflation. The first is of the kind which arises in non-monetary dynamic models but inflation may make the problem worse. Indeed, if the monetary authority uses the money issued to buy goods, the classic "inflationary tax", they would have an incentive to increase the distortion. The second is present in any economy where holding real cash balances is costly but inflation, by increasing the cost of holding money, increases the distortion. Neither example depends on assumptions which are in any way unusual and, in particular, they are entirely consistent with the view of the economy put forward in the rational expectations literature. The equilibria are characterized by perfect foresight (a form of rational expectations), market clearing prices and so on. It follows that the model used to illustrate the LSP is at best incomplete. In a more general model, the rate of change of the money supply has a real effect even if the absolute level does not. It is only by ignoring the cost of holding money and its effect on the level and composition of demand for assets generally that the pure neutrality result can be obtained.

The various types of inefficiency caused by inflation have been known for a long time. It seems, therefore, a trifle odd that they should have been ignored in the literature on rational expectations and the neutrality of monetary policy. There are two possible explanations: that it was not thought to be relevant and that the effect was thought to be "small". Although the LSP and related results do claim to show that monetary policy has either a transitory effect or no effect at all, the real target of their critique is the use of expansionary monetary policy to increase output, cure unemployment, etc. One can quite consistently hold the view that there is no useable trade-off between inflation and unemployment without denying that monetary policy has any effect whatsoever on the economy. For the purposes of illustrating the absence of a useable trade-off it is legitimate to use a model from which some real effects of monetary policy have been eliminated, as long as these effects do not constitute a useable trade-off themselves. And no one has suggested that the establishment of an "optimum quantity of money" rule would cure unemployment. Whatever the magnitude of the inefficiency caused by inflation, it is most unlikely that these real effects have any significant impact on stabilization policies. It is right, of course, to point out that the claim that monetary policy has no effect at all is false. But this does not disprove the essential lesson of the LSP that monetary policy is of limited use for stabilization policy. Still less does it prove the contrary.

Concluding remarks

In the thumbnail sketch of monetary theory contained in this chapter, the question of the neutrality of money predominates. The impression has no doubt been created in part by the bias of the author but it is mainly, I think, a fair reflection of the preoccupations of theorists over a considerable part of the period under discussion. The curious thing is the resilience of the idea that money is neutral. Under the most generous interpretation, the conditions which must be satisfied if money is to be be strictly neutral are impossibly restrictive. But if that is the case, why do theorists keep returning to the concept, either as believers or sceptical or hostile critics? The issue behind the theoretical controversies is whether monetary policy is useful as a means of regulating the economy. The view of the neutralist camp appears to be that it is not. Sometimes they seem to be casting doubt on the effectiveness of any kind of stabilization policy, or so they have been accused. The simplistic models that have appeared in the literature belie the seriousness of the underlying issues. If, for the sake of argument, one imagines that there are only two intellectual camps, neutralist and anti-neutralist, there would seem to be three points, on which they are divided, which matter. The first is the importance of the long run, the second is the efficiency of the economy when left to itself and the third, much harder to make precise, is a prejudice against discretionary policy *per se*.

Despite the theoretical flimsiness of the original treatment by Archibald and Lipsey, the idea that money must be neutral in the long run has survived. At one level the argument is quite robust. In a stock equilibrium the distribution of assets is determined, almost by definition, by real factors. At another level it is very shaky. There may be many equilibria, they may be unstable, repeated monetary shocks may keep the economy permanently out of stock equilibrium, and so on. But these arguments cut both ways. Given how little we know about dynamics, there is not much hope for controlling the economy if these points are valid. When economists cannot rely on equilibrium arguments they usually have little to say. The long-run neutrality of money is a durable idea precisely because it is hard to find anything else to put in its place, not because it is based on realistic assumptions. The real issue has become the relevance of long-run results. In other words, does it really matter what happens in the long run?

To the extent that this is an empirical question, it cannot be answered here. A theoretical observation may help to put the matter in perspective, though. There is a *prima facie* case for dismissing the long run on the grounds that it never arrives. Even if there were theoretically persuasive results which showed that, under plausible conditions, the economy would converge to a long-run equilibrium, it would only do so as time approached infinity. Put another way, since the long run is made up of a sequence of short runs, it is sufficient to analyse the short run. There is a fallacy of composition in this argument, however. What may be true of one short period need not be true of a sequence of short periods. For example, it may be legitimate to treat expectations as more or less given in one short period but it is not legitimate to ignore the effect of a policy, carried on for several periods, on the expectations held in the succeeding periods. Likewise, the fact that the economy is never in long-run equilibrium does not make it irrelevant to ask what will happen in the long run. It may only be from such questions that we get a theoretical insight into the sustained effect of economic policy.

On the second issue, the neutralist camp is often portrayed as believing that we live in the best of all possible worlds. If the *status quo* is inefficient, they want to know, why has not someone done something about it? Rational agents would always take advantage of the opportunity to make themselves genuinely better off. Although this sort of argument may seem absurd in a practical context it is an extremely useful question to ask. In the first place, there may be some hitherto uncounted cost which makes an apparent Pareto-inefficiency not an inefficiency at all. In the second place, if there is an inefficiency then the neutralist argument suggests that it must result from non-cooperative[41] behaviour. By insisting that all sorts of transactions costs be taken into account and by locating the source of inefficiency in non-cooperative behaviour, the neutralist argument may be suggesting another limitation of the scope of monetary policy. In any case, there is more to the argument than a simple belief in *laisser-faire*.

The prejudice against discretionary policy as such seems to spring from similar sources. But there must be more to it than that. If rational agents can always be counted on to achieve a Pareto-efficient outcome in the private sector, why not in the public sector too? If the world is populated with rational, maximizing agents the failure of government intervention must be explained in terms of rational maximizing behaviour too. The usual approach of both sides is to treat government policy as a parameter, or at best as a rule, and sometimes to optimise with respect to this policy. Clearly a more sophisticated model is required to explain where government policy goes wrong, if indeed it does. The answer may lie in the informational constraints on the government or it may lie in the sort of non-cooperative game the government is playing.

I am not sure that much remains to be said on the issue of the long run versus short run view of the economy. On the other hand, something does remain to be said about the way in which the government is portrayed in economics and in the theory of economic policy in particular. The REH literature has begun to question the traditional conception of the policy-maker as an omniscient central planner. For the first time the government is assumed to be a destabilizer but there is no real theory to back this up. If we want to go further it will be necessary at the very least to treat the government as a maximizing agent whose behaviour is determined, like that of other agents, as the outcome of a (non-cooperative) policy game. Some tentative steps in this direction are taken in Chapter 3.

The intervening pages are devoted to the logically prior question: what are the efficiency properties of the rational expectations equilibrium, with and without government intervention?

Notes

1. A. Phillips, "The Relation Between Unemployment and the Rate of Change of Money Wage Rates in the United Kingdom, 1862–1957", *Economica*, **25** (1958), pp. 283–99.

2. R. Lipsey, "The Relation Between Unemployment and the Rate of Change of Wage Rates in the United Kingdom, 1862–1952: a Further Analysis", *Economica*, **27** (1960), pp. 1–31.

3. C. Schultze, *Recent Inflation in the U.S.*, Study Paper No. 1, Study of Employment, Growth and Price Levels (Joint Economic Committee, 86th Congress: 1st Session, 1959).

4. M. Friedman, "The Role of Monetary Policy", *American Economic Review*, **58** (1968), pp. 1–17; E. Phelps, "Phillips Curves, Expectations of Inflation and Optimal Unemployment Over Time", *Economica*, **34** (1967), pp. 254–81.

5. If a firm hires labour today at a money wage w and produces goods which it assumes it can sell at the current price, the demand for labour depends on the real wage rate only. Inflation changes the values of w and p in the same proportion and leaves demand for labour unchanged.

6. Suppose that wages are set for a period of time on the assumption that the current price level will be maintained. An increase in goods prices will lower the real wage and increase demand for labour.

7. In the long run, that is.

8. R. Lucas and L. Rapping, "Real Wages, Employment and Inflation", *Journal of Political Economy*, **77** (1969).

9. The information set is defined to be the set of variables (GNP, price level, etc.) which an individual can observe, i.e. whose values he knows, at some point of time.

10. "Closed" in the sense that it is a complete account of expectation formation and "consistent" in the sense that an individual with rational expectations has no incentive to alter his expectations.

11. T. Sargent and N. Wallace, "Rational Expectations, the Optimal Monetary Instrument and the Optimal Money Supply Rule", *Journal of Political Economy*, **83** (1976), pp. 241–57; R. Lucas, "Expectations and the Neutrality of Money", *Journal of Economic Theory*, **4** (1972) pp. 103–24.

12. Suppose money wages paid in period t are set in period $(t-1)$. If the logarithm of the money wage equals ${}_{t-1}p_t$ (or is proportional to it) the supply function says that real income is a function of the real wage as in traditional theory.

13. Since velocity is a random variable this is not quite the usual version but the demand for money is homogeneous of degree one in the price level. This is the important point as it turns out.

14. In practice this means that one solves for x_t in terms of all the exogenous variables and then substitutes their true values (if in Φ_{t-1}) or their expectation to get ${}_{t-1}x_t$.

15. Even this can be weakened a lot. See the discussion of homogeneity below.

16. This suggestion was put to me by David Hendry.

17. Cf. R. Radner, "Existence of Equilibrium of Plans, Prices and Price Expectations in a Sequence of Markets", *Econometrica*, **40** (1972), pp. 289–303.

18. Again this can be weakened a bit. It is homogeneity that counts.

19. An economy with origin at $-\infty$ differs from one which starts at a finite point in time in only two important respects, there is no initial state and at any date there is, perforce, an infinite number of events (partial histories) to be observed.

20. A state-dependent policy is one in which the government's action depends in a non-trivial way on the state of nature. For example, a policy of increasing the money supply by a constant proportion at each date would *not* be state-dependent.

21. That is, $\mathscr{F}_{t+1}$ refines $\mathscr{F}_t$ for each t. If F belongs to $\mathscr{F}_{t+1}$ it is also contained in some element of $\mathscr{F}_t$.
22. A trivial example of a sequence economy (with no uncertainty) is provided by the simple model discussed in connection with the optimum quantity of money.
23. In a public lecture delivered at the London School of Economics in November 1978. He attributed the original idea to J. Stiglitz.
24. A security in this context is sometimes defined as a bundle of commodities for future delivery. The set of final net trades in commodities which can be attained by trading in all possible securities is called the trade set. The security to which a unit of money corresponds depends on prices. Thus the definition of the trade set is endogeneous to the model.
25. I.e. the trade set.
26. Cf. the homogeneity assumption in the proposition above.
27. The analysis does not consider the question of how the government expands the money supply. As in the discussion of the Patinkin controversy it turns out that the stock of securities offered in exchange for money must increase in proportion with the money supply. Suppose individuals issue a bond to the government in exchange for money, i.e. they are borrowing from the government.
28. This is the same problem encountered in the discussion of the Patinkin controversy.
29. For example, purchasing a good on credit entails the exchange of a good and a stream of money payments. This could be defined as a commodity and thus included within the standard sequence economy framework. But a change in "price" would seem to require a change in the definition of the commodity, especially if monetary policy is to be neutral.
30. S. Fischer, "Long Term Contracts, Rational Expectations and the Optimal Money Supply Rule", *Journal of Political Economy*, **85** (1977) 191–205; E. Phelps and J. Taylor, "Stabilizing Powers of Monetary Policy Under Rational Expectations", *Journal of Political Economy* **85** (1977) 163–90.
31. This may be a slight lapse from rational expectations, for if ${}_{t-1}w_t = {}_{t-1}p_t$ it does not follow that the mathematical expectation of the real wage is unity.
32. If y_{ti} is the supply of firms in the i-th period of their contract then $y_{ti} = \frac{1}{2}(k_t + \alpha(p_t - {}_{t-i}p_t) + u_t^1)$ and $y_t = y_{t1} + y_{t2}$.
33. *Proof* Without essential loss of generality and to simplify the arithmetic it will be assumed that $k_t = 0$ and $\alpha = \beta = 1$. Without these assumptions the calculations are much more tedious but follow the same lines. The model is now defined by the equations:

$$e_t = \bar{m}_t - p_t - u_t^2$$

$$y_t = \frac{1}{2}\sum_{i=1}^{2}(p_t - {}_{t-i}p_t) + u_t^1$$

and

$$e_t = y_t.$$

Since

$$\underset{t-2}{E}\,({}_{t-1}p_t) = {}_{t-1}p_t$$

$${}_{t-2}p_t = {}_{t-2}\bar{m}_t - {}_{t-2}(u_t^1 + u_t^2).$$

But $\bar{m}_t = {}_{t-1}\bar{m}_t$ so

$$
{}_{t-1}p_t = \frac{2}{3}({}_{t-1}\bar{m}_t) + \frac{1}{3}({}_{t-1}\bar{m}_t) - \left(\frac{1}{3}\right)_{t-1}(u_t^1 + u_t^2) - \frac{2}{3}(u_t^1 + u_t^2)
$$

Accordingly

$$
2p_t = \frac{4}{3}\bar{m}_t + \frac{2}{3}({}_{t-2}\bar{m}_t) - (u_t^1 + u_t^2) - \left(\frac{1}{3}\right)_{t-1}(u_t^1 + u_t^2) - \left(\frac{2}{3}\right)_{t-2}(u_t^1 + u_t^2)
$$

and

$$
y_t = \frac{1}{3}(\bar{m}_t - {}_{t-2}\bar{m}_t) + \frac{1}{2}(u_t^1 - u_t^2) + \left(\frac{1}{6}\right)_{t-1}(u_t^1 + u_t^2) + \left(\frac{1}{3}\right)_{t-2}(u_t^1 + u_t^2).
$$

From the money supply function:

$$
{}_{t-2}\bar{m}_t = a_1\rho_1 u_{t-2}^1 + \sum_{i=2}^{\infty} a_i u_{t-i}^1 + b_1\rho_2 u_{t-2}^2 + \sum_{i=2}^{2} b_i u_{t-i}^2
$$

so

$$
\begin{aligned}
\bar{m}_t - {}_{t-2}\bar{m}_t &= a_1(u_{t-1}^1 - \rho_1 u_{t-2}^1) + b_1(u_{t-1}^2 - \rho_2 u_{t-1}) \\
&= a_1\varepsilon_{t-1}^1 + b_1\varepsilon_{t-1}^2.
\end{aligned}
$$

Output is clearly unaffected by the values a_i and b_i for $i \geq 2$. Putting these equal to zero:

$$
\begin{aligned}
y_t &= \frac{1}{3}[a_1(u_{t-1}^1 - \rho_1 u_{t-2}^1) + b_1(u_{t-1}^2 - \rho_2 u_{t-1}^2)] \\
&\quad + \frac{1}{2}(u_t^1 - u_t^2) + \left(\frac{1}{6}\right)_{t-1}(u_t^1 + u_t^2) + \left(\frac{1}{3}\right)_{t-2}(u_t^1 + u_t^2) \\
&= \frac{1}{2}(\varepsilon_t^1 - \varepsilon_t^2) + \frac{1}{3}(\varepsilon_{t-1}^1(a_1 + 2\rho_1) + \varepsilon_{t-1}^2(b_1 - \rho_2)) \\
&\quad + \rho_1^2 u_{t-2}^1
\end{aligned}
$$

The asymptotic variance of y is easily calculated to be

$$
\sigma_y^2 = \sigma_{\varepsilon 1}^2\left[\frac{1}{4} + \frac{4}{9}\rho_1^2 + \rho_1^4(1 - \rho_1^2)^{-1} + \frac{a_1}{9}(4\rho_1 + a_1)\right] + \sigma_{\varepsilon 2}^2\left[\frac{1}{4} + \frac{1}{9}\rho_2^2 - \frac{b_1}{9}(2\rho_1 - b_1)\right].
$$

The variance is minimized by setting $a_1 = 2\rho_1$ and $b_1 = \rho_2$ in which case the variance becomes

$$
\sigma_y^2 = \sigma_{\varepsilon 1}^2\left[\frac{1}{4} + \rho_1^4(1 - \rho_1^2)^{-1}\right] + \sigma_{\varepsilon 2}^2\left[\frac{1}{4}\right]. \quad \square
$$

34. There is a substantial literature but the main early contributions are P. Samuelson, "What Classical and Neoclassical Monetary Theory Really Was", *Canadian Journal of Economics*, **1** (1968), pp. 1–15; M. Friedman, *The Optimum Quantity of Money*, Chicago: Aldine, 1969; H. Johnson, "Inside Money, Outside Money, Income, Wealth and Welfare in Monetary Theory", *Journal of Money, Credit and Banking*.

35. In a stationary equilibrium in which the money price of consumption is constant and there is a bond which sells at price q and yields one pound after one period, one unit of consumption today can be transformed into $(1/q)$ units tomorrow. One unit of consumption exchanged for money today can be transformed into one unit of consumption tomorrow. Thus there must be some real benefit derived from holding money balances. Precisely,

$$\left(\frac{1}{q} - 1\right) \partial u/\partial x = \partial u/\partial(m/p),$$

where the left hand side refers to marginal utility tomorrow and the right hand side to marginal utility today. $\partial u/\partial(m/p) = 0$ only if $q = 1$, i.e. the interest rate is zero.

36. Since in that case bonds would be held only if there was no non-pecuniary benefit from holding money.

37. Suppose the consumer maximizes a utility function of the form $\sum_{t=0}^{T} u(x_t)$, where x_t is consumption on day t, subject to the constraints $p_t(x_t - e_t) + m_t - m_{t-1} \leq 0$ if the bond market is closed at date t and $p_t(x_t - e_t) + m_t - m_{t-1} + q_t b_t - b_{t-30} \leq 0$ if it is open. Here e_t denotes this endowment at date t and b_t is the net purchase of bonds at t. q_t is the price of bonds.

38. If $m_t > 0$ at each t then $\lambda_{t+1} = \lambda_t$ for each $t < T$ where λ_t is the marginal utility of income. If the bond market is open at t then $\lambda_t q_t = \lambda_{t+30}$ since sales of bonds are allowed, but the previous relation implies $\lambda_t = \lambda_{t+30}$.

39. For some consumer 1, say, and some t', $\lambda_{t'}^1 > \lambda_{t'+1}^1$ since otherwise $\lambda_t^1 \leq \lambda_{t+30}^1$ which contradicts $\lambda_t^1 q_t = \lambda_{t+30}^1$. But since someone must hold money balances at the end of date t', say consumer 2, $\lambda_{t'}^2 = \lambda_{t'+1}^2$. Thus the marginal rates of substitution between consumption at t' and at $(t'+1)$ are different for 1 and 2.

40. When the rate of interest is zero there is effectively a single budget constraint so the equilibrium is like a Walrasian one.

41. A cooperative game is one in which there is unlimited pre-play communication and players are able to make self-binding commitments. The outcome of such a game is expected to be Pareto-efficient, almost by definition. A non-cooperative game is one which is not cooperative. Non-cooperative behaviour refers to the play of a non-cooperative game.

CHAPTER 2

Informational efficiency and economic efficiency

2.1 Rational expectations hypothesis

In the last chapter it was argued that the Rational Expectations Hypothesis (REH) is not logically necessary for the Lucas–Sargent Proposition (LSP) and, more generally, for propositions characterizing the neutrality of money. It might seem natural to abandon the REH, together with its ideological overtones, but there are a number of reasons for retaining it.

First, it is not clear that anything is gained by replacing the REH with a weaker or more plausible condition which leads to the same conclusion. For example, it was pointed out during the discussion of the LSP that, instead of assuming agents know the "true" model, one could assume they knew some "subjective" model, as long as there was no differential information. In that case, adopting the REH entails no essential loss of generality and avoids an awkward circumlocution.

In the second place, there is much more to the REH than the assumption of perfect foresight. In general-equilibrium theory it has generally been assumed that economic agents have a fixed quantity of information about their environment. More recently it has been recognized that by observing endogenous variables agents may infer something about the state of nature. For example, prices may reveal to an agent information held by others. The study of these phenomena raises all sorts of technical and conceptual problems. Under the REH these problems have turned out to be tractable.[1] The insights gained do not appear to depend crucially on the REH although the methods do. When we come to the study of strategic behaviour and its interaction with endogenous information, the complications mount and it is even more helpful then to have the REH.

The third reason for retaining the REH is that it avoids *ad hocery*. The trouble with *ad hoc* assumptions about expectations is simply that there are too many of them. The REH acts as an "organizing principle" in much the same way as the assumption that agents are maximizers. It is of some interest to study the REH as a "benchmark" case. It provides a test of the logical consistency of the claims of Monetarists and others and, in the absence of controlled experiments, this test may be extremely valuable. A hypothetical and well-behaved world provides a perspective on the "real" one. By noting the discrepancies between them it is possible to see where the hypothetical argument might break down when applied to a practical problem.

The usefulness of economic theory lies in showing what can or cannot legitimately be said, not in establishing "facts". The case for using the REH rests on its being part of a fruitful research strategy, not on its literal accuracy. The first step in the strategy is to understand precisely what the hypothesis means in a model of economic equilibrium.

To begin with I shall consider a very simple economy without money because the basic issues are the same for monetary and non-monetary economies. The economy consists of two individuals or *agents* who are labelled $i = 1, 2$. It is a *pure exchange* economy, i.e. there is no production, and there are two commodities, labelled $h = 1, 2$, which can be traded by the agents. Each agent has an initial endowment of the two commodities. Let e_{ih} denote the i-th agent's endowment of the h-th commodity and call the vector $e_i = (e_{i1}, e_{i2})$ his *endowment*. Uncertainty is introduced into the economy by way of *states of nature*. There are assumed to be two states, labelled $\omega = 0, 1$. The states can be thought of as exogenous variables; they represent outside influences on the economy. More formally, a state is a complete description of the environment of the economy. Once the state of nature is known, everything else is determined. In practice, states of nature represent any information about which agents may be uncertain: the weather, tastes, technology, etc. In the present example it is tastes which are uncertain. The i-th agent has a utility function $u_i(x_i, \omega)$ where $x_i = (x_{i1}, x_{i2})$ is a *consumption bundle* and x_{ih} is his consumption good h. If the i-th agent consumes x_i and the true state of nature is ω his utility will be $u_i(x_i, \omega)$. The appearance of ω in the utility function merely indicates that tastes are uncertain, i.e. depend on the state of nature.

If it seems odd that consumers do not know their own preferences, the following illustration may help. Suppose the two commodities were actually machines which produced different amounts of a homogeneous consumption good in each state of nature. Let $r_h(\omega)$ be the amount of consumption produced by a machine of type h in state ω. If the i-th agent owns x_{ih} units of the

h-th machine his consumption in state ω will be $x_{i1}r_1(\omega) + x_{i2}r_2(\omega)$. Clearly, the utility he will derive from owning x_i will depend on the state of nature and, if trading takes place before the state is known, he will be uncertain about his true preferences, i.e. uncertain about the amount of utility he will actually get from x_i.

To bring the example closer to reality we might imagine that the machines referred to above are shares in companies and the consumption produced is profits. The agents are interested in maximizing the utility gained from holding a particular portfolio. There may be many factors affecting the profitability of a company which are unknown to them. When trading takes place the agents will be uncertain about the utility which a particular portfolio will yield.

A final example is the case where commodities of uncertain quality are traded. A consumer may not have consumed this particular commodity before or he may be unable to determine at the time of purchase whether the goods are exactly the same as those he has sampled previously. In either case, he will not know how much utility the bundle x_i will yield until he has actually consumed it, i.e. until the state of nature is revealed.

In all the illustrations given above it is easy to imagine that some agents are better informed than others. In other words, there is *differential information*. This is easily represented in the model by making appropriate assumptions about the observability of states of nature. An *informed* agent is one who can observe the true state before trading takes place. An *uninformed* agent is one who cannot. I shall assume that agent 1 is informed and agent 2 is not. An immediate implication is that agent 1 always maximizes $u_1(x_1, \omega)$ when state ω occurs whereas agent 2, unless he can obtain more information, will maximize the expected value of $u_2(x_2, .)$ whichever state occurs.

It will also be assumed that there is no direct communication between the two agents and that agent 2 cannot observe agent 1's behaviour before making his own demand. All that agent 2 can observe is prices but prices may reveal information. Prices are determined by demand and supply which in turn are influenced by agents' information. If an agent has private information which leads him to believe a commodity is worth more than the market price, he may bid up the price. Other agents, observing this, may infer that the high price is a sign of high quality. In other words, they may infer the true state of nature. If the commodities are interpreted as shares, agent 1 may have inside information about the company's profits but if he tries to exploit this information by buying or selling the shares he is effectively announcing the fact by driving prices up or down. Thus prices have a dual role of representing terms of trade as well as disseminating information. It is not too hard to think of other examples where prices have this dual function, though the most convincing illustrations undoubtedly come from financial markets.

To make precise the notion of deriving information from prices we need a more sophisticated kind of REE than the one we met in Chapter 1. Trades and prices depend in general on the state of nature and this leads to new concepts. Let $\phi(\omega)$ denote the vector of prices ruling in state ω. Then ϕ is a function associating a price vector p to every state of nature. If $\phi(0) \neq \phi(1)$ and if agent 2 knows the function ϕ, then by observing the vector $p = \phi(\omega)$ he can infer which state has occurred. Information should only be disseminated by relative prices since absolute prices have no meaning in this context. For this reason prices are normalized: $\phi_1(\omega) + \phi_2(\omega) = 1$ for each value of ω. Let $z_i(\omega)$ denote the vector of excess demands of the i-th agent in state ω. Then z_i is a function associating a vector ξ_i of excess demands with each state of nature. The agent may choose the same vector of excess demands in each state. For example, agent 2 will do this if the true state is not revealed by prices.

A *revealing equilibrium* is a REE in which the price function ϕ reveals the true state of nature to the uninformed agent. Formally, it is an ordered triple (ϕ, z_1, z_2) consisting of a price function ϕ and a pair of trade plans z_i, one for each agent $i = 1, 2$, satisfying the following conditions:

(i) $z_i(\omega) + z_2(\omega) = 0$ for $\omega = 0, 1$;
(ii) for each $i = 1, 2$ and $\omega = 0, 1$, $z_i(\omega)$ maximizes $u_i(e_i + \xi, \omega)$ subject to $\phi(\omega).\xi \leq 0$ and $e_i + \xi \geq 0$;
(iii) $\phi(0) \neq \phi(1)$.

(i) simply says that demand equals supply; (ii) says that each agent maximizes utility in each state of nature subject to the usual constraints; (iii) says ϕ is a sufficient statistic for ω. A *non-revealing equilibrium* is one in which the true state is not revealed to the uninformed agent. Formally, it is a triple (ϕ, z_1, z_2) satisfying the following conditions:

(i) $z_1(\omega) + z_2(\omega) = 0$ for $\omega = 0, 1$;
(ii)′ for each $\omega = 0, 1$, $z_1(\omega)$ maximizes $u_1(e_1 + \xi, \omega)$ subject to $\phi(\omega).\xi \leq 0$ and $e_1 + \xi \geq 0$;
(ii)″ $z_2(0) = z_2(1)$ maximizes $Eu_2(e_2 + \xi, \omega)$ subject to $\phi(\omega).\xi \leq 0$ and $e_2 + \xi \geq 0$;
(iii)′ $\phi(0) = \phi(1)$.

The difference, of course, is that in the non-revealing equilibrium agent 2 has to choose the same excess demand to maximize the expected value of his utility function whereas in the revealing equilibrium he could choose his excess demand contingently to maximize the appropriate function in each state. The description of agent 1's behaviour is the same in both cases but his excess demands will in general be different because prices are different.

Some remarks are in order. Agents are assumed to know the price *function* ϕ, otherwise they could infer nothing about the true state. It is not enough to observe the price vector $\phi(\omega)$. They must know that this is the price vector which occurs in state ω and that a different price vector occurs in other states. How are they to know the function ϕ? It might be that from a knowledge of the structure of the economy, preferences, endowments, etc., they can deduce the equilibrium prices that go with each state. In limited circumstances this might be possible but in general it would require enormous, not to say incredible, analytical powers. Or it might be that the agents found themselves repeatedly in this situation and gradually learned to associate the vector $\phi(\omega)$ with the state ω. This interpretation is less demanding, although there are pitfalls along the path to full knowledge of ϕ, as we shall see in Chapter 3. Another explanation might be that although agents are only believed to have very imperfect knowledge of ϕ in reality they do draw inferences, however imperfectly. The assumption that ϕ is known acts then as a benchmark, designed to give us some insights into the general case, in the absence of a theory of how "imperfect" inferences are drawn. (Cf. the discussion at the beginning of this chapter).

Another oddity, closely related to the first is the simultaneity of the inferences about the state of nature and the determination of equilibrium prices. The excess demands expressed by agent 2 depend on whether he knows the true state of nature and at the same time help determine whether the equilibrium prices will reveal information or not. A dynamic story would be preferable but it would have to be a peculiar sort of dynamic story. Agents might have to forget information that was revealed at some point in order to end up in a non-revealing equilibrium.

There may not exist an equilibrium of either variety. The usual way to prove the existence of a REE is to assume that the state is or is not revealed and then determine market clearing prices for each state. One then checks whether the price function so determined is consistent with the informational assumption. In the first case, prices should be different in the two states and in the second the same. It may be that when agent 2 knows the true state, prices are the same in both states and that when he does not, they are different. Then there is no price function which is consistent with the information possessed by agents. This possibility only arises when rather special conditions are met. Unless there are reasons for thinking that these special conditions will hold the possibility can safely be ignored. In fact, one can go further. In the example described above where there are two states and two commodities one would almost always expect the existence of a revealing equilibrium. Both agents will in general have different demand functions in the two states when the true state is known and it is only when the changes in demand offset each other that prices will be the same in each state.

There are circumstances where the conditions for the existence of a non-revealing equilibrium are met, not by coincidence but by design. This can happen when money is introduced. Consider the following very simple model. There is only one agent, a consumer, but there is also assumed to be a monetary authority which exchanges goods for money. There are two dates, labelled $t = 0, 1$ and two states of nature, labelled $\omega = 0, 1$. There is a single consumption good, at each date, and money. At the first date the consumer has an endowment of e_0 units of consumption, independently of the state. At the second date his endowment is $e_{1\omega}$ in state ω. The consumer cannot observe the true state at date 0; only at date 1 when he observes his endowment is the true state revealed to him.

The monetary authority can issue any amount of money it likes in exchange for goods. It can store these goods until the second date when they are exchanged for money again. The consumer is assumed to be unable to store goods so he is happy to hold money instead. Suppose that m is the amount of money purchased by the consumer at date 0, p is the price of consumption at date 0 and q is the price of consumption at date 1. The consumer gives up m/p units of consumption at date 0 and receives in exchange m/q units at date 1. The amount of consumption available in this way at date 1 is just what was given up by the consumer at date 0. Then in equilibrium $m/p = m/q$ and when $m > 0$ (the only case considered in the sequel) $p = q$. Thus, without loss of generality, the money price of consumption is the same at both dates, in each state of nature.

The consumer is assumed to have a utility function $u(x_0, x_1)$ where x_t is consumption at date t and he maximizes the expected value of this function, conditional on the information available to him. If he buys m units of money at date 0 his consumption at date

0 will be $e_0 - m/p$ and at date 1 it will be $e_{1\omega} + m/p$ in state ω. If the consumer knows the true state he will choose m to maximize

$$u(e_0 - m/p, e_{1\omega} + m/p)$$

given the price p. If he does not know the state of nature then he will choose m to maximize

$$Eu(e_0 - m/p, e_{1\omega} + m/p)$$

where E denotes the expectation operator. Two points should be noted. First, the consumer is only interested in real balances, which represent the exact counterpart of the goods stored. An equiproportional change in m and p leaves utility unchanged. Second, a change in the price level may affect the demand for real balances if it transmits information about the state of nature.

Let m denote the consumer's demand for money and $\bar{m}$ the amount supplied by the monetary authority. If $m = \bar{m}$ then all markets will clear. The budget constraint at the first date ensures that the goods market clears at date 0 and at the second date, given the same money-price of consumption, the trades carried out are simply the mirror-image of what happened at the first date. Let μ denote the level of real balances demanded by the consumer when he is uninformed about the state of nature, i.e. μ maximizes $Eu(e_0 - \mu, e_{1\omega} + \mu)$. If $\bar{m}$ is the amount of money supplied by the authorities, independently of ω, then the equilibrium price level is $p = \bar{m}/\mu$. Clearly, $\bar{m}$ and p define a non-revealing equilibrium since the consumer is maximizing his expected utility, markets clear and no information is revealed by the price level, which is the same in each state. Thus, as long as certain mild conditions are satisfied which guarantee the existence of an optimal $\mu > 0$ there will be a non-revealing, monetary REE.

There will also be a revealing REE. Let μ_ω denote the demand for real balances when the consumer knows the state is ω, i.e. μ_ω maximizes $u(e_0 - \mu_\omega, e_{1\omega} + \mu_\omega)$. Let $\bar{m}_\omega$ denote the money supply in ω. The equilibrium price level in ω is then $\bar{m}_\omega/\mu_\omega = p_\omega$ say. Clearly, as long as $\mu_\omega > 0$ for $\omega = 0, 1$ it is possible to choose $\bar{m}_\omega > 0$ so that p_ω is different in each state. Then $(\bar{m}_0, \bar{m}_1, p_0, p_1)$ define a revealing, monetary REE. For consistency's sake it must be assumed that the authority knows the true state at date 0. The existence of two equilibria, one revealing the other non-revealing, allows the monetary authority to choose whether or not to reveal the information it possesses about the state of nature by adjusting the price level. The homogeneity of demand with respect to the price level in a given state of information leaves the price level free to carry messages. The neutrality of money, in a given state of information, can be exploited to make money *non-neutral*.

2.2 Efficiency

In an Arrow–Debreu model the relationship between efficiency and equilibrium is quite easy. Under standard assumptions every equilibrium is efficient and every efficient allocation can be decentralized as a competitive equilibrium if some lump sum transfers are made. In a REE, things are more complicated. In most monetary models, markets are *incomplete*. It is not possible to buy and sell all commodities (where commodities are distinguished by the date and state in which they are delivered) at the first date. Equilibrium is rarely Pareto-efficient in these circumstances and it is often difficult to make general statements about efficiency. To complicate matters further, it is not always clear how efficiency ought to be defined. The two examples examined in Section 2.1 illustrate the difficulties and pitfalls in choosing an efficiency concept as well as the complicated relationship between equilibrium and efficiency.

Consider first the simple monetary model. There are two possible equilibria, one revealing, the other non-revealing. In the non-revealing equilibrium the consumer chooses a level of real balances μ to maximize $Eu(e_0 - \mu, e_{1\omega} + \mu)$. In the revealing equilibrium he chooses μ_ω in state ω to maximize $u(e_0 - \mu_\omega, e_{1\omega} + \mu_\omega)$, Therefore,

$$(1) \qquad u(e_0 - \mu_\omega, e_{1\omega} + \mu_\omega) \geq u(e_0 - \mu, e_{1\omega} + \mu)$$

and, taking the expected value of both sides,

$$(2) \qquad Eu(e_0 - \mu_\omega, e_{1\omega} + \mu_\omega) \geq Eu(e_0 - \mu, e_{1\omega} + \mu).$$

The first inequality shows that whichever state occurs the consumer is at least as well off *ex post*, i.e. once the true state is revealed, in the revealing equilibrium as in the non-revealing one. In fact, he is probably better off. The reason is quite simple. In the revealing equilibrium he is free to choose a different level of real balances in each state while in the non-revealing equilibrium he is constrained to choose the same level. The extra freedom is clearly an advantage. The second inequality shows that he is better off *ex ante*, i.e. before the true state has been revealed, in the revealing equilibrium.

These results accord with our intuition that more information is a good thing. Furthermore it is hardly necessary to worry about the appropriate concept of efficiency to use. In every sense the revealing equilibrium yields the best result that could be achieved. Now consider the economy with two goods and two agents described at the beginning of Section 2.1. Suppose that neither agent can observe the true state of nature at the time when trading takes place. Prices cannot reveal what neither agent initially knows so suppose there is some authority which knows ω and can choose to reveal it to both agents or neither. The question then is whether the equilibrium in which ω is revealed is better than the one in which it is not. Assume that both agents have the same preferences, defined by a function $u(x, \omega)$, where

$$u(x, 0) = \sqrt{x_1}$$
$$u(x, 1) = \sqrt{x_2}.$$

In other words, only commodity 1 (resp. 2) is desired in state 0 (resp. 1). Each agent thinks each state is equally likely *a priori.* Agent 1 has one unit of commodity 1 and none of commodity 2 and agent 2 has one unit of 2 and none of 1, i.e. $e_1 = (1, 0)$ and $e_2 = (0, 1)$. Suppose the true state is revealed to be $\omega = 0$. Then neither agent desires commodity 2 and its price falls to zero. The price of commodity 1 is positive so there can be no trade. Similarly, if the true state is revealed to be $\omega = 1$. If agents do not know the state they will maximize $Eu(x, \omega)$, or equivalently, $\frac{1}{2}(\sqrt{x_1} + \sqrt{x_2})$. From symmetry, it is clear that the price vector $p = (1, 1)$ will yield a non-revealing equilibrium in which both agents, having the same income, will have the same consumption. In fact, they will choose x to maximize $\sqrt{x_1} + \sqrt{x_2}$ subject to $p.x \leq 1$ and this results in $x = (\frac{1}{2}, \frac{1}{2})$. *Ex post*, agent 1 is worse off in state 1 and better off in state 0 in the revealing equilibrium. *Ex post* agent 2 is worse off in state 0 and better off in state 1 in the revealing equilibrium. It does not seem to be possible to make any comparison *ex post* in either state. *Ex ante* however both agents are better off in the non-revealing equilibrium since $\frac{1}{2}(\sqrt{\frac{1}{2}} + \sqrt{\frac{1}{2}}) = 1/\sqrt{2} > \frac{1}{2}(1 + 0)$. In this case, information seems a bad thing. The reason is that when there is uncertainty both agents are prepared to hedge against the possibility that he has the worthless endowment. In effect, they are providing insurance for each other by pooling their endowments. When the true state is known, however, the agent with the valuable commodity has no incentive to share it with the other.

These examples show quite graphically the difficulty of making general statements about the value of information about the state of nature. In the first example, information is helpful because it enables the agent to tailor his savings-behaviour to his circumstances. In the second example, information is harmful because it prevents hedging. In general, both factors will be at work. These negative results are important because there is a tendency to equate revealing equilibrium with efficiency (cf. the "efficient markets hypothesis", which in some contexts is another name for the REH). As we shall see in the next section, it has been suggested that (a) the non-neutrality of money works through the ability of the price level to transmit information about ω, (b) a k-per cent rule is full-revealing and (c) this is efficient. The above results suggest that these claims are not very robust, at least as far as (c) is concerned.

Of course, it depends to some extent on whether one compares equilibria *ex ante* or *ex post*. In the second example the revealing equilibrium was efficient *ex post* and hence could not be dominated. *Ex post* efficiency is generally the weaker concept and hence makes it more difficult to discriminate between equilibria. There are arguments in support of using either concept, and these are discussed in some detail in part 2 of this Chapter. Very briefly, the argument in favour of the *ex post* concept is that individuals in different states are different individuals from the point of view of the Pareto-criterion. The argument in favour of the *ex ante* concept is that if agents were consulted about whether they wished to have ω revealed or not, they would decide on an *ex ante* basis.

2.3 Noise and the Lucas model

In 1972, Robert Lucas published what turned out to be one of the most important papers in recent monetary theory: *Expectations and the Neutrality of Money*. In many ways it is the seminal paper on rational expectations and the information revealed by prices. In his paper, Lucas describes a model in which prices are determined by the condition that markets clear and in which agents have rational expectations, in a sense to be made precise. And yet there appears to be a positive correlation between inflation and employment. There is no structural trade-off in the model; the Phillips curve is an illusion caused by the fact that the price level is a "noisy" signal which only imperfectly reveals the state of nature.

The structure of the model is deceptively simple. Agents make consumption and labour supply decisions over a two period horizon. One unit of labour produces one unit of consumption good. An agent is only productive in the first of his two periods and the consumption good is perishable, so in order to consume in the second period he has to hold money. There is an infinite sequence of elementary time periods or dates, indexed by $t = 0, 1, 2, \ldots,$ which are linked by over-lapping generations. At each date there are $2N$ (divisible) agents; N of these agents are in the first half of their lives and N in the second. These groups are referred to as the young and old generation respectively. All agents have identical preferences so they can be replaced by representative consumers.

There are two *submarkets* in the economy. These can be thought of as geographically isolated markets, each of which has a uniform price ruling in it. Since there is no trade between the submarkets the same price is observed in both only by sheerest coincidence. In each period, young agents are allocated between the two submarkets in the proportions $\theta/2$ and $(1 - \theta/2)$, respectively, where θ is a random variable with a continuous, symmetric probability density function $g(\theta)$, concentrated on the interval $[0, 2]$. The old generation is allocated so that the money supply is the same in each submarket. Since the submarkets are treated symmetrically in the theory, an equilibrium can be completely analysed by looking at just one of them.

Fiat money is issued by a government which has no other function. The government makes a *transfer payment* to the old generation at the beginning of each period. This transfer is assumed to be proportional to the pre-transfer holdings of the agents. Let $\bar{m}_t$ denote the pre-transfer money supply, per member of the old generation, at date t. All agents know $\bar{m}_t$ at date t. Post-transfer money balances, per member of the older generation, are given by the equation

$$\bar{m}_{t+1} = \bar{m}_t x$$

where x is a random variable. $\bar{m}_{t+1}$ is not generally known, except to the extent that it is revealed by prices, until the next period. This is because x, like θ, is unobservable at date t. It is assumed that x is independently and identically distributed at each date and has a continuous probability density function f on $(0, \infty)$. The state of the economy at any date t is described by the values of the per capita money supply $\bar{m}_t$, the transfer variable x_t and the allocation variable θ_t. The transition from state to state is completely determined by the equation $\bar{m}_{t+1} = \bar{m}_t x_t$ and by the density functions f and g of x and θ respectively.

The old generation has a trivial decision problem at date t. The consumption good is always desirable, they have no labour to sell, there is no inheritance and money yields no direct utility so the old generation supply money inelastically in exchange for consumption. The young generation has a more complicated decision problem. A young agent's utility depends on his consumption c_t at date t, his consumption c_{t+1} at date $(t+1)$ and on his supply of labour n_t at date t. His utility is measured by a Neumann–Morgenstern utility function which has the form $U(c_t, n_t) + V(c_{t+1})$. At date $(t+1)$ the currently young agent will supply the money he holds inelastically in exchange for consumption. If m_t denotes his demand for money at date t and p_{t+1} denotes the price of consumption at date $(t+1)$, his consumption at date $(t+1)$ will be $(m_t x_{t+1}/p_{t+1})$. Let the distribution function $F(x_{t+1}, p_{t+1} \mid \bar{m}_t, p_t)$ formally represent the joint probability distribution of (x_{t+1}, p_{t+1}) conditional on $(\bar{m}_t, p_t)$. If a young agent chooses to demand (c_t, m_t) units of consumption and money respectively and supply n_t units of labour-consumption, his expected utility will be:

$$U(c_t, n_t) + \int V(m_t x_{t+1}/p_{t+1})\, \mathrm{d}F(x_{t+1}, p_{t+1} \mid \bar{m}_t, p_t).$$

His decision problem is to choose a non-negative triple (c_t, n_t, m_t) to maximize this expression, subject to the budget constraint:

$$p_t(c_t - n_t) + m_t \le 0\,.$$

Now consider the submarket which receives the fraction $\theta_t/2$ of young consumers at date t. Since consumption and labour are indistinguishable there are effectively two commodities being traded, money and consumption. If the excess demand for one of them is zero the excess demand for the other is zero by Walras's law. If the state of the economy is $(\bar{m}_t, \theta_t, x_t)$ then the demand for goods by the old generation is $(N\bar{m}_t x_t/2p_t)$ since old consumers are allocated so as to equate the money supply in the two submarkets. A typical young agent solves the problem described above and chooses an excess demand for consumption: $(c_t - n_t) = \zeta(p_t; F(\,.\mid p_t, \bar{m}_t))$. The total demand from young consumers will be $N\theta_t\zeta/2$, since $N\theta_t/2$ is the number of young consumers in this submarket. The submarket will clear if

$$\frac{N\bar{m}_t x_t}{2p_t} = \frac{N\theta_t}{2}\zeta(p_t; F(\,.\mid p_t, \bar{m}_t))\,,$$

that is,

$$\frac{\bar{m}_t x_t}{\theta_t} = p_t\zeta(p_t; F(\,.\mid p_y, \bar{m}_t))\,.$$

Define an *equilibrium price system for* F to be a function $\phi(\bar{m}, x, \theta)$

such that, for each state $(\bar{m}, x, \theta)$, ϕ satisfies

$$\frac{\bar{m}x}{\theta} = \phi(\bar{m}, x, \theta)\zeta(\phi(\bar{m}, x, \theta); F(.\,|\,\phi(\bar{m}, x, \theta), \bar{m}))$$

In other words, $\phi(\bar{m}, x, \theta)$ clears the goods market in state $(\bar{m}, x, \theta)$.

To determine the distribution function F Lucas appeals to the REH. Agents are assumed to know the true distribution function conditional on their observations of $\bar{m}$ and p. The "true" conditional distribution is endogenous to the model, of course, and this means that ϕ and F must be determined simultaneously. To find F it is necessary to use the relation:

$$\begin{aligned} p_{t+1} &= \phi(\bar{m}_{t+1}, x_{t+1}, \theta_{t+1}) \\ &= \phi(\bar{m}_t x_t, x_{t+1}, \theta_{t+1}). \end{aligned}$$

Then

$$\begin{aligned} F(x_{t+1}, p_{t+1}\,|\,\bar{m}_t, p_t) &= \text{Prob}\,\{(x, p) \leq (x_{t+1}, p_{t+1})\,|\,\bar{m}_t, p_t\} \\ &= \text{Prob}\,[A\,|\,\bar{m}_t, p_t], \end{aligned}$$

where $A := \{(x, x', \theta)|\phi(\bar{m}_t x, x', \theta) \leq p_{t+1}$ and $x' \leq x_{t+1}\}$. The probability that $(x, x', \theta) \in A$ depends on $(\bar{m}_t, p_t)$ in two ways. First, through the appearance of $\bar{m}_t$ in the definition of A and second, through the information revealed by $(\bar{m}_t, p_t)$ about the true value of x_t. Let $G(x_t|p_t, \bar{m}_t)$ denote the distribution of x_t conditional on $(p_t, \bar{m}_t)$. Then

$$G(x_t\,|\,p_t, \bar{m}_t) = \text{Prob}\,\{(x, \theta)\,|\,x \leq x_t, \phi(\bar{m}_t, x, \theta) = p_t\}$$

which is easily calculated from f, g and ϕ. A REE is defined to be an ordered pair (ϕ, F) where ϕ is an equilibrium price system for F and F is derived using the REH as above.

From the form of the market clearing condition it seems plausible that one might be able to find a price system ϕ which depended only on the quantity $(\bar{m}_t x_t/\theta_t)$. This turns out to be the case. Indeed, Lucas is able to show that any equilibrium price system is a sufficient statistic for x_t/θ_t, if $\bar{m}_t$ is known. The distribution of (x, x', θ) conditional on $\phi(\bar{m}, x, \theta)$ is the same as the distribution conditional on x/θ for all possible equilibrium price systems ϕ. This suggests the equilibrium price system might have the form $\bar{m}_t\phi(x_t/\theta_t)$. Lucas is able to show under certain conditions that this is the case, i.e. there exists a REE (ϕ, F) having this form.

The money supply term $\bar{m}_t$ factors out of the price function because a fully announced increase in the money supply does not, in this model, have any real effects. When the price function has this special form, the market clearing condition reduces to

$$\frac{x_t}{\theta_t} = \phi\left(\frac{x_t}{\theta_t}\right)\zeta\left(\bar{m}_t\phi\left(\frac{x_t}{\theta_t}\right); \quad F\left(\cdot|\bar{m}_t\phi\left(\frac{x_t}{\theta_t}\right), \bar{m}_t\right)\right.$$

i.e. the demand for goods facing the average producer is a function of x_t/θ_t alone. Excluding the case where the disturbance was a purely monetary one, the price function was found to be positive, with an elasticity between zero and one. This implies that the equilibrium employment function has the form $n(x/\theta)$ and that $n'(x/\theta) > 0$. Increases in demand induce increases in *real* output, whether the initial increase in demand is monetary (an increase in x) or real (a reduction in θ, which increases demand per producer by reducing the number of young agents in the submarket).

The relevance to the Phillips curve debate is fairly clear now. In this model there is no useable trade-off between inflation and employment and yet inflation and employment appear to be positively correlated. Indeed, Lucas shows that if the Phillips curve relation

$$\ln Y_t = \beta_0 + \beta_1(\ln P_t - \ln P_{t-1}) + \varepsilon_t,$$

where Y_t is real GNP (or employment) and P_t is the implicit price deflator, were fitted to data generated by this model, the estimate of β_1 will be positive. In other words, econometric evidence in the form of fitted Phillips curves cannot establish the existence of a useable trade-off between inflation and employment.

Lucas next turns to welfare questions and asks whether a policy of increasing the money supply by a constant, k per cent each period is Pareto-efficient. The k-per cent rule is equivalent to putting $x \equiv 1$ because of homogeneity. Lucas attempts to show that in some sense the k-per cent rule is actually Pareto-efficient. The sense in which this is shown to be true is very special and not entirely reasonable.

Each generation can be indexed by the ordered pair (θ_t, θ_{t+1}) of values of θ observed during its lifetime. An allocation rule can be described by a triple of real-valued functions $\{c, n, c'\}$, each defined on the interval [0, 2]. If θ is observed at some date, the allocation rule specifies that the young generation should consume $c(\theta)$ and supply $n(\theta)$ units of labour and that the old generation should consume $c'(\theta)$. An allocation rule $\{c, n, c'\}$ is *attainable* if and only if c, n, and c' are non-negative functions and

$$c'(\theta) + \theta c(\theta) \leq \theta n(\theta).$$

An attainable allocation $\{c, n, c'\}$ is defined to be efficient in Lucas's sense if there is no attainable allocation, $\{\bar{c}, \bar{n}, \bar{c}'\}$ say, such that:

$$U(\bar{c}(\theta), \bar{n}(\theta)) \geq U(c(\theta), n(\theta))$$
$$\bar{c}'(\theta) \geq c'(\theta)$$

for all θ in [0, 2] and at least one of the inequalities is strict for a set of values of θ which has positive probability.

The definition is odd in a number of respects. In the first place, why should the old generation's consumption be independent of the value of θ which was observed in the first period of its life? In a REE in which $x \equiv 1$, the quantity of money in each submarket is a constant at each date. Suppose it is equal to $N/2$ units. Then each young consumer in a submarket with a fraction $\theta/2$ of the young generation ends up with $1/\theta$ units of money. If an agent observes (θ_t, θ_{t+1}) during his lifetime his second period consumption must be $1/\theta_t p(\theta_{t+1})$ where $p(\theta_{t+1})$ is the price ruling at date $(t + 1)$, now a function of θ only. Hence the equilibrium consumption of old agents depends on both values of θ, not just one. It is not clear, therefore, how this notion of efficiency is to be applied.

In the second place, the definition does not require that *ex ante* or *ex post* utility should be increased by the alternative allocation $\{\bar{c}, \bar{n}, \bar{c}'\}$. It requires that an agent's "one period utility", if it is possible to conceive of such a thing, be increased. This is a sufficient condition for an agent to be better off both *ex post* and *ex ante* but it is not necessary for either. Here "*ex post*" should be interpreted as referring to expected utility conditional on the first period value of θ. That is, an agent is better off *ex post* if

$$U(c(\theta), n(\theta)) + E\{V(c'(\theta'))\}$$

is increased. It is unlikely that *ex post* efficiency could be established here because of the extreme incompleteness of markets. In the example of an economy with two agents given in Section 2.2, markets are complete *ex post* (i.e. once ω is known) and this guarantees efficiency *ex post*. If *ex post* efficiency is out of the question so is *ex ante* efficiency because the latter implies the former.

In the model studied in the preceding sections there does not appear to be any "noise" in the system. The monetary authority can choose to reveal or not to reveal information it possesses to the consumers but it cannot "confuse" them. In a formal sense, this is easily rectified. Consider the two-person economy described in

Section 2.1 generalized to admit several states of nature. Let Ω denote the set of states and assume that $\Omega = \Omega_0 \times \Omega_1$. Every state of nature ω is identified with an ordered pair (ω_0, ω_1) where ω_0 represents a real disturbance and ω_1 represents a nominal one. The i-th agent's utility is denoted by $u_i(x_i, \omega_0)$, i.e. it depends only on his consumption bundle x_i and the real part of the state of nature. The nominal part ω_1 has no effect on the structure of the economy; it simply represents noise.

A trade plan z_i is called *noisy* if, for any pair of states ω and ω' (which occur with positive probability), $z_i(\omega) \neq z_i(\omega')$ and $\omega_0 = \omega'_0$. In other words, the trade plan depends in a non-trivial way on the noise component. Let (z_1, z_2) be an attainable set of trade plans, i.e. $z_1 + z_2 = 0$, for the two agents. If both agents are risk averse (u_i is strictly concave in x_i) and z_i is noisy, then the trade plans (z_1, z_2) are Pareto-inefficient. If they average their consumption over the states with the same real component (which is clearly attainable since e_i does not depend on ω) they will be better off *ex ante* because of the concavity of u_i. In fact, they will be better off *ex post* if *ex post* is taken to mean before ω_1 is observed but after ω_0 is observed.

The result, which is mathematically trivial, probably explains something of the intuitive hostility to a noisy policy felt by some economists. By definition, the uncertainty introduced by noise can always be removed. Risk-averse consumers will always prefer a non-noisy allocation, so a noisy policy appears to be a gratuitous burden on consumers. In an ideal (First Best) world, all noise would be removed. But it does not follow that in the world of the Second Best, a noisy equilibrium is worse than a non-noisy one.

Notes

1. J. Muth, "Rational expectations and the theory of price movements", *Econometrica*, **29** (1961) 315–35; R. Lucas, "Expectations and the neutrality of money", *Journal of Economic Theory*, **4** (1972) 103–24; T. Sargent and N. Wallace, "Rational expectations, the optimal monetary instrument and the optimal money supply rule", *Journal of Political Economy*, **83** (1975) 241–57; R. J. Barro, "Rational expectations and the role of monetary policy", *Journal of Monetary Economics*, **2** (1976) 1–32.

CHAPTER 2: PART 2

Informational efficiency and economic efficiency

2.4 Rational Expectations Equilibrium (REE)

The model developed in this section extends and generalizes the examples encountered in Part 1 of this Chapter. As a model of a monetary economy it is rather rudimentary, but it suffices for the purpose of analysing the relationship between information and efficiency. The model describes a *pure exchange economy*; there is no production. This considerably simplifies matters without affecting the central issues. There is a finite number of economic *agents*, comprising a monetary authority and several consumers, who trade goods and money. The authority can create money at will. Money has no intrinsic utility; it consists of pieces of paper, say. In order to give money a role to play as an asset, it is assumed that there are two *dates*, indexed $t = 0, 1$, at which trading takes place. Uncertainty is represented by a set of *states of nature* and each agent has an information structure, defined on this set, which represents his information in the first period. In the second period the true state is revealed to everyone.

Consumers can trade goods on spot markets (i.e. for immediate delivery) at each date but no forward trading is allowed. Neither is it possible to store commodities from one date to the next. However, the monetary authority can store any amount of goods costlessly. Consumers sell part of their endowment to the monetary authority in exchange for money at the first date. The authority stores the goods it has purchased until the second date, when it offers them to consumers in exchange for money. The authority behaves passively in all this. It chooses the amount of money it wishes to issue at date 0 and accepts whatever goods are offered in exchange. The price level will adjust so that the "money market" clears. At the second date, consumers supply their money inelastically because money has no intrinsic utility. The authority likewise supplies its goods inelastically (the authority is not allowed to consume) and so receives back its initial issue of fiat money. Again, the price level adjusts to clear the money market. Apart from the choice of the amount of money to issue, the authority's behaviour is determined by the behaviour of the consumers.

In the resulting market equilibrium, the general price level may reveal information about the state of nature. By influencing the price level the quantity of money can affect the information revealed to agents and hence their (real) behaviour. This is the only way the monetary authority can have a real effect on the economy (under the REH) and depends on the assumption that the authority possesses differential information. Without differential information the LSP can be shown to hold.

There are assumed to be l *goods*, distinguished by their physical characteristics, available for delivery at each date. Commodities are distinguished by the date and state in which they are delivered. If Ω denotes the set of states of nature and $|\Omega|$ the number of elements in Ω, there are $2l.|\Omega|$ commodities. Every consumer chooses to consume a non-negative bundle of goods at each date, i.e. his *consumption set* is $\mathbb{R}^l_+ \times \mathbb{R}^l_+$. A consumption *plan* is a function x from Ω to $\mathbb{R}^{2l}_+$. For each ω in Ω, $x(\omega)$ is the consumption bundle the agent plans to consume in state ω. Let X dènote the set of plans. Each consumer's preferences are represented by a *preference relation* $\prec$ on X. $\prec$ is a transitive, irreflexive binary relation on X. The consumer also has an endowment of initial goods represented by an element e of X. To complete the description of the consumer, it is only necessary to describe his initial information. An information structure is a partition[1] $\mathscr{F}$ of the set Ω. If two states ω and ω' belong to the same element of $\mathscr{F}$, the consumer cannot distinguish them at date 0. He can only observe a set F in $\mathscr{F}$, in which case he knows the true state belongs to F but nothing more. The sets F in $\mathscr{F}$ are sometimes called *events*. The i-th consumer is completely described by the ordered triple $(\prec_i, e_i, \mathscr{F}_i)$ consisting of a preference relation $\prec_i$, an endowment e_i and an information structure $\mathscr{F}_i$. (The set of plans X is understood to be given.) For the sake of consistency, the function e_i^0 representing the i-th agent's first-period endowment must be $\mathscr{F}_i$-measurable.[2] Otherwise, he could obtain new information about the state of nature by observing the value of $e_i^0(\omega)$. In the sequel, measurability is always tacitly assumed.

The monetary authority's only function is to issue money at the first date in exchange for goods and redeem it at the second. It chooses a *monetary policy*, i.e. a function $\bar{m}$ from Ω to $\mathbb{R}_+$; if ω is the true state then the quantity of money issued is $\bar{m}(\omega)$. The authority is assumed to be indifferent to the outcome of the exchange process. This assumption, which is dropped later, is made in order to avoid discussing game-theoretic problems for the moment. Since the authority is indifferent to the outcome, every monetary policy is optimal and this justifies treating the choice of policy as parametric.

At date 0 every agent observes a price vector p in $\mathbb{R}^l_+$ which lists the prices of all goods in the first period. But in order to infer anything from this observation he must know which vector goes with which state. For example, if p is observed when the true state is ω and p' when the true state is ω' and the agent knows this, then if $p \neq p'$ he can always discriminate between ω and ω'. If p is observed he infers that the true state is *not* ω' and similarly if p' is observed the true state is *not* ω. This suggests that information is revealed not by a price vector alone but by a price function which associates a price vector with each state of nature. Formally, a *price system* is a function ϕ from Ω to $\mathbb{R}^l_+ \times \mathbb{R}^l_+$. For every ω in Ω, $(p, q) = \phi(\omega)$ is a pair of price vectors in $\mathbb{R}^l_+$ representing the prices of goods at date 0 and date 1 respectively. It will be convenient to write ϕ as the ordered pair (ϕ^0, ϕ^1) of functions from Ω to $\mathbb{R}^l_+$ representing, respectively, price systems at date 0 and 1. The first period price system is the only one to reveal information since there is full information at date 1. The information contained in ϕ^0 can be represented by an information structure. Let the *information structure* generated by ϕ^0 be denoted by $\mathscr{F}[\phi^o]$ and defined as the family of non-empty subsets of Ω which are inverse images of points in $\mathbb{R}^l_+$. In other words, two states ω and ω' belong to the same element of the partition $\mathscr{F}[\phi^0]$ if and only if $\phi^0(\omega) = \phi^0(\omega')$.

In order to make sense of the theory, restrictions must be placed on admissible price systems. The first period price system should not, for example, reveal information which no group of agents possessed initially. There is a unique information structure $\mathscr{F}$ which is defined to be the coarsest partition[3] that is at least as fine as $\mathscr{F}_i$ for all $i = 0, 1, \ldots, n$. A typical element of $\mathscr{F}$ is a non-empty subset A of Ω which is the intersection of sets $\bigcup_{i=0}^n \mathscr{F}_i$, i.e. $A = \bigcap_{i=0}^n A_i$ where $A_i \in \mathscr{F}_i$ for each $i = 0, 1, \ldots, n$. Two states ω and ω' are indistinguishable at date 0 according to $\mathscr{F}$ if and only if they are indistinguishable according to every $\mathscr{F}_i$ $(i = 0, 1, \ldots, n)$. This is precisely what is meant by saying that $\mathscr{F}$ represents the total information available to the agents collectively. Then ϕ^0 will be said to be *admissible* if and only if ϕ^0 is $\mathscr{F}$-measurable, i.e. ϕ^o is constant on elements of $\mathscr{F}$. Similarly, $\phi \equiv (\phi^0, \phi^1)$ is called admissible if ϕ^0 is admissible.

A trade plan is an ordered pair (z, m) consisting of a function z from Ω to $\mathbb{R}^{2l}_+$ and a function m from Ω to $\mathbb{R}_+$. For each ω, $z(\omega)$ represents the excess demand for goods at each date if state ω occurs and $m(\omega)$ represents the demand for money at the first date if state ω occurs. An agent's action may depend at most on the information initially available to him plus what is revealed by prices. The i-th agent initially knows $\mathscr{F}_i$ and can observe $\mathscr{F}[\phi^0]$ so the information available to him is the join of $\mathscr{F}_i$ and $\mathscr{F}[\phi^0]$, denoted by $\mathscr{F}_i \vee \mathscr{F}[\phi]$, i.e. the coarsest partition of Ω which is finer than both $\mathscr{F}_i$ and $\mathscr{F}[\phi^0]$. It is denoted by $\mathscr{F}_i[\phi^0]$. A plan (z, m) is said to be *admissible for the i-th consumer at the price system* ϕ if z^0 and m are $\mathscr{F}_i[\phi^0]$-measurable. Similarly the policy $\bar{m}$ is *admissible for the authority at the price system* ϕ if $\bar{m}$ is $\mathscr{F}_0[\phi^0]$-measurable, where $\mathscr{F}_0$ is the authority's information structure and $\mathscr{F}_0[\phi^0] = \mathscr{F}_0 \vee \mathscr{F}[\phi^0]$. When there is no risk of confusion I shall refer to admissible plans or admissible policies, without specifying the prevailing price system ϕ.

Suppose the price system is ϕ. The authority can choose any admissible policy $\bar{m}$ but consumers have various constraints on their choice of trade plan. First, the plan must be admissible. Second, a consumer cannot supply goods he does not have:

(1) $$e_i + z_i \geq 0\,.$$

Third, he must satisfy a budget constraint at each date. At the first date the value of his sales of goods to the authority must pay for the money he demands:

(2) $$\phi^0(\omega) . z(\omega) + m(\omega) \leq 0 \qquad (\omega \in \Omega)\,.$$

At the second date, the money carried forward from the first is supplied inelastically in exchange for goods since money yields no direct utility. Each consumer chooses an excess demand whose value is no greater than the value of his money holdings from the first period:

(3) $$\phi^1(\omega) . z^1(\omega) \leq m(\omega) \qquad (\omega \in \Omega)\,.$$

The i-th consumer's budget set is denoted by $\beta_i(\phi)$ and defined to be the set of trade plans (z, m) which are admissible for the consumer at the price system ϕ and satisfy (1)–(3) above. If the i-th consumer chooses a trade plan (z_i, m_i) his consumption plan is uniquely determined: $x_i = e_i + z_i$.

The preceding discussion is summed up in two formal definitions.

2.4.1 Definition *An exchange economy* $\mathscr{E}$ *is an* $(n + 1)$*-tuple* $\{\mathscr{F}_0,$

$(\prec_i, e_i, \mathscr{F}_i)\}$ consisting of information structures $\mathscr{F}_i$, preference relations $\prec_i$ and endowments e_i $(i = 1, \ldots, n)$.

2.4.2 Definition *A rational expectations equilibrium (REE) for the exchange economy $\mathscr{E}$ defined above is an array $\{\phi, \bar{m}, (z_1, m_1), \ldots, (z_n, m_n)\}$, consisting of a price system ϕ, a monetary policy $\bar{m}$ and the trade plans (z_i, m_i) for $i = 1, \ldots, n$, which satisfies the following conditions:*

(i) *for each $i = 1, \ldots, n$, (z_i, m_i) is maximal with respect to $\prec_i$ in the budget set $\beta_i(\phi)$;*
(ii) *$\bar{m}$ is admissible;*
(iii) *$\sum_{i=1}^{n} z_i^0 \leq 0$, $\sum_{i=1}^{n} m_i = \bar{m}$ and $\sum_{i=1}^{n} (z_i^0 + z_i^1) = 0$.*

One oddity in this definition is the market-clearing condition (iii) which requires that the *sum* of market excess demands at dates 0 and 1 be zero. The more usual condition is that market excess demands at each date be zero. The difference here is accounted for by the fact that the monetary authority does not have an explicit excess demand for goods even though it implicitly demands goods at the first date and supplies goods at the second. Condition (iii) is just a shortcut, made possible by the fact that the authority has no strict preferences and so passively accepts the goods offered to it at $t = 0$ and resells them at $t = 1$. The condition that aggregate excess demand (including the authority's) be zero at each date collapses to the condition (iii). Similarly, the condition $\sum_{i=1}^{n} z_i^0 \leq 0$ indicates that the authority cannot supply goods at date 0. Expressing the market-clearing conditions in this way emphasizes that although the authority formally trades goods its only actual decision is the quantity of money to supply. It can thus be said to carry out a pure monetary policy. It is also clear that the authority influences the equilibrium allocation of goods only by altering the information revealed to agents by prices. For suppose that all agents had full-information to start with so that prices could reveal nothing further. Then traditional homogeneity arguments could be used to show that equilibrium is invariant to the choice of $\bar{m}$. This follows easily from the definition.

The equilibrium thus defined is characterized by rational expectations in the sense that agents know what will happen in each state of nature. More precisely, each agent knows the prices $\phi(\omega)$ that will rule in each state ω. Consumer i also knows his endowment $e_i(\omega)$ in each state ω as well as his preferences, and this is all the information he needs in order to make a choice. But agents still have very limited information about the true state of nature and there is no requirement that they know the "true probability" of a state occurring. Agents may differ widely in the subjective probabilities they attach to states and hence to future prices.

2.4.3 Proposition *Let $\{\phi, \bar{m}, (z_i, m_i)_{i=1}^n\}$ be a REE for the exchange economy $\mathscr{E}$. If λ is a function from Ω to $\mathbb{R}$ such that $\lambda(\omega) > 0$ for every $\omega \in \Omega$ and $\mathscr{F}_i[\lambda \otimes \phi^0] = \mathscr{F}_i[\phi^0]$ for every $i = 0, 1, \ldots, n$, then $\{\lambda \otimes \phi, \lambda \otimes \bar{m}, (z_i, \lambda \otimes m_i)_{i=1}^n\}$ is also a REE for $\mathscr{E}$.*

Proof Recall that the notation $(\lambda \otimes \phi^0)$ refers to the function from Ω to $\mathbb{R}_+^l$ which maps ω to $\lambda(\omega)\phi^0(\omega)$ and similarly with the other expressions. The proof follows trivially by the usual homogeneity arguments since, by hypothesis, the information available to each agent is unchanged by the change in policy from $\bar{m}$ to $\lambda \otimes \bar{m}$. □

2.4.4 Corollary *Let $\{\phi, \bar{m}, (z_i, m_i)_{i=1}^n\}$ be a REE for the exchange economy $\mathscr{E}$. For any positive, real number λ, $\{\lambda\phi, \lambda\bar{m}, (z_i, \lambda m_i)_{i=1}^n\}$ is also a REE for $\mathscr{E}$.*

The corollary shows that equilibrium is invariant to positive, scalar changes in the policy *function* but this does not mean that the quantity of money is neutral, as Proposition 2.4.3 points out.

2.5 Efficiency

In ordinary general-equilibrium analysis there is one natural efficiency-concept: Pareto-efficiency. Let $\mathscr{E}$ be an exchange economy and define an *allocation* for $\mathscr{E}$ to be an n-tuple $(x_1, \ldots, x_n)$ where x_i belongs to X_i for $i = 1, \ldots, n$. An allocation is said to be attainable for $\mathscr{E}$ if and only if $\sum_{i=1}^n x_i = \sum_{i=1}^n e_i$. An allocation $(x_1', \ldots, x_n')$ *strongly* (resp. *weakly*) *Pareto-dominates* the allocation $(x_1, \ldots, x_n)$ if $x_i' \succ_i x_i$ for $i = 1, \ldots, n$ (resp. $x_i' \succsim_i x_i$ for $i = 1, \ldots, n$ and $x_i' \succ_i x_i$ for some i). In this case, the allocation $(x_1', \ldots, x_n')$ would be called *strongly* (resp. *weakly*) *Pareto-superior* to $(x_1, \ldots, x_n)$ and $(x_1, \ldots, x_n)$ would be called *strongly* (resp. *weakly*) *Pareto-inferior* to $(x_1', \ldots, x_n')$. An allocation for $\mathscr{E}$ is defined to be *strongly* (resp. *weakly*) *Pareto-efficient* if it is attainable for $\mathscr{E}$ and is not weakly (resp. strongly) Pareto-dominated by an attainable allocation. In Walrasian equilibrium, the equilibrium allocation is always weakly Pareto-efficient and under a mild condition (local non-satiability of preferences) it can be shown that the allocation is strongly Pareto-efficient.

In a REE, things are more complicated. In the present model

consumers cannot buy goods at date 0 and they cannot make trades contingent on the state revealed at date 1 (i.e. trades arranged at date 0 but delivered at date 1 conditional on the true state being the one specified in the contract). Restrictions of this sort are generally described by saying that markets are "incomplete". When markets are incomplete, efficiency breaks down and it is hard to say much in general. To complicate matters further, it is not always clear how efficiency ought to be defined when there is differential information.

These problems can be made much clearer with the aid of some simplifying assumptions. First, assume that the expected utility hypothesis holds, so that the relation $\succsim_i$ can be represented by a function having the form $\sum_{\omega \in \Omega} u_i(x(\omega), \omega)$. Second, assume that the monetary authority can observe the true state of nature at date 0 ($\mathscr{F}_0 = \{\{\omega\} : \omega \in \Omega\}$) whereas the consumers have no initial information ($\mathscr{F}_i = \{\Omega\}$ for $i = 1, \ldots, n$). The first assumption makes it possible to talk about a consumer's welfare *conditional on a certain piece of information*, e.g. the information that the true state is ω. The second assumption is really equivalent, for present purposes, to assuming that consumers all have the same initial information, which is less than the authority's information. This more general case involves rather cumbersome notation, however. Both assumptions are maintained, sometimes without an explicit statement to this effect, throughout the section.

I distinguish two concepts of efficiency: *ex ante* efficiency and *ex post* efficiency. In what follows, only "strong" efficiency concepts are used so the prefix will be suppressed. Both efficiency-concepts answer the same question: "Is it possible to make some individuals better off without making anyone worse off?" The difference lies in the information available when the question is asked. *Ex ante* efficiency applies before any information about the state of nature is available. A consumer's preferences are defined on a set of consumption *plans*. The consumer is better off with the prospect of x' than with the prospect of x if and only if

$$\sum_{\omega \in \Omega} u(x'(\omega), \omega) > \sum_{\omega \in \Omega} u(x(\omega), \omega)$$

assuming he has no information about the true state. *Ex post* efficiency on the other hand applies to a situation in which the true state is already known. Then a consumer's preferences are defined on a set of consumption bundles. The consumer is better off consuming $x'(\omega)$ than $x(\omega)$ if and only if

$$u(x'(\omega), \omega) > u(x(\omega), \omega)$$

assuming he knows the true state to be ω. Formally, $u(.)$ can be thought of as defining preferences over plans, but the planned consumption in states other than the true one is irrelevant. This would not be true without the expected utility hypothesis however.

An allocation of consumption plans $(x_1, \ldots, x_n)$ is *efficient ex ante* if and only if it is attainable and Pareto-efficient in the sense defined above. An allocation $(x_1, \ldots, x_n)$ is *efficient at* ω if and only if it is attainable and there is no attainable allocation $(x'_1, \ldots, x'_n)$ such that

$$u_i(x'_i(\omega), \omega) \geq u_i(x_i(\omega), \omega)$$

for all $i = 1, \ldots, n$, with strict inequality for some i. An allocation is *efficient ex post* if and only if it is efficient at every ω in Ω.

Prima facie, *ex ante* efficiency seems the more natural concept. Its definition is formally the same as that of Pareto-efficiency in the static environment. Also, the definition of equilibrium seems to favour *ex ante* efficiency. A REE is an equilibrium of *plans*. In the usual way, one can think of plans as having been chosen at the end of some sort of *tâtonnement* but before trading has started at date 0. At this point all agents, including the authority are ignorant of the true state, which is why they make plans for each possible ω in Ω. The relevant question to ask is whether, *at the point where the decision was made*, a different choice of plans could have made some individuals better off without making any individuals worse off.

The appeal of the concept of Pareto-efficiency is that it rests on the *unanimity principle*. It is taken as axiomatic that if one allocation is Pareto superior to another, there will be unanimous agreement to choose the first (when offered a choice of the two). An allocation which is not Pareto-efficient is therefore held to be unsatisfactory. In an exchange economy of the sort discussed here, if an allocation is not efficient *ex ante* then there will be unanimity about choosing another, Pareto-preferred one at the time the agents make their choice of plans, i.e. before date 0. The argument for *ex ante* efficiency appears to be a strong one. Anyone who wishes to defend the *ex post* concept is reduced to saying that if an equilibrium is efficient *ex post* then a change will make someone worse off in some state of nature. Since all agents vote for the change *ex ante*, this seems a very weak argument against a change.

Unfortunately, this story depends on the assumption that there is something like a Rawlsian "initial position" in which agents make decisions in ignorance of ω. Suppose on the other hand that plans are chosen at date 0, when the monetary authority knows the true value of ω. The authority might ask itself whether say, a fully-revealing equilibrium would be preferable to a non-revealing one. Clearly, efficiency at ω is a relevant concept now. There is a slight difficulty in interpreting a REE in this way. If the authority knows the true value of ω, say ω_0, when it chooses $\bar{m}$ then $\bar{m}$ may depend on ω_0 and hence ϕ may depend on ω_0. The REH may then allow consumers to deduce ω_0 from the auctioneer's announcement of ϕ. To avoid this problem it can be assumed that the authority's behaviour, i.e. its choice of function $\bar{m}$, is independent of ω_0.

To make the point very concretely, imagine a finite set of economies, one for each $\omega \in \Omega$, which are identical except that the true state of nature is different in each one. There is a single authority common to all economies which is constrained to choose the same policy in each one. Ignoring the problem of multiple equilibria, the same allocation of consumption plans will be observed in each economy. The allocation will be efficient if there is no way of making every agent in every economy better off i.e. all $n.|\Omega|$ of them. This is precisely the same, from a formal point of view, as the definition of *ex post* efficiency.

The distinction between *ex ante* and *ex post* efficiency may seem slightly pedantic in a two period framework but it is quite forcefully brought out in models of repeated exchange. Consider the following story, for example. There is a finite number of agents $i = 1, \ldots, n$ and a sequence of independent, identically distributed, random drawings from a finite set Ω of states of nature. The agents are faced with two prospects $\underset{\sim}{a}$ and $\underset{\sim}{b}$. Under $\underset{\sim}{a}$, if the state ω at Ω is drawn at the t-th date then agent i receives utility $a_i(\omega)$, $(i = 1, \ldots, n)$. The interpretation of $\underset{\sim}{b}$ is similar. Agents maximize long run expected utility:

$$u_i(\underset{\sim}{a}) := \lim_{T \to \infty} \frac{1}{T} E\left\{\sum_{t=1}^{T} a_i(\omega_t)\right\}$$

and

$$u_i(\underset{\sim}{b}) := \lim_{T \to \infty} \frac{1}{T} E\left\{\sum_{t=1}^{T} b_i(\omega_t)\right\}$$

where the expectation is taken over all possible sequences $\{\omega_1, \omega_2, \ldots\}$ of drawings from Ω. The law of large numbers immediately implies that:

$$u_i(\underset{\sim}{a}) = \sum_{\omega \in \Omega} \pi(\omega) a_i(\omega)$$

and

$$u_i(\underset{\sim}{b}) = \sum_{\omega \in \Omega} \pi(\omega) b_i(\omega)$$

for all $i = 1, \ldots, n$, where $\pi(\omega)$ denotes the probability of drawing ω in Ω at any trial. But this means that $u_i(\underset{\sim}{a})$ (resp. $u_i(\underset{\sim}{b})$) is simply the *ex ante* expected utility the i-th agent achieves from the prospect $\underset{\sim}{a}$ (resp. $\underset{\sim}{b}$) when there is only one trial. There will be unanimity in preferring $\underset{\sim}{a}$ to $\underset{\sim}{b}$ if and only if $\underset{\sim}{a}$ is *ex ante* Pareto-superior to $\underset{\sim}{b}$ when there is one trial.

Now suppose that instead of there being n agents there is a countably infinite number, indexed by the ordered pairs (i, t), where $i = 1, \ldots, n$ denotes the individual's type and $t = 1, 2, \ldots$ denotes the trial. Agent (i, t)'s utility is determined in the t-th trial: with prospect $\underset{\sim}{a}$ (resp. $\underset{\sim}{b}$) the (i, t)-th agent receives $a_i(\omega_t)$ (resp. $b_i(\omega_t)$) if ω_t is drawn at the t-th trial. One can still define the expected utility of agent (i, t) and it shows, before the drawings take place, there will be unanimous preference of $\underset{\sim}{a}$ over $\underset{\sim}{b}$ if and only if $\underset{\sim}{a}$ is *ex ante* Pareto-superior to $\underset{\sim}{b}$. But note this: if $\underset{\sim}{a}$ is not Pareto-superior to $\underset{\sim}{b}$ *ex post* then the probability that some agent is worse off with $\underset{\sim}{b}$ than with $\underset{\sim}{a}$ is one! For, assuming $\pi(\omega) > 0$, if $a_i(\omega) < b_i(\omega)$, for some $i = 1, \ldots, n$, then

$$P\{(\omega_t): a_i(\omega_t) < b_i(\omega_t) \quad \text{for some } (i, t)\} = 1$$

In fact the proportion of agents who are worse off under $\underset{\sim}{a}$ is $\pi(\omega)/n > 0$. Moreover, in this case the fiction of the initial position seems rather artificial. Suppose the trials correspond to dates and agent (i, t) is born on date t. Then it may be that (i, t) knows ω_t as soon as he is born. There is no *ex ante* for him, only *ex post*. Furthermore, the appeal to unanimity which motivates *ex ante* efficiency in the static case has no meaning if the choice between $\underset{\sim}{a}$ and $\underset{\sim}{b}$ is to be made by a central planner who cannot enquire of (i, t) which he prefers until after (i, t) knows ω_t.

This example makes it fairly clear what the appeal of *ex post* efficiency is. It is a conservative concept: $\underset{\sim}{b}$ is efficient if it cannot be guaranteed that every agent will be made better off, or at least no worse off. In the example above, if $\underset{\sim}{a}$ is not *ex post* superior to $\underset{\sim}{b}$ in the one-trial case then with probability one in an infinite sequence of trials a positive proportion of agents is actually made worse off under $\underset{\sim}{a}$. This is very striking as an argument against calling $\underset{\sim}{a}$ Pareto-superior to $\underset{\sim}{b}$. But it is important to realize that the reason *ex ante* efficiency fails us here is because the unanimity test is difficult to apply and hence the Pareto principle involves a much stronger value judgement here than it normally does.

In the one trial case, applying the *ex post* concept is like treating the "same" agent, in different states, as different agents. That is, agents, like commodities, are distinguished by the state of nature in which they are delivered. Whether this is more reasonable than assuming an initial position is a question which strays beyond the boundaries of economics. Bearing in mind how conservative the Pareto criterion is in making comparisons between allocations it may seem attractive to use the stronger of the two efficiency-concepts, *ex ante* efficiency. Unfortunately, the only general result appears to hold for *ex post* efficiency.

2.5.1 Proposition *If* $\{\phi, \bar{m}, (z_i, m_i)_{i=1}^n\}$ *is a REE for an exchange economy* $\mathscr{E} = \{\mathscr{F}_0, (\succsim_i, e_i, \mathscr{F}_i)_{i=1}^n\}$ *and if* $\succsim_i$ *is monotonic, for each* $i = 1, \ldots, n$, *then the equilibrium is efficient ex post.*

Proof Let $(x_1, \ldots, x_n)$ be the equilibrium allocation and suppose there is an attainable allocation $(x'_1, \ldots, x'_n)$ differing only at ω, say, such that $x'_i \succsim_i x_i$ for all i and $x'_i \succ_i x_i$ for some i. If $x'_i \succsim_i x_i$ then x_i must be too expensive at ω, i.e.

$$\phi^1(\omega).x'_i(\omega) > \phi^1(\omega).(e_i(\omega) + z_i^0(\omega)) + m_i(\omega).$$

By monotonicity $m_i(\omega) = -\phi^0(\omega).z_i^0(\omega)$ so

$$(1) \qquad \phi^1(\omega).x'_i(\omega) > \phi^1(\omega).e_i(\omega) + (\phi^1(\omega) - \phi^0(\omega)).z_i^0(\omega).$$

Suppose now that $x'_i \succsim_i x_i$. Then I claim that

$$(2) \qquad \phi^1(\omega).x'_i(\omega) \geq \phi^1(\omega).e_i(\omega) + (\phi^1(\omega) - \phi^0(\omega)).z_i^0(\omega).$$

since otherwise by monotonicity there would exist $x''_i \succ_i x_i$ such that

$$\phi^1(\omega).x''_i(\omega) \leq \phi^1(\omega).e_i(\omega) + (\phi^1(\omega) - \phi^0(\omega)).z_i^0(\omega).$$

This inequality contradicts (1), thus establishing (2). If the REE were not efficient *ex post* then for some $\omega \in \Omega$ and some attainable allocation $(x'_1, \ldots, x'_n)$ differing from $(x_1, \ldots, x_n)$ only at ω, (2) is satisfied for all i and (1) is satisfied for some i. Summing over i from 1 to n and using the attainability condition $\sum_{i=1}^n x'_i = \sum_{i=1}^n e_i$ gives:

$$(3) \qquad 0 > (\phi^1(\omega) - \phi^0(\omega)).\sum z_i^0(\omega).$$

But since the value of goods bought back from the authority at date 1 equals the value of money held by agents at the beginning of date 1:

$$-\phi^1(\omega).\sum_{i=1}^n z_i^0(\omega) = \sum_{i=1}^n m_i(\omega) = -\phi^0(\omega).\sum_{i=1}^n z_i^0(\omega)$$

contradicting condition (3). □

The main question waiting to be answered is this: is a monetary policy which reveals information "better" than one which conceals it? If it could be shown that a non-revealing policy was inefficient, or dominated by a revealing one, this would be an argument for using control of the money supply as a tool of policy even in an essentially homogeneous system. Proposition 2.5.1 shows that in an *ex post* sense, a revealing equilibrium cannot be either Pareto-superior or Pareto-inferior to a non-revealing equilibrium. However, as was shown above, this is a rather weak defence of the *status quo*. Putting the point more symmetrically, the fact that two types of equilibria cannot be ranked using the *ex post* criterion is only a weak reason for regarding them as equivalent.

Using the *ex ante* criterion one finds that nothing can be said in general. A REE is not *ex ante* Pareto-efficient in general because markets are incomplete. Furthermore, full information is not necessarily desirable. The incompleteness of markets means that the REE is subject to the theory of Second Best. Full information is a necessary condition for full Pareto-efficiency but it is not sufficient. When markets are incomplete increasing the amount of information may make things worse rather than better. Thus it should be no surprise that a revealing equilibrium may be Pareto-superior to or Pareto-inferior to a non-revealing equilibrium.

Let $\mathscr{E}$ be an exchange economy satisfying the expected utility hypothesis. Equilibrium prices at date 1 are said to be *independent of the distribution of income*, if, for every ω in Ω and for every n-tuple of non-negative numbers (w_i), there exists a *unique* price vector $\phi^1(\omega)$ in $\mathbb{R}^l_+$ and an n-tuple of consumption vectors $(x_i(\omega))$ such that $x_i(\omega)$ is maximal for $u_i(.,\omega)$ in the budget set $\{\xi \in \mathbb{R}^l_+ \mid \phi^1(\omega).\xi \leq w_i\}$ for $i = 1, \ldots, n$, *and if* $\phi^1(\omega)$ *is independent of* (w_i) *up to a scalar multiple*. In other words, income transfers among consumers will not alter relative prices. This is the case, for example, if agents have identical, linear, Engel curves passing through the origin. It is an extremely strong assumption and is useful only for the purposes of illustration. Under these assumptions a general comparison of revealing and non-revealing policies can be made.

2.5.2 Proposition *Let $\mathscr{E}$ be an exchange economy in which $(\succsim_i)$ satisfy the expected utility hypothesis and equilibrium prices are independent of the distribution of income at date* 1. *Let $(x_1, \ldots, x_n)$ (resp. $(x'_1, \ldots, x'_n)$) be the consumption allocations corresponding to a revealing (resp. non-revealing) equilibrium. Then $x'_i \succsim_i x_i$ for all $i = 1, \ldots, n$.*

Proof The essential argument can be sketched without entering into much detail. In both equilibria consumers will face the same relative prices $\phi^1(\omega)/\|\phi^1(\omega)\|$ in each state $\omega \in \Omega$. This is because the only effect of trading at date 0 is to alter the distribution of a consumer's income across states and, by hypothesis, relative prices are independent of the distribution of income among agents in each state. In the revealing equilibrium nothing is to be gained by selling forward. In the non-revealing equilibrium, a consumer may always *choose* not to sell forward, in which case his budget set at date 1 will be the same as in the revealing equilibrium. By revealed preference he must be at least as well off in the non-revealing equilibrium as in the revealing equilibrium. □

The intuition behind this result is straightforward. Holding money provides a kind of insurance against fluctuations in prices. For a given set of future prices consumers will only choose to buy insurance if it makes them better off. Since relative prices are given independently of the income distribution, consumers must be at least as well off when they can buy insurance (non-revealing equilibrium) as when they cannot (revealing equilibrium). To get a contrary result, that revelation is better than non-revelation, it is necessary to have distribution effects (on future prices) which outweigh the value of having insurance in the non-revealing equilibrium.

2.6 A characterization of REE

The results on the preceding pages are suggestive but not very precise. What is needed is a *characterization* of the REE, that is, a concept of efficiency such that every REE is "efficient" in this sense and every "efficient" allocation can be decentralized as a REE with lump sum transfers. The word 'efficient" has to be put in inverted commas because a REE is not efficient in the ordinary sense of the word and no definition can make it so. What is involved in characterizing an equilibrium is inventing a concept which is formally like a notion of efficiency but which really only tells us, in a precise way, in which *directions* the equilibrium is efficient.

The ordinary notion of Pareto-efficiency does not refer to prices but the degree of efficiency in a REE with money does depend on prices. This sort of problem is rather messy so I am going to leave it for the moment and analyse a non-monetary economy instead. In fact, it is a generalization of one of the examples first encountered in Chapter 2. The problem of characterizing equilibria when there is no differential information is dealt with thoroughly in Chapter

5, so in what follows I shall only sketch those bits of the theory which deal with the effect of information revealed by prices. The reader who is unfamiliar with this sort of analysis may wish to read this section after Chapter 5 (Part 2).

Consider a very simple model of equilibrium in which agents make inferences about the state of nature after observing prices. There is a finite set Ω of states of nature and a finite number l of securities labelled $h = 1, \ldots, l$. The value of securities depends on the state of nature. Each agent $i = 1, \ldots, n$ has a utility function u_i which maps $\mathbb{R}^l \times \Omega$ to $\mathbb{R}$. If the i-th agent has a bundle x of securities and state ω occurs, his utility is $u_i(x, \omega)$. The i-th agent is assumed to have an initial bundle of securities e_i, independently of the state of nature. He is also assumed to have an information structure, that is, a partition $\mathscr{F}_i$ of the set of states of nature Ω. Each cell $\mathscr{F}_i$ is an event which the i-th agent can observe. If the set A in $\mathscr{F}_i$ is "observed" it means the agent knows that the true value of ω belongs to A but that is all he knows. Agents are imagined to trade securities at date 0, when all they know about the state of nature is the information contained in $\mathscr{F}_i$. At date 2 the securities produce their "revenue" and consumption takes place. Thus agents make their choices in partial ignorance but are eventually informed about the true value of every security.

A price function is a function ϕ from Ω to $\mathbb{R}^l$. If state ω occurs then $\phi(\omega) = (\phi_1(\omega), \ldots, \phi_l(\omega))$ is the vector of prices of securities which prevails. The information available to agents collectively will be represented by a partition $\mathscr{F}$. The function ϕ is called admissible if it is $\mathscr{F}$-measurable, i.e. if it is constant on each cell of $\mathscr{F}$. The choices of agents similarly must depend at most on the information available from their own personal observation and the information revealed by prices. The information available to the i-th individual is represented by a partition $\mathscr{F}_i[\phi]$. A trade plan is a function z from Ω to $\mathbb{R}^l$; $z(\omega)$ is the agent's net trade in state ω. The trade plan z_i chosen by the i-th agent is required to be $\mathscr{F}_i[\phi]$-measurable, i.e. z_i is constant on every cell of $\mathscr{F}_i[\phi]$. The i-th agent's budget set is defined to be the set of trade plans z such that

(1) z is $\mathscr{F}_i[\phi]$-measurable, i.e. $z(\omega) = z(\omega')$ if i cannot distinguish ω and ω';

(2) $\phi(\omega) . z(\omega) \leq 0$ for all ω in Ω.

It is denoted by $\beta_i(\phi)$.

A REE consists of an admissible price function ϕ and a n-tuple $(z_1, \ldots, z_n)$ of trade plans, one for each agent $i = 1, \ldots, n$, such that

(3) $\sum_{i=1}^{n} z_i = 0$ (demand equals supply)

and for each $i = 1, \ldots, n$,

(4) z_i maximizes $Eu_i(e_i' + z_i(\omega), \omega)$ in the set $\beta_i(\phi)$.

A fully revealing equilibrium is a REE $(\phi, z_1, \ldots, z_n)$ in which $\mathcal{F}_i[\phi] = \mathcal{F}$ for $i = 1, \ldots, n$. In other words, prices reveal all the information which is collectively available to the agents.

Is more information a "good thing" in this context? Not necessarily, as the following argument shows. Suppose that $\mathcal{F} = \{\{\omega\}: \omega \in \Omega\}$. Agents collectively have enough information to identify the true state of nature. Suppose that $(\phi, z_1, \ldots, z_n)$ is fully revealing and that the h-th security delivers $r_h(\omega)$ units of a homogeneous consumption good if ω occurs. Let $r(\omega) = (r_1(\omega), \ldots, r_l(\omega))$, for every ω in Ω. In each state ω which occurs with positive probability, $\phi(\omega)$ will be proportional to $r(\omega)$ and no trade will occur. (The example is just a generalization of the one given in Section 2.2.) In *any* equilibrium, every agent is at least well off (*ex ante*) as he would be if he consumed his initial endowment. Thus, the fully-revealing equilibrium is unambiguously the worst that can occur.

The intuition behind this result is fairly transparent. The function of securities in the model is to allow agents to insure themselves. If the true state of nature is revealed then the value of every security is known with certainty and there is no point in trade. In this very special case it is possible to reach an unambiguous conclusion about the value of information. In more general cases such general comparisons are impossible.

To study the role of information in determining efficiency I shall make the assumption that $\mathcal{F}_i = \mathcal{F}$ for $i = 1, \ldots, n$. This assumption has the immediate consequence that all REEs are fully revealing and eliminates differential information. The amount of information available in equilibrium varies only if the initial information structure $\mathcal{F}$ varies. This case is much simpler than the general case in which ϕ may reveal some but not all of the available information; yet it allows me to draw out the essential relationship between information and efficiency. Since I am proposing to compare different economies with different information structures I need some way of describing how efficient an equilibrium is. The concept of V-efficiency is one way of characterizing an equilibrium's efficiency.

An n-tuple of trade plans $(z_1, \ldots, z_n)$ is called an *allocation* if z_i is

$\mathscr{F}$-measurable, for $i = 1, \ldots, n$. An allocation is *attainable* if $\sum z_i = 0$. Let Z denote the set of $\mathscr{F}$-measurable trade plans, i.e. $Z = \{z: \Omega \to \mathbb{R}^N | z(\omega) = z(\omega') \text{ when } \omega, \omega' \in A \in \mathscr{F}\}$, and let V denote a subset of Z, usually a linear subspace. An allocation $(z_1, \ldots, z_n)$ is *strongly V-dominated* if there exists an attainable allocation $(z'_1, \ldots, z'_n)$ such that, for every $i = 1, \ldots, n$.

$$(z'_i - z_i) \in V$$

$$Eu_i(e_i + z_i(\omega), \omega) < Eu_i(e_i + z'_i(\omega), \omega).$$

V is the set of admissible variations in trade plans. When $V = Z$, strong V-domination coincides with strong Pareto-domination, which concept it obviously generalizes. An attainable allocation $(z_1, \ldots, z_n)$ is *weakly V-efficient* if it is not strongly V-dominated. Weak V-efficiency obviously corresponds to weak Pareto-efficiency when $V = Z$ but it is a mistake to think of V-efficiency as an efficiency concept in the normative sense. Any allocation will be V-efficient for some specification of V, for example $V = \{0\}$. The problem is to find the largest set of admissible variations and use this set to characterize the efficiency of the allocation. The usefulness of the idea of V-efficiency is that it provides a measure of the efficiency (or inefficiency) of an allocation or class of allocations. In what follows I shall use V-efficiency to mean weak V-efficiency.

To find out how efficient the REE is I want to find a set V and a corresponding notion of V-efficiency which characterizes the REE in the sense that every allocation is V-efficient and every V-efficient allocation is a REE allocation (with lump sum transfers). Let

$$V = \{z \in Z | \text{for some } A \in \mathscr{F}, \quad z(\omega) = 0 \text{ if } \omega \notin A\}.$$

V is the set of trade plans which exhibit non-zero trade in at most one observable event A in $\mathscr{F}$. If z and z' are trade plans and $(z' - z)$ belongs to V then z and z' differ in at most one observable event A in $\mathscr{F}$. With this definition of V it is easy to prove that

2.6.1 Proposition *If $(\phi, z_1, \ldots, z_n)$ is a REE then $(z_1, \ldots, z_n)$ is weakly V-efficient.*

The converse requires the notion of an equilibrium with lump sum transfers. Let $t_i(\omega)$ denote the net transfer (in units of account) to the i-th agent in state ω. A *transfer system* is a n-tuple of functions $(t_1, \ldots, t_n)$ where, for each $i = 1, \ldots, n$, t_i is a $\mathscr{F}$-measurable function from Ω to $\mathbb{R}$, such that $\sum_{i=1}^{n} t_i = 0$. A *REE with lump sum transfers* is a $(2n + 1)$-tuple $(\phi, z_1, \ldots, z_n, t_1, \ldots, t_n)$, consisting of a price function ϕ, an attainable allocation $(z_1, \ldots, z_n)$ and a transfer system $(t_1, \ldots, t_n)$, such that, for each $i = 1, \ldots, n$.

> z_i maximizes $Eu_i(e_i + z_i(\omega), \omega)$ subject to the constraints that z be $\mathscr{F}$-measurable and $\phi(\omega) . z(\omega) \leq t_i(\omega)$ for all ω in Ω.

Suppose that an allocation $(z_1, \ldots, z_n)$ is V-efficient. Can it be sustained as a REE with lump sum transfers, for some price function ϕ and transfer system $(t_1, \ldots, t_n)$? Clearly it would be enough to show that for some ϕ and every $i = 1, \ldots, n$, if $z \in Z$ and $Eu_i(e_i + z(\omega), \omega) > Eu_i(e_i + z_i(\omega), \omega)$ then $\phi(\omega) . z(\omega) > \phi(\omega) . z_i(\omega)$ for some ω. An allocation $(z_1, \ldots, z_n)$ with this property is called *competitive*. The utility function u_i is called locally non-satiable if, for any x and ω there exists x' arbitrarily close to x such that $u_i(x', \omega) > u_i(x, \omega)$.

2.6.2 Proposition *For $i = 1, \ldots, n$, the function u_i is continuously differentiable, quasi-concave and locally non-satiable. If $(z_1, \ldots, z_n)$ is V-efficient then it is competitive for some ϕ.*

The proofs of the two propositions are not given here partly because of the technicalities involved but mainly because the whole subject of characterizations is treated much more thoroughly in Chapter 5. Once the reader has mastered the material in Chapter 5 he should be able to provide the necessary arguments himself.

The two propositions show that V-efficiency *characterizes* the REE. Every REE is V-efficient and under certain conditions every V-efficient allocation is competitive, i.e. can be sustained as a REE with lump sum transfers. The concept of V-efficiency must be treated with care, however. A particular type of V-efficiency characterizes a *class* of allocations. A smaller set V characterizes a larger class of allocations. If $\mathscr{Z}(V)$ denotes the set of V-efficient allocations then obviously $\mathscr{Z}(V_0) \subset \mathscr{Z}(V_1)$ if $V_0 \supset V_1$. Unambiguously, enlarging the set V "strengthens" the efficiency concept and in this sense the larger V is, the more efficient the allocations are. But if we are given two allocations $(z_1, \ldots, z_n)$ and $(z'_1, \ldots, z'_n)$, which are respectively V_0-efficient and V_1-efficient, it is impossible to rank them, even if it is known that $V_0 \subset V_1$. Indeed, it may be the case that $(z_1, \ldots, z_n)$ Pareto-dominates $(z'_1, \ldots, z'_n)$ even when both are characterized by the same notion of V-efficiency. So comparisons can really only be made between classes of allocations and not within classes using the concept of V-efficiency.

Nonetheless, it is possible to show why the value of information is ambiguous, using the idea of V-efficiency. Consider two versions of the economy described above which differ only in their initial information structures. Let $\mathscr{F}_0$ and $\mathscr{F}_1$ denote the two information structures and suppose that $\mathscr{F}_1$ refines $\mathscr{F}_0$, i.e. for any cell A in $\mathscr{F}_1$ there exists a cell B in $\mathscr{F}_0$ such that $A \subset B$. Thus, $\mathscr{F}_1$ contains or reveals at least as much information as $\mathscr{F}_0$. Let V_0 and V_1 be corresponding sets of admissible variations. It is tempting to imagine that $V_0 \subset V_1$ *but this is not so.* Neither set includes the other. Consider an extreme case where $\mathscr{F}_0 = \{\Omega\}$ is the trivial partition and $\mathscr{F}_1$ is the discrete partition. Then V_0 contains only constant functions and V_1 contains functions which are zero except possibly for one value of ω. The only case in which V_0 is contained in V_1 is when $\mathscr{F}_0$ is the same as $\mathscr{F}_1$.

Notes

1. A partition is a family of subsets which are pairwise disjoint and whose union is the whole set. If $\mathscr{F}$ is a partition of Ω then $\bigcup_{F \in \mathscr{F}} F = \Omega$ and $F \cap F' = \phi$ if F, $F' \in \mathscr{F}$

2. In this very simple case, a function f on $(\Omega, \mathscr{F})$ is measurable if the inverse image of any set in the range of f is the union of some sets in $\mathscr{F}$. Equivalently, f is constant on F, for any F in $\mathscr{F}$.

3. Let $\mathscr{F}_1, \ldots, \mathscr{F}_n$ be a set of partitions of Ω. The coarsest partition refining $\mathscr{F}_i (i = 1, \ldots, n)$ is the unique partition which contains $\mathscr{F}_i (i = 1, \ldots, n)$ and is contained in every partition containing $\mathscr{F}_i$ $(i = 1, \ldots, n)$. It is called the join of $\mathscr{F}_i$ $(i = 1, \ldots, n)$ and denoted by $\mathscr{F}_1 \vee \ldots \vee \mathscr{F}_n$. The finest partition refined by $\mathscr{F}_i$ $(i = 1, \ldots, n)$ is the (unique) partition which is contained in $\mathscr{F}_i$ $(i = 1, \ldots, n)$ and contains every partition containing $\mathscr{F}_i$ $(i = 1, \ldots, n)$. It is called the meet of $\mathscr{F}_i$ $(i = 1, \ldots, n)$ and denoted by $\mathscr{F}_1 \wedge \ldots \wedge \mathscr{F}_n$.

CHAPTER 3

Expectations and economic policy

Many of the issues which have arisen in the debate over rational expectations are relevant to a wider range of problems than the emphasis on monetary policy would suggest. Monetary policy is a natural place to begin to consider the role of expectations and the connection between policy formation and expectations, since future prices play a large role in business decisions. But expectations about government decisions play an important role in many areas of economic policy and it is worth having a look at the theory of economic policy generally, without specific reference to monetary problems.

The theme of this chapter is that when expectations are taken seriously into account, it limits the scope of economic policy. As the rational expectations debate showed, changes in policy influence expectations, which will influence the success or failure of the policy. The LSP is the most striking illustration of this principle but it has a much wider application. For example, Robert Lucas has used it as the basis of a wide-ranging critique of econometric methods of policy evaluation. The two problems which are discussed in this chapter are both, in different ways, extensions of the Lucas critique.

The methods used are essentially game-theoretic. The first problem concerns credible commitments or how the government makes people believe it will do what it says it will do. This is an important problem, although it has been largely ignored. If agents have rational expectations, not only in the sense that what actually happens is what they expected but also in the sense that they expect the government to behave rationally in all circumstances, then it turns out that the government's power to influence events may be surprisingly limited.

The second problem concerns the distinction between rules and discretionary behaviour. Rules can be learned in a way that discretionary behaviour, which is constantly evolving, cannot. As Lucas argues, when individuals have no firm basis for predicting government behaviour, their expectations are liable to be volatile. As a result, the impact of the government's chosen policy will be hard to predict and this is another limitation on the scope of economic policy.

3.1 Expectations and the theory of economic policy

As a starting point, I take "the theory of economic policy" in Tinbergen's sense. Despite recent criticisms, to which I shall return below, it remains the framework in which most quantitative analysis of economic policy is conducted. For the sake of concreteness, consider an explicit version borrowed from Lucas. The state of the economy is described by three kinds of variables. A vector x of control variables or "policy instruments" describes the government's action. A vector ω of exogenous variables describes those factors, including random shocks, which are entirely outside the government's influence. The endogenous variables, represented by the vector y, are determined jointly by x and ω, possibly with a lag. At any time t, the state of the economy is described by the ordered triple (y_t, x_t, ω_t). The evolution of $\{\omega_t\}$ is described by some prescribed stochastic process (for example, $\{\omega_t\}$ are i.i.d.)[1] and $\{x_t\}$ is chosen by the government. The evolution of the endogenous variables $\{y_t\}$ is perhaps described by a difference equation:

$$(1) \qquad y_{t+1} = f(y_t, x_t, \omega_t).$$

Once $\{x_t\}$ has been chosen, the stochastic properties of $\{y_t, x_t, \omega_t\}$ can be determined and the government can evaluate the policy $\{x_t\}$ by looking at a functional, defined on $\{y_t, x_t, \omega_t\}$, such as the expected value of a social welfare function:

$$(2) \qquad \sum \beta^t u(y_t, x_t, \omega_t).$$

In the briefest terms, the government's problem is to choose $\{x_t\}$ to maximize the expected value of (2), subject to (1) and the independent specification of the stochastic process which generates $\{\omega_t\}$. This is Tinbergen's "theory of economic policy" in a nutshell.

The view of the world implicit in this formulation of the policy problem is noteworthy. The economy is a machine which can be controlled by pressing the right buttons. The whole problem of policy formulation is reduced (in principle) to a simple problem of maximization subject to constraints. The simplicity of the problem thus formulated probably explains the attractiveness of the paradigm. There are still a lot of modelling problems to be solved, of course. The econometricians have to discover the true structure represented by the function f. Even the classification of variables is problematical. Is the government deficit a control variable or an endogenous one, for example? It is not clear what social welfare function should be used. And so on. These are serious problems but they are the problems inherent in carrying out any serious research programme. To a greater or lesser extent they affect any quantitative analysis of economy policy; they cannot be adduced as criticisms of the "theory of economic policy" as such. The same is not true of other aspects of the paradigm.

One serious criticism is levelled by R. Lucas in his important paper *Econometric Policy Evaluation: A Critique*. In estimating the structural equation (1) it is generally assumed that the true function f belongs to a family of functions which may be paramaterized thus:

$$f(.) = F(., \theta).$$

For example, θ might be the vector (α, β) and f might be a linear function:

$$y_{t+1} = f(y_t, x_t, \omega_t) = \alpha y_t + \beta x_t + \omega_t,$$

where y_t, x_t and ω_t are assumed to be scalars, of course. The function F is specified in advance and the econometrician's job is to estimate θ. Once an estimate of θ has been found, the theory of economic policy, as outlined above, comes into operation. But as Lucas points out there are good reasons for thinking (a) that θ is not fixed over time and (b) that it may even be systematically related to $\{x_t\}$. As an example of the first possibility, it has been suggested that θ might follow a random walk. Although at first sight this appears to be an extreme assumption, it is actually consistent with some aspects of econometric practice (such as *ad hoc* adjustments to the intercepts) if not the theory. If θ does follow a random walk, long-run policy simulations will have infinite variance even though the model performs well in the short run.[2]

The LSP (Chapter 1) is a dramatic example of the importance of studying the feedback between government policy and the private sector's expectations. Lucas provides other examples from the analysis of consumption, taxation and investment demand, and the Phillips curve to show the sensitivity of the conclusions to the specification of how expectations are formed. By leaving out of account the impact of policy on expectations it is possible to derive bogus structural relations and policy conclusions. Trade-offs appear where none exist and governments are led to rely on "stable" relationships which prove unstable in the event.

The implications for the conduct of economic policy are not as dire as this précis might suggest. The quantitative analysis of policy is feasible but it must model explicitly the impact of policy on expectation-formation. To do this requires a restriction of the class of policies which may be followed. If the government can choose arbitrary sequences $\{x_t\}$ which are unknown to the agents who make up the economy, then the optimal-decision problems of those agents are not well defined. No one should be surprised if, in that case, the parameters θ appear to take a random walk. It is necessary that government policy be systematic, in an appropriate sense, in order that agents' decision problems be well defined. Then there may be a chance that the relationship between policy and expectations will be discovered econometrically. Lucas suggests that policies should be characterized as a parameterized family of functions, say

$$x_t = G(y_t, \lambda, \omega_t). \tag{3}$$

The point then is to choose λ to maximize the expected value of (2) subject to (1) and (3) and the stochastic specification of $\{\omega_t\}$. If changes in λ are clearly announced and G is known, it may be possible to discover the relationship, if any exists, between θ and λ. The simpler the function G and the less frequent the changes in λ, the more stable the long-run relationship between λ and θ is likely to be. From this point of view, the case against discretionary policy, as represented by the Tinbergen paradigm, is that it undermines its own effectiveness by "destabilizing" the structure of the economy.[3] A more modest policy might, in the long run, prove more effective.

Another difference between the traditional approach to policy analysis and Lucas's, which is already implicit in the discussion above, is that Lucas regards the economy as a collection of agents whose behaviour is determined by optimization. To a pure theorist, this seems the natural way to look at the economy. Indeed, he would go further. The government is an optimizing agent too. The model of policy formation presented above, whether in the original Tinbergen-format or in the revisionist Lucas-format, does describe the government's behaviour as a kind of optimization, but it is a very special kind. In the language of game theory, the government is treated as a leader and the rest of the agents are followers. The agents in the private sector take the government's "policy" λ as given—they treat it as a parameter—and optimize accordingly. The government, knowing the private sector's best response for each value of λ, will optimize by taking into account the reaction of the private sector. In more formal language, the policy game is analysed as a leader-follower equilibrium. Agents in the private sector behave non-cooperatively, maximizing their own payoffs while taking the actions of all the other agents as given. Solving for their behaviour as a function of λ yields the reaction curve (as described in (1) and (3)). The leader (government) then maximizes in the obvious way. The justification for this solution concept would run something like this.

The government is a very large agent. The private sector consists of relatively small and disorganized agents, especially if for analytical purposes the economy is assumed to be competitive. Because of the disparity in size, individuals assume they cannot affect the payoff of either the government or of most other individuals and hence assume they cannot affect the behaviour of either the government or of most other individuals. The government, on the other hand, sees only too clearly its impact on the private sector and hence may expect to influence its behaviour. If the government perceives that private individuals treat its own actions as a parameter, which seems reasonable when this is how they actually behave, then it will clearly act as a leader. The rest of the agents, perforce, become followers. This is the essential argument for using the leader-follower solution and I do not think there is a better argument. Now, what are its defects?

In the first place, the argument about relative size is far from being convincing, though it obviously has some force. The government may be the largest actor on the economic stage but it is not the only large one. Large firms, trade unions, ginger groups, political parties and the like, all have sufficient power in certain areas to influence government behaviour. In any case, they do not treat the government's behaviour as a parameter but actively seek to change it. For some purposes the assumption that the economy is competitive may be innocuous but it is certainly misleading to assume that government policy, as well as prices, is always taken as given.

A related criticism is that governments are also, to some extent, the creatures of those they seek to control. A parliament which is elected for a fixed term may be autonomous in the short run but sooner or later it has to face a day of reckoning. Expectations about changes of party or policy following an election may be very important in determining the private sector's behaviour. There is no way of modelling this within the theory of policy framework. The leader's preferences (social welfare function) are constantly being reshaped by the consequences of his own actions. It could be argued, in defense of the leader-follower assumption, that even though governments are not autonomous in practice, it is legitimate to treat them as if they were for the purposes of determining the optimal policy. The theory of policy is after all a normative exercise aimed at discovering what an ideal government would do. To this end it is appropriate to treat the government as if it were a central planner or benevolent dictator, unaffected by political currents. One can sympathize with the desire to separate economics from politics in order to reach a purely economic conclusion about the optimal policy, but the argument is fallacious. Even a central planner has to take into account the private sector's expectations and these expectations may be largely determined by some idea of what is politically feasible for the government. Though the central planner might not be concerned with political pressures *per se*, he still has to cope with the private sector's view of whether his current policy, if implemented by a democratic government, could be sustained. An example will make this distinction clearer.

Economists sometimes recognize the existence of a political business cycle. Governments are said to prefer deflationary measures when elections are a long way off. More precisely if governments have preference orderings over combinations of unemployment and inflation rates, then their preferences are assumed to "tilt" in favour of inflation as the election draws near. Suppose that in the first year of a government's term, an economist is asked to draw up an optimal economic policy, given a fixed social welfare function. Being well trained in the theory of economic policy he chooses $\{x_t\}$ or λ to maximize the social welfare function, ignoring "political" considerations. But the electorate, having grown used to the political business cycle, expect reflation towards the end of the government's term and make their optimal decisions accordingly. Even if the economist were secretly made a dictator he would still have to cope with the fact that individuals expect a U-turn and this must help determine what is optimal for him to do. Thus, even for normative purposes, it is not correct to abstract entirely from the fact that governments are sometimes technically followers.

So far I have been questioning whether the leader-follower assumption is empirically a good one. The points discussed may have cast some doubt on the assumption but they do not add up to a decisive case for rejecting it. At best they suggest that the leader-follower assumption is sometimes misleading and should not be adopted unthinkingly, as it often is. There is a purely theoretical criticism, however, which has a lot in common with the empirical points discussed above and which shows that the leader-follower assumption can be very misleading indeed.

Unless it is assumed that the government can make a once-for-all, self-binding commitment to a comprehensive future policy, the government must at some point be following the private sector's actions. For example, if the government commits itself to a particular course of action today but cannot choose tomorrow's action before tomorrow, then the private sector will treat today's action as a parameter (the government is a leader) but recognize that tomorrow's action is influenced by its (the private sector's) behaviour today. This may have far-reaching consequences even if private individuals never imagine that they can influence the government's present or future course of action and even if the government continues to act as a leader at each date when it chooses its action.

To illustrate, suppose there were a run on sterling and the government announced large sales of foreign exchange to peg the rate. None of the speculators believes he is large enough to influence the government's behaviour so they all treat this decision as a parameter. But the government cannot make a self-binding commitment to behave in the same way tomorrow or next week or the week after and everyone knows its action then will depend on how much sterling is sold today. It may be assumed that the government has large reserves and that, if it could commit itself to using as much of these reserves as necessary to defend the current rate, the speculators would fade away, allowing the rate to stabilize at the current value. Now here is the paradox. If the government is rather timid about losing reserves and it is known that at some point in the future it would devalue if the loss of reserves were high enough today, then there may be an equilibrium in which the government devalues immediately, rather than face a continuing loss of reserves. And this is true in spite of the fact that each day the speculators treat the government's decision as a parameter. The government is undone by its failure to make a credible threat. Because it cannot make a self-binding commitment about its future plans and because it is known to have a preference for devaluation when reserves fall sharply, no one believes the rate will be defended to the limit and it falls. If everyone believed the rate would be defended to the limit, the policy might easily succeed at no cost to the government. It is important to see that it is not assumed in this story that individual speculators believe they can influence the government's behaviour, though collectively they can of course.

A formal example will make this last point clear. Suppose that there is a large number of identical speculators who are identified with the points on the unit interval [0, 1]. Collectively they can behave like one large individual but each assumes he has no influence on the economy. Time is divided into elementary intervals or *dates* which are indexed $t = 0, 1, 2, \ldots,$ *ad inf.* At each date a speculator can raise up to one pound sterling which he then sells for dollars. He pays a fixed charge of £c per period for the money raised in this way. There is a limit on the amount that speculators can sell in one period because it takes time for the speculator to liquidate other assets or raise money by borrowing. The charge c represents the opportunity cost of holding speculative balances of dollars. If a devaluation occurs the benefit is assumed to be £π per pound sterling sold up to that point. Thus, if the devaluation occurs at date t the profit on £1 sold at date 0 is $\pi - ct$. The government has reserves of dollars worth £R at the current rate. It is forced to devalue when it runs out of reserves but may choose to do so earlier. For a given level of reserves the government is assumed to prefer maintaining the present rate to devaluation and for a given exchange rate it prefers more reserves to less. Assume also that

$$2 < R < 3$$

and

$$\frac{\pi}{2} < c < \pi .$$

The first inequality says that the government can hold off for two periods but not three if all the speculators exert maximum pressure on the rate. The second states that a speculator can make a profit selling today if devaluation occurs tomorrow but not if it occurs the next day or later.

To say what happens in this game we need a solution concept. I assume that each speculator takes the actions (present and future) of the government and other speculators as given and chooses to sell or sit tight at each date to maximize profit. The government takes into account the reaction of the speculators when choosing its action. This means the speculators' behaviour must be specified for each possible action of the government.

The structure of the game can be represented most transparently if a *tree diagram* is used. Figure 3.1.1 below shows such a diagram, in which each node represents a decision to be made by a particular player and the branches represent the possible choices. (The diagram is drawn as if there were only one speculator. In this particular case, there is no harm in treating the speculators as one

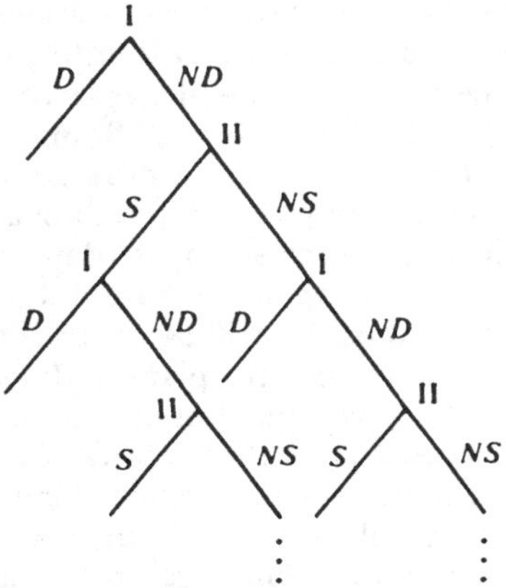

Figure 3.1.1

player. In general, however, one has to have a separate node for *each* player's decision.) The government is identified as Player I and the speculator(s) as Player II. A node which has I (resp. II) beside it represents a decision to be made by the government (resp. speculators).

For example, the node at the top represents the government's decision, on the first day, whether to devalue (D) or not to devalue (ND). If the government chooses to devalue the game is effectively over, so the branch marked D leads nowhere. If it chooses the branch marked ND then the speculators (Player II) must choose whether to sell (S) or not to sell (NS). Then the government has another decision to make, whether to devalue at the next date, and so the game continues. Each node has a unique path leading to it and hence uniquely represents the history of the game to that point. The decision made on a particular day (i.e. the branch chosen) will depend on the node that has been reached and not just on the date. Furthermore, at each node it is possible to tell, by looking at the past decisions of both players, how large the remaining reserves are. The important point is that, since reserves are finite, every path must come to an end if speculators choose S more than a certain number of times (in this instance, three). The tree is very large, however. In fact, for any N there is an infinite number of paths of length N or longer.

I claim the following is an equilibrium for this game. The speculators sell until the government decides to devalue and sit tight thereafter. The government chooses to devalue immediately

($t = 0$). All players are behaving rationally. If the government were to delay devaluation it could at most delay it until date 2. In that case, devaluation would be inevitable but the reserves would be lower. The speculators are being rational as well. Suppose the government does not devalue at $t = 0$. Then it can devalue at $t = 1$, in which case the speculators have been justified in selling at date 0, or it can delay devaluation, in which case selling at date 0 was a bad idea. However, if speculators sell again at date 1 then devaluation is inevitable at date 2. In that case it will be rational for them to sell at date 1 regardless of the government's plans at date 1. If devaluation is inevitable at date 2 the government prefers to devalue at date 1 in order to save its reserves. It was therefore rational for speculators to sell at date 0. But if the best the government can hope for by delaying devaluation at date 0 is to devalue at date 1, it would rather devalue straight away. This argument can clearly be extended to any value of R, however large. Higher reserves do not strengthen the government's hand.

Suppose on the other hand that the government can nail its colours to the mast by somehow committing itself not to devalue until its reserves are gone. Then devaluation will never occur. For reserves cannot be exhausted unless speculators have been selling sterling for at least three periods and it would never be profitable for them to sell in the first of those periods.

Although the informality of the discussion hides the fact, the use of a notion of *perfect equilibrium* is a crucial element in the analysis. If the ordinary leader-follower solution had been used the first case, where devaluation occurs, would be eliminated. The structure of these examples is quite trivial but their analysis requires a certain delicacy nonetheless. Every player's strategy is assumed to be a sequence of functions, one for each date, which indicates what action he will take as a function of the information he has at that date. In the case of the government, this information comprises the history of the game up to and including the previous date. In the case of the speculators this information consists of the history of the game and the decision of the government, at that date, of whether to devalue. The notion of perfectness requires that each player's action at date t be an optimal response to what has gone before, for every possible history of the game up to that point. This means that the only credible threats are those which it would actually be optimal for a player to carry out if his bluff were called.

The game described in Figure 3.1.2 illustrates the rationale for using the concept of perfect equilibrium. The ordered pairs at the end of each path represent the payoffs to the respective players.

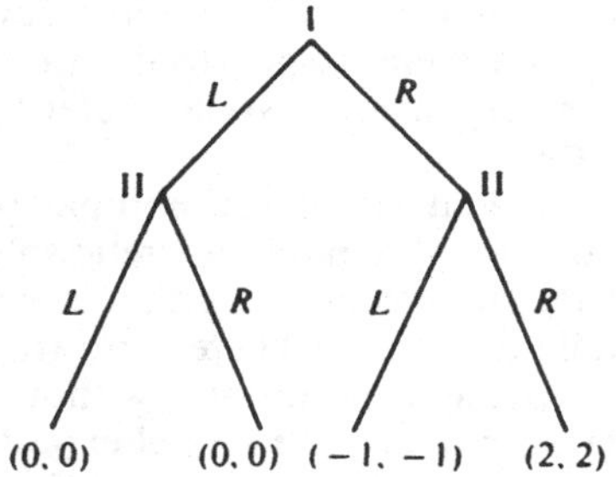

Figure 3.1.2

Each player has two possible moves, left (L) or right (R). Player I moves first.

The game has two Nash equilibria. In one of them, both players move right and in the other, both move left. The payoffs are (2, 2) and (0, 0) respectively. Going left is a Nash equilibrium because, given that I goes left, II is indifferent between his two moves and, given that II moves left, I prefers the outcome (0, 0) to (−1, −1) so he goes left too. There is something wrong with this equilibrium, however. If Player I, who moves first, were to choose R, so that Player II finds himself at the right hand node, faced with a choice between (−1, −1) and (2, 2), will he (Player II) choose L? Of course not, for he prefers R in this case and can be sure of getting it. But if Player I knows this he will not believe that Player II is going to go left at each node. The concept of perfect equilibrium requires that each player choose an optimal move at *each* node and not just at the nodes which are actually arrived at in the course of the game. This allows us to solve the game backward. At the right hand node, II must choose R. At the left hand node, II may choose L or R. At the first node, I will clearly choose R because he knows how II will play and he prefers (2, 2) to (0, 0).

The game between the government and the speculators is more difficult to analyse, mainly because there is no limit to how long the game can be, depending on when and if the speculators choose to sell. In particular, the game cannot be solved backwards. But the intuition behind the use of the perfect equilibrium concept is the same in both games. For example, it is not credible for the government to announce at date 0 that it will never devalue unless reserves have run out. For as was shown above, speculators will sell today because it is optimal for the government to devalue tomorrow if it does not do so today. And the reason for that is that if the government refused to devalue tomorrow it would then be optimal for speculators to sell at dates 1 and 2, forcing devaluation at date 2. The government would prefer to get the devaluation over with at date 1, but by the same argument it would prefer to get it over with still sooner, i.e. at date 0.

In this example, the analysis of the optimal policy cannot be carried out without the use of a game-theoretic solution concept. It is not simply a matter of remembering that expectations matter, although they certainly do matter. There is no way of saying what are rational or reasonable expectations without reference to a solution concept. Here I am using "rational expectations" to mean not just "correct expectations" but also expectations derived from a theory of what a rational agent would do in all circumstances. The speculators in the example have certain expectations about the government's future behaviour not just because this is what the government will do but also because it is what a rational government must do. The Lucas critique of the theory of economic policy can be extended by the observation that the traditional theory of policy treats the appropriate solution concept, as well as the process of expectation formation, as part of the structure of the economy. The criticism which was made of the failure to analyse expectations properly can be extended to the failure to analyse solution concepts.

In the example analysed above, there are in fact two perfect equilibria,[4] in both of which the government acts as a leader. Which of these is observed depends largely on the expectations with which agents begin, but each outcome is self-fulfilling, rational and highly stable. A change of government might switch the economy from one equilibrium to another simply through its effect on expectations. Even more seriously, the government might be able to change the solution concept itself, that is, change the rules of the game. In either case, it is rather misleading to assume the economy has an immutable structure, independently of the government and the policy.

An obvious illustration of this point is the argument in favour of monetary targets, that is, a commitment by the government to keep the growth of the money supply within stated limits. The point of having targets is partly to break inflationary expectations. If a government takes office with a credible commitment to monetary targets then it has changed the rules of the game. Likewise if a government which was previously in the grip of the political business cycle finds some way of making a self-binding commitment to targets. In either case the "structure" of the economy has changed.

The preceding discussion suggests three tentative conclusions. First, solution concepts matter. Second, even if it is accepted that the government is a leader, the inability to make self-binding commitments may reduce the leader's apparent power considerably. Third, when governments cannot or will not make public commitments, the possibility of several rational expectations solutions seems greater than when commitments are made.[5]

3.2 The importance of commitments: an example

What a player threatens to do during a game is often as important as what he actually does. By making threats a player can influence the behaviour of other players to his own advantage. It is important to know, therefore, which threats are credible and which are not. It is often to a player's advantage to commit himself to a particular strategy or set of strategies. A self-binding commitment makes a threat credible and thereby increases its effectiveness. One can imagine various ways of making a self-binding commitment. A player may arrange for some heavy penalty to be imposed on himself if he does not carry out his threat. Or the commitment may be automatic, as in the case where one player can choose his strategy first. When one player chooses his strategy first the game is a *leader-follower game*, the leader being the player who moves first. The simplest case is a two-person game. The follower takes the first player's strategy as given and chooses an optimal response. For each strategy of the first player, the second's optimal response is well-defined. Thus the first player knows the second's reaction function and takes the second player's optimal response into account when choosing his own strategy. It makes a great difference which player is leader.

As an illustration consider a stylized contest between two players representing the government on the one hand and workers or trade unions collectively on the other. The government has to choose the level of the money supply for the coming year and the unions the level of wage settlements in the coming round of negotiations. Both government and unions have preferences defined over combinations of inflation and unemployment and the level of real wages. Suppose that all these variables are determined once the money supply m and level of money wages w are chosen. Then both players can be treated as having preferences over ordered pairs like (w, m). A well known argument claims that faced with high wage claims and the prospect of unemployment, governments tend to increase the money supply. For this reason the money supply proves a weak tool of anti-inflationary policy. Against this position it is argued that if the government announces monetary targets the effect will be to "moderate" wage claims. The argument is really about who is the leader.

To make this more precise, define a game with two *players*, the workers ($i = 0$) and the government ($i = 1$). The i-th player's utility is denoted by $v_i(w, m)$ where w is the money wage and m the money supply. The workers choose a number $w \geq 0$ and the authority chooses a number $m \geq 0$. An *outcome* is any non-negative ordered pair (w, m).

The i-th player's reaction function is denoted by f_i. A *reaction function* f_i maps $\mathbb{R}_+$ to $\mathbb{R}_+$ and has the property that:

(i) for each m in $\mathbb{R}_+$, $v_0(f_0(m), m) \geq v_0(w, m)$ for every w in $\mathbb{R}_+$;
(ii) for each w in $\mathbb{R}_+$, $v_1(w, f_1(w)) \geq v_1(w, m)$ for every m in $\mathbb{R}_+$.

Clearly, $f_0(m)$ (resp. $f_1(w)$) is the workers' (resp. authority's) optimal response when the monetary authority (resp. workers) is committed to m (resp. w). The diagram below illustrates the way in which these curves may be derived graphically.

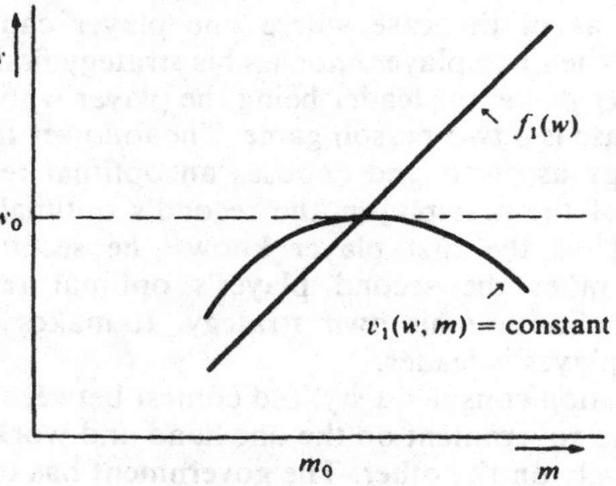

Figure 3.2.1

For each level of money wages w_0 the government's optimal response is at a point like (w_0, m_0), where an indifference curve is tangent to the horizontal line. The upward sloping line passing through (w_0, m_0) is the graph of the reaction function, i.e. the locus of points derived in the same way for different values of w. The workers' reaction function can be derived similarly.

In Figure 3.2.1 it is implicitly assumed that the government prefers a *caet. par.* fall in the money wage rate. It is also assumed that $f_1(w)$ is increasing in w. These turn out to be crucial assumptions later on. Suppose that two reaction functions have been obtained and have the properties illustrated below, *viz.* both are increasing and their graphs have a unique point of intersection at (m_0, w_0).

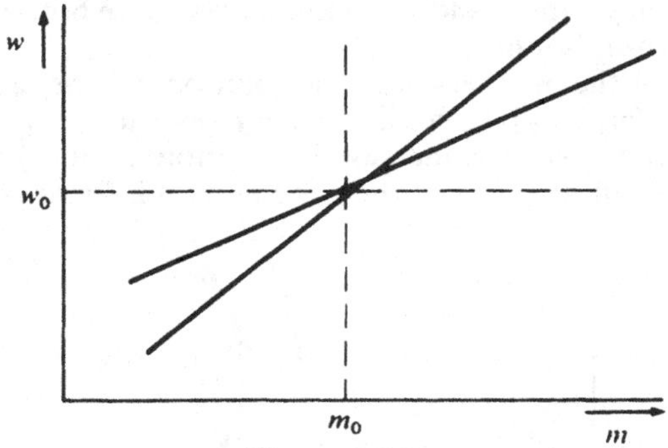

Figure 3.2.2

A *Nash equilibrium* of the game is an ordered pair (m_0, w_0), say, such that $m_0 = f_0(w_0)$ and $w_0 = f_1(m_0)$, i.e. m_0 is an optimal response to w_0 and *vice versa*. If (m_0, w_0) is a Nash equilibrium then the indifference curves of the authority and workers are tangent at (m_0, w_0) to the horizontal and vertical lines through (m_0, w_0) respectively.

Consider the game in which the government is the leader. Since the government can predict the workers' response to every choice of the money supply m, it will choose m to maximize $v_1(f_0(m), m)$. Diagrammatically this means the authority will move along the graph of the workers' reaction function until it reaches the point it most prefers. This is illustrated in Figure 3.2.3. Formally, the *solution* of

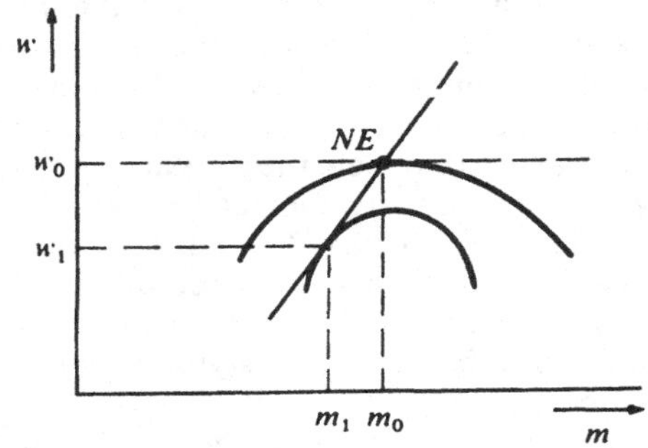

Figure 3.2.3

a game in which the government leads is an ordered pair (m_1, w_1) such that m_1 maximizes $v_1(f_0(m), m)$ and $w_1 = f_0(m_1)$. If a *caet. par.* decrease in w makes the authority better off at (m_0, w_0) then, as Figure 3.2.3 makes clear, the solution is a point like (m_1, w_1) at which the money supply and the nominal wage are both lower than at the Nash equilibrium.

Similarly, if the workers lead, a solution of the game is an ordered pair (m_2, w_2) such that $m_2 = f_1(w_2)$ and w_2 maximizes $v_0(w, f_1(w))$. If a *caet. par.* increase in the money supply makes the workers better off at (m_0, w_0) then as Figure 3.2.4 makes clear, the

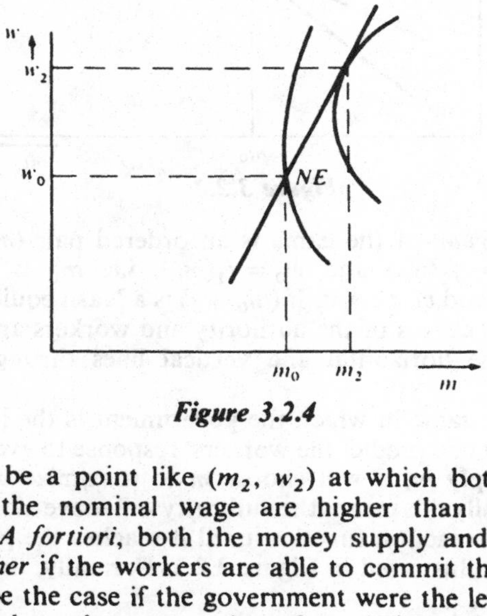

Figure 3.2.4

solution will be a point like (m_2, w_2) at which both the money supply and the nominal wage are higher than at the Nash equilibrium. *A fortiori*, both the money supply and the nominal wage are *higher* if the workers are able to commit themselves first than would be the case if the government were the leader.

This result depends on a number of restrictive assumptions. It is assumed that the Nash equilibrium exists and is unique, that both reaction functions are increasing and that, at the Nash equilibrium, $\partial v_0/\partial w < 0$ and $\partial v_1/\partial m > 0$. When these assumptions are relaxed almost anything can happen, as the reader can easily convince himself by considering a few cases. Nonetheless, the assumptions are no more implausible than any other set which would allow a definite conclusion to be drawn and they permit a precise formulation of the difference between the stylized "monetarist" and "anti-monetarist" positions.

There is a lesson here which concerns the REH as well. To make a binding and credible commitment the government may wish to make a public announcement about its plans and the information on which they are based. Conversely, if it wishes to follow discretionary policy which cannot be anticipated by the private sector it may find itself faced with a kind of *fait accompli*. There is a complementarity between rational expectations and commitment which restricts the government's room to manoeuvre, at least in the case where fully anticipated monetary policy has little effect.

3.3 Rules, commitments and rational expectations

In the paper cited earlier, Lucas put forward an interpretation of the REH which treated it not as a factual assumption but as a necessary condition for an effective, long-run economic policy. Only when changes in policy take the form of fully discussed and understood changes in rules will the resulting changes in the structure of the economy be econometrically predictable.

> It is perhaps necessary to emphasize that this point of view towards conditional forecasting, due originally to Knight and, in modern form, to Muth, does not attribute to agents unnatural powers of divining instantly the true structure of policies affecting them. More modestly, it asserts that agents responses become predictable to outside observers only when there can be some confidence that agents and observers share a common view of the nature of the shocks which must be forecast by both. [Lucas *op. cit.*]

To this end the government ties its hands by choosing rules rather than making *ad hoc* policy decisions. Furthermore, if the government can only evaluate a policy by trial and error because each rule leads to different expectations and different structure, the process of finding a nearly optimal policy is likely to be a lengthy one. Most economists would probably reject such a pessimistic view. There must be some underlying structure which explains how agents react to policy changes, how expectations are formed and so on. Once this structure has been uncovered the optimal policy can be calculated much as the theory of economic policy suggests, even if it is limited by the need to adopt reasonably simple rules and make them understood to the public. Lucas himself seems to have tacitly adopted an approach not too different from this one. But the argument does not go to the heart of the critique against discretionary policy as a simple example will show.

Two players α and β play a repeated game. For concreteness think of β as the government and α as a group of agents. Each player has a choice of two moves to make at each date. α's payoffs are described by a 2×2 matrix:

$$\begin{array}{cc} & \beta\text{'s move} \\ \alpha\text{'s move} & \begin{bmatrix} 1 & 0 \\ 0 & 1 \end{bmatrix} \end{array}$$

The rows correspond to α's move and the columns to β's. The entries indicate α's payoff when α and β make the corresponding moves. In this case, α is rewarded if he makes the same move as β. For α the game consists of trying to predict β's move. β's payoff depends on the state of nature as well as on the moves made by α and β. There are two states $\omega = 0, 1$ and the corresponding payoff matrices are

$$\begin{array}{ccc} & \multicolumn{2}{c}{\beta\text{'s move}} \\ \alpha\text{'s move} & \begin{bmatrix} -10 & 0 \\ 1 & -10 \end{bmatrix} & \begin{bmatrix} -10 & 1 \\ 0 & -10 \end{bmatrix} \\ & \omega = 0 & \omega = 1 \end{array}$$

If α correctly anticipates β's move then β's payoff is independent of his own move. If β's move is not anticipated by α then β will prefer his first (resp. second) move in state 0 (resp. state 1).

There is an infinite sequence of dates $t = 0, 1, 2, \ldots,$ *ad inf.* and the state of nature at each date is generated by a Markov process.[6] The transition matrix is

$$T = \begin{bmatrix} t_{00} & t_{01} \\ t_{10} & t_{11} \end{bmatrix}$$

where the entry t_{ij} is the probability of observing state j at date $t+1$ if state i was observed at date t. α cannot observe the state of nature at any date but β is assumed to observe the true state before he makes his move. What α can observe indirectly is β's move, for α knows his own move and infers from his payoff whether his move was the same as β's. Both players are assumed to be interested in maximizing their expected, long-run average payoffs.

It is not clear what sort of solution concept would be appropriate in the absence of rational expectations. Perhaps the place to start is with minimal assumptions about what the respective players can do. For example, β, not knowing how α intends to play, assumes that either move by α is equally likely. In that case, β will unambiguously maximize his expected payoff by choosing move 0 in state 0 and move 1 in state 1. α, not knowing how β intends to play, may assume that he will make each move with probability 1/2 in which case it will be optimal for α to make each move with probability 1/2. These are not equilibrium strategies, however, for although β's conjecture about α's play is confirmed, α's conjecture about β's play is not. To see this, note that the probability of β choosing move i at any date is the same as the probability of observing state i at that date. Let p_i^t denote the probability of state i occurring at date t. Under the assumption that every entry in the matrix T is positive, it can be shown that p_i^t will converge to a stationary value p_i^*, as t approaches ∞. These long-run values have the property

$$p_0^* + p_1^* = 1$$

and

$$p_0^* = t_{10}p_1^* + t_{00}p_0^*.^7$$

These two equations are easily solved to show that

$$p_0^* = t_{10}/(t_{01} + t_{10})$$

and

$$p_1^* = t_{01}/(t_{01} + t_{10}),$$

using the fact that $t_{00} + t_{01} = 1$. Since α conjectures that β chooses each move with probability 1/2, his conjecture is verified in the long run only if $p_0^* = p_1^* = 1/2$. Only when $t_{01} = t_{10}$ will α's conjecture be confirmed. In the case where $t_{01} \neq t_{10}$, α will surely notice that β chooses one move more often than the other. When he does notice, he will choose that move with probability 1. Then when β notices that α is making a particular move with probability 1, he (β) will start to make the opposite move with probability 1.

The two players may cycle around each other indefinitely but if they do settle down to an equilibrium it will most likely be the Nash equilibrium in which each player's conjecture about the other's play is confirmed. It is not too difficult to calculate the equilibrium strategies. Note first of all that there cannot be an equilibrium in which α chooses one of his moves with probability 1. For β will then choose the other with probability 1 and α's strategy will then be suboptimal. However, α will only choose each move with positive probability if he is indifferent between them, i.e. if he expects β to choose each of *his* moves with probability 1/2. Let λ_ω denote the probability with which β chooses move 0 in state ω, where $\omega = 0, 1$. The probability that β chooses move 0 will tend, in the long run, to $p_0^* . \lambda_0 + p_1^* . \lambda_1$. Player β's equilibrium strategy must be one which satisfies the equation

$$p_0^* . \lambda_0 + o_1^* . \lambda_1 = 1/2 .$$

With β using this strategy, α will observe that β makes each of his two moves with probability 1/2. Then α will be indifferent between each of his possible moves. In equilibrium, of course, α's strategy must be chosen so that β is happy using the probabilities λ_0 and λ_1. There are two such strategies. α will choose his first move either with probability $\mu = 11/21$ or with probability $\mu = 10/21$, according as $0 < \lambda_0 < 1$ or $0 < \lambda_1 < 1$.[8] Exactly one of these conditions will be satisfied. If $0 < \lambda_0, \lambda_1 < 1$ were true, β would be indifferent between his two possible moves in each state; but this is impossible (see fn. 8). If $\lambda_0 = \lambda_1 = 1$ or $\lambda_0 = \lambda_1 = 0$, the equation $p_0^* . \lambda_0 + p_1^* . \lambda_1 = 1/2$ is violated. Hence, either $0 < \lambda_0 < 1$ or $0 < \lambda_1 < 1$ but not both. In the case where $\lambda_0 \neq \lambda_1$, β's moves will be serially correlated. By taking account of this correlation, α may be able to improve on his Nash equilibrium payoff by using β's move at one date to predict his move at the next.

Suppose that α uses the following estimation procedure. He notes the proportion of times that move j follows i up to date t and uses this as his estimate of the transition probability at that date. As time passes the law of large numbers ensures that these estimated probabilities will approach the true ones almost surely. In general the probability that β chooses j after i will not equal 1/2. If it does not then α, maximizing the likelihood of a correct prediction, will predict one or other of β's moves with probability one, i.e. α's behaviour has become certain, conditional on β's previous move. But β can observe this regularity and, when he does so, will exploit it. There is no need to extend the argument; a more general treatment is provided in Section 3.5. What seems intuitively clear is that there need be no limit to the process of learning. The form of the strategies used by each player may become more and more complicated and sophisticated and may never settle down to a stationary equilibrium. The problem is that there is no way of predicting when a player will change the form of his strategy, for example, when α will drop the assumption that β chooses each move with a fixed probability and realizes that the probability of β's move depends on the move that went before. As long as an agent is using a rule of thumb his behaviour is to some extent predictable. But what if he changes rules of thumb? The problem is evidently quite a general one and it is not very easy to get a handle on it. One way of dealing with it is to ask under what conditions an agent could successfully learn the strategy of his opponent without thereby upsetting the equilibrium and changing his opponent's strategy. If these conditions were very mild, one might conclude the problem is not a serious one. In fact, the conclusion is likely to be the opposite.

At the beginning of the game, α has before him the possibility of making an infinite number of observations of β's behaviour. From these observations he wants to learn β's strategy and thus predict his behaviour. But there are two prerequisites to learning from repeated observation. First, he must have a theory and second the theory must have a stationary structure. Suppose, for example, that α hypothesizes that the probability of β making a move at date t depended on ω_t and on the value y_τ of β's move for $\tau = t - T, \ldots, t - 1$. Let this probability be denoted by $P(y_t | \omega_t, y_{t-T}, \ldots, y_{t-1})$. ω_t is unobservable by α but y_τ is observable. α might hope to estimate the probability of y_t conditional on $(y_{t-T}, \ldots, y_{t-1})$ but only if the function P is the same for all t. In any case, α must commit himself to some assumption about the form of β's strategy and the complexity of this form must be definitely limited. Otherwise, repeated observation will gain him nothing. Although this conclusion seems quite innocuous it has far-reaching consequences. It implies that if a situation is ever reached in which learning has stopped and α and β are satisfied both with their models of each other's behaviour and with their own strategies, then they must be using stationary strategies. For example, suppose that α uses as his model of β's behaviour the function $P(y_t | y_{t-T}, \ldots, y_{t-1})$ giving the probability of y_t as a function of $(y_{t-T}, \ldots, y_{t-1})$. If α uses his estimate of P to choose his own optimal strategy then α's move will also be a function (perhaps a random function) of $(y_{t-T}, \ldots, y_{t-1})$. Similar remarks apply to β. If, after repeated observation, both players have acquired a fairly high degree of confidence in their estimates of the other's behaviour, then both players will be using stationary strategies which are known, insofar as they are observable, to the other player. The stationarity of these strategies is crucial for while it will be true that there exists an equilibrium when the players are *required* to adopt a particular form of stationary strategy, an equilibrium may not exist if they are not. Suppose that β's true strategy is $P(y_t | \omega_t, y_{t-T}, \ldots, y_{t-1})$. α cannot observe ω_t so he uses the model $P(y_t | y_{t-T}, \ldots, y_{t-1})$ instead. The vector $(y_{t-T}, \ldots, y_{t-1})$ does not contain all the information available to α however. In equilibrium, it must be the case that knowledge of y_{t-T-1}, for example, would not improve the prediction of y_t. But if β is really following a strategy $P(y_t | \omega_t, y_{t-T}, \ldots, y_{t-1})$ then knowledge of y_{t-T-1} may alter the probability implicitly assigned to ω_t and hence to y_t. Then α would be better off using a more sophisticated[9] model (and strategy) and the situation described could not be an equilibrium. In fact, there may not be an equilibrium. If each player knows the other's model, insofar as this is possible, then there may always be an incentive for one of them to adopt a more sophisticated model and by so doing upset the equilibrium.

The way to ensure that an equilibrium exists is to prescribe the *form* of the stationary strategy used by each player. Sooner or later each player is almost bound to decide that his strategy is sub-optimal compared to some more sophisticated strategy but unless the form of the strategies is restricted it is impossible to play the game rationally at all. The difference between discretionary policy and a policy based on rules is that in the latter the form of the strategies adopted is restricted. There is no limit to the complexity of the models on which discretionary policy is based, on the other hand. An agent's behaviour is predictable when he uses a fixed model but almost by definition there is no way of predicting when he will change models.

These conclusions apply when the prerequisites of the REH are not satisfied and agents do not know government policy in advance. If the government wishes the private sector's behaviour to be predictable it must encourage conditions under which the private sector will have confidence in a stable model. One way for the government to do this would be to commit itself to a stationary, though sub-optimal, policy which could be learned. An alternative would be to ensure the REH held by announcing its policy in advance.

Notes

1. i.i.d. means the random elements $\{\omega_t\}$ are independently and identically distributed.

2. Suppose that f has the form $y_{t+1} = \alpha y_t + \beta x_t + \omega_t$. Using the data available at date t, values of α and β are estimated. Using these estimates, $\hat{\alpha}_t$ and $\hat{\beta}_t$, it is possible to estimate future values of y for any policy $\{x_\tau\}$. This can be done recursively by putting $\hat{y}_{t+1} = \hat{\alpha}_t y_t + \hat{\beta}_t x_t$, $\hat{y}_{t+2} = \hat{\alpha}_t y_{t+1} + \hat{\beta}_t x_{t+1}$ and so on. But since the true values of α and β take a random walk, the variance of the true value of y_τ about the estimated value $\hat{y}_\tau$ will get unboundedly large as $\tau \to \infty$. This follows simply from the fact that the variance of the true values α_τ and β_τ about the estimates $\hat{\alpha}_t$ and $\hat{\beta}_t$ grows without limit as $\tau \to \infty$.

3. I am using "discretionary policy" as a rather loose catch-all to describe policy-making procedures which are not very well understood by those on the outside and whose outcomes are hard to anticipate even in a probabilistic sense. When

individuals have no firm basis for predicting government behaviour, their own expectations are liable to be volatile. If the government cannot predict how its policy will affect individuals' expectations it cannot fully predict the impact of its own policy. This obviously limits the chances of success.

4. Namely, the one in which the government devalues immediately without a fight and the one in which speculators never sell and the government never devalues.

5. In fact, in a leader-follower game there is usually a unique outcome, at least in terms of payoffs.

6. In a Markov process, the probability of observing state s at date t depends on the state which was observed at date $(t - 1)$. The process is characterized by the probabilities of transition from one state to another.

7. For any t, $p_0^t = t_{10}p_1^{t-1} + t_{00}p_0^{t-1}$ and $p_0^t + p_1^t = 1$. The corresponding relations for p_0^* and p_1^* are obtained by passing to the limit.

8. Since $p_0^* . \lambda_0 + p_1^* . \lambda_1 = \frac{1}{2}$ and $p_0^* + p_1^* = 1$ we must have $0 < \lambda_\omega < 1$ for at least one $\omega = 0, 1$. But this is only possible if β is indifferent between his two moves in that state. Let μ be the probability that α chooses his first move (i.e. move 0). From β's payoff matrices, the expected payoff to β in state $\omega = 0$ will be $-10 . \mu + 1 . (1 - \mu) = 1 - 11\mu$ if β chooses his first move and $0 . \mu - 10 . (1 - \mu) = -10 + 10\mu$ if he chooses his second. Equating these expected payoffs shows that β will be indifferent between his two moves in state $\omega = 0$ if and only if $\mu = \frac{11}{21}$. By a similar argument it can be shown that β is indifferent between the two possible moves in state $\omega = 1$ if and only if $\mu = \frac{10}{21}$.

9. Here and elsewhere I use "more sophisticated" to denote a model or strategy depending on a larger number of past observations. In more general situations, an increase in "sophistication" could take other forms, of course.

CHAPTER 3: PART 2

Expectations and economic policy

This part of the chapter deals with two aspects of the theory of repeated games as they apply to economic policy. Unlike one-shot games, repeated games present the player with an environment in which he can learn. The sort of learning which may go on is rather sophisticated since the structure of the system being observed by the player, i.e. his opponents' strategies, need not be constant over time. The analysis of such games has some important lessons for the way we theorize about expectations in economic models. The REH is often interpreted as being the assumption that agents make the correct prediction or draw the correct inference in a given set of circumstances. In static models there is often an unambiguously correct way of proceeding, but in repeated games where learning occurs this need not be so. What then?

Another interesting characteristic of repeated games is the central role of threats. An agent's behaviour is influenced as much by threats of future retaliation as it is by the current behaviour of his opponents. Sometimes he is unreasonably influenced by threats, as for example when he is dissuaded from a particular course of action by a threat which a rational opponent would not carry out if his bluff were called. To eliminate these bogus equilibria, which would not be sustained by rational players, we introduce the notion of *perfect equilibrium* which essentially requires that every agent's behaviour or threatened behaviour must be optimal in every eventuality and not merely those which actually occur. Expectations are assumed to be rational not just in the sense of being self-fulfilling but also in the sense of ascribing rational behaviour to players in all possible future circumstances, those which will not arise as well as those which will. The relevance to economic policy arises when governments cannot commit themselves to a course of action in advance. A commitment is like a threat and a government which is expected to behave rationally in the future may find its ability to make credible commitments severely limited.

A repeated game consists of a subgame and a supergame. For the sake of illustration, suppose there are two players α and β who have *action sets* X and Y and *utility functions* u and v, defined on $X \times Y$. The *subgame* is defined by the 4-tuple (X, Y, u, v). It is just an ordinary game in normal form. The play of the supergame consists of repeated moves in the subgame but the move which is made in any particular play of the subgame will depend on what has gone before. Let the successive plays of the subgame be indexed $t = 0, 1, \ldots,$ *ad inf.* and let x_t (resp. y_t) denote the move made by α (resp. β) at t. A *partial history* of the game up to t is a finite sequence $(x_0, y_0, \ldots, x_{t-1}, y_{t-1})$ of moves. Let these sequences be generically denoted by H_t. A strategy for α (resp. β) in the supergame is a sequence of functions $\{f_t\}$ (resp. $\{g_t\}$) such that for every t, $f_t(H_t) \in X$ (resp. $g_t(H_t) \in Y$) for every H_t. In other words, the strategy chooses an action for the player at each t as a function of what has gone before. Given a pair of strategies $\{f_t\}$ and $\{g_t\}$ a unique play of the supergame is defined recursively by the equations

$$(x_0, y_0) = (f_0, g_0)$$

$$(x_t, y_t) = (f_t(H_t), g_t(H_t))$$

and

$$H_{t+1} = (x_t, y_t, H_t).$$

Payoffs can be assigned to the players in the supergame by aggregating the payoffs in the individual subgames. For example, one might take the long-run averages.

$$U(\{f_t, g_t\}) := \lim_{T \to \infty} T^{-1} \sum_{t=0}^{T} u(x_t, y_t)$$

$$V(\{f_t, g_t\}) := \lim_{T \to \infty} T^{-1} \sum_{t=0}^{T} v(x_t, y_t)$$

The game defined in this way is fairly representative of repeated games analysed by game-theorists. The games introduced in the sequel can be seen as variants of this standard form. In Section 3.4 one of the players is allowed to be a leader and in 3.5 one of the players has incomplete information, but the basic structure is the same.

3.4 The repeated leader-follower game

The concept of a leader-follower game was used in the first part of this chapter so the intuition behind the definition should be fairly clear. The leader-follower equilibrium is used when one player moves first and the other(s) have to take his move as given. It may also be appropriate when one player is very large in relation to the others. Strictly speaking, this is true if the small players form a continuum and act non-cooperatively. In that case, a small player perceives that his actions have no effect on the payoffs of the other players (large and small) so he reasonably assumes that his actions will have no effect on their actions either. The large player, on the other hand, does affect the payoffs of the others by his actions. Furthermore, he knows they treat his action as a parameter and can therefore anticipate their optimal response. If he takes the optimal response into account when choosing his own action then he is behaving as a leader.

The second case is of some importance for the theory of economic policy. The government is typically assumed to be a leader in the policy game. The rationale for this assumption is unclear since solution concepts are rarely discussed in the literature. It seems to be based on the difference in size between the government and the members of the private sector, together with the assumption that agents behave non-cooperatively. I have not discovered a better explanation. The assumption that the government is the leader is important because it increases the government's power to control the game, as measured by its payoff. The examples in Chapter 3 (Part 1) illustrate this fact. What is true of a one-shot game need not be true of a repeated game, however, and in particular the size of the government does not give it the power to commit itself, in advance, to a course of action. The government, however large, may only be a leader in a very limited sense in a repeated game.

Consider a subgame played by a single large player (β) and a continuum of small players (α) who are uniformly distributed over the unit interval. The action sets of large and small players are Y and X respectively. I shall only consider outcomes in which the small players, who are assumed to be identical, choose the same action. Let x be the action of a typical small player, $\bar{x}$ the action of all the other small players and y the action of the large player. The payoff of the large player depends on the actions chosen by himself and by the small players, i.e. on $\bar{x}$ and y. The payoff of the typical small player depends on his own action (x), that of the other small players ($\bar{x}$) and that of the large player (y). In effect, it is being assumed that any agent's payoff depends on his own action and the *distribution* of other agents' actions. Since only symmetric outcomes are being studied here, there is no loss of generality in replacing the distribution of other small players' actions by the typical action $\bar{x}$.

The game is formally defined by the 4-tuple (X, Y, u, v) where u (resp. v) is a utility function mapping $X \times X \times Y$ (resp. $X \times Y$) to $\mathbb{R}$. If β chooses y, α chooses x and the rest choose $\bar{x}$ then α's payoff is $u(x, \bar{x}, y)$ and β's is $v(\bar{x}, y)$. The *leader-follower equilibrium* of this game is the ordered pair $(\phi, \bar{y})$, consisting of an optimal response function $\phi: Y \to X$ and an action $\bar{y}$ in Y, such that:

(i) $u(\phi(y), \phi(y), y) \geq u(x, \phi(y), y)$ for any $(x, y) \in X \times Y$;
(ii) $v(\phi(\bar{y}), \bar{y}) \geq v(\phi(y), y)$ for any $y \in Y$.

To measure the advantage gained by β by virtue of his leadership we need some sort of benchmark. Suppose the roles were reversed, that is, that β made his choice after the small players made theirs. He would then have to treat $\bar{x}$ as given. For the reason given earlier, the small players would still treat the actions of all other players as given. The result would be a *Nash equilibrium*, i.e. an ordered pair $(\bar{x}, \bar{y})$ in $X \times Y$ such that:

(iii) $u(\bar{x}, \bar{x}, \bar{y}) \geq u(x, \bar{x}, \bar{y})$ for any $x \in X$;
(iv) $v(\bar{x}, \bar{y}) \geq v(\bar{x}, y)$ for any $y \in Y$.

Comparing the two equilibria it is fairly obvious that

if (x, y) is a Nash equilibrium there is a leader-follower equilibrium $(\phi, \bar{y})$ such that $v(\phi(\bar{y}), \bar{y}) \geq v(x, y)$

(and usually the inequality is strict).[1] The government is clearly able to "manipulate" the private sector as a leader to an extent which it cannot in a Nash equilibrium. Concrete examples (cf. Chapter 3, Part 1) make the distinction even more graphically.

As I have already argued, α treats β as a leader because of their difference in size. While this argument retains its force in a repeated game as far as current actions are concerned it does not extend to future actions. More precisely, the leader will choose his action at each date taking into account the optimal response of the small agents at that date, but he may have no influence or "leadership" over their expectations or plans for the future. Let the game (X, Y, u, v) defined above be taken as a subgame. Let x_t, $\bar{x}_t$, and y_t denote, respectively, the actions chosen by α, the rest of the small agents and β. A partial history is a finite sequence $H_t = (\bar{x}_0, \bar{y}_0, \ldots, \bar{x}_{t-1}, \bar{y}_{t-1})$ describing the play of the game up to date t.[2] Note the actions of a single α are ignored. A *strategy for* α is a sequence $\{f_t\}$ of functions such that $f_t(H_t, y_t)$ belongs to X for every t, H_t and y_t. The appearance of y_t as an argument of f_t indicates that α responds to β's current action and this allows β to act as leader at each date. The set of α's strategies is denoted by F. A *strategy for* β is a sequence $\{g_t\}$ of functions such that $g_t(H_t)$ belongs to Y for every t and H_t. G is the set of β's strategies. Let f and $\bar{f}$ be the strategies in F chosen by α and the rest of the small players respectively and let g be the strategy in G chosen by β. A unique play of the supergame $\{x_t, \bar{x}_t, y_t\}$ is defined, in the usual way, by putting

$$(x_0, \bar{x}_0, y_0) = (f_0, \bar{f}_0, g_0)$$

$$y_t = g_t(H_t)$$

$$(x_t, \bar{x}_t) = (f_t(H_t, y_t), \bar{f}_t(H_t, y_t)).$$

Rather than define a utility function for each player in the supergame in terms of corresponding functions in the subgame I shall assume, more generally, that utility functions are defined on the strategies of the supergame directly. Let $V(\bar{f}, g)$ be β's payoff and $U(f, \bar{f}, g)$ be α's payoff when f, $\bar{f}$ and g are given the same interpretation as above. When there is no risk of confusion, the payoffs may be denoted by $V(\{\bar{x}_t, y_t\})$ and $U(\{x_t, \bar{x}_t, g_t\})$ in an obvious notation. The supergame is formally defined by the 4-tuple (F, G, U, V).

Let $H_t = (\bar{x}_0, y_0, \ldots, \bar{x}_{t-1}, y_{t-1})$ be a partial history of the supergame and f a strategy in F. Then $f|(H_t, y_t)$ denotes the unique strategy f' in F defined as follows:

(i) for any $\tau < t$ and any (H'_τ, y'_τ) $f'(H'_\tau, y'_\tau) = \bar{x}_\tau$
(ii) for any $\tau \geq t$ and any (H_τ, y_τ) $f'(H_\tau, y_\tau) = f(H_\tau, y_\tau)$

Up to date t, f' agrees with H_t. From date t onwards f' agrees with f. In a similar way, $g|H_t$ is defined for every g in G and partial history H_t. The strategies $f|(H_t, y_t)$ and $g|H_t$ describe the behaviour of players who are forced to play according to H_t up to t and then according to f and g respectively from t onwards.

3.4.1 Definition *A Nash equilibrium outcome of the game (X, Y, U, V) is a pair of sequences $\{\bar{x}_t\}$ and $\{\bar{y}_t\}$ in X and Y, respectively, such that*

(i) $U(\{\bar{x}_t, \bar{x}_t, \bar{y}_t\}) \geq U(\{x_t, \bar{x}_t, \bar{y}_t\})$ *for any* $\{x_t\}$;
(ii) $V(\{\bar{x}_t, \bar{y}_t\}) \geq V(\{\bar{x}_t, y_t\})$ *for any* $\{y_t\}$.

A perfect leader-follower equilibrium of (F, G, U, V) is an ordered pair $(\bar{f}, \bar{g})$ in $F \times G$ such that

(iii) $U(\bar{f}|(H_t, y_t), \bar{f}|(H_t, y_t), \bar{g}|H_t) \geq U(f|(H_t, y_t), \bar{f}|(H_t, y_t), \bar{g}|H_t)$ *for any t, (H_t, y_t) and f in F;*

(iv) *$V(\bar{f}|(H_t, \bar{y}_t), \bar{g}|H_t) \geq V(\bar{f}|(H_t, y_t), g|H_t)$ for any t, H_t and g in G, where $\bar{y}_t = \bar{g}_t(H_t)$ and $y_t = g_t(H_t)$.*

The definition of the Nash equilibrium is straightforward; (i) and (ii) simply require that every player choose a best response to the actions of the other players, taking those actions as given. The perfect leader-follower equilibrium is more complicated. Condition (iii) requires two things: that α's strategy be optimal from t onwards whatever the history of the game up to t and whatever action is chosen by β. The first requirement imposes the "perfectness" property: α's behaviour must be optimal in every eventuality and not just in the play which actually occurs. This rules out the possibility of making threats or commitments which are not credible. The second requirement means that α responds optimally to any current action by β: α must be a follower at each date. Condition (iv) is analogous to the first part of (iii). β is required to choose a strategy which is optimal from t onwards, given any history of the game up to t. In doing so he takes into account the response of the small players to his current and future actions. To the extent that every player must respond optimally to any history of the game up to t, they may all be considered followers. In particular, α responds optimally to past as well as current choices of y_t. However, none of the small players has any perceptible influence on β since β's behaviour depends on past values of $\bar{x}_t$ and y_t which are both taken as given by α. In other words, the small agents collectively influence β's future behaviour but individually they cannot exploit this influence.

The play of the game from t onwards is called the *sequel* and is denoted by $S_t = (\bar{x}_t, y_t, \ldots)$. The utility function V is called *forwardly separable* at t if and only if

$$V(H_t, S_t) \geq V(H_t, S_t')$$

implies

$$V(H_t', S_t) \geq V(H_t', S_t')$$

for every H_t, H_t', S_t and S_t'. In other words, preferences over the sequel at t are independent of the history up to t. The definition of forward separability for U is more awkward. Let x generically denote a sequence $\{x_t\}$ in X and y generically denote a sequence $\{y_t\}$ in Y. U is said to be *forwardly separable* at t if and only if

$$U(x^0, \bar{x}, y) \geq U(x^1, \bar{x}, y)$$

implies

$$U(x^2, \bar{x}', y') \geq U(x^3, \bar{x}', y')$$

for any x^0, x^1, x^2, x^3, $\bar{x}$, y, $\bar{x}'$ and y' such that

$$\begin{aligned} x^0_\tau &= \bar{x}_\tau = x^1_\tau && (\tau < t) \\ x^2_\tau &= \bar{x}'_\tau = x^3_\tau && (\tau < t) \\ x^0_\tau &= x^2_\tau && (\tau \geq t) \\ x^1_\tau &= x^3_\tau && (\tau \geq t) \\ \bar{x}_\tau &= \bar{x}'_\tau && (\tau \geq t) \end{aligned}$$

and

$$y_\tau = y'_\tau \qquad (\tau \geq t+1)$$

In other words, α's preferences over values of x_τ $(\tau \geq t)$ are independent of the history of the game up to t and of y_t when $\bar{x}_\tau$ and y_τ are constant for $\tau \geq t$ and $\tau \geq t+1$ respectively.[3] If V is defined by putting

$$V(\{\bar{x}_t, y_t\}) = \sum_{t=0}^{\infty} \delta^{-t} v(\bar{x}_t, y_t)$$

then V is obviously forwardly separable. If U is defined by putting

$$U(\{x_t, \bar{x}_t, y_t\}) = \sum_{t=0}^{\infty} \delta^{-t} u(x_t, \bar{x}_t, y_{t+1})$$

then U is also forwardly separable. There are much more general functional forms which have the property of forward separability, of course.

3.4.2 Theorem *Let (F, G, U, V) be a supergame in which U and V are forwardly separable at each t. If $\{\bar{x}_t, \bar{y}_t\}$ is a Nash equilibrium outcome of the game (X, Y, U, V) then there is a perfect, leader-follower equilibrium $(\bar{f}, \bar{g})$ of the supergame which yields the same outcome.*

Proof Define f and g by putting

$$\begin{aligned} \bar{f}_t(H_t, y_t) &= \bar{x}_t && \text{for any } t, H_t \text{ and } y_t; \\ \bar{g}_t(H_t) &= \bar{y}_t && \text{for any } t \text{ and } H_t. \end{aligned}$$

To show that condition (iii) of Definition 3.4.1 is satisfied let $\bar{H}_t = (\bar{x}_0, \bar{y}_0, \ldots, \bar{x}_{t-1}, \bar{y}_{t-1})$ and note that condition (i) implies that

$$U(\bar{f}\,|\,(\bar{H}_t, \bar{y}_t), \bar{f}\,|\,(\bar{H}_t, \bar{y}_t), \bar{g}\,|\,\bar{H}_t) \geq U(f\,|\,(\bar{H}_t, \bar{y}_t), \bar{f}\,|\,(\bar{H}_t, \bar{y}_t), \bar{g}\,|\,\bar{H}_t)$$

for any f in F. Then forward separability implies that for any (H_t, y_t)

$$U(\bar{f}\,|\,(H_t, y_t), \bar{f}\,|\,(H_t, y_t), \bar{g}\,|\,H_t) \geq U(f\,|\,(H_t, y_t), \bar{f}\,|\,(H_t, y_t), \bar{g}\,|\,H_t)$$

which is precisely condition (iii). A similar argument shows that condition (iv) is satisfied also. □

Although the proof of the theorem is mathematically trivial the theorem itself is not. It is not hard to imagine situations in which it is the government's future actions which matter to the private sector's current decisions. In these situations, when expectations are paramount, the theorem suggests the government has little power to manipulate the members of the private sector, despite their difference in size, as long as the criterion of "perfectness" is used to decide which commitments are credible. Such a stark result cannot be expected to hold in general but it suggests a further limitation of the scope for economic policy.

The exchange rate example discussed in Section 3.1 belongs to a different class of games which also emphasize the limitations imposed on economic policy by the inability of governments to make arbitrary, self-binding commitments. In one respect it is more general than the supergame described above: the set of actions from which β may choose at date t depends on the history of the game up to that date. Let $Y(H_t)$ denote the set of actions available to β at date t given the partial history of the game is H_t. A strategy g in G is called *admissible* if $g_t(H_t)$ belongs to $Y(H_t)$ for every t and H_t. The definition of a perfect, leader-follower equilibrium is easily adapted by replacing condition (iv) in Definition 3.4.1 with the condition:

(iv)′ $V(\bar{f}\,|\,(H_t, \bar{y}_t), \bar{g}\,|\,H_t) \geq V(\bar{f}\,|\,(H_t, y_t), g\,|\,H_t)$

for any admissible g in G, where $\bar{y}_t = \bar{g}_t(H_t)$ and $y_t = g_t(H_t)$, for any t and H_t.

Of course, it is understood that $\bar{g}$ must be admissible too.

In other respects, the exchange rate example is much more special. It has a great deal of structure which the forwardly separable supergames lack. Nonetheless, in some ways it represents a paradigm of the struggle between a government which wishes to commit itself to a particular course of action and a private sector which believes the government will be "blown off course" or "make a U-turn". The government, which is identified with β, has two options. In the exchange rate example, these were to devalue or maintain the rate but in general the options are to hang on or to give in. The small agents can exert pressure on the large agent. In the exchange rate example they do this by selling sterling. The government can maintain its position for a certain length of time, perhaps indefinitely, depending on the amount of pressure exerted by the small agents. Whether or not the small agents choose to exert pressure depends on whether or not they expect the government to give in. The closer the proximity to a "U-turn" the greater is their incentive to apply pressure. These are the "stylized facts" of the confrontation and they are easily formalized. Under surprisingly mild assumptions the capitulation observed in the exchange rate example is shown to be a perfect, leader-follower equilibrium.

Let x denote the amount of "pressure" a small player exerts on the government. The set X must be compact and there is then not much loss of generality in assuming $X = [0, 1]$. β, on the other hand, has a binary choice so there is no loss of generality in letting $Y = \{0, 1\}$, where $y = 1$ signifies holding on and $y = 0$ signifies giving in. In the exchange rate example, 0 and 1 correspond to devaluation and maintenance of the rate respectively. Let H_t be a partial history of the game up to t. $Y(H_t)$ is defined by two rules:

(i) $Y(H_t) = \{0\}$ if $t > T$ and $(\bar{x}_\tau, y_\tau) = (1, 1)$ for all $\tau < t$;
(ii) $Y(H_t) = \{0, 1\}$ otherwise.

T is a fixed but arbitrary integer (presumably large). Condition (i) says that β is only forced to give in if he has not done so previously and if the small players have exerted maximum pressure in all previous periods and for at least T periods. This condition is about as restrictive as one could reasonably get and weights the game substantially in β's favour. Condition (ii) allows β to choose $y = 1$ after he has chosen $y = 0$. This may seem odd but it is immaterial since, as will become clear below, the game effectively ends when β first chooses $y = 0$. The definition of $Y(H_t)$ given above is convenient, however.

Let $\{x_\tau, \bar{x}_\tau, y_\tau\}$ be any sequence in $X \times X \times Y$. I assume that U has the form

$$U(\{x_\tau, \bar{x}_\tau, y_\tau\}) = U_t(x_0, \ldots, x_{t-1})$$

where $t = \inf\{\tau : y_\tau = 0\}$ and that U_t is non-decreasing in x_τ if $\tau = t - 1$ and strictly decreasing otherwise. In other words, α's utility depends on his own actions and the value of t at which β gives in. α always prefers not to exert pressure except in the case $\tau = t - 1$ when he may prefer it. (Values of x_τ for $\tau \geq t$ do not matter.) V is assumed to have the form

$$V(\{\bar{x}_\tau, y_\tau\}) = \begin{cases} V_\infty & \text{if } t = \infty \\ V_t(\bar{x}_0, \ldots, \bar{x}_{t-1}) & \text{if } t < \infty \end{cases}$$

where $t = \inf\{\tau : y_\tau = 0\}$. It is also assumed that for any $t < \infty$

$$V_t(\bar{x}_0, \ldots, \bar{x}_{t-1}) < V_\infty$$

and that for any $t' < t$

$$V_t(\bar{x}_0, \ldots, \bar{x}_{t-1}) \leq V_{t'}(\bar{x}_0, \ldots, \bar{x}_{t'-1})$$

with strict inequality if $\bar{x}_\tau > 0$ for any $t' \leq \tau < t$. The most preferred alternative is to hold on indefinitely, regardless of the cost, if it is possible to do so. If the government is going to give in at some finite date anyway and the private sector is applying pressure then it would prefer to give in sooner and avoid a futile struggle.

With these assumptions it is possible to show that the game has two perfect, leader-follower equilibria. Define the pair $(\bar{f}, \bar{g})$ in $F \times G$ as follows:

$$\bar{f}_t(H_t, y_t) = 1 \qquad \text{for any } t, H_t \text{ and } y_t;$$

$$\bar{g}_t(H_t) = 0 \qquad \text{for any } t \text{ and } H_t.$$

α applies maximum pressure in every circumstance and β gives in at the earliest opportunity. α's behaviour is rational given β's behaviour but it seems paradoxical that β, though a leader, should give in. For β prefers to hold out indefinitely if possible and if he were to hold out it would never be rational for the small agents to force him to give in. Yet $(\bar{f}, \bar{g})$ is a perfect, leader-follower equilibrium. The proof is fairly simple.

Consider first of all whether condition (iii) of Definition 3.4.1 is satisfied. Let t, H_t and y_t be arbitrary but fixed. If $y_\tau = 0$ for any $\tau \leq t$ then α's utility is independent of what happens from t onwards and condition (iii) is automatically satisfied. If $y_\tau = 1$ for all $\tau \leq t$ then the definition of $\bar{g}$ implies that $\bar{g}_{t+1}(H_t, \bar{x}_t, y_t) = 0$ for any choice of $\bar{x}_t$ in X. Hence, by our assumption on the form of U

$$U(f|(H_t, y_t), \bar{f}|(H_t, y_t), \bar{g}|H_t) = U_{t+1}(\bar{x}_0, \ldots, \bar{x}_{t-1}, x_t)$$

for any f in F, where $x_t = f_t(H_t, y_t)$. Since U_{t+1} is non-decreasing in x_t, condition (iii) is satisfied because $\bar{f}_t(H_t, y_t) = 1$.

Now consider β's strategy, letting t and H_t be arbitrary but fixed as before. If $y_\tau = 0$ for some $\tau < t$ then β's utility is independent of what happens from t onwards and condition (iv) is automatically satisfied. Suppose then that $y_\tau = 1$ if $\tau < t$ and let g be any admissible strategy in G. Let $\{\bar{x}_\tau, y_\tau\}$ be the play of the game associated with the strategies $\bar{f}|(H_t, y_t)$ and $g|H_t$, where $y_t = g_t(H_t)$. Let $t_0 = \inf\{\tau : y_\tau = 0\}$. Clearly, $t_0 \geq t$. There are two cases to be considered. If $t_0 = \infty$ then, from the definition of $\bar{f}$, $\bar{x}_\tau = 1$ for all τ.

Then for some τ, $Y(H_\tau) = \{0\}$, where $H_\tau = (\bar{x}_0, y_0, \ldots, \bar{x}_{\tau-1}, y_{\tau-1})$ by part (i) of the definition of $Y(H_\tau)$ contradicting the admissibility of g. If, on the other hand, $t_0 < \infty$ then

$$\begin{aligned} V(\bar{f}\,|\,(H_t, y_t), g\,|\,H_t) &= V_{t_0}(\bar{x}_0, \ldots, \bar{x}_{t_0-1}) \\ &\leq V_t(\bar{x}_0, \ldots, \bar{x}_{t-1}) \\ &= V(\bar{f}\,|\,(H_t, \bar{y}_t), \bar{g}\,|\,H_t) \end{aligned}$$

where $\bar{y}_t = \bar{g}_t(H_t) = 0$. Hence condition (iv) is satisfied, i.e. $\bar{g}$ is at least as good as g.

The intuition behind the result can be seen most easily in terms of a concrete illustration like the exchange rate example. Suppose the government only has $\frac{1}{2}$ unit of reserves left and yet it decides not to devalue this period. An optimal response by the speculators would be to sell sterling, for if they do so the government will be forced to devalue next period. Remember that the speculators behave non-cooperatively, i.e. they take the behaviour of the others as given, but given that the others sell it is rational for each individual to sell as well.[4] But the government, perceiving this response and that it must devalue tomorrow would rather devalue today and avoid the drain on its reserves. Thus it is optimal for the government to devalue when its reserves stand at $\frac{1}{2}$ unit. Now suppose that it has reserves of $1\frac{1}{2}$ units and decides not to devalue. Then it is optimal for speculators to sell because they know that the government will devalue, i.e. it is *optimal* for the government to devalue, when its reserves stand at $\frac{1}{2}$ unit, which they will do at the next date. The government, seeing that it will devalue at the next date, would rather devalue today and spare the drain on its reserves. Applying this argument repeatedly, we see that, however large the government's reserves, it will choose to devalue immediately, rather than delay devaluation for one period and lose reserves. The government's problem is that it does not have a credible threat. It can delay devaluation so long that it would never be rational for the speculators to sell sterling. But because the speculators know the government will devalue (and soon) it is optimal for them to speculate and hence for the government to devalue immediately. The speculators always expect devaluation tomorrow if it does not occur today and they are rational to do so because the government finds it optimal to devalue. The government is trapped, not by the irrationality of the speculators, who are quite rational, but by its own rationality.

The general conclusion is that the "perfectness" concept cuts two ways. By making it impossible for the government to commit itself in a credible way to holding on, it makes it credible—that is to say rational—for the small players to threaten maximum pressure. The argument is symmetric, however, so it is not surprising that there exists another perfect, leader-follower equilibrium. Define the pair $(\bar{f}, \bar{g})$ in $F \times G$ by putting

$$\bar{f}_t(H_t, y_t) = 0$$
$$\bar{g}_t(H_t) = 1$$

for any t, H_t and y_t. The proof that $\bar{f}$ and $\bar{g}$ are equilibrium strategies is left to the reader.

The crucial element in the analysis is the assumption that the government cannot commit itself to a course of action. In a true leader-follower equilibrium of the game the large player β would choose a sequence $\{y_t\}$ at the beginning of the game and the small players would respond by choosing an optimal sequence $\{x_t\}$, taking $\{y_t\}$ as given. In that case, there can only be one outcome—*the government never gives in*. By introducing the requirement of perfectness, which is really just a rationality property, we have added an extra equilibrium in which the government's advantage disappears.

The assumption that the government only cares, *caet. par.*, about whether it has to give in or not, and not when, is obviously crucial. If delay were valued for its own sake the conclusions might be somewhat different. The analysis of the limiting case above has enough in common with practical problems such as the control of the money supply to be relevant to the debate on the scope of economic policy. To the extent that it shows the advantages of self-binding commitments, to a k-per cent rule, for example, over discretionary policy, it provides another argument against using the money supply for stabilization policy. Of course, the government might commit itself to a very complicated stabilization rule but it would be very difficult to do so. The more complicated the rule, the more likely it is that the public will believe there are "loopholes" for the government to get out of its commitment. In any case, it seems unlikely that the government could find a satisfactory rule to which it was prepared to commit itself. The k-per cent rule represents the abandonment of one aspect of stabilization policy and that is much easier than carrying on stabilization policy using a fixed rule.

3.5 Rules and the existence of REE

The results in the last section provide no more than a hint that there may be some advantage for a government in contriving a credible self-binding commitment, even at the cost of giving up some flexibility and discretion. The real point of the analysis was to show that solution concepts matter and that this neglected aspect of the theory of economic policy might provide further limits on the scope of effective policy. The present section takes up the discussion of rules *versus* discretionary policy which started in Section 3.3. Lucas's critique of the traditional theory of economy policy is based on the belief that expectations matter and that they depend on government policy. When policy takes an unpredictable course the private sector's expectations will be similarly unstable and hence, so will the structure of the economy. On these grounds, there is a case for adopting well understood policy rules rather than making *ad hoc* decisions which take the structure of the economy as given. It does not follow that government policy should be predictable with certainty. And some economists would argue that the imposition of the rule-format does not restrict discretion at all, that any policy ought to be describable as a rule. This view is incorrect. There is one important respect in which rules, as these are normally understood, are quite different from discretionary behaviour. A rule, once chosen, puts very definite limits on the government's ability to adopt new forms of behaviour. There is, on the other hand, no limit to the complexity of the discretionary behaviour the government may exhibit, even if, at each stage in its evolution the behaviour can be represented by an appropriately chosen rule. In an economy where agents have to learn by trial and error, using rules of thumb, the structure of the economy is continually changing. Discretionary policy may evolve and adapt in ways which a rule, however complex but chosen once-for-all, cannot imitate. Precisely because of this constant evolution discretionary policy may be impossible to predict. It may be necessary for the government to restrict its flexibility in ways which, *ex post*, appear suboptimal in order to be predictable. The policy rule is then a rule of thumb. According to this view, the trouble with discretionary policy is precisely the fact that it is a maximizing policy and the attempt to maximize at each date leads to unpredictability. This criticism of discretionary policy is more fundamental than Lucas's remarks might have suggested. These ideas are not easy to make precise but it is possible to go some way in the right direction using the simple example first introduced in Section 3.3. It will be recalled that there are two players, α and β, each of whom has two possible moves at each date. Player α's payoffs are described by the 2 × 2 matrix

$$\alpha\text{'s move} \overset{\beta\text{'s move}}{\begin{bmatrix} 1 & 0 \\ 0 & 1 \end{bmatrix}}$$

where the rows correspond to α's move and the columns to β's. α is rewarded by a payoff of one unit if he makes the same move as β and nothing otherwise. β's payoffs depend on the state of nature. There are two possible states, labelled $\omega = 0, 1$, at each date. The values of ω are generated by a Markov process with the transition matrix

$$T = \begin{bmatrix} t_{00} & t_{01} \\ t_{10} & t_{11} \end{bmatrix}$$

The entry $t_{\omega\omega'}$ stands for the probability of observing ω' at date t, given that ω is observed at date $t-1$. β's payoffs, in the respective states of nature, are described by the matrices:

$$\alpha\text{'s move} \quad \underset{\omega = 0}{\begin{bmatrix} -10 & 1 \\ 1 & 0 \end{bmatrix}} \quad \overset{\beta\text{'s move}}{} \quad \underset{\omega = 1}{\begin{bmatrix} 0 & 1 \\ 1 & -10 \end{bmatrix}}$$

Each player makes a move at each date. β observes the state of nature at date t before he makes his move but α does not. α can observe β's move, however, since he knows his own move and his payoff which tells him whether it was the same as β's. The game is technically a game of perfect but incomplete information.

When the REH is not satisfied each player must begin to play the game on the basis of weak assumptions about the form of the other's strategy, which allows him to learn the true strategy from repeated observation. In other words, each player chooses a model of the other's behaviour and proceeds to use repeated observation to estimate the parameters. As was pointed out in Section 3.3, a necessary condition for the success of this procedure is that the other player's behaviour should be stationary in some sense. And this hypothesis must be built into the model, giving it a stationary structure. Each player's behaviour depends on the model he uses and if the model's structure is stationary so will its user's behaviour be. This does not mean that it does not change over time. It only means, for example, that if α's strategy at some date depends only on what happens at the preceding date then the same is true at all subsequent dates. In other words, the *form* of the strategy is constant. This implies that if the learning process ever comes to an end, i.e. if both players are satisfied with their estimated models of the other's behaviour, the result must be an equilibrium in which both player's "know" the other's strategy and do not want to change their own.

To formalize this idea I shall use the concept of a *Nash equilibrium with stationary strategies.* The stationary strategies are assumed to have the form suggested in Section 3.3. This is not the only possibility and to that extent the following results should be treated with caution. Let X (resp. Y) denote the set of moves or actions available to α (resp. β) at each date and let Z denote the T-fold product of Y. A *strategy for* α is a function f from $X \times Z$ to $[0, 1]$. For any move x in X if α observes $z = (z_1, \ldots, z_T)$, where z_τ is β's move τ periods earlier, then α chooses x with probability $f(x|z)$, i.e. $f(x|z)$ is the conditional probability of x given z. β can observe ω directly and this will affect his play. Apart from this he is only concerned with what α will do and since α's strategy is a function of z it makes sense to assume that β's is too. There appears to be no loss of generality in this, especially as T is arbitrary. A strategy for β is formally defined to be a function $g: Y \times \Omega \times Z \rightarrow [0, 1]$, where $g(y|\omega, z)$ is the probability of β playing y when ω and z are observed.

Both players would normally be assumed to maximize the expected value of their long-run average payoffs. If β then took into account the dependence of α's future play on his (β's) current play the analysis would become rather complicated and, in any case, would not be in the spirit of the simple Nash equilibrium that seems most natural for players who have arrived at the equilibrium by trial and error. For this reason, I ignore the link between β's choice of y and α's future behaviour in describing β's decision problem. Both players are assumed to maximize the expected value of their current payoffs conditional on their information. There are two information sets, one for each player, at each date. The information set of player α (resp. β) at date t is denoted Φ_t^α (resp. Φ_t^β) and defined by putting

$$\Phi_t^\alpha = \{y_{t-i}: i = 1, 2, \ldots\}$$

(resp. $\Phi_t^\beta = \{\omega_t, y_{t-i}: i = 1, 2, \ldots\}$). Let $u(x, y)$ (resp. $v(x, y, \omega)$) denote the payoff to player α (resp. β) when α chooses x, β chooses y and the state of nature is ω. Then α wants to maximize

$$E[u(x, y)|\Phi_t^\alpha, g]$$

and β wants to maximize

$$E[v(x, y, \omega) | \Phi_t^\beta, f].$$

A *long-run, Nash equilibrium* is a pair of strategies (f, g) which maximize the objective functions of α and β respectively, as described above, at each date t, for each possible value of the variables in the information sets.

If the two agents are ever to settle down to a predictable pattern of behaviour, as a result of the learning process, then the outcome must, I think, be something like the Nash equilibrium with stationary strategies. The next question is whether such an equilibrium can exist. In the remainder of this section I show that it may not.

Since f and g are known to both players all probabilities are conditioned on them, even when there is no explicit reference. Let $p(\omega | \Phi^\alpha)$ denote the probability of ω occurring at date t given Φ^α. The optimality of f means that

$$(1) \quad \sum_{x,y,\omega} u(x, y) g(y|\omega, z) p(\omega|\Phi^\alpha) f(x|z) \geq \sum_{y,\omega} u(\bar{x}, y) g(y|\omega, z) p(\omega|\Phi^\alpha)$$

for any $\bar{x}$ in X. Similarly, the optimality of g means that

$$(2) \quad \sum_{x,y} v(x, y, \omega) f(x|z) g(y|\omega, z) \geq \sum_{x} v(x, \bar{y}, \omega) f(x|z)$$

for any $\bar{y}$ in Y. Returning to the example, let the two possible moves of a player α (resp. β) be denoted by x_0 and x_1 (resp. y_0 and y_1). A player will be called *predictable* if the probability of one of his moves, as perceived by the other player, is greater than $\frac{1}{2}$. Suppose that, at some date, β is predictable. For example, suppose that $\sum_\omega g(y_0|\omega, z) p(\omega|\Phi^\alpha) > \frac{1}{2}$. Then optimality requires $f(x_0|z) = 1$, from (1), in which case (2) requires that $g(y_0|\omega, z) = 0$, a contradiction. Hence β is always unpredictable, i.e. $\sum_\omega g(y|\omega, z) p(\omega|\Phi^\alpha) = \frac{1}{2}$ for all y and z. In particular, at each date both of β's moves occur with positive probability, given α's information Φ^α, regardless of the history of the game to that point.

The next point to notice is that in at least one of the two states, β will make a move with probability one. When $\omega = 0$, β is indifferent between y_0 and y_1, if and only if

$$-f(x_0 | z) 10 + f(x_1 | z) = f(x_0 | z).$$

i.e. $f(x_1 | z) = 11/12$, using the condition that $f(x_0 | z) + f(x_1 | z) = 1$.

Similarly, when $\omega = 1$ indifference implies that $f(x_1 | z) = 1/12$. It is impossible to satisfy both conditions simultaneously so in at least one state β is not indifferent and in that state one of his moves occurs with probability one. Since β is not predictable the other move must occur with positive probability in the other state. Now, if α observes that move he will know which state has occurred. Furthermore at every date there is a positive probability that the true state will be revealed (*ex post*).

Suppose that at some date the true state is revealed (*ex post*) to be $\omega = 0$. The opposite case is exactly symmetrical so there is no loss of generality in the assumption. Let z denote the sequence of moves by β up to *and including* date t, i.e. $z = (y_{t-T+1}, \ldots, y_t)$, and assume that $t_{ij} > \frac{1}{2}$ for $i \neq j$, i.e. the probability of changing to a new state is greater than $\frac{1}{2}$ in each state. I claim that $f(x_1 | z) = 1/12$. If not, then at date $(t + 1)$ in state 1, either $g(y_0 | 1, z) = 1$ or $g(y_1 | 1, z) = 1$ since β cannot be indifferent between y_1 and y_2. But since β is unpredictable

$$\begin{aligned}
\tfrac{1}{2} &= \sum_{\omega} g(y \,|\, \omega, z) p(\omega \,|\, \Phi^{\alpha}_{t+1}) \\
&\geq g(y \,|\, 1, z) p(1 \,|\, \Phi^{\alpha}_{t+1}) \\
&= g(y \,|\, 1, z) t_{01}
\end{aligned}$$

for all y, which is impossible since $t_{01} > \frac{1}{2}$. If $f(x_1 | z) = 1/12$, however, then $g(y_1 | 0, z) = 1$, i.e. y_1 is chosen with probability one in state 0. If y_0 is observed at $(t + 1)$ then the true state is revealed to α as $\omega = 1$. The argument can be extended to the next date and the next and so on.

The reference to date t is immaterial: at any date either state may be revealed by the observation of y_1 (in the case of $\omega = 0$) or y_0 (in the case of $\omega = 1$). Consider two possible situations which can occur at some date (I shall refer to both as arising at date t).

Situation I:

In the first y_1 is observed at t and this reveals the true state to be $\omega = 0$. At date $(t + 1)$, y_1 is observed again, which leaves α uncertain as to the true state. In the second situation, y_0 is observed at t and this reveals the true state to be $\omega = 1$. At $(t + 1)$, y_1 is observed, which reveals the true state to be $\omega = 0$. At any date there is a positive probability of observing either of β's moves since β is unpredictable. Hence, any sequence of moves $(y_{t+1}, \ldots, y_{t+T})$ may be observed with positive probability between t and $t + T + 1$.

At date $(t+1)$ the probability that $\omega = 0$ can easily be calculated. It is

$$p(\omega_{t+1} = 0 \mid y_{t+1} = y_1) = \frac{p(\omega_{t+1} = 0, y_{t+1} = y_1)}{p(y_{t+1} = y_1)}$$

$$= \frac{g(y_1 \mid \omega_{t+1} = 0, y_{t-T+1}, \ldots, y_t) \cdot t_{00}}{p(y_{t+1} = y_1)}$$

$$= 2t_{00}$$

since unpredictability implies $p(y_{t+1} = y_1) = \frac{1}{2}$ and, as we have seen before, $\omega = 0$ at t implies y_1 is chosen with probability one at $(t+1)$ if $\omega = 0$. Now suppose that $t_{00} = \frac{1}{4}$ so $p(\omega_{t+1} = 0 \mid y_{t+1} = y_1) = \frac{1}{2}$. This is consistent with the earlier assumption $t_{01} > \frac{1}{2}$. Then unpredictability implies that in each state at date $t+2$ one of β's moves is chosen with probability one if T is symmetric. For suppose not. As has been shown before in at least one state it must be true that one move is chosen with probability one, so the hypothesis amounts to saying that for some y, the probability of y in one state is one and in the other is positive. If we suppose the transition matrix T is symmetric then $p(\omega_{t+1} = 0 \mid y_{t+1} = y_1) = \frac{1}{2}$ implies $p(\omega_{t+2} = 0 \mid y_{t+1} = y_1) = \frac{1}{2}$. Then the probability of observing y at date $(t+2)$ is greater than $\frac{1}{2}$, contradicting unpredictability. It is fairly easy to see that at $(t+2)$ β chooses y_1 (resp. y_0) with probability one if $\omega = 0$ (resp. $\omega = 1$). α will choose each move with probability $\frac{1}{2}$. If y_1 is observed at $(t+2)$ then the true state is revealed to have been $\omega = 0$.

Situation II:

In the second situation if y_0 is observed at $(t+2)$ then α is uncertain about the true state. In fact, the situation is exactly the same for him as in the first situation at $(t+1)$. The probability that the true state is $\omega = 0$ is exactly $\frac{1}{2}$. It should be fairly clear by now that at each date the equilibrium strategy of each agent is completely determined, once α has attached implicit prior probabilities to each state ω. In either situation, if y_1 is observed at some date then either the true state is revealed to be $\omega = 0$ or the probability that $\omega = 1$ is $\frac{1}{2}$. At each date, however, the probabilities in the two situations are different, being one in one and $\frac{1}{2}$ in the other. Now suppose that y_1 is observed at each date from $(t+1)$ to $(t+T)$. From the form of β's strategy, at date $(t+T+1)$ he must assign the same probability to a given move in a given state, in both situations. But the probabilities α assigns to $\omega = 0$ in the two situations are different. Then unpredictability requires that β assign the same probability to a given move in each state, which is clearly suboptimal. This establishes the impossibility of a long-run Nash-equilibrium in the case

$$T = \begin{bmatrix} \frac{3}{4} & \frac{1}{4} \\ \frac{1}{4} & \frac{3}{4} \end{bmatrix}$$

What has been shown is that there is no way of expressing α's maximizing behaviour, given all the information available to him, as a function of z, however large T is. If α knows g then α can always make inferences, based on information not in z, which will influence his behaviour if he is a maximizing agent. It may be thought that the form which the strategies of the two players are assumed to take is unnecessarily restrictive but this is not the case. If α, for example, starts out not knowing β's strategy, he can only learn by observing β's behaviour and trying to model it. The only way that α can use these data is by hypothesizing a stationary structure. The actual parameters of this model may depend on all the observed values of y from the start of the game to the present. For example, α may hypothesize that the probability of observing $y = 1$ at t depends on $y_{t-1}, \ldots, y_{t-T}$ and he may estimate this probability by the proportion of times $y = 1$ follows $z = (y_{t-1}, \ldots, y_{t-T})$. But if this model, i.e. the transition matrix, converges at all it must converge to a stationary probability $p(y|z)$. Furthermore, unless α makes the hypothesis that the structure of the process he is observing is stationary, there is no way he can use repeated observations to deduce anything about it. Far from being arbitrary, the stationarity of the strategies in long-run equilibrium is a necessary condition for the whole exercise to make sense.

If β is interpreted as the government and α the private sector the moral of the story is fairly clear. The only way that the government can ensure stable behaviour on the part of both players is to commit itself to a stationary strategy even if, at some date in the future, the strategy appears non-optimal. The example makes precise the crucial distinction between discretionary and "rule" behaviour. Discretionary behaviour can evolve in ways that rules cannot and the possibility of constant evolution must make the behaviour of both agents unpredictable.

Notes

1. The inequality may not be strict if the follower's strategy x is a dominant strategy, i.e. if $u(x, \bar{x}, \bar{y}) \geq u(x', \bar{x}, \bar{y})$ for any x', $\bar{x}$ and $\bar{y}$. In that case $\phi(\bar{y}) = x$ for all $\bar{y}$ is an optimum response for the follower, in which case the Nash equilibrium (x, y) is also a leader-follower equilibrium.

2. The reader should note that a bar above a letter is used to denote both the actions of small players other than α and the actions of the partial history. This does not lead to any ambiguity because the partial history is only taken to describe the past actions of β and the typical alphas, i.e. it is independent of what any single α has done.

3. The condition $y_\tau = y'_\tau$ holds for $\tau \geqslant t + 1$ only and not $\tau = t$. This means that β's action at t does not influence α's preferences over strategies from date t onwards. This is like saying that an optimal strategy $\{x_\tau\}_{\tau \geq t}$ from t onwards is "dominant" (see fn. 1) but only against y_t. It is not "dominant" against $\{y_\tau\}_{\tau \geq t+1}$.

4. If the others do not sell, of course, it would not be optimal for this agent to sell, but that is a different story.

CHAPTER 4

The economic costs of inflation

4.1 Traditional theory

The sustained inflation of the nineteen-seventies was quite remarkable in the history of the West. Economists focussed their attention on the causes and possible cures of inflation, rather than on an explanation of the costs of inflation. On the surface this seems quite reasonable. Businessmen, trade unionists and housewives all know very well the costs of inflation. Politicians justify the unpleasant medicine needed to cure it by pointing to the heavy damage inflicted on industry by inflation: unemployment, low investment, bankruptcies and so on. Few seem to doubt the reality of the economic convulsions "caused" by rising prices. And yet pure theory is hard pressed to explain the consequences which are popularly attributed to prolonged and steady inflation. Certainly the neoclassical account seems rather tame.

In equilibrium the cost of holding money is equal to the real rate of return plus the rate of price inflation. A change in the rate of inflation will, *caeteris paribus*, reduce the demand for real balances. Since real balances are below the optimal level this leads to a further loss of consumer surplus. This is the Optimum Quantity of Money argument. A reduction in the demand for real balances will usually be accompanied by a shift in the demand for other assets and in savings and investment behaviour generally. Under certain circumstances this may also lead to inefficiency. These arguments were briefly surveyed in Chapter 1, Part 2 and, although they seemed as substantial as some other sources of inefficiency in general equilibrium, they hardly justified the common view of inflation as a monster.

Of course, inflation has effects on distribution as well as on efficiency. It may be that a certain amount of the grumbling comes from sections of the community that feel they have lost out in the race to keep up with inflation. It is sometimes suggested that there is a systematic tendency for individuals to overestimate the extent to which they have fallen behind inflation and this may explain the general impression that everyone is being cheated by inflation. While it may be possible to explain the unhappiness about inflation in this way, one cannot explain the very real change in the economy's performance by appealing to a change in the distribution of income. In any case, the causation seems to go the other way. The induced rise in unemployment is a major factor in determining the size of labour income just as falling sales are in profits. If inflation has an important impact on distribution it is probably because inflation first has an impact on employment, output, etc.

To return to the efficiency argument, it has already been noted (cf. Chapter 1, Part 2) that there is an incongruity between the assumption, found in the monetarist and REH literatures, that the interest-elasticity of the demand for real balances is small and the attempt to explain the costs of inflation in terms of portfolio adjustment. From one point of view, the steeper the demand-for-real-balances curve, the smaller the loss of consumer surplus from inflation. From another point of view, the smaller the change in real balances caused by inflation the smaller the change in holdings of other assets and hence, the smaller the reallocation of resources generally. It seems difficult to reconcile the low-interest-elasticity of demand for real balances with the idea that inflation matters, in a neo-classical framework.

These doubts, or something similar, have led some economists to the conclusion that the model of perfectly anticipated inflation, accompanied by costless adjustment of relative prices to clear markets, simply trivializes inflation. It concentrates on marginal adjustments occasioned by an increase in the cost of holding real balances while ignoring larger issues. These "larger issues" range from the claim that inflation tends to be ragged and so increases uncertainty to the claim that it places great strain on the political and economic institutions of the country as individuals and groups struggle to cope with the effects of rising prices. When the economy is in dire straits, it is tempting to search for explanations which are equally dramatic. These explanations are not necessarily more insightful or helpful to the theorist. The uncertainty hypothesis is a case in point. Suppose, for the sake of argument, that inflation *does* tend to be ragged in practice. More precisely, the fluctuations of the actual inflation rate around the trend rate increase, in some sense, as the trend rate of inflation increases. From this assumed empirical fact, it might be inferred that inflation tends to increase uncertainty about the future price level. An increase in uncertainty could in turn be held responsible for discouraging investment, encouraging miscalculation, provoking industrial unrest and so on. Although the argument has its attractions it rests on rather shaky foundations. In the first place, uncertainty is an *ex ante* concept. It does not follow from the fact that observed inflation is uneven that individuals were uncertain about its course *ex ante*. Even ragged inflation can be perfectly anticipated, in principle. Second, it does not follow that inflation *per se* causes greater uncertainty. For example, it may be that uncertainty increases because individuals are uncertain how the government will cope with inflation. The solution in that case is to make the government behave in a way which is consistent with greater certainty. Instead of making sporadic attempts to reduce inflation, the government might relax its opposition to inflation and let it smoothly run its course. The existence of a logically consistent, general-equilibrium model in which fully anticipated inflation is nearly neutral does suggest that inflation *per se* may not be at fault. In any case, it is clear that a serious theory is wanted to explain the link between inflation and greater uncertainty. Casual empiricism is not enough.[1]

If the only objection to the traditional account was that it seemed unrealistic, then it might be possible to mount a rescue operation by telling an "as if" story. But the case against the theory goes deeper than that. The demand-for-money paradigm itself is unimpeachable and maximizing behaviour requires that demand, in general, depends on the cost of holding real balances, which includes the rate of inflation. But when these ideas, which arise so naturally in a static setting to explain the demand for money, are used as a basis for explaining inflationary processes, the results are somewhat eccentric. In particular, there is an instability problem very similar to the one found in growth models with heterogeneous capital goods.[2] It is a symptom, perhaps, of the inappropriateness of the paradigm as the basis of an account of inflationary processes.

The instability of monetary economies, as depicted in the standard theory, is well illustrated by the model of overlapping generations described at the end of Chapter 1. There is a doubly infinite sequence of dates and at each date a new generation is born. All agents are assumed to have identical characteristics so a generation can be identified with a representative individual. A consumer born at date t lives for two periods, t and $t + 1$. There is a single, perishable consumption good at each date. The consumer has an endowment of $e > 0$ units of the consumption good in the first period of his life and none in the second. His utility is represented by a function $u(c_t, c_{t+1})$, where $c_t \geq 0$ is consumption at date t. In order to consume at date $(t + 1)$ he must hold money at the end of date t. Let m_t denote the amount of money held at the end of date t. The consumer chooses a consumption bundle $(c_t, c_{t+1}) \geq 0$ and a cash balance $m_t \geq 0$ to maximize $u(c_t, c_{t+1})$ subject to the budget constraints

$$p_t c_t + m_t \leq p_t e$$

and

$$p_{t+1} c_{t+1} \leq m_t$$

where p_t and p_{t+1} denote the price of consumption in terms of money at dates t and $t+1$ respectively. Under standard assumptions, when the price of consumption is positive at each date there is a unique, optimal value of m_t for each pair (p_t, p_{t+1}), which determines the optimal $(c_t, c_{t+1}) = (e - m_t/p_t, m_t/p_{t+1})$. Let the optimal value of m_t be denoted by $f(p_t, p_{t+1})$ for all strictly positive pairs (p_t, p_{t+1}).

The function f is homogeneous of degree one by construction. This allows us to write

$$c_{t+1} = m_t/p_{t+1} = f(p_{t+1}, 1).$$

Two other useful properties may be assumed:

(1) $$f(p_t/p_{t+1}, 1) \uparrow \infty \quad \text{as} \quad p_t/p_{t+1} \uparrow \infty$$

and

(2) $$f(p_t/p_{t+1}, 1) \downarrow 0 \quad \text{as} \quad p_t/p_{t+1} \downarrow 0.$$

It may as well be assumed for good measure that $f(p_t/p_{t+1}, 1) > 0$ for all $p_t/p_{t+1} > 0$.

New money is introduced by the government which issues the amount $\bar{m}_t - \bar{m}_{t-1} \geq 0$ at date t in exchange for consumption goods. The money supply at t is denoted by $\bar{m}_t$, of course, and the government's monetary policy is identified with the (non-decreasing) sequence $\{\bar{m}_t\}_{t=-\infty}^{\infty}$, where $\bar{m}_t$ is assumed positive at each t. Given a monetary policy $\{\bar{m}_t\}$, an equilibrium is defined to be a sequence of prices $\{p_t\}_{t=-\infty}^{\infty}$ such that

(3) $$\bar{m}_t = f(p_t, p_{t+1})$$

for every t (and $p_t > 0$). (3) is a system of implicit difference equations. In order to determine the sequence $\{p_t\}$ a single boundary condition is required. Unfortunately there are no natural boundary conditions and this means that equilibrium is indeterminate. More precisely, choose an arbitrary date, say $t = 0$, and let $p_0 = \bar{p}$ where $\bar{p}$ is an arbitrary positive number. By (1) and

(2) and continuity there exists a value of $p_1 > 0$ such that

$$\bar{m}_0/p_0 = \bar{m}/\bar{p} = f(1, p_1/\bar{p}).$$

Continuing in this way, backwards and forwards, one can find at each date t prices which equate the demand for money with the supply. For example, going backwards from $t = 0$, suppose that p_{t+1} has been determined to equate demand and supply at $t + 1$. Then there is a unique p_t such that

$$\bar{m}_t/p_t = f(1, p_{t+1}/p_t)$$

and this is the equilibrium value of p_t. For every choice of $p_0 = \bar{p}$ there is an equilibrium price sequence $\{p_t\}$ and a different level of real balances and consumption at each date. This indeterminacy is a worrying aspect of the theory but it is not as worrying as the actual nature of the equilibrium paths suggested in some cases.

To illustrate the problem I shall consider a simple example. If there is a constant proportionate rate of growth of the money supply at each date, it is easy to see that under the assumptions made above there is an equilibrium in which prices grow at the same steady rate. This equilibrium is undoubtedly the natural one to choose. Intuition suggests that when the rate of monetary growth is constant the rate of inflation should be the same or at least should converge to the same rate, but this is not the case. Suppose that the money supply grows at a constant and positive rate up to date 0 and is held constant thereafter. The intuitive solution is to have prices climbing at the same rate up to date 0 and remaining steady or converging to some fixed level from date 0 onwards. Certainly this is the intuition on which the monetarist cure for inflation is based. However, there is no equilibrium with this property. This could be demonstrated in general but I shall take a specific functional form for f in order to make the point as quickly and transparently as possible.

Suppose that

$$\frac{m_t}{p_t} = f(1, p_{t+1}/p_t) = (p_{t+1}/p_t)^{\alpha} \qquad (\alpha < 0).$$

Letting $\hat{m}_t$ and $\hat{p}_t$ denote the natural logarithms of m_t and p_t respectively, the money-demand equation can be rewritten in the following convenient form:

(4) $$\hat{m}_t = \alpha\hat{p}_{t+1} + (1 - \alpha)\hat{p}_t.$$

Solving (4) for $\hat{p}_{t+1}$ and using successive substitutions yields:

$$
\begin{aligned}
(5)\qquad p_{t+1} &= \frac{1}{\alpha}\,[\hat{m}_t - (1-\alpha)\hat{p}_t] \\
&= \frac{1}{\alpha}\left[\hat{m}_t - \left(\frac{1-\alpha}{\alpha}\right)\hat{m}_{t-1} + \frac{(1-\alpha)^2}{\alpha}\,\hat{p}_{t-1}\right] \\
&= \frac{1}{\alpha}\left[\sum_{i=0}^{t} \hat{m}_{t-i}\left(\frac{1-\alpha}{-\alpha}\right)^{i}\right] + \left(\frac{1-\alpha}{-\alpha}\right)^{t+1}\hat{p}_0,
\end{aligned}
$$

where it is assumed that $t+1>0$. Similarly, one can solve the system "backwards" by first solving (4) for $\hat{p}_t$ and then using successive substitutions.

$$
\begin{aligned}
(6)\qquad \hat{p}_t &= \frac{1}{1-\alpha}\,[\hat{m}_t - \alpha\hat{p}_{t+1}] \\
&= \frac{1}{1-\alpha}\left[\hat{m}_t - \left(\frac{\alpha}{1-\alpha}\right)\hat{m}_{t+1} + \left(\frac{\alpha^2}{1-\alpha}\right)p_{t+2}\right] \\
&= \frac{1}{1-\alpha}\left[\sum_{i=0}^{t} \hat{m}_{t+i}\left(\frac{-\alpha}{1-\alpha}\right)^{i}\right] + \left(\frac{\alpha}{1-\alpha}\right)^{t}\hat{p}_0,
\end{aligned}
$$

where it is assumed that $t<0$.

It is assumed that the money supply grows at a constant proportional rate up until $t=0$ and remains constant thereafter. Suppose, without loss of generality, that

$$
\begin{aligned}
(7)\qquad \hat{m}_t &= \mu t \qquad (t \le 0) \\
&= 0 \qquad (t \ge 0).
\end{aligned}
$$

Let $\{p_t\}$ be a sequence of equilibrium prices satisfying (4). If prices grow at the same rate as the money supply for $t \le 0$, i.e. $\hat{p}_t = \hat{p}_{t-1} + \mu$ for $t \le 0$, then (4) and (7) imply

$$\mu t = \alpha\mu + \hat{p}_t$$

or $\hat{p}_t = \mu(t-\alpha)$ for $t<0$. Then $\hat{p}_0 = \hat{p}_{-1} + \mu = -\mu\alpha > 0$. Substituting this value of $\hat{p}_0$ into (5) and using the fact that $\hat{m}_t = 0$ for $t \ge 0$ yields:

$$(5)'\qquad \hat{p}_t = \left(\frac{1-\alpha}{-\alpha}\right)^{t}(-\mu\alpha)$$

Since $(1-\alpha)/-\alpha > 1$ and $-\mu\alpha > 0$ it is clear that $\hat{p}_t \to \infty$ as $t \to \infty$. Thus, holding the money supply constant does not, in this case, bring inflation to a halt. In fact, it leads to hyperinflation. From (5)′ it is easy to see that

$$\hat{p}_{t+1} - \hat{p}_t = \left(\frac{1-\alpha}{-\alpha} - 1\right)\hat{p}_t$$
$$= \left(\frac{1}{-\alpha}\right)\hat{p}_t$$

so $(\hat{p}_{t+1} - \hat{p}_t) \to \infty$ as $t \to \infty$.

The reason why inflation "takes off" at date 0 is perfectly clear. Since prices have been growing at the same rate as money supply up to $t = 0$, the real money supply at date 0 is the same as at the preceding dates. In order to persuade individuals to hold this level of real balances, the rate of inflation expected at date 0 must be the same as at preceding dates, *viz.* μ. But if $\hat{p}_1 = \hat{p}_0 + \mu$, as required by the REH, the real money supply at date 1 will be smaller than at date 0 since $\hat{m}_1 = \hat{m}_0 = 0$. In order to persuade individuals to hold this level of real balances, the rate of inflation expected at date 1 must be higher than at date 0, i.e. $\hat{p}_2 - \hat{p}_1 > \hat{p}_1 - \hat{p}_0$. And so it goes on. The source of the instability is the fact that an increase in the price level will, *caeteris paribus*, reduce the real money supply and this must lead, in a rational expectations equilibrium, to an increase in the rate of inflation, if the demand for real balances is to equal the supply. This phenomenon, sometimes called the *Wicksell effect* is quite robust. It is found in a large variety of models of equilibrium with (myopic) perfect foresight as well as in rational expectations models.

From (5) it is clear that when $\hat{m}_t = 0$ for all $t \geq 0$, the "stability" of prices depends on the value of $\hat{p}_0$. There is a unique equilibrium sequence of prices $\{\hat{p}_t\}$ corresponding to each value of $\hat{p}_0$ and

$$\hat{p}_t \to \infty \quad \text{if} \quad \hat{p} > 0\,;$$
$$\hat{p}_t = 0 \quad \text{if} \quad \hat{p}_0 = 0\,;$$
$$\hat{p}_t \to -\infty \quad \text{if} \quad \hat{p}_0 < 0\,.$$

The case in which $\hat{p}_0 = 0$ corresponds to the intuitively plausible outcome in which both price level and money supply are constant from date 0 onwards. Equation (6) can be used to solve backwards for prices from $t = 0$ to $t = -\infty$. Substituting $\hat{p}_0 = 0$ and $\hat{m}_t = \mu t$ in (6) gives

$$\text{(6)}' \qquad \hat{p}_t = \frac{1}{1-\alpha}\sum_{i=0}^{-t} \mu(t+i)\left(\frac{-\alpha}{1-\alpha}\right)^i \qquad (t < 0)\,.$$

From (6)′ it is clear that $\hat{p}_t \to -\infty$ as $t \to -\infty$. Also,

$$\hat{p}_t - \hat{p}_{t-1} = \frac{\mu}{1-\alpha}\left[\sum_{i=0}^{-t}\left(\frac{-\alpha}{1-\alpha}\right)^i\right]$$

$$\to \mu \text{ as } t \to -\infty .$$

As t approaches $-\infty$ the inflation rate approaches μ. This is somewhat more plausible than the first case considered; but it puts a lot of weight on the REH: for the change in the rate of growth of the money supply has to be anticipated at every preceding date from 0 to $-\infty$ and will have some impact on the inflation rate at each of those dates. This is a far cry from the use of the REH, encountered in Chapter 1, to isolate those phenomena which do not depend on agents making mistakes, or to study the limits of policy when agents can learn about the policy by repeated observation. There is no learning here since agents cannot "learn" about the arbitrary future behaviour of money supply. The fact that agents do not make mistakes is made less interesting by the fact that there is no explanation of how they could form any views whatever about so distant a future.

One way of ruling out the indeterminacy of equilibrium is to assume "stability". There is only one equilibrium in which prices do not explode after date 0 and that is the equilibrium in which prices are constant from date 0 onwards (the second of the two examples given above). If accelerating inflation with a constant money supply really is counter-intuitive then the *assumption* of stability, it might be argued, is only natural. The objection then is the need to allow that the government's decision to halt monetary growth at date 0 will influence inflation rates at every date prior to date 0. Alternatively, it can be argued that the limiting case in which a change in the rate of growth of the money supply is anticipated at all preceding dates is an approximation to the more realistic case in which the change is anticipated a finite number of periods before it occurs. For example, if the change at date 0 is not anticipated before date $T < 0$ then prices will grow at the rate μ up to date T, they will remain constant from date 0 onwards and from date T to date 0 there will be gradually decelerating inflation. Qualitatively the two cases are very similar and quantitatively they will be similar for sufficiently large $|T|$. The trouble with this sort of argument is that it reintroduces the sort of arbitrariness that the REH is supposed to eliminate. It is not clear how T is determined; nor is it clear why agents have the (incorrect) expectations they have prior to T. In very simple cases like the present one, where there is one constant rate of growth up to a particular date and another constant rate thereafter it is fairly easy to make reasonable-sounding guesses about what expectations should be. But when the rate of monetary expansion is constantly varying it does not make sense to assume that agents antipate a change correctly $|T|$ periods before it happens, for the implication is that, before that, they anticipated the change incorrectly and there is no obvious way of assigning "incorrect" expectations. Finally, the "stability" of the model could be assured by assuming $\alpha > 0$. Although this would not prevent indeterminacy (indeed, it would make the problem worse since there would no longer be a distinguished, stable equilibrium) it would ensure that prices converge to a long-run stationary value as $t \to \infty$. There are two disadvantages, however. Prices may explode as $t \to -\infty$ and the demand-for-money curve is now upward sloping so it is impossible to calculate the efficiency loss of inflation in the usual way.

The traditional theory very neatly explains the impact of inflation on the economy by making the expected rate of inflation one of the determinants of the demand for real balances. Its weakness lies not in the way this link is constructed but in the treatment of expectations. The REH leaves equilibrium indeterminate unless a stability assumption is imposed, in which case the REH requires a change at date 0 to affect the economy at all preceding dates. The REH can be modified so that agents only anticipate a change T periods ahead, but only at the cost of opening up the model to too many possibilities as far as expectations are concerned. If expectations are important it is essential that we be able to model them in a precise and convincing way. The theory I have been discussing does not do this and that is a serious weakness. Of course, it does not follow from this that the expected rate of inflation does not matter. All that "follows" is that the traditional theory, whatever its empirical attractions, lacks a satisfactory account of expectation-formation in the short run to convert the demand-for-money paradigm into a convincing account of inflationary processes.[3]

There may be solutions to some of the problems which have been raised in this section. If so, the neoclassical model of inflationary processes may yet prove to be helpful in explaining the costs of inflation. As it stands, however, the theory suffers from a number of weaknesses and at the same time appears to trivialize the costs of inflation. The case for looking at less orthodox explanations seems rather strong.

4.2 Other explanations

Once we move away from theories of inflation which are formalized as quantitative models, there is no lack of explanations of why inflation damages the economy. Some of them are rather journalistic, but there is a lot of good sense in them nonetheless. I shall consider briefly three ideas: that inflation increases uncertainty, that the energy crisis is the cause of the present inflation and the associated economic problems and, finally, that wage increases play the same role as higher energy prices in generating (costly) inflation.

Uncertainty

The criticisms of the traditional theory (i.e., the model of inflation based on perfect foresight and a demand-for-money function with the inflation rate as an argument) which were given in the preceding section do not imply that the model is useless. Even if the criticisms are all accepted as valid there may still be a role for the model to serve as a benchmark. By defining the conditions under which inflation is innocuous it provides a guide to those missing factors which might explain the real costs of inflation. It has been argued repeatedly in earlier chapters that the REH is useful because it gives an indication of the "long run" impact of a systematic policy pursued over a sufficiently long period for agents to learn about it. If a long-run model of fully anticipated inflation does not give a realistic picture, then it suggests the real problems arise from unanticipated inflation in the short run. Opening this door leads perhaps to too many possibilities. There is virtually no end to the problems caused by incorrect expectations. However they all depend on the fact that when agents write long-term contracts in terms of money, unexpected changes in the price level have real (and sometimes disastrous) effects. Examples of non-neutrality were given in Chapter 1. To that list one might add the non-neutrality of the tax system and the impact of inflation on the balance of payments; but there is little to be gained from multiplying these illustrations. Any one of them would serve as an object lesson on the costs of inflation. But the more fundamental and intriguing questions are not answered by these examples. Why is inflation unanticipated? Why do individuals write long-term contracts in terms of money? Why should inflation pose a more serious problem than deflation? And so on.

The first question has a ready-made answer, already encountered in Chapter 2. One way for the government to have a real impact on the economy is by introducing noise into the system, that is, by adopting a stochastic monetary policy. There is no reason to expect the policy to be inflationary, though, and to this extent the answer is unsatisfactory. There are actually two questions requiring an answer here. The first is why the price level is uncertain and the second is why uncertainty and inflation go together. In the normal course of events, even if the money supply were held constant, one would not expect the price level to be steady. A host of exogenous, real factors—the balance of trade, strikes, the size of the harvest, "animal spirits", the discovery of new technology and natural resources, demographic changes, and so on—will ensure that the real demand for money, and hence the price level, behaves like a random variable. There is no mystery in this; in fact one might expect the price level to fluctuate more than it does. When there is inflation, uncertainty about the price level is translated into uncertainty about the inflation rate. This can only be part of the answer, however, because it does not explain why a low trend rate of growth in the price level is to be preferred to a higher one in the sense that the low trend rate leads to greater certainty. It may turn out that it does not, of course, but the general consensus holds that it does, so let us try to find a rationale for that point of view.

To begin with, is there any reason to think that fluctuations in the price level might be smaller when the trend rate of change is very small? If not, one would expect to find substantial decreases as well as increases in the price level. Now there is an asymmetry between increases and decreases. One benefits creditors and the other debtors but, whereas creditors merely suffer a capital loss when the price level rises, debtors may be bankrupted by a fall in the price level. The existence of debts which are fixed in money terms may provide a very strong incentive for firms to resist price reductions. However the ability of a firm to resist price reductions may not be very strong. *In extremis*, the firm's desire to maximize profits will be as strong as ever and profit maximization may recommend a fall in prices rather than an increase. In any case, it is the general price level which is of interest here so it will not be enough to look at each firm in isolation. In fact, this is the key to the problem for, if all prices and wages fall, the only effect is to redistribute wealth to creditors and push debtors closer to bankruptcy. The actual outcome depends on the reaction of the banking system. Suppose that all firms are net debtors and the banking system can increase the money supply at will. For example, under the system long used in the U.K. the interest rate was fixed and the central bank, acting almost as a lender of first resort, adjusted the supply of money to the quantity demanded by the clearing banks at that rate of interest. Firms with heavy commitments in the form of interest charges and loan repayments would face losses if prices fell. This in turn led to increased borrowing, i.e. an increase in the supply of money. For this reason the money supply is a decreasing function of the price level and this negative correlation, working through the real balance effect, will tend to offset fluctuations in the price level, at least when they operate in a downward direction.

In this way, the banking system may act as an automatic stabilizer on the price level when the trend rate of inflation is zero but there is no reason to expect it to do so when the trend rate of inflation is high. During an inflationary period the asymmetry between increases and decreases in the rate of inflation tends to disappear. This is not a *necessary* consequence of inflation; it depends very much on the convention of spreading the repayment of a debt evenly over the term of the debt. This leads to "front-end loading" in which the real burden is heaviest in the early years. Any inflation, however small, reduces the burden, so a mere fall in the rate of inflation need not cause difficulties for the debtor firms. In particular, it need not lead to the sort of involuntary borrowing occasioned by an actual fall in prices. The absence of an automatic stabilizer when the trend rate of inflation is positive may be one possible explanation of the greater variability of prices—more precisely, of the rate of inflation—when the trend rate of inflation is high. It is, furthermore, an explanation consistent with strictly neoclassical assumptions: rational expectations, market-clearing prices, etc. How serious an explanation it is will depend on how significant the empirical link between price changes and borrowing turns out to be. In the absence of hard evidence, the argument remains little more than an interesting possibility. Yet something like this argument seems to be unavoidable if the link between inflation and uncertainty is to be explained in terms of a model in which the price level is determined by the demand and supply of money.

The emphasis on uncertainty also provides the key to the answer to the second question: why do individuals make long-term contracts in terms of money? An alternative formulation of the question might be: why don't they index all contracts completely? When prices are relatively stable, that is, when the trend rate of inflation is near zero, changes in the price level are small relative to changes in the determinants of individual prices. In these circumstances, contracts which are fixed in money-terms represent a kind of insurance. A manufacturer who has contracts to produce various lines of goods at fixed prices and who has similar contracts with his workforce and suppliers, has removed a substantial amount of uncertainty from his everyday calculations. The lack of flexibility implied by long-term contracts may itself cause problems but at least the manufacturer "knows where he stands". By replacing market-clearing prices with "fixed prices" individuals help to reduce the variability of prices. It is easier for other agents to write long-term contracts when prices are predictable than when they are very uncertain.

When the price level is relatively stable, a long-term contract in terms of money represents a kind of insurance because the basket of goods which a unit of money will purchase is fairly constant. When there is steady inflation money cannot serve as a standard of value, quite obviously, but there seems to be no reason why long-term contracts in terms of a basket of goods should not take over the role of long-term contracts in money. In principle, there is no reason why they should not. The difficulty is in getting the economy as a whole to switch over from one standard to another. If the rate of inflation were fully anticipated, long-term contracts in money would be useful as before. If the economic system were completely indexed the rate of inflation would be a matter of indifference (except to holders of large cash balances). But when inflation is uncertain, an individual who has only partially indexed his future transactions is taking enormous risks which may be worse than simply avoiding long-term contracts altogether. For example, an employer who enters into a long-term fully indexed contract with his workers bears the full weight of any uncertainty about the price of his product relative to the general price level. He may even risk bankruptcy if the price he is able to charge fails to keep pace with inflation.

The analysis of inflation here touches on the importance of conventions. When individuals' behaviour is governed as much by rules of thumb (however efficient) as it is by explicit maximization, there can be a Nash equilibrium of *rules* in which each individual is satisfied with his own rule as long as the others do not change theirs.[4] He may be well aware at the same time that if they were all to adopt a different set of rules they could all be better off. In the case of inflation, the impossibility of simultaneous indexation of all contracts is an effective bar to the introduction of even fairly small-scale indexation when the rate of change of the price level is uncertain. Individuals find themselves in a kind of equilibrium in which they would like to change from long-term contracts in terms of money to completely indexed ones but they cannot do so unilaterally without running great risks. Inflation does place great strains on the convention of writing long-term contracts in fixed money prices, however, and the greatest possible cost of inflation would be the breakdown of this convention, were it not replaced by another.

However interesting these various possibilities may turn out to be, they do not at the moment add up to a solid theory explaining how inflation leads to greater uncertainty. More important than this fact, however, is the apparent necessity of incorporating long-term contracts, conventions, etc., into the theory. These are things which fit rather uncomfortably into the neo-monetarist view of the world.

The energy crisis

Because of the dramatic political events associated with the first increase in the price of oil, the continuing "energy crisis" has had greater prominence than the other putative causes of the present inflation. The "stylized facts" of the episode are quite simple. The supply of some resource is controlled by a small cartel. The demand for it is highly inelastic. An administered increase of several times the original price resulted, after a period in which emergency measures to conserve fuel were hastily adopted, in generally higher prices and wages in the developed countries. There followed a longer period in which successive increases in the price of oil attempted to keep up with the pace of inflation in the importing countries. What puzzles the layman and sometimes, to judge by newspaper reports, even the principals involved, is how an increase in the price of a factor of production which, however important, represents a smallish fraction of input costs, can lead to an equal or greater proportionate increase in the general level of prices. As an elementary exercise in homogeneity-economics, this need not puzzle us but there are some subtleties in the chain of causation which require closer inspection. Also, there is the central question of why, if it is all a matter of homogeneity, the economies of the West have been thrown into such disarray. This is a major problem for any theory which attempts to explain inflation as a purely monetary phenomenon.

From the point of view of monetary economics, the important issue is the recycling of the revenues earned by the petroleum-exporting countries and its effect on the money supply of the importing countries. The following *scenario* may be too simplistic but it brings out the major issues and problems. In the beginning there was equilibrium and an oil price which had remained stable (in dollar terms) for a suspiciously long period of time. Then the price of oil went up. Interim conservation measures and borrowing give firms time to decide what to do about prices. In the meantime, the new revenues of the exporting countries must find a home. Suppose for simplicity that the entire increase were left in the importing country to be invested in some form or other. The sudden appearance of these liquid funds presents a problem. If borrowing is to increase to absorb these funds the money supply will have to increase since deposits = reserves plus advances. But that is all right because by now firms have decided that the prices of their product must rise to cover the increased cost of oil and that means the demand for cash balances will increase. Short-term borrowing by firms whose profit margins have been reduced will absorb some of the funds. The rest will have to find their way into liquid assets since new investment projects are unlikely to be encouraged by the increase in the cost of oil. After a while the increase in output prices is likely to have an effect on the price of factors of production. In particular, money wages go up as workers try to maintain the real value of wages. As costs go up, the price of output must go up and this leads to a further rise in costs and so on. At each step, however, an increase in the money supply is needed and this is provided by governments anxious to recycle oil revenues to their own economies. The process comes to an end when relative prices have been restored to their original level and the price level and money supply have increased correspondingly, so that real money balances are unchanged. Before this point is reached there has been a temporary increase in the savings ratio because the oil exporters are assumed to save their revenues. This autonomous increase in savings may cause a temporary failure of effective demand. The Keynesian consequences may last for a long time if the inflationary process is halted.

The story represents inflation as a safety valve. Sufficiently rapid inflation, assuming that it does not itself have undesirable domestic consequences, is perhaps the surest defence against an increase in the price of a commodity like oil. The slower the inflation, the greater the chance of Keynesian factors coming into play.[5] It is not the only story which could be told, however, even under the rather unrealistic assumptions made above. Suppose that the oil exporters choose to use the pounds they gain from the sale of oil to purchase government securities (gilts). Other things being equal, the result will be a rise in the price of gilts and hence a fall in the rate of interest. If domestic holders of gilts were forced to sell their assets because of the rise in the price of oil, the fall in the rate of interest might be small but there would be no reason at all to expect an increase in the money supply. Nor, if inflation is accepted as a purely monetary phenomenon, is there any reason to expect inflation. On the contrary, the fall in the rate of interest, if any, should increase the demand for money. If the money supply is constant this will put a downward pressure on prices.

In order to explain, in terms of the traditional model, how the increase in oil prices generates inflation it is necessary to include an increase in the money supply as part of the story. The behaviour of the money supply is extremely sensitive to the assumptions which are made about the allocation of the oil revenues so the story cannot be very robust. Also, the impact of the oil revenues was complicated by a number of factors which have not yet been mentioned. Oil revenues are unlikely to be distributed among importing countries according to their needs. Unwelcome funds raise a currency's value and reduce exports while a scarcity of funds may reduce the exchange rate too much, thus increasing the burden of paying for the oil. The only consolation is that a country cannot suffer from both afflictions at once. A great deal of damage must have been caused by the inappropriate and changeable, international allocation of oil revenues, however.

The simplest sequence of events described above, in which a rise in the price of oil leads to an equiproportionate increase in all other prices after a short interval, is not what actually happened. An ingrained resistance to inflation combined with successive price rises by the oil exporters ensured that the real price of oil remained substantially above its previous level in spite of what was, by historical standards, fairly rapid inflation. The consequent rise in unemployment and fall in the rate of growth could have been caused not by inflation but by insufficiently rapid inflation. While this view has a pleasant irony about it, it is perhaps unfair to the policy-makers involved. Even if it were true that all importing countries, by inflating simultaneously at the same rate, could have removed the effects of the oil-price rise, they could not unilaterally have done so. Any country which inflates faster than the rest will suffer a decline in the value of its currency relative to that of the other importers. This has the effect of worsening the current account deficit and increasing the real cost of oil. At best, the country can be no better off in the long run than by inflating at the same rate as the other countries. And even if all the importing countries inflated rapidly at the same rate, the attempt by the oil exporters to catch up might well lead to leap-frogging and hyperinflation.[6]

Simple parables and stories must not be taken too seriously. However, two lessons may be drawn from the preceding discussion. One is that although it is possible to tell stories about the oil crisis and the ensuing inflation which are consistent with the traditional model, it is just as easy to tell stories which are not. Second, if the inflation was caused by an expansion of the money supply, as the traditional theory has it, then the problems would appear to have been caused not by inflation but by insufficiently rapid inflation. The oil crisis does not seem to bring us any closer to reconciling the traditional model of inflation with the popular view of the costs of inflation.

Wage-inflation

In many ways the charges made against trades unions (for demanding "inflationary" increases in wages) are very similar to those made against the oil-exporting countries. Although they were preceded by and mixed up with the effects of the increase in the price of oil, it is instructive to consider the role of wage increases in isolation. The principal difference is that wage increases do not involve the problem of the international allocation of revenues in the same way that the oil-price rise does. The same general conclusion holds, however: if inflation were allowed to cancel out the change in relative prices caused by the initial change in some wages, the impact of that change would be limited to the effect of a general inflation on the economy. When the leading sectors increase wages by more than the subsequent inflation there will be additional real effects. Even if the average rate of wage increases is the same as the subsequent rate of inflation these real effects will be present unless all wages and prices increase in the same proportion. There is, of course, no reason to expect that all wages and prices will increase in the same proportion. Indeed we should expect the contrary for two reasons. The government will resist inflation to a greater or lesser extent by refusing to let the money supply expand at the required rate. Since something has to give, some sections of the community will gain at the expense of others. Second, the importance of international competition is different for different sectors of the economy and, depending on how the government manages the exchange rate, the incentive to resist wage and price increases will vary from one sector to another. The existence of long-term contracts, though it does not affect this question more than any other, does have an influence on how quickly any particular wage or price is changed. It may lead to changes in relative prices, even if only temporarily.

The main question which arises in connection with wage-induced inflation, assuming there is such a thing, is its connection with unemployment. The traditional textbook account of the relationship between wages and employment depends on the marginal productivity theory of the demand for labour. When the real wage rises above its equilibrium (market-clearing) level, an excess supply of labour results. If wages on the whole rose by more than the prices of goods then this explanation would carry some weight. When the wages of substantial sections of the labour force have risen by less than output prices a more involved explanation is required. One would expect, perhaps, that those groups whose wages have risen fastest would be most at risk of losing their jobs but such does not appear to be the case. Most of the unemployed are not even union members. This may not be a great obstacle to the theory. Assuming that unions in different sectors wield different amounts of monopoly power, it might be possible to show that wage and price increases in one industry reduce the profitability of another industry to the point where layoffs became inevitable unless the workforce is prepared to accept a massive cut in wages. But the problem then is to explain why prices in that industry did not rise sufficiently to offset any changes in factor prices. The answer again must be the government's restrictive attempt to curb inflation, other things being equal.

4.3 Inflation and the rate of interest

While the energy crisis and the behaviour of trades unions are both widely believed to have contributed to the present inflation, there is no consensus about why this particular sort of inflation should be harmful. I have tentatively suggested that it may be the cure rather than the disease which is the worst part of inflation, but that leaves unexplained the general fear of unrestrained but steady inflation. The hypothesis that inflation tends to be ragged goes some way to explaining why inflation is a bad thing but there is as yet no complete theory of why a higher trend rate of inflation should be associated with greater uncertainty. Where there does seem to be a consensus, at least among the public, is in the view that high interest rates, whether they are the result of government policy to curb inflation or come about merely because lenders insist on the same real rate of interest as before, are a very bad thing indeed. To the economist who automatically thinks in terms of real rates, it is hard to see why high nominal rates of interest, which may even be below the rate of inflation, cause such distress in the business community. When this habit of thought is reinforced by personal experience of the declining real value of mortgage repayments, say, it becomes very hard to see what all the fuss is about. As an antidote it may be helpful to try to see things from the businessman's point of view.

Consider the (trivial) example of a small manufacturer of a single, homogeneous good. To keep the story simple it is assumed that the production period and the payments period coincide. At the beginning of every production period, the manufacturer buys raw materials and hires labour which he uses to produce the output which appears, and is sold, at the end of the period. The raw materials are financed by overdraft facilities at his local bank and wages are paid at the end of the period. The manufacturer also has a long term loan at variable interest which he took out in order to set up his plant.[7] To begin with, the economy is in a stationary state, prices are constant and the manufacturer conducts his business in the same way each period. The real rate of interest (which is equal to the nominal rate) is assumed to be five per cent per period. The value of output, measured in units of account, is 100, wages were 69, raw materials are 20 and the value of the manufacturer's loan is 200. These facts are summarized in more convenient form in the table below.

	Income	*Expenditure*
Sales	100	
Wages		69
Materials (incl. interest on overdraft)		21
Interest on debt		10
	100	100

The manufacturer is just breaking even and will continue doing so indefinitely.

Now suppose that at the beginning of a period it is announced that all prices will be twenty per cent higher at the end of the period. It is assumed that the real rate of interest remains the same since this will provide a test of the proposition that fully anticipated inflation has no effect. These two assumptions imply that the nominal interest rate must rise to twenty-six per cent. Materials are purchased at the beginning of the period so their cost is the same as before. However, the interest rate on overdrafts has increased to twenty-six per cent so the cost of materials including interest rises to 25.2. Wages are paid at the end of the period and the labour force will want the same real wage as before so the wage bill rises by twenty per cent to 82.8. The interest on the debt will now be twenty-six per cent of 200 or 52. The value of sales will rise to 120, of course. Thus, if the manufacturer wishes to make the same trades as before, his balance sheet will look like this.

	Income	*Expenditure*
Sales	120	
Wages		82.8
Materials (incl. interest)		25.2
Interest on debt		52
	120	160

Instead of breaking even there is now a loss of 40 on a turnover of 120. A brief inspection of the figures reveals why. The culprit is the item "Interest on debt". This sum has increased by over 500 per cent as a result of the rate of inflation rising from zero to twenty per cent. Even if materials were financed free using trade credit it would do little more than dent the loss.

It could be argued that this is not really a case of perfectly anticipated inflation since the rise to 20 per cent should have been anticipated in all previous periods, in which case the debt might be different. But this argument merely reinforces the conclusion that perfectly anticipated inflation has very real effects on business. The example given above could equally well be interpreted as a comparison of two identical economies, each in a steady state, differing only in the fact that the rate of inflation in one is 20 per cent and in the other is zero. If it really were true that anticipated inflation had no effect then the real rate of interest, the real indebtedness of the firm and the price level ought to be the same in each economy at corresponding points in time. As the example shows, in one economy the firm will be facing bankruptcy even though in both economies the rate of inflation has been assumed constant and perfectly anticipated at all dates.

The example captures sufficiently well the popular view of the impact of inflation. *They* all seem to be convinced that inflation costs jobs and leads to bankruptcy. It is only economists who have difficulty in reconciling this common sense view with general equilibrium habits of thought. To see where the difference lies it is helpful to retell the story, still further simplified, in general equilibrium terms.

An entrepreneur purchases a perfectly durable machine which will, without further expenditure on inputs, produce a steady stream of q units of output, say, a homogeneous consumption good, in every period. The economy is in a stationary state with constant prices and there is no loss of generality in choosing the consumption good as numeraire. There is a perfect capital market on which the interest rate is constant and is expected to remain so. In these circumstances the entrepreneur will not be prepared to pay more than the present value of the stream of output because he could do better lending the money at interest. Likewise, in a competitive market the price of the machine must be at least as high as the present value of the stream of output. Otherwise it would pay someone to borrow money at the going rate ρ, say, and bid up the price of the machine. Hence the price is just equal to the present value, which is q/ρ. If the entrepreneur does borrow q/ρ and buy the machine, his balance sheet will look like this:

	Income	*Expenditure*
Sales	q	
Interest on debt		q
	q	q

Now suppose that there is a steady and positive rate of inflation π. There is no loss of generality in assuming once again that the price of consumption is unity at date 0 when the entrepreneur is considering purchasing his machine. However, money is now the numeraire. The real rate of interest is ρ as before so the nominal rate must be $r = \rho + \pi$. The revenue produced by the machine at date t is $e^{\pi t} q$ (where the present is taken to be date 0).[8] The present value of this stream is q/ρ as before. Using an arbitrage argument it can be shown that the price of the machine at date 0 must be q/ρ in a competitive market. Assuming once again that the entrepreneur borrows the money to buy the machine, his balance sheet at date 0 will look like this:

	Income	*Expenditure*
Sales	q	
Interest on debt		$(\rho + \pi)q/\rho$
	q	$(\rho + \pi)q/\rho$

He appears to be making a loss. The reason is that the real value of the initial amount borrowed is falling over time as a result of the inflation. At some point in the future, revenues will outstrip interest payments, yielding surpluses from that date onwards. In order for the entrepreneur's present net wealth to be zero he must start off making "losses".

If the entrepreneur balances his budget at each date then initially his indebtedness must grow. Let b denote his indebtedness at date t and let $\dot{b}$ denote the rate of change of b (both in money terms). The deficit at date t is the difference between interest due (rb) and revenue ($e^{\pi t} q$). Formally,

$$\dot{b} = rb - e^{\pi t} q \, .$$

This is a differential equation from which we can solve for b, using the initial condition $b_0 = q/\rho$. It can easily be checked that $b = e^{\pi t} q/\rho$. Nominal indebtedness grows at the same rate as the price level.[9] To see what is happening in real terms, one simply multiplies the nominal terms by $e^{-\pi t}$. Then real income is q, real indebtedness is q/ρ, the real value of interest paid (as opposed to interest due) is q, which equals the real interest due on a real debt of q/ρ, when there is no inflation. In fact all the magnitudes are the same as their corresponding values in the non-inflationary case.

Inflation has no effect when there is a perfect capital market because the existence of such a market allows agents to *index* their debts. The rentier's income can be broken down into two parts. ρb is the reward for lending and πb is compensation for the capital loss (decline in real value) of his asset due to inflation. The entrepreneur can afford to pay ρb out of current receipts but not πb. By borrowing more money to pay πb he is simply maintaining the real value of his indebtedness, which is just what his creditor wants. It is exactly the same as if the two agents had signed a contract in which the nominal value of the debt was index-linked to inflation and the nominal rate of interest held constant at ρ. When debts are indexed in this way it is not surprising that inflation has no real effects.

This example allows us to see what was happening in the earlier one. Inflation causes a reduction in the real value of the manufacturer's indebtedness and this increase in net wealth ought, in some sense, to have counted as income. Had there been some way to realize this income, he would have been able to meet his interest payments without difficulty. If he had had access to a perfect capital market or if his banker had paid more attention to present values than to current profits, he would have borrowed to meet the interest payments. In practice, capital markets are highly imperfect and a banker who is asked to lend increasingly large amounts to a firm which, if inflation continues, will always have a negative cash flow, will certainly decline to do so. Present values have little meaning when capital markets are imperfect. Again, if there existed a perfect market for equity, it might be possible, by issuing new shares, to capitalize the value of the reduction in real indebtedness but this too is not observed in practice.

In terms of its predictions, this account of the effects of inflation seems to accord with reality quite well. High inflation rates mean high interest rates and in the absence of adequate access to fresh borrowing the higher interest charges have a direct impact on profitability. This may lead either to insolvency or the need to contract the firm's operations in order to remain solvent. In the absence of compensating changes in factor prices the demand for factors of production will fall as well. But however plausible these conclusions seem, the basic hypothesis that cash-flow problems result from constraints on borrowing begs a number of important questions. If inflation is fully anticipated then so must be the balance sheet effects of inflation. Account will have been taken of them when saving and investment decisions are made. Consider the example of the entrepreneur purchasing an infinitely durable machine. Fully anticipated inflation raises the real value of interest charges above what he can afford to begin with. If he is not able to borrow to meet the interest charges he will have to borrow less, meaning that unless the price of capital goods falls he will have to find part of the purchase price from his own resources. Moreover, the higher the rate of inflation the higher the proportion that he will have to meet from his own resources. So unless the entrepreneur can borrow to meet interest payments, an anticipated increase in the rate of inflation is likely to have a restrictive effect on investment decisions, other things being equal.

Under the assumption of perfect foresight it is very difficult to explain why imperfections in the capital market should exist. If the real situation of the firm is unchanged it seems irrational for the bank to want to reduce the real value of its loans to the firm. The more serious problem, however, is to explain, as we must do, how there can be a general shortage of liquidity at the same time as general inflation. Imagine a steady-state in which the money supply and the general level of prices are increasing at the same rate. Then bank advances are growing at the same rate but somehow these funds do not find their way into industry's bank accounts where they are needed. For if borrowing increased at the same rate as the price level there would be no problem, as we have already seen, about high interest rates. So a crucial question is to explain where the money goes.

There would seem to be two main explanations. The first is that the rate of expansion of the money supply may not be equal to the rate of inflation. If there are long lags between a fall in the rate of monetary growth and the consequent fall in the rate of inflation, there may be a period when money is tight in the sense of being unavailable even at high interest rates. This explanation indicates that, once again, it is the attempt to reduce inflation which hurts rather than unrestricted steady state inflation itself. As a variation on this theme, rather than appealing to credit-rationing it might be assumed that the real rate of interest rises in order to choke off excess demand for loans. In that case, it is the rise in the real rate which is causing the trouble. This increase in the real rate may be disguised by the tendency of commentators to compare current rates of interest with current rates of inflation, whereas it is future inflation rates, and more precisely expected future rates, which are appropriate. There may well be something in this explanation though the difficulty the authorities have had in controlling the money supply over the past year (1979–1980) may argue against it. The period has also witnessed a substantial increase in unemployment and bankruptcies.

The other explanation is that the loanable funds available are simply not channelled in the right direction. In other words, the fault lies with the banking system. This is not entirely fair. If government borrowing tended to rise in real terms along with inflation then the private sector might be squeezed out of the market whatever the banking system did. In view of what has been said above, a real increase in government borrowing which had this effect would be highly undesirable. But this is, theoretically at any rate, a side issue. The more interesting question is whether inflation itself leads to an undesirable change in the pattern of lending and whether the consequent rationing of firms can be reconciled with rational behaviour.

4.4 Inflation and the supply of loanable funds

Two types of explanation are available for the effect of inflation on the pattern of lending. The first assumes that the decisions of potential lenders are governed by rules of thumb which may be quite sensible in a non-inflationary environment but are quite misleading when there is rapid inflation distorting a company's balance sheet. For example, when inflation is negligible, profits, cash-flow and similar indicators may be a reliable guide to a firm's medium- or long-term creditworthiness. It is therefore reasonable to suppose that lending institutions will develop criteria for extending credit based on these figures. As we have seen the same criteria applied without alteration in an inflationary environment will lead to a drastic cut in lending to the same firms because the reduction in real indebtedness does not count as income. So here is a case where a rule of thumb leads to a shift in the pattern of lending when the rate of inflation changes even though, by hypothesis, there has been no real change in the economy. Whether this sort of explanation is realistic or not, it is not a very satisfactory one from a theoretical point of view. The trouble is that when people are not optimizing almost anything can happen. An explanation which attributes an agent's actions to "irrational" motives has little content since almost anything can be explained in this way. This is not to say that rules of thumb are irrational: in the example above the rule may have been quite efficient when it was adopted. But it remains to be explained why no one perceives that there would be a profit from changing the rule. In other words, we need to show why rational agents should behave in this way.

One possibility is to use a kind of "bootstraps" argument. Suppose one of the agents encountered in the last section wants to borrow money in order to pay the interest on his debts and discovers that no one will lend to him because of his prospective permanent negative cash-flow. Why doesn't some agent find it profitable to lend to him? In the case where all the agents have perfect foresight and are prepared to lend forever it is hard to answer this question. If, on the other hand, agents with money to lend only wish to have it tied up for a limited period, the picture is quite different. For at the end of that period it will be impossible for the borrower to repay the loan unless someone else is prepared to step into the first lender's shoes. A single lender, therefore, may be dissuaded from lending by the knowledge that, since no one else will lend in those circumstances, his money will be tied up indefinitely. Since every potential lender finds himself in the same position there is a Nash equilibrium in which it is (individually) optimal for no one to lend. Under different circumstances it may be possible to repay the loan in a finite period of time, in which case a lender with perfect foresight might go ahead with the loan. But when there is uncertainty about the profitability of the enterprise it may be impossible to predict how much has to be borrowed *in toto* before the loan is repaid in full, or how long it will take. In these circumstances it becomes more likely that the initial lender will take into account the possibility that it will be necessary for the borrower to find extra funds elsewhere. This may occur not only because the first lender is "small" but also because he can only allocate a small fraction of his resources to any particular borrower. Large institutions such as banks, pension funds, insurance companies and the like have commitments which force them to remain fairly flexible. Once again the attractiveness of a particular borrower depends on the attitude of all the other potential lenders.

In the most general terms then, it may be rational for a lender to reject a potential borrower simply because he believes that all the other lenders will do the same. Once the *assumption* of perfect capital markets is dropped, every lender must take into account not only the real characteristics of the firm or individual to whom he lends but also the constraints on their future borrowing. So far the story has nothing to do with inflation but it is clear how it will enter. Beginning from a period of relatively stable prices, if inflation begins to accelerate lending institutions will lose confidence in industry and commerce as borrowers, either because they react in a conventional way to the effect of inflation on their (the borrowers') balance sheets or because they have a theory that says that inflation is bad for business. If all the lending institutions react in a similar way then it will be rational for each of them individually to react in this way. For to depart from the behaviour of the herd is to expose themselves to possible insolvency in the future. And, of course, this lack of confidence tends to be justified or self-fulfilling. Some firms will go bankrupt, others will have to cut back their operations in order to remain solvent (e.g. by selling assets) and this initial shock to the system will have further "Keynesian" repercussions later on. Once the process begins in earnest the borrowing requirements of remaining firms will be even greater. For this reason and because of the drying-up of other sources of funds, it may even be that the money supply and short-term bank advances to industry continue to grow at the same rate as before (which is also the rate of inflation), thus belying the real shortage of credit.

Whether this story has anything to do with the predicament of the United Kingdom in the late 'seventies remains to be seen. There is no doubt that in its broad outlines it captures the symptoms of the current situation. One final question remains. Loanable funds must find a home somewhere, presumably by shifting into gilts and other liquid assets. There is an echo here of Keynes's notion of speculative hoarding, but that is another story.

Notes

1. Sheshinski and Weiss have provided an explanation of why prices do not change smoothly, in their paper "Inflation and Costs of Price Adjustment". When changing price involves a fixed cost, changes will occur at discrete intervals. When there are many commodities, it may be costly to predict when each price will change. This is not the same as uncertainty about the aggregate price level, however, and it may be that the "law of large numbers" does some smoothing here. For example, a manufacturer may regard his many inputs as constituting a composite commodity if, on average, relative prices are constant. The "price" of this "commodity" will be an index number which adjusts smoothly if the dates at which individual input-prices change are independently distributed.

2. See, for example, the papers by S. Goldman, M. Kurz and F. Hahn in the *Review of Economic Studies*, 1968.

3. The fault does not lie entirely with the REH, though. Similar problems can arise when the *adaptive expectations hypothesis* is used, as Cagan pointed out in his classic study of the demand for money during hyperinflations.

4. An example is found in Chapter 4, Part 2.

5. Of course, instant inflation would bring a swift response from the oil producers in the form of another price increase. In any case, in a decentralized economy it would be impossible to organize a general price increase though a devaluation would have similar effects.

6. In fact, it has been suggested to me by R. Jackman that the possibility of the oil producers suffering from money illusion of any sort is so remote that the discussion might well run in terms of the effects of an increase in the real price of oil. But this approach, by assuming that inflation doesn't matter, begs the question I want to answer. An analysis conducted in real terms allows no role for inflation.

7. There is no equity in this example but it could be introduced without changing the conclusions fundamentally.

8. To make the calculations easier I am now assuming that time is continuous.

9. To check that this solution for b is correct, simply differentiate with respect to time, thus:

$$\begin{aligned}\dot{b} &= \pi e^{\pi t} q/\rho \\ &= (\rho + \pi) e^{\pi t} q/\rho - \rho e^{\pi t} q/\rho \\ &= rb - e^{\pi t} q\,.\end{aligned}$$

CHAPTER 4—Part 2

The economic costs of inflation

The "bootstraps" argument to which I appealed at the end of Section 4.4 requires closer inspection. It appears to be contradicted by one of the central conclusions of traditional capital theory, namely that the value of every asset is determined by its productivity. Suppose that a capital-asset is characterized by a stream of outputs of a homogeneous consumption good. The income stream is formally represented by a sequence $\{a_t\}_{t=1}^{\infty}$, where $a_t \geq 0$ denotes the output at date t. The value of the asset at date t (v_t) is related to its value at date $t + 1$ (v_{t+1}) and output at date $t + 1$ (a_{t+1}) by the familiar relationship

(1) $$(1 + r_t)v_t = a_{t+1} + v_{t+1},$$

where r_t is the rate of return on a riskless bond held between dates t and $t + 1$. (1) is established by an arbitrage argument. If the RHS of (1) were greater than the LHS, it would profit some individual to sell bonds and purchase an asset at a price greater than v_t.[1] And if the RHS were less than the LHS it would profit him to sell the asset and buy bonds. The assumptions required for the argument to go through are not very strong.

Using (1), the present value v_0 of the asset can be expressed as a discounted sum of output at the first t dates plus the value of the asset at date t:

$$v_0 = \sum_{k=1}^{t} \delta_k a_k + \delta_t v_t$$

where

$$\delta_k := \frac{1}{(1 + r_0)(1 + r_1)\ldots(1 + r_{k-1})}.$$ [2]

Under the "stability" assumption that $\delta_t v_t \to 0$ as $t \to \infty$, v_0 can be expressed as the present value of the entire income stream:

$$v_0 = \sum_{t=1}^{\infty} \delta_t a_t.$$

Equation (1) taken by itself suggests that the value of an asset today depends as much on the value the market chooses to place on it tomorrow as it does on productivity. But (2) dispels this illusion. There is no support here for the "Keynesian" notion that the value of an asset is determined by what the market thinks it is worth, independently of productivity.

One possibility which has not been considered so far is that $\lim_{t\to\infty} \delta_t v_t \neq 0$. For example, suppose that for all t, $a_t = 0$. For any v_0 there exists a sequence $\{v_t\}_{t=1}^{\infty}$ satisfying $v_{t+1} = (1 + r_t)v_t$ for $t = 0, 1, 2, \ldots$ The value of the asset is indeterminate in this case. To that extent there is a role for market opinion independent of productivity. The indeterminacy is limited by a number of factors, however. The price of the asset can only go up. If $r_t \geq \varepsilon > 0$ then $v_t \to \infty$ as $t \to \infty$ (unless $v_0 = 0$). Unless the economy is growing very rapidly the value of the asset is going to outstrip the economy's income at some point. The appreciation of the asset represents mere accounting profits unless it can be realized. Any attempt to sell the asset for consumption goods will drive down the price. For example, in an overlapping generations model with constant population and no inheritance, the only equilibrium price is $v_t = 0$. The well known "tulip mania" phenomenon, which characterizes growth models with heterogeneous capital goods, can only occur if agents are tacitly assumed to live forever or to bequeath all their assets to their children. Since neither assumption is likely to be satisfied in practice it seems safe to disregard the case where $\lim \delta_t v_t \neq 0$.

I have only rehearsed the argument for the simplest case where there is complete certainty but the argument is quite robust. Introducing uncertainty, for example, means that (1) has to be replaced by a sequence of market-clearing conditions; but the force of the argument is unaffected. The implications for the credit-rationing story told in 4.4 are clear. When there is perfect foresight, the size of a loan is limited by the amount of security the borrower can offer because of the problem of moral hazard. If an entrepreneur wishes to borrow money in order to purchase an asset and he has no other resources, the amount he can borrow will be limited by the (future) value of his asset. If the value of this asset is uniquely determined by its productivity, i.e. the discounted sum of the outputs it produces, then the entrepreneur's creditworthiness is also well defined. In Section 4.4 it was assumed that the amount a bank would lend to a firm today depended on the amount it expected other banks to lend to this firm in the future. From this it was inferred that the amount a firm could borrow was indeterminate, in the sense that it resulted from a Nash equilibrium of lending policies in the money market. There could be many such equilibria. But this inference appears to be false if the value of an asset is uniquely determined by its productivity. For any rational bank will then be willing to lend a firm a unique amount, namely the value of its assets, independently of the behaviour of the other banks.

The trouble with this argument is that it treats a complex firm as though it were the same kind of asset as a house or a machine. A firm is really quite different. It may *own* physical assets but its value as a going concern may be much greater than the value of the plant and equipment it owns. There are several reasons for this. The book value of capital goods represents their original worth to the firm. Their resale or scrap value may be much less, not only because of depreciation but also because their usefulness may be quite specific to the firm which first bought them. Part of a firm's assets consists of unsold goods and goods in progress. If the firm ceases production and cannot guarantee to provide servicing or spare parts, the value of these goods will be greatly reduced. Finally, a considerable part of a firm's value as a going concern may consist of goodwill, accumulated expertise in its chosen line of business, a particular style of management, things which are not easily transferred. All these components of a firm's value as a going concern are reflected in its profitability. When a banker uses a firm's profitability as a measure of its creditworthiness, he is prepared to lend more than the future market value of the firm's physical assets. The same is true if he is prepared to use the book value of the firm's assets as a measure of its creditworthiness.

None of these considerations would make any difference to the traditional story if it were always possible to realize the full value of a firm as a going concern. There are, of course, stock markets on which individual shareholders can exchange their equity in firms which are going concerns but these do not meet the banks' needs. If a bank wishes, for whatever reason, to have a loan repaid and the borrower is unable to do so, the stock market provides no means of recouping the loss. The bank cannot requisition shares in the firm and sell them on the stock market. The creditor really has only two choices. It can extend the loan, hoping it will be repaid in the future, or it can force the firm into bankruptcy. If it chooses the latter course of action it may find that the realizable value of the firm's assets is insufficient to cover the debts. On the other hand, if it tries to realize the value of the firm as a going concern it must find someone who will provide new management and pay enough for the firm to pay for its debts. As was suggested above it may be difficult to transfer a business intact from one management and ownership to another. The loss of goodwill and experienced personnel occasioned by bankruptcy as well as lack of information on the part of the new owners and managers may lead them to offer far less for the firm as a going concern than its past profitability might suggest. In short, the bank may not be able to get the money owed by realizing either the scrap or resale value of the physical assets or the value of the firm as a going concern. In such cases, forcing bankruptcy on a firm is a measure to be used in the last resort and does not provide much security for the bank's loan.

The circumstances described above can be summarized by saying that there may be no adequate market for the firm as a going concern. In the absence of such a market, the ability of a lender to realize his investment may depend on the willingness of others to lend to the debtor. For if he wishes to recall his loan his best prospect is to get someone else to take his place, rather than force the debtor into bankruptcy. This means that when a bank initially extends a loan a prime consideration must be the amount which other banks would be willing to lend on the same security. And the amount which those banks are prepared to lend will be determined by similar considerations.

Even if the bank decided the best course of action were to force a firm into bankruptcy and try to sell it as a going concern, it is unlikely that the prospective purchaser would acquire the firm entirely from his own resources. If he has to borrow, the amount will be limited by the value which the lender places on his security (the firm). So even in this case we cannot escape from the fact that the amount which it is safe to lend on the security of an asset like a firm depends ultimately on the amount which others are prepared to lend. This particular case contains the clue as to why the traditional argument breaks down here. As was indicated at the beginning of this section, the traditional theory of the valuation of assets depends on an arbitrage argument. If an asset is "undervalued" according to this theory, someone will be willing to borrow the money to purchase the asset at a slightly higher price. But suppose the amount he can borrow is limited by the value the lender places on his security. He may not be able to borrow enough to purchase the asset at a higher price. Furthermore, the prospective lender may not be irrational to place the value he does on this asset. If other prospective lenders place the same value on it, he knows it will be unsafe to lend more. In the event that he wishes to recall his loan unexpectedly, no one would be prepared to take his place. The difference between the traditional story and the present one is that here I am not prepared to *assume* perfect capital markets. Once this assumption is dropped the usual arbitrage arguments break down, even though everyone is assumed to be acting rationally.

It may be thought (mistakenly) that the preceding analysis depends on the implicit assumption that prices are fixed. In neo-Keynesian models of disequilibrium, it is often assumed that prices do not adjust in the short run and that markets are cleared by quantity-rationing. It is typical of such models that there exists an equilibrium with quantity-rationing for every given vector of prices. Equilibrium is indeterminate in the absence of a theory of how prices are set. Although quantity-rationing in this sense sounds a bit like the rationing in the loan market discussed earlier, it is actually quite different. Banks are free to adjust rates of interest and change their lending policy, but in equilibrium will choose not to do so. A simple, formal model will help to make this important distinction clear.

I shall make some extreme assumptions to simplify the analysis. To capture the idea that firms are difficult to sell as going concerns, I assume that every firm is run by an entrepreneur who is the only person who knows how to operate the business. Also, each firm's plant and equipment are useful to that firm alone. They have no resale or scrap value. Finally, the entrepreneur who sets up a firm has no personal resources and does not have access to a stockmarket. All investment in the company is financed by borrowing from banks. From these assumptions it follows that the only way banks can recover their investment in a firm to which they have lent money is to keep it going (under the same management). If they do not want to wait for their loan to be repaid they must find another bank to provide the money in their stead.

Consumers

The model is a dynamic one. Time is divided into dates indexed by the integers $t = 0, \pm 1, \ldots$, *ad inf.* At each date there are two commodities, labour and a consumption good. There are two types of agents in the economy, consumers and entrepreneurs. A consumer is assumed to live for two periods. In the first period, he has an endowment of $l > 0$ units of labour. In the second period he has nothing. Labour is supplied inelastically in exchange for consumption goods which are either saved or consumed immediately. Savings earn interest at the market rate and savings plus interest are consumed in the second period. A consumer's preferences are represented by a utility function $u: \mathbb{R}_+ \times \mathbb{R}_+ \to \mathbb{R}$. If $c_t = (c_t^0, c_t^1)$ denotes the consumption plan of an individual born at date t (c_t^i is his consumption at date $t + i$) then his utility is $u(c_t)$. Let ω_t and ρ_t be, respectively, the real wage measured in units of consumption goods and the real rate of interest on savings between dates t and $t + 1$. The consumer's decision problem is to choose $c_t \geq 0$ to

$$\text{maximize } u(c_t)$$
$$\text{subject to } c_t^0 + (1 + \rho_t)^{-1} c_t^1 \leq \omega_t l.$$

If u is monotonic, continuous and strictly quasi-concave there is a unique value of c_t which solves this problem for any $(\rho_t, \omega_t) \gg 0$. Let $s(\rho_t, \omega_t)$ be the savings of the consumer at (ρ_t, ω_t). The savings function provides all the information we need about consumer behaviour since his consumption plan can be calculated from the budget constraints:

$$c_t = [\omega_t . l - s(\rho_t, \omega_t), (1 + \rho_t) . s(\rho_t, \omega_t)].$$

Finally, there are assumed to be N_t identical consumers born at date t, where $N_t = N_0(1 + n)^t$ and N_0 and n are positive numbers.

Firms

There is an unlimited supply of entrepreneurs who are formally identical, in the sense that they have the same mathematical characteristics. They are economically distinct in the sense that no entrepreneur can do another's job and their capital goods cannot be transferred from one firm to another. An entrepreneur has no resources but he does have access to a production technology represented by a production function $f: \mathbb{R}_+ \times \mathbb{R}_+ \to \mathbb{R}_+$. If the entrepreneur has invested k_t units of consumption goods in plant and equipment and hires l_t units of labour, then he can produce $f(k_t, l_t)$ units of consumption good at date t. At each date the entrepreneur must take his capital stock as given and choose l_t to maximize profits. Instead of working with the production function we can describe the entrepreneur's profit possibilities in terms of the profit function π defined by putting

$$\pi(k, \omega) = \max_{l \geq 0} f(k, l) - \omega . l$$

for every (k, ω). If f is continuous and bounded above then π is well defined for every value of $\omega > 0$. If f is strictly concave in l then for every $(k, \omega) \gg 0$ there is a unique optimal value of l which will be denoted by $l(k, \omega)$.

At any date there is a finite number of entrepreneurs who are actually producing. The rest are inactive and have yet to accumulate any capital. Consider an entrepreneur who decides to "enter the market" at date 0. His objective is to maximize the discounted value of the stream of income he generates. Let b_t denote the level of his borrowing at the end of date t and let k_t be the stock of capital available at the beginning of date t. After paying for labour costs the entrepreneur has a surplus of $\pi(k_t, \omega_t)$. Fresh borrowing provides an extra income of $b_t - b_{t-1}$. Out of this he must meet interest charges (ρb_{t-1}) and the cost of new investment $(k_{t+1} - k_t)$. The net income available for his own use is

$$y_t = \pi(k_t, \omega_t) + (b_t - b_{t-1}) - \rho b_{t-1} - (k_{t+1} - k_t). \tag{3}$$

By an earlier assumption $k_{t+1} - k_t \geq 0$ for all t and $k_t = 0$ for $t \leq 0$. The restriction $y_t \geq 0$ may be treated either as part of the definition of y_t or as a budget constraint. It says that the entrepreneur cannot generate income except through his business.

The entrepreneur seeks to maximize the discounted sum of the y_ts, that is,

$$\sum_{t \geq 0} \delta_t y_t \tag{4}$$

where $\delta_t = [(1 + \rho_0) \ldots (1 + \rho_{t-1})]^{-1}$, subject to the constraints $k_{t+1} \geq k_t$ and $y_t \geq 0$. These constraints must be supplemented by a constraint on borrowing, however. Otherwise (4) can be made arbitrarily large simply by increasing b_t substantially at each date.[3] Let the borrowing constraint be the value of the entrepreneur's collateral. In this case, his collateral is not k_t (which only represents investment to date rather than a saleable asset) but the value of the firm as a going concern. The profitmaking possibilities of the firm from date t onwards depend at most on three things:

(i) the capital stock k_t;
(ii) present and future prices $\{\rho_t, \omega_t\}$;
(iii) future lending behaviour of banks.

Since (ii) and (iii) are taken as given by entrepreneurs at date t, it seems reasonable to express the entrepreneur's credit limit as a function of (i). Let $v_t(k_{t+1})$ denote the maximum the entrepreneur can borrow at date t given that his capital stock at the end of date t will be k_{t+1}. A change in prices or expected future behaviour of the banks will of course change the *function* v_t.

The entrepreneur's decision problem is to choose a sequence $\{(k_t, b_t)\}_{t=0}^{\infty}$ in $\mathbb{R}_+ \times \mathbb{R}_+$ to

$$(4)\quad \begin{cases} \text{maximize} \sum_{t \geq 0} \delta_t y_t \\ \text{subject to } y_t \geq 0 \\ \qquad k_{t+1} - k_t \geq 0 \qquad (k_0 = 0) \\ \qquad b_t \leq v_t(k_{t+1}) \end{cases}$$

Banks

The only function of banks is to channel savings from consumers to entrepreneurs. Their existence is notional: I need them to explain how v_t is chosen. Each bank is assumed to adopt a lending policy which maximizes the discounted value of profits (which are zero in equilibrium, assuming free entry) taking as given the future choice of the function v_t. This is a crucial assumption which can be defended in two ways. A bank can be thought of as a syndicate of consumers. Since consumers last only two periods, so do banks. Future choices of v_t are taken as given because they will be made by other banks. Alternatively, even if a bank lasts for more than two periods, its current depositors will wish to withdraw their entire deposits next period. Since the bank cannot be sure it will be able to replace these deposits with fresh ones, it acts conservatively as if it had to wind up its affairs after two periods. In that case, the choice of v_t is effectively made by other banks, the ones with deposits. Whichever assumption we adopt, taking future choices of v_t as given amounts to the Nash hypothesis of taking other agents' behaviour as given.

The question now arises, what is an optimal choice of v_t? The market for bank loans is competitive. Each bank is so small that its own behaviour has no effect on the prevailing rate of interest or the lending policy of other banks. Consider a symmetric equilibrium in which all banks initially choose v_t and earn zero profits (i.e. the deposit rate equals the lending rate). Suppose the constraint $b_t \leq v_t(k_{t+1})$ is not binding on the bank's customers. In other words, firms would choose to borrow the same amount from this bank even if there were no constraint at date t. Now, consider the impact of a change in the bank's lending policy and the rate it charges borrowers from v_t and ρ_t to v_t' and ρ_t', respectively. The change will have no effect unless it causes borrowers to borrow less since it cannot force them to borrow more than they wish to. Since customers always have the option of using another bank, they cannot be any worse off than they were initially, i.e. when the bank chose (v_t, ρ_t). This means that $\rho_t' < \rho_t$, since an increase in the rate of interest must make the borrower worse off when he was initially unconstrained. However the bank is no better off if $\rho_t' \leq \rho_t$. Thus, a sufficient condition for v_t to be optimal is that the constraint $b_t \leq v_t(k_{t+1})$ is not binding. This may seem a very strong condition but it is actually necessary as well.

Suppose the constraint were binding at date t. This means that if there were no constraint at date t, the firms would want to borrow more. They would only do so if they could increase the value of discounted profits (equation (4)). But if (4) can be increased, a firm will be prepared to pay a slightly higher rate of interest to borrow the larger amount at date t. Thus, both the bank and the firm can be made better off if the constraint $b_t \leq v_t(k_{t+1})$ is binding. Hence v_t cannot be optimal.[4]

Using the preceding argument it is possible to eliminate the bank's behaviour entirely from the description of equilibrium. When the deposit rate equals the lending rate, as it must in equilibrium, a bank can increase its profit by changing v_t if and only if the borrower can increase his profit by increasing his borrowing. Optimality for the banker is therefore equivalent to optimality for the entrepreneur *when the current v_t-constraint is removed.* The theory of banking and entrepreneurial behaviour can be summarized in the following definition. The sequence $\{(k_t, b_t)\}_{t=0}^{\infty}$ is said to be *jointly optimal for banks and entrepreneurs* if and only if, for every $T \geq 0$, $\{(k_t, b_t)\}_{t>T}$ is optimal for the problem:

$$(5)\quad \left\{ \begin{array}{l} \text{maximize } \sum_{t \geq T} \delta_t y_t \\ \text{subject to } y_t \geq 0 \\ \qquad\qquad k_{t+1} - k_t \geq 0 \quad (k_T \text{ fixed}) \\ \qquad\qquad b_t \leq v_t(k_{t+1}) \quad \text{for } t \geq T+1\,. \end{array} \right.$$

If $\{(k_t, b_t)\}$ solves (4) it is obviously optimal from every date T onwards by the Principle of Optimality. What (5) requires is that it be optimal from T onwards when the borrowing constraint $b_t \leq v_t(k_{t+1})$ is dropped for $t = T$.

Equilibrium

Equilibrium requires two things, that demand equal supply in each market and that every agent be acting optimally at the given prices. There are only two markets: the labour market and the goods market. The market for loans has been effectively eliminated in the definition (5) and there is no need to consider it further.

It has already been noted that optimal consumer behaviour is completely characterized by the savings function s, which is assumed to be well-defined, and the fact that consumers supply labour inelastically. Thus, equilibrium can be defined entirely in terms of the two market-clearing conditions and a characterization of optimal behaviour for firms. In the sequel, I shall only be concerned with *stationary equilibria* in which $(\rho_t, \omega_t, k_t, b_t) = (\rho, \omega, k, b)$ for all t.

At each date there are two generations, the old and the young. The income of the old consists entirely of interest payments, which they consume. The income of the young consists entirely of wages, part of which they save. The only other demand for consumption goods comes from entrepreneurs wishing to invest. If profits are zero, total output is the sum of wages and interest payments, so the demand for consumption equals supply if savings equals investment. In a stationary equilibrium $b = k$. ($y_t \geq 0$ implies $k \leq b$ and $\pi(k, \omega) - \rho b \geq 0$ so the zero-profit condition $\pi(k, \omega) - \rho k = 0$ implies $b = k$.) Let F_t be the number of firms in existence at the *end* of date t. Total demand for loans will be $F_t b = F_t k$ and total supply of savings will be $N_t s(\rho, \omega)$. Let $F_t = (1 + n^t)F_0$ and $\alpha = F_0/N_0$. The condition "savings = investment" at each date reduces to

$$(6) \qquad s(\rho, \omega) = \alpha k\,.$$

Total labour supply at date t is $N_t l$. The demand for labour is $F_{t-1}l(k, \omega)$. (F_{t-1} appears in place of F_t because only firms which already have a capital stock at the beginning of date t can produce in that period.) Then demand for labour equals supply if and only if

$$(7) \qquad (1 + n)l = \alpha l(k, \omega)\,.$$

It should be clear from (6) and (7) that there is no loss of generality in assuming that the ratio F_t/N_t is constant in a stationary equilibrium.

Entrepreneurs have two decisions to make: whether to enter the market and what to do if they do enter. Since there is free entry and an unlimited number of potential entrepreneurs, equilibrium requires that entrepreneurs who do not enter are at least as well off as those who do, i.e. $0 \geq \sum \delta_t y_t$ for any feasible sequence $\{y_t\}$. Since

$y_t \geq 0$, for all t, this implies that

(8) $$\sum_{t=0}^{\infty} \delta_t y_t = 0$$

for any feasible $\{y_t\}$. From equation (8) it follows that:

(9) *for any number k satisfying* $0 \leq k \leq v(k)$, $\quad \pi(k, \omega) \leq \rho k$.

To see this suppose the contrary and define the sequence $\{(k_t, b_t)\}$ by putting $k_0 = 0$ and $k_t = b_{t-1} = k$ for all $t \geq 1$. At each date $t \geq 0$,

$$y_t = \pi(k_t, \omega) - (k_{t+1} - k_t) - (1 + \rho)b_{t-1} + b_t$$
$$= \begin{cases} 0 & \text{if } \ t = 0 \\ \pi(k, \omega) - \rho k > 0 & \text{if } \ t \geq 1 . \end{cases}$$

By construction and the hypothesis that $0 \leq k \leq v(k)$, the sequence $\{(k_t, b_t)\}$ satisfies all the constraints in (5), so $\sum \delta_t y_t > 0$ contradicts (8). This contradiction establishes the truth of (9).

Using the inequality in (9), for any feasible $\{y_t\}$,

$$\sum_{t \geq 0} \delta_t y_t = \sum_{t \geq 0} \delta_t[\pi(k_t, \omega) - (k_{t+1} - k_t) - (1 + \rho)b_{t-1} + b_t]$$

(11)
$$\leq \sum_{t \geq 0} \delta_t[\rho k_t - (k_{t+1} - k_t) - (1 + \rho)b_{t-1} + b_t]$$
$$= \sum_{t \geq 0} (1 + \rho)^{-t}[(1 + \rho)(k_t - b_{t-1}) - (k_{t+1} - b_t)]$$
$$= \sum_{t \geq 1} \{(1 + \rho)^{-t}[(1 + \rho)(k_t - b_{t-1})] - (1 + \rho)^{-(t-1)}(k_t - b_{t-1})\}$$
$$= 0 .$$

The inequality in (11) is strict if, for any date t, the inequality in (9) is strict. But (8) implies that the inequality in (11) is an equation, so $\pi(k_t, \omega) = \rho k_t$ for every $t \geq 1$. The equilibria in the sequel have the property that

(12) *there is a unique value of* $0 \leq k \leq v(k)$ *such that* $\pi(k, \omega) = \rho k$.

When (12) holds there is no loss of generality in assuming that, if $\{(k_t, b_t)\}$ solves (5), then $k_t = k$ for all $t \geq 1$. Finally, note that since

$y_t = 0$, for all t, in equilibrium (this follows from (8) and $y_t \geq 0$) $b_t = k_{t+1}$ for all $t \geq 0$. This is easily proved by induction.

$$0 = y_0 = -k_1 + b_1$$

and if $k_t = b_{t-1}$ then

$$\begin{aligned} 0 = y_t &= \pi(k_t, \omega) - (k_{t+1} - k_t) - (1 + \rho)b_{t-1} + b_t \\ &= \pi(k_t, \omega) - \rho k_t + (k_t - k_t) - k_{t+1} + b_t \\ &= -k_{t+1} + b_t . \end{aligned}$$

If (12) is satisfied and $\{(k_t, b_t)\}$ is optimal in equilibrium then $k_t = b_{t-1} = k$ for $t \geq 1$. There is no loss of generality consequently in including this restriction in the definition of equilibrium.

Now define a *stationary equilibrium* to be an array $(\rho^*, \omega^*, k^*, v^*, \alpha^*)$ such that:

(i) the sequence $\{(k_t, b_t)\}$, defined by putting $k_0 = 0$ and $k_t = b_{t-1} = k^*$ for $t \geq 1$, solves (5) when $(\rho_t, \omega_t) = (\rho^*, \omega^*)$ for all t;
(ii) $\pi^*(k^*, \omega^*) - \rho^* k^* = 0$;
(iii) $s(\rho^*, \omega^*) = \alpha^* k^*$;
(iv) $(1 + n)l = \alpha^* l(k^*, \omega^*)$.

(iii) and (iv) are market clearing conditions, (ii) is the no-profit condition implied by free entry and (i) requires joint optimality in the sense of definition (5).

Formally, a stationary equilibrium looks like an equilibrium with quantity-rationing. Consider a stationary equilibrium in which $v^*(k) = k^*$ for all $k \geq 0$. The entrepreneur's optimum is illustrated in the figure below.

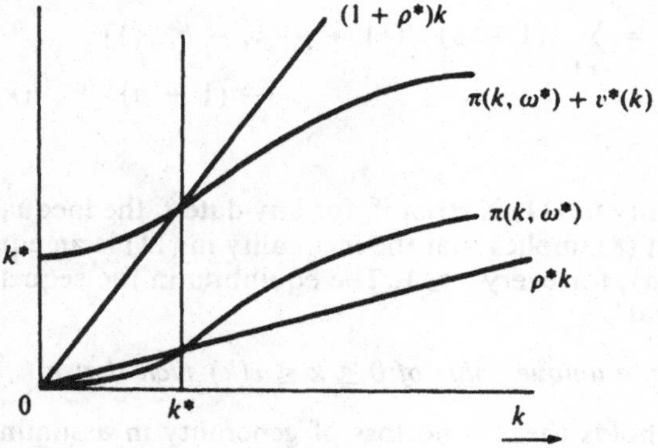

Figure 4.1

From the diagram,

$$(13)\quad \begin{cases} k < k^* \Rightarrow \pi(k, \omega) < \rho k, \\ k > k^* \Rightarrow (1+\rho)k > \pi(k, \omega) + k^*. \end{cases}$$

Define the sequence $\{(k_t^*, b_t^*)\}_{t=0}^{\infty}$ by putting $k_0 = 0$ and $k_t = b_{t-1} = k^*$ for all $t \geq 1$. I claim that $\{(k_t^*, b_t^*)\}$ solves the entrepreneur's problem described in (5). To prove this it is necessary to show that, beginning at any date T, there is no better sequence even when the borrowing constraint at date T is removed. Consider first the case $T = 0$. Let $\{(k_t, b_t)\}$ be an alternative feasible sequence. Then (5) implies that

$$(14)\quad \begin{cases} k_0 = 0 \quad \text{and} \quad k_t \geq k_{t-1} \quad \text{for all} \quad t \geq 0; \\ b_t \leq v(k_{t+1}) = k^* \quad \text{for all} \quad t \geq 0; \\ 0 \leq y_t = \pi(k_t, \omega^*) - (k_{t+1} - k_t) - (1+\rho^*)b_{t-1} + b_t \\ \qquad\qquad\qquad\qquad\qquad\qquad\qquad \text{for all} \quad t \geq 0. \end{cases}$$

At date 0, (14) implies that

$$0 \leq y_0 = -k_1 + b_0$$

so $k_1 \leq b_0$. At date 1, (14) implies that

$$\begin{aligned} 0 \leq y_1 &= \pi(k_1, \omega^*) - (k_2 - k_1) - (1+\rho^*)b_0 + b_1 \\ &\leq \pi(k_1, \omega^*) - (1+\rho^*)k_1 + k^* \end{aligned}$$

since $k_2 - k_1 \geq 0$, $k_1 \leq b_0$ and $b_1 \leq v(k_2) = k^*$. From (13) it follows that $k_1 \leq k^*$ and hence $\pi(k_1, \omega^*) \leq \rho^* k_1$. Using this inequality and (14) gives

$$\begin{aligned} 0 \leq y_1 &= \pi(k_1, \omega^*) - (k_2 - k_1) - (1+\rho^*)b_0 + b_1 \\ &\leq \rho^* k_1 - (k_2 - k_1) - (1+\rho^*)k_1 + b_1 \\ &= b_1 - k_2. \end{aligned}$$

Hence $k_2 \leq b_1 \leq k^*$. Now suppose that for every $t = 1, \ldots, T$,

$$k_{t+1} \leq b_t \leq k^*.$$

Then (14) implies

$$\begin{aligned} 0 \leq y_T &= \pi(k_T, \omega^*) - (k_{T+1} - k_T) - (1+\rho^*)b_{T-1} + b_T \\ &\leq \rho^* k_T - (k_{T+1} - k_T) - (1+\rho^*)k_T + b_T \\ &= b_T - k_{T+1}. \end{aligned}$$

By induction it has been proved that $k_{t+1} \le b_t \le k^*$ for all $t \ge 1$. Then

$$\begin{aligned}
\sum_{t \ge 0} \delta_t y_t &= \sum_{t \ge 0} \delta_t \{\pi(k_t, \omega^*) - (k_{t+1} - k_t) - (1 + \rho^*) b_{t-1} + b_t\} \\
&\le \sum_{t \ge 0} \delta_t \{\rho^* k_t - (k_{t+1} - k_t) - (1 + \rho^*) b_{t-1} + b_t\} \\
&= \sum_{t=1}^{\infty} \delta_t \{(1 + \rho^*)(k_t - b_{t-1}) - (k_{t+1} - b_t)\} \\
&= \sum_{t=1}^{\infty} \{(1 + \rho^*)^{-t}(1 + \rho^*)(k_t - b_{t-1}) \\
&\qquad\qquad - (1 + \rho^*)^{-(t-1)}(k_t - b_{t-1})\} \\
&= 0,
\end{aligned}$$

as required.

The case where $T > 0$ is very easy to handle. Let $\{(k_t, b_t)\}$ be any feasible sequence such that $k_0 = 0$ and $k_t = b_{t-1} = k^*$ for $t = 1, \ldots, T$. From (14),

$$\begin{aligned}
0 \le y_T &= \pi(k_T, \omega^*) - (k_{T+1} - k_T) - (1 + \rho^*) b_{T-1} + b_T \\
&= \pi(k^*, \omega^*) - (k_{T+1} - k^*) - (1 + \rho^*) k^* + b_T \\
&= b_T - k_{T+1}
\end{aligned}$$

so $k_{T+1} \le b_T$. Now suppose $b_T > k^*$. Then (14) implies

$$\begin{aligned}
0 \le y_{T+1} &= \pi(k_{T+1}, \omega^*) - (k_{T+2} - k_{T+1}) - (1 + \rho^*) b_T + b_{T+1} \\
&\le \pi(k_{T+1}, \omega^*) + k^* - (k_{T+2} - k_{T+1}) - (1 + \rho^*) b_T
\end{aligned}$$

(since $b_{T+1} \le k^*$)

$$\le (1 + \rho^*)(k_{T+1} - b_T) - (k_{T+2} - k_{T+1})$$

(with strict inequality if $k_{T+1} > k^*$)

$$\begin{aligned}
&\le -(k_{T+2} - k_{T+1}) \\
&\le 0.
\end{aligned}$$

If any of the inequalities were strict, it would lead to a contradiction. Hence $k_{T+1} = b_T = k^*$. By induction it can be shown that $k_t = b_{t-1} = k^*$ for all $t \ge 1$. Once an entrepreneur has chosen $k_1 = b_0 = k^*$ he has no choice but to put $k_t = b_{t-1} = k^*$ for all t, even if the borrowing constraint is removed at any subsequent date. It has already been shown that it is optimal to choose $k_1 = b_0 = k^*$ at date 0 so it follows trivially that $\{(k_t^*, b_t^*)\}$ solves (5), when (13) is satisfied.

The diagram (Fig. 4.1) shows clearly why the entrepreneur is not effectively constrained by his current borrowing constraint. The inequality

$$b_t \leq k^*$$

is exactly equivalent to the inequality

$$(1 + \rho^*)b_t \leq \pi(b_t, \omega^*) + k^*$$

when (13) is satisfied. Supposing that $b_{t-1} = k_t = k^*$, (14) implies that

$$(15) \quad 0 \leq y_t = \pi(k_t, \omega^*) - (k_{t+1} - k_t) - (1 + \rho^*)b_{t-1} + b_t$$
$$= b_t - k_{t+1}.$$

Then (14) and (15) imply that

$$(16) \quad y_{t+1} = \pi(k_{t+1}, \omega^*) - (k_{t+2} - k_{t+1}) - (1 + \rho^*)b_t + b_{t+1}$$
$$\leq \pi(b_t, \omega^*) - (1 + \rho^*)b_t + k^*$$

As noted above, (16) implies that $b_t \leq k^*$ but the inequality $b_t \leq k^*$ was not used to obtain (15) or (16). The inequality $b_{t+1} \leq k^*$ was used to obtain (16), however. What this argument shows is that, even if there is no borrowing constraint today, the existence of a borrowing constraint tomorrow forces the entrepreneur to satisfy the inequality $b_t \leq k^*$ today.

There is evidently a continuum of stationary equilibria when there is at least one (making the usual regularity assumptions). There are three equations to determine the four variables $(\rho^*, \alpha^*, \omega^*, k^*)$. More precisely, suppose that $(\rho^*, \omega^*, k^*, \alpha^*)$ satisfy equations (ii) to (iv) of the definition of a stationary equilibrium and (13) is also satisfied. Suppose that ρ^*, ω^*, k^* and α^* are all strictly positive numbers and that the functions π, s and l involved in equations (ii) to (iv) satisfy the conditions required for the Implicit Function Theorem to apply. Then, for any k in some small neighbourhood of k^*, there exist numbers ρ, ω and α such that $(\rho, \omega, k, \alpha)$ satisfies (ii) to (iv). But it is clear that for all k in some small neighbourhood of k^*, if (ii) is satisfied then (13) is also satisfied. This "proves" that $(\rho, \omega, k, \alpha)$ is also a stationary equilibrium since (13) implies that (i) is satisfied. This indeterminacy is quite unlike the one already encountered in models of inflation. There the stationary equilibria were determinate though there existed many unstable, non-stationary equilibria. Here it is the stationary equilibria which form a continuum, a much more remarkable result.

The specification $v^*(k) = k^*$ is not the only possible one. An alternative is $v^*(k) = k$ for all $k \geq 0$. It is left to the reader to show that with this choice the only stationary equilibrium is the traditional one. Furthermore it is determinate as illustrated below.

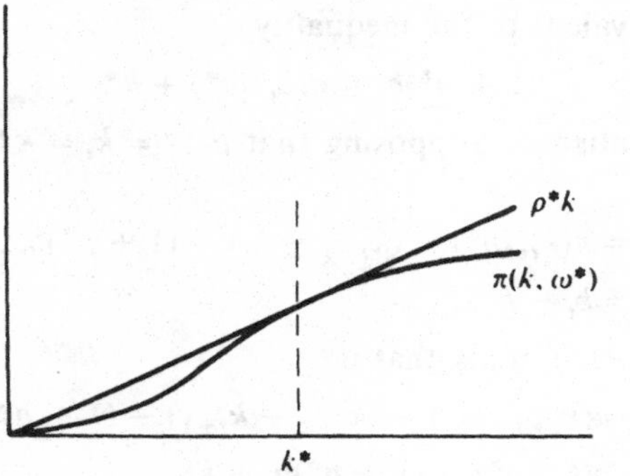

Figure 4.2

(i) and (ii) determine both ρ^* and k^* in terms of ω. Then (iii) and (iv) can be used to solve for α^* and ω^*.

What sort of equilibria we obtain depends on the nature of the policies v^* which are entertained. The important point, however, is that in equilibrium only optimal policies are allowed. Each bank chooses v_t to maximize profits jointly with the borrower, taking as given the future lending policy of other banks. The "bootstraps" argument depends only on this Nash equilibrium property and not on any "fix-price" assumption of the sort found in disequilibrium theory.

The entire story has been told in real terms. To link it to the problem of inflation we must return to the idea of conventional behaviour. When there is a continuum of Nash equilibria, a *convention* is needed to select one. For example, there may be a conventional idea of how much it is safe to lend on certain types of security. This amount will be expressed in terms of money. Inflation will reduce the real value of this nominal amount. The economy slides along the continuum of Nash equilibria as a result, but there is no money illusion at work here. Each agent is behaving rationally but since he must take the behaviour of other agents as given, he must also take the convention as given. When the "real" convention changes, the "nominal" convention remaining the same, everyone's real behaviour must adjust. Thus, inflation may have real consequences simply because agents believe it will have real consequences. The fault lies not with inflation but with the nature of our beliefs.

Remarks

The indeterminacy of the equilibrium (real) rate of interest is not simply a product of capital market imperfections. It is a general-equilibrium property of the system and depends on the institutional structure of the model. This point is well illustrated by an example earlier in this Chapter. Suppose an entrepreneur with no resources of his own wishes to purchase a machine which costs c units and produces q units at each date from tomorrow onwards. The real rate of interest is expected to remain constant at ρ, although this is not essential to the story. The income-stream represented by this machine is assumed to have a present value of zero, i.e., $c = q/\rho$. In order to purchase this machine the entrepreneur must borrow from a consumer, but consumers only live for two periods whereas the machine only yields up its output over an infinite number of periods. The only way the entrepreneur can repay his initial borrowing tomorrow is to obtain another loan at that date. In other words, he must continually "roll over" his debt. The amount he can afford to borrow today clearly depends on the amount he will be able to borrow tomorrow and so on. Let v_t denote the amount he is able to borrow at date t. At date t a rational consumer will be prepared to lend the entrepreneur as much as he can *certainly* repay, with interest, at the next date. In that case,

$$v_t = (1 + \rho)^{-1}(q + v_{t+1}) .$$

Assuming $\lim_{t \to \infty} v_t < \infty$,

$$v_0 = q/\rho .$$

The entrepreneur can borrow precisely what he needs to purchase the machine, so the traditional story is unchanged by the introduction of capital market imperfections.

The reason why the general-equilibrium model gives a different answer is that the amount the entrepreneur is allowed to borrow actually affects the profitability of his asset. In equilibrium, the amount an entrepreneur can borrow is equal to the present value of the stream of income he produces (his net present wealth is zero). But the size of his firm and hence its profitability depend initially on how much he can borrow. It is crucial in this respect that firms are only valuable as going concerns and that their capital goods are non-transferable. If firms could pool their capital the results would break down. Also, if there were constant returns to scale the only effect of capital-market imperfections of the sort described above would be to alter the number of firms (relative to the number of consumers). And, of course, the fact that capital goods only yield up their product over an indefinitely long period of time is essential too.

Thus, the results obtained in this chapter depend as much on the assumed "illiquidity" of capital (in Keynes's sense, cf. Leijonhufvud, *On Keynesian Economics and the Economics of Keynes*, Chapter 3) as on imperfections in the lending market. Whether Keynes understood the importance of the interaction of these two factors is doubtful, however, for in his discussion of the indeterminacy of asset-values he did not go any further than the fallacious argument based on equation (1).

Notes

1. Suppose the individual borrows v_t (sells bonds worth v_t) at the rate of interest r_t. At date $t+1$ he receives a coupon worth a_{t+1} and sells the asset for v_{t+1}. He also repays the loan with interest, which costs him $(1+r_t)v_t$. The net gain is $a_{t+1}+v_{t+1}-(1+r_t)v_t$ which is positive hy hypothesis.

2. By successive substitutions, using (1), we get,

$$v_0 = \frac{1}{1+r_0}(a_1+v_1)$$

$$= \frac{1}{1+r_0}a_1 + \frac{1}{(1+r_0)}\frac{1}{(1+r_1)}(a_2+v_2)$$

$$= \frac{1}{1+r_0}a_1 + \frac{1}{(1+r_0)}\frac{1}{(1+r_1)}a_2 + \frac{1}{(1+r_0)}\frac{1}{(1+r_1)}\frac{1}{(1+r_2)}(a_3+v_3)$$

and so on.

3. Suppose the entrepreneur chooses not to invest in capital goods at all, i.e. $k_t = 0$ for $t = 0, 1, \ldots,$ *ad inf.* Then equation (3) becomes $y_t = b_t - (1+\rho_{t-1})b_{t-1}$. For *any* non-negative sequence $\{y_t\}_{t=0}^{\infty}$, there exists a sequence $\{b_t\}_{t=0}^{\infty}$ such that this equation is satisfied. Simply define b_t recursively by putting $b_0 = y_0$ and $b_t = y_t + (1+\rho_{t-1})b_{t-1}$ for $t \geq 1$. Since the economy never comes to an end the entrepreneur can always borrow to pay back his old debts and meet the cost of interest charges and consumption. Clearly there is no best sequence $\{y_t\}$.

It is often thought that an economy with no uncertainty and a perfect capital market is essentially the same as an Arrow–Debreu economy. This belief is based on the idea that the existence of perfect capital markets at each date allows a sequence of budget constraints to be amalgamated into a single budget constraint. The argument is correct when every agent has a finite life span. Otherwise, as the example above shows, a sequence of constraints does not ultimately constrain the agent's behaviour at all.

4. This argument begs two, possibly important, questions. Because I have not assumed that the profit function is concave it may be that the firm can make itself better off only if it increases its borrowing by a large amount. Since the supply of bank deposits is not assumed to be perfectly elastic, it may be that the bank cannot accommodate this level of borrowing. This problem may not be serious if firms are small relative to banks or the degree of increasing returns to scale is not too great. The second problem concerns the continuity of the firm's objective function. In order for the firm to share with the bank the surplus it obtains from increased borrowing it may be necessary for the firm to adjust its new optimal plan slightly. It must be assumed that the value of discounted profits is continuous with respect to such changes. The assumption of continuity is not trivial when the firm has an infinite horizon.

Neither problem affects the sufficiency of the optimality condition, however, and the sufficient condition is all that is needed in the sequel. By treating the sufficient condition as part of the definition of equilibrium I may be eliminating some legitimate equilibria but this only strengthens the "bootstraps" argument I wish to make.

CHAPTER 5

Sequences of budget constraints

5.1 The general equilibrium view of money

Many different sorts of general equilibrium models have been used to describe monetary economies and they hardly provide a unified view of what money is or how it functions. What I choose to mean by "the general equilibrium view" is one strand in this large literature. It is the attempt, associated with the names of Patinkin, Hahn and others, to develop a theory of money as part of a unified theory of value, taking as starting point the Walrasian model of equilibrium. Money is "different" from other commodities, of course, and no sensible theory could pretend otherwise. What unifies the theory is an application of certain principles and a particular way of representing the economy. Starting from a Walrasian point of view imposes certain limitations. The Arrow–Debreu model, to choose a non-monetary example, is hardly recognizable as the world we live in. Indeed, there is a mystical school of monetary thought which holds that the existence of money has something to do with uncertainty (as distinct from risk) and the impossibility of rational calculation. Money would never be found in a Walrasian world of rational agents and smoothly functioning markets. This last is false, as I try to show in Chapters 6 and 7, but even apart from this, the mystical view misses the point. It may be of interest to economic historians to discover how money came into being but that is a different matter from analysing the functioning of money in a modern economy. It is simply fallacious to argue that a model which does not explain why money came into existence cannot be used to gain insights into the working of monetary economy. The contrary case must be argued as well, of course, and that is done in the sequel. But first, let us see what a general equilibrium model with money looks like.

The model on which the theory is based is a generalization of the Arrow–Debreu model. There are parametric prices which clear markets and all agents (in the case of a pure exchange economy) maximize utility subject to budget constraints. Unlike the Arrow–Debreu model, there is not a complete set of markets at the first date. There is no need for money in the Arrow–Debreu model because all trading takes place at the first date. There are markets for commodities to be delivered at any date or even delivered contingently on some future event, so agents balance sales against purchases once and for all without the use of a store of value. In a monetary economy markets are highly incomplete, just as they are in reality, but even this is not enough. When markets are incomplete, trading must continue after the first date. But if agents have rational expectations (in a sense made precise in Part 2 of this Chapter) the fact that they must trade at several dates makes no essential difference unless they are forced to satisfy a budget constraint at each date. The essential characteristic of a sequence economy, or more precisely of a sequence equilibrium, is that there is a sequence of budget constraints. At each date there is a set of markets, generally incomplete, and a vector of parametric, market clearing prices. Agents choose a trade plan, which indicates what trades they will make at each date, to maximize utility subject to a sequence of budget constraints, one for each date.

It may help to have a concrete example at this point. A consumer who lives for T periods has an initial cash balance $\bar{m}$ and, at each date $t = 1, \ldots, T$, an initial endowment e_t of goods. At each date, his wealth is the sum of $p_t . e_t$, the value of his endowment and m_{t-1}, the amount of money brought forward from the last period. By convention, put $m_0 = \bar{m}$. At each date, the consumer chooses a bundle x_t of consumption goods and an amount m_t of money which he carries forward to the next period. His utility can be written as a function $U(x_1, x_2, \ldots, x_T)$ of his consumption at the various dates. Money does not enter the utility function. In an Arrow–Debreu economy, he would choose $(x_1, \ldots, x_T)$ to maximize $U(x_1, \ldots, x_T)$ subject to single budget constraint:

$$\sum_{t=1}^{T} p_t x_t \leq \sum_{t=1}^{T} p_t e_t + \bar{m}$$

There is no need for money here. In a sequence economy, by contrast, he chooses $(x_1, \ldots, x_T)$ and $(m_1, \ldots, m_T)$ to maximize $U(x_1, \ldots, x_T)$ subject to the *sequence* of constraints

$$p_t . x_t + m_t \leq p_t . e_t + m_{t-1},$$

one for each date $t = 1, \ldots, T$.

The role of money in this context is to help consolidate the budget constraints. Money allows an agent effectively to reduce expenditure at one date and increase it at another. In this way the effect of the several budget constraints is relaxed. There is no doubt that money does perform this function in reality but so do many other assets. It is probably this fact that has led so many authors to look for other explanations of the usefulness of money. These other explanations are really unnecessary, however. One fact about money which is undeniable is that it is accepted almost everywhere. In other words, trades in money appear in almost all budget constraints, which is not true of other assets. If one enters a shop one confronts an incomplete set of markets, in the sense used earlier. The commodities traded include the goods sold in the shop and money in various forms. The budget constraint for this set of markets requires that the value of trades in these commodities alone should balance. One does not have to look further for a rationale for money than the fact that it appears in so many budget constraints. Having established that fact, it seems legitimate to simplify the story by looking at models where, for example, there are only two dates and two budget constraints and money is the only asset.

These assumptions are not intended to be taken literally. Indeed, taken literally they lead to absurd results. Anyone who really believed the world had only two dates and two budget constraints would find it rather hard to explain why money could not be replaced by bonds, say. The point is that we cannot sensibly introduce another asset without further refining the market structure. Money can be traded on some markets where bonds are not traded. This distinction cannot be made in a simple model with only two sets of markets so we need to have more markets. For example, we might divide commodities into possibly overlapping groups which are traded in different submarkets. Money would be traded in each submarket but bonds in only one. If each submarket had its own budget constraint, there would be a role for money in spite of the presence of bonds. The resulting model would be very complicated but that complexity would not add anything very important to the story of money. The role of money in the complicated model is the same as in the simplest two-period model: it allows wealth to be transferred from one market (or submarket) to another. This is the problem which has to be analysed and it might as well be done in the simplest model possible.

5.2 Borrowing and Lending

The simple framework adopted in the preceding section allows a story to be told in which money has a role to play. That role may seem a rather narrow one but it is nonetheless important. Even the restricted analysis which is possible in a two-period economy shows that the efficiency properties of an economy with money may be quite different from the efficiency properties of one without money. It could be argued, however, that this way of modelling money does not really capture the essence of a monetary economy. In the first place (one could argue) the role of money here is simply that of an asset and it could be replaced by any other asset. More generally, the function of transferring wealth between periods is usually ascribed to stores of value and money is not the only store of value. In the second place (it could be argued) there are many essential features of money which are omitted from the highly simplified story told in the preceding section.

Now, it is certainly true that there are many aspects of an actual monetary economy which are not explicitly represented. There is no banking sector, there are no alternative assets, the trading process is modelled in a simplistic way and so forth. But the claim that there is something essential missing requires careful scrutiny. Any investigation of the foundations of monetary theory is bound to leave out of account many details. These may or may not be important in some practical way but to say they are essential requires proof. A number of aspects of a monetary economy are ruled out simply by the adoption of a general equilibrium framework. For example, the "search theories" developed in recent years may be relevant but they lie outside the scope of the present investigation. An important question is being begged here; that is a pity but there is nothing for it. Within the self-imposed restriction of a general equilibrium framework, it seems to me that it is possible to capture the essence of the monetary economy by looking at simple economies of the type described in Section 5.1. This is not to say that these models can answer every question in the general equilibrium theory of money. Far from it. But as far as the study of what is sometimes called the "micro-foundations of monetary theory", which I would prefer to call the fundamental properties of money, is concerned, they serve quite well. It must be emphasized, however, that this is only true if we ignore problems that lie outside the general equilibrium framework. These may turn out to be more interesting or important, but general equilibrium theory provides enough insights to justify a separate study.

Even within the limited sphere of general equilibrium theory the claim that money is just a store of value may seem unjustified. Consider the argument mentioned above, that other assets would serve just as well as money in the simple two-period economy and lead to the same results. For example, introducing a bond market into a two-period economy at date 0 would give a sequence equilibrium the same efficiency properties as a monetary equilibrium. Does this mean that money and "bonds" are indistinguishable? A theory which implied this would be unsatisfactory. Fortunately, even within the context of a simple two-period economy it is possible to illustrate a crucial difference, if we avoid taking literally the simplifying assumptions of the model.

Bonds are what are known as *named commodities*, that is, they are distinguished by the names of the individuals who trade them. The bonds issued by different agents are regarded as different commodities because the risk of default differs from one agent to another. In the preceding example, a bond is a promise to deliver one unit of account at the second period but the promise is treated as being as good as the thing itself. The possibility of default is not even considered. One way of describing this is to say that agents are—or are assumed to be—trustworthy. This assumption does not make sense in a model with a sequence of markets. As was pointed out earlier, the real difference between an economy with incomplete markets and an Arrow–Debreu economy lies in the sequence of budget constraints which is assumed to accompany a sequence of markets. With a single budget constraint the two economies are essentially the same. If agents were really trustworthy, however, there would be no need for a sequence of budget constraints. That is to say, each agent could be trusted to take out of the economy, in value terms, exactly what he put in and this is the definition of a single budget constraint. The presence of a sequence of budget constraints implies that agents are not completely trustworthy and this has dramatic consequences for the theory of equilibrium.

In the next chapter, I shall consider the limiting case in which agents are completely untrustworthy, i.e. they always renege on their debts if they can get away with it. In that case, of course, bond markets simply cannot function in a two-period model. In more realistic models there would be a role for bonds either because agents were somewhat trustworthy (e.g. because they feel unhappy when they break an agreement) or because there is some means of enforcing agreements (e.g. a legal system). Both these innovations lead to transaction costs, in the one case the costs of gathering information about the trustworthiness of the individual selling the bond, in the other the costs of collecting a debt. In each case there is a motive for using money instead, for money is not a named commodity. Because money is a claim on the economy as a whole rather than on a single individual, there is no need to acquire information about the individual who offers it in exchange.[1]

This distinction, which is both clear and quite precise in the case of money and personal bonds, applies broadly to money and other assets in one way or another. In order to form an estimate of the value of any asset one needs more information than one does to form an estimate of the value of money. This rather vague generalization becomes precise in any particular context. Imagine a consumer paying for goods in a shop. A personal I.O.U. is not accepted because the shopkeeper lacks information about the consumer's creditworthiness. A cheque is accepted but only with a banker's card. Here the bank bears the cost of ensuring the consumer's creditworthiness because it makes a profit on his current account. A credit card may not be accepted because the shopkeeper does not wish to pay the commission which the credit card company demands as payment for ensuring the creditworthiness of the consumer. Share certificates, mortgages, etc., are unacceptable because, like personal I.O.U.s, they impose a tremendous information cost on the recipient. Thus one can imagine a continuum of assets, with money at the left, increasing in information costs as one moves to the right.

It may be argued, however, that while information costs are important they are not the only or most important distinction between money and other assets. I shall consider a number of arguments in turn.

(1) Indivisibility Money comes in smaller denominations than other assets, e.g. Treasury bills. This is not an independent reason for the use of money. If the information costs mentioned above did not exist there would be nothing to stop me splitting a bill and paying my tailor with a small fraction, the publican with another and so on.

(2) Liquidity It may be argued that the shopkeeper accepts money (whether in the form of cash, a cheque from someone he knows or whatever) because he knows it is acceptable to everyone else so that he can spend it in turn. To argue that money is accepted because it is acceptable (i.e. liquid) is just to push the argument back one stage. It is true that there is something of a Nash equilibrium about a monetary economy, but since this can be explained in terms of information costs there is no need to regard it as a separate, independent characteristic of money. Money is liquid because of lower or non-existent information costs (including the cost of anticipating the future price level).

(3) Transaction costs The information costs described above are certainly a kind of transaction cost but it could be argued that they are not the only ones and that money reduces transaction costs in ways not accounted for above. This is too large an objection to be dealt with briefly here so I return to it in Section 5.5 below. The conclusion is the same, however: it is information costs that lie at the bottom of any difference between money and other assets.

Even if all these objections are rejected it might still be argued that less information is required to evaluate money than other assets. In a two-period economy the fact that money is a claim on society rather than an individual does not explain why society as a whole should be regarded as trustworthy. Nor is it clear that other information costs (for example, about the future value of money) do not make money as expensive as bonds, say. Let us consider these arguments in turn.

(4) Price information In an economy with rational expectations these costs are ignored but if they do exist they should still not affect the cost of using money. In the first place, this information must be gathered anyway to make a rational consumption-decision. There is no *extra* cost imposed by using money. Second, what is in question is the distinction between money and its closest substitutes. A bond or other security denominated in money would impose exactly the same informational costs as money in this respect. The use of money involves no *extra* cost.

The argument stated in the beginning of this section and elaborated above can be summarized as follows. In a monetary economy, money is accepted in part because it is expected to be acceptable in future. But what distinguishes money most from other assets is that the potential substitutes for money impose higher information costs. Whatever other superficial differences there may be reduce themselves to differential information costs in the end. This is clearest in the case of the closest possible substitutes for money, securities denominated in money (I.O.U.s etc.). Here information costs are simply the costs of determining how likely default is. The cost of enforcement, if such is necessary, can always be shifted to the seller if there is perfect information. What cannot be shifted are information costs.

In general equilibrium, as we have seen, there is no justification for a sequence of budget constraints if agents are completely trustworthy. (There may be other justifications for a sequence of constraints in a different sort of economy, but it is only general equilibrium that is considered here.) Without a sequence of budget constraints there is no need for money or any other financial asset. The absence of trust explains both the need for a sequence of budget constraints and the difference between money and its closest substitutes. In this sense and in a theory of general equilibrium it appears to be the fundamental distinguishing characteristic of money as an asset.

In short, in general equilibrium models, the absence of trust leads to a sequence of budget constraints which leads to the use of assets. Money is the asset which imposes the least cost of gathering information and, in general equilibrium, these information costs must be chiefly the costs of determining the trustworthiness (in the broadest sense) of the issues of the asset. This disposes of the question of why other assets will not do just as well as money at least in the context of the sort of model described in Section 5.1. The second question posed at the beginning of this section is thornier. Are there not other characteristics of money which are "essential" and yet are left out of account in this account? More precisely, is there not a role for money as a *medium of exchange* as distinct from its role as a store of value? As far as general equilibrium theory is concerned—and probably other theories as well—*there is no useful distinction to be drawn between money's functions as a store of value and a medium of exchange*. Money is an asset, nothing more.

5.3 Cash constraints and incomplete markets

The view that money is a medium of exchange, as if this explained its special role in the economy, is widely accepted but rarely expressed in a form sufficiently precise to be attacked. The view is not so much wrong as contentless. I think one particularly precise and outspoken example will allow me to make the general point without discussing every manifestation of this school of thought.

In a well known paper entitled *A Reconsideration of the Microfoundations of Monetary Theory*, R. W. Clower launched an energetic attack on Patinkinesque monetary theory. In fact Clower's arguments are directed almost exclusively at the account of consumer behaviour contained in Patinkin's book. Consider a consumer whose utility is a function u of his consumption of goods $x = (x_1, \ldots, x_l)$ and his real balances (m/P), where P is some price index. The consumer has an initial endowment $e = (e_1, \ldots, e_l)$ of goods and $\bar{m}$ of money. He seeks to maximize his utility $u(x, m/P)$ within the budget set $\{(x, m) \in \mathbb{R}^l_+ \times \mathbb{R}_+ \mid p.x + m \leq p.e + \bar{m}\}$ where $p = (p_1, \ldots, p_l)$ is the prevailing vector of money-prices of goods. Clower did not attack the appearance of money in the utility function as he might well have done. Rather he directed his attention at two implications of this model of consumer behaviour. He pointed out first that there is nothing in the model to ensure that consumers hold money. (Clower was prescient in seeing that the standard assumptions about maximizing behaviour and the convexity and curvature of preferences do not impose non-trivial empirical restrictions on demand functions. It is the form of the budget constraint which does this.) Second, he noted that demand for every commodity is a function of prices and income alone. An increase in the initial endowment $\bar{m}$ of money affects demand for commodities only by affecting total wealth. Clower criticized the Patinkin theory on both counts because it fails to assign a special role to money. Apart from the appearance of the price index P in the utility function—it is real balances rather than nominal balances that count—money is treated like any other commodity. The same is true of the model described in Section 5.1. At date 0, utility can be expressed *indirectly* as a function of first-period consumption x^0, money balances m and future prices $\{p_t\}$. Clower's analysis applies to this consumer *mutatis mutandis*.

The criticism derives its force from the implicit assumption, never justified, that money should have a distinct role as a medium of exchange. Clower and other writers, before and since, have presumably taken this point to be axiomatic or intuitively obvious. What Clower offers instead of an argument is something called an *exchange relation*. Two commodities are "related" if and only if they can be exchanged one for the other. An example of an exchange relation is provided by his maxim that:

> *money buys goods and goods buy money; but goods do not buy goods.*

From this restriction which, he claims, ought to be the central theme of the theory of a monetary economy, Clower deduces an additional constraint on the consumer's choices. Let $z := (x - e)$, $z_h^+ := \max(z_h, 0)$ $(h = 1, \ldots, l)$ and $z^+ := (z_1^+, \ldots, z_l^+)$. Then the cash constraint requires that the consumer have enough cash on hand at the beginning of the period to pay for all his purchases, i.e. $p.z^+ \leq \bar{m}$. The consumer now maximizes $u(x, m/P)$ within the budget set $\{(x, m) \in \mathbb{R}^l_+ \times \mathbb{R}_+ | p.x + m \leq p.e + \bar{m},\ p.z^+ \leq \bar{m}\}$. With this change, the model of consumer behaviour will not have either of the properties Clower dislikes so much in Patinkin's account.

Clower's innovation certainly has dramatic results, not least of which is the fact that it reduces utility *caeteris paribus*. The cash constraint may be lacking in subtlety but it certainly captures the flavour of what many economists must mean when they say that money is a medium of exchange. There are many questions one might ask of this theory but one particularly relevant one is: what is really *new* here? What does this theory tell us that Patinkinesque ones cannot? Not a lot. Consider the following points. Trading takes place over some period of time. The consumer starts with an endowment $(e, \bar{m})$ and ends up with (x, m). If all trading were compressed into a single instant there would be no need for the cash constraint. Sales could be used to pay for purchases with money being held only instantaneously to bridge a virtual gap. Wicksell realized this long ago. If trading takes place over time, however, there is a role for money to bridge the gap between sales and purchases. During the trading period, the consumer visits various submarkets, in each of which there is a budget constraint. Money is traded in all submarkets but in each submarket only a subset of goods is traded. It is this incompleteness of markets which prevents all trades from taking place simultaneously. But on what assumption would the incompleteness of markets lead to Clower's cash constraint? Only if the consumer first visited submarkets in which he made purchases and then visited those in which he made his sales. There is nothing in the story so far to explain why he does not reverse the order, in which case the cash constraint disappears.

In practice, of course, there are carrying costs, transaction costs, simultaneous consumption and trading and the consumer is not free to sell his labour whenever he likes. In a complete model these factors would have to be included and then the order in which submarkets are visited would be endogenous. In fact, this is precisely the kind of story that Patinkin told to justify the appearance of money in the utility function. Clower on the other hand wants to have his bun and his ha'penny. He wants to take the Hicksian week as the elementary unit during which demand is to be explained but he also wants the structure of the budget constraints to reflect the fact that trading takes place on various days of the week. The proper way to do this would be to model trading days explicitly. In that case, the cash constraint amounts to nothing more than the fact that each day has its own budget constraint. This constraint has the usual form and money serves merely as a store of value between trading days.

What the Clower model shows, albeit inadvertently, is that there is no role for money as a medium of exchange as distinct from its role as an asset. This point is quite general. In any model of equilibrium, however elaborate, the incompleteness of markets together with a sequence of budget constraints may lead to demand for money. But money serves as an asset here, nothing more. In a complete model there would be many assets, an endogenous market structure and all sorts of costs arising from the trading process would be modelled explicitly; agents could choose which markets to visit and when; but the role of money would be essentially the same as in the simple two-period model.

None of this is intended to deny that money is a medium of exchange, of course. The argument is simply about what is meant by saying that money is a medium of exchange. In a general equilibrium model, a medium of exchange is an asset which appears in almost every budget constraint, nothing more.

5.4 Digression on flexibility

A different sort of argument suggests that money differs from other assets in allowing greater "flexibility". It is not always clear just what flexibility means. It is not just the fact that money has lower transaction costs than other assets. Agents do not want to plan too far into the future and to some extent holding money relieves them of the need to do so.

This is a rather peculiar argument. To get the flavour of its peculiarity, it may be helpful to contrast it with a more traditional argument. In their classic analyses of the demand for money, Baumol and Tobin addressed the question: why does an individual hold money when it can be let out at interest until it is needed? The answer lies in the existence of brokerage fees for the sale of bonds. When there are fixed fees it is optimal to sell bonds at discrete intervals. Since consumption expenditure takes place relatively continuously, a positive stock of money is held on average.

In this story individuals know exactly what they are going to do at each point in time, yet they plan to hold money. The fixed costs of trading bonds impose a constraint which is similar in its effects to incompleteness of markets. Adding uncertainty does not change the story fundamentally. There is nothing here that cannot be modelled using a sequence economy. Indeed the Tobin–Baumol model is an example of the sort of economy described at the end of the last section. Agents can visit the goods market or the bond market but not both simultaneously. There is a cost to visiting the bond market so they do so occasionally. The market structure, that is, the set of markets in which an agent can trade at any date, is endogenous. In a sequence economy the structure is exogenous. This is the only difference.

Flexibility involves quite different considerations. In the Tobin–Baumol model, brokerage fees are essential to explain the holding of money but if, for example, bonds were available in a continuum of maturities and there were no cost to redeeming a bond at maturity, then there would be no demand for money. An agent could plan his initial portfolio to provide exactly the stream of money receipts required to pay for his consumption plan. An agent wants flexibility if he is unwilling or unable to plan this precisely. He wants to leave his options open in some sense and money, it is argued, allows him to do this. To get any further with the argument it is necessary to be more precise about what is meant by a "desire for flexibility".

Let X be a finite set from which a choice is to be made and let $\mathscr{X}$ be the set of all non-empty subsets of X. Suppose that an individual has a complete, transitive preference-or-indifference relation $\gtrsim$ on X. The relation $\gtrsim$ induces a relation on $\mathscr{X}$ as follows. Let X' and X'' be non-empty subsets of X, i.e. they belong to $\mathscr{X}$. Then write $X' \gtrsim X''$ if and only if, for any $x'' \in X''$ there exists $x' \in X'$ such that $x' \gtrsim x''$. This relation on $\mathscr{X}$ has the following property:

$$(1) \qquad X' \gtrsim X'' \quad \text{implies} \quad X' \gtrsim X' \cup X''$$

In other words all that matters is the most preferred element in the set, not the size of the set from which a choice is made. A relation $\gtrsim$ on $\mathscr{X}$ is said to exhibit *a desire for flexibility* if $X'' \subset X'$ implies $X' \gtrsim X''$ but the property (1) does not hold in general. Clearly, this relation cannot be derived from a preference-or-indifference relation on X. Some change is required in the underlying model of consumer behaviour.

The change which suffices turns out to be quite a simple one. If $\gtrsim$ exhibits a desire for flexibility then it can be treated "as if" it were generated by uncertainty about preferences. More precisely, there is a set Ω of "states of nature" and a utility function u on $X \times \Omega$ which generates a utility function V on $\mathscr{X}$ *via* the relationship:

$$V(X') := \sum_{\omega \in \Omega} \left[\max_{x \in X'} u(x, \omega) \right].$$

V is a representation of $\succsim$ on $\mathscr{X}$. u is like a stochastic utility function; if the agent chooses x and the state of nature is ω then his utility is $u(x, \omega)$. If the agent chooses a set X' before ω is known and then chooses an element from X' after ω is known, the "expected utility" associated with the choice of X' is $V(X')$. Thus, a desire for flexibility can be mimicked by uncertainty about tastes. An agent whose preferences over sets are given by V is just like an agent who acts so as to maximize his "expected utility"

$$Eu = \sum_{\omega} u(x, \omega).$$

Uncertainty about tastes can certainly be incorporated in models of sequence economies.

It appears that a desire for flexibility is not a separate explanation of the demand for money. Uncertain tastes, together with brokerage fees, can make the demand for money more robust, however. When tastes are uncertain one cannot, or rather does not wish to, plan as precisely as one does in the Tobin–Baumol model. This will mean that some brokerage fees are pretty well unavoidable unless money is held so the Tobin–Baumol argument is strengthened by uncertainty. In a complete model of a sequence of markets, the choice of which market to visit and the costs of trading in any particular market would be modelled explicitly. As was argued in the last section this does not represent a departure from the outline given in Section 5.1. It is merely an elaboration of it.

5.5 Transaction costs revisited

Transaction costs are broadly defined as the costs of transferring ownership of goods or assets from one individual to another. It has been argued that one of the essential features of money is that its use in exchange reduces these costs. In one sense, this is true. The use of money allows the development of institutions whose function is, among other things, to reduce transaction costs. The function of money in this case is the same as in general equilibrium models without transaction costs, however. Money serves as an asset which allows agents to consolidate the sequence of budget constraints which they face as they go from market to market. This role of money is extremely important and corresponds broadly to what economists typically consider the medium of exchange function of money. But it is a mistake to think that the service performed by money as a "medium of exchange" is any different from its asset role in general equilibrium models without transaction costs.

Every advanced economy depends on the use of money in exchange. The only non-monetary economies which exist are very primitive indeed. The great productivity of economies which are commercially and technologically advanced depends crucially on specialization and the division of labour. In turn, specialization depends on trade and trade is greatly facilitated by the use of money. This is because agents must trade in markets where only a subset of commodities is accepted in exchange. Each market has its own budget constraint and this restricts the pattern of trades which can be carried out. Money is accepted in almost every market whereas other assets are not. The use of money allows agents to avoid lengthy and costly intermediate exchanges. A man with money can simply go out and buy what he wants. There is no problem of the double coincidence of wants here but it is important to see that the problem of the double coincidence of wants presents itself as a sequence of budget constraints. Money's usefulness in an economy with segregated markets and transaction costs consists of helping to relax these constraints.

The same point can be made even more forcefully in connection with the many institutions which have grown up to facilitate exchange. There is a vast network of firms and individuals in the business of distributing goods: brokers, wholesalers, retailers, shippers and, less directly, advertisers, insurers and bankers. The costs of distributing goods *per se* should not be included in transaction costs. For example, shipping goods from one place to another is a production process (remember that goods are distinguished by their location) and the cost of shipping goods is just another cost of production. Similarly, the cost of storing, packaging and insuring goods is just part of the cost of producing the finished product, namely, the commodity which appears in the shop window. Nonetheless, the activity of the distributive trades as a whole does tend to reduce transaction costs. For example, if I want groceries, I go to a grocer. The mere fact that he specializes in a particular range of goods and has them available provides useful information. It reduces the cost of making the transaction by eliminating the need to search. Clearly, money is essential to the grocer's business and to this extent money can be said to reduce transaction costs. But money does this by serving as an asset. To explain why money helps to reduce transaction costs in this case, it is necessary and sufficient to explain why there should be a budget constraint at the grocer's and why money enters the budget constraint. In other words, why the value of net trades at the grocer's should be zero and why money is accepted in exchange.

These are the very questions that must be answered about any sequence economy with money. The explicit introduction of transaction costs does not seem to involve anything new as far as money is concerned.

This is not to say that there are no advantages specifically connected with the use of money in exchange. There are computational advantages. Even where individuals trust one another, so that I.O.U.s are acceptable, the use of money relieves the parties to a transaction of the need to remember who owes whom what. The use of money as a numeraire has similar advantages since money is one of the goods traded in any market. These advantages seem small, however, beside money's central role as an asset.

There is now a vast literature on transaction costs, much of it dealing with money. This theory is largely concerned with the determination of which markets will be operative and which will not. A sequence of budget constraints is taken for granted. The need for an asset then depends on the incompleteness of markets at the first date. This has led many writers to the conclusion that by explaining the incompleteness of markets they were explaining the demand for money, whereas the real explanation lay somewhere else again, namely with the sequence of budget constraints. To the extent that the set of operative markets was made endogenous the introduction of transaction costs was a step towards realism. But the story is essentially the same as one in which the market structure is simply given (i.e. markets are either free or infinitely expensive). Moreover, there are a number of difficulties about the way in which transaction costs are modelled.

In the first place, transaction costs are modelled as if they were production or distribution costs. In order to exchange a certain bundle of goods another bundle of resources must be used up. The set of feasible pairs of bundles defines a transactions technology, by analogy with the production set of the traditional Arrow–Debreu model. How this technology is determined is not explained and in particular it is not explained why the transaction costs associated with a particular transaction should be treated as a technological datum. If transaction costs are almost exclusively information costs, as I have argued, then the amount of information gathered should be a matter of choice not technique.

Furthermore, it would seem inappropriate to retain the usual definition of market-clearing. If the information costs are generated by differences between individuals (e.g. their trustworthiness) then two different individuals selling the "same" commodity should do so on different markets. But this change would destroy the general equilibrium flavour of the model, replacing it with something closer to pairwise exchange. It would no longer be sufficient to have a simple transaction technology. A theory of search would be required as well.

While these doubts about the representation of transaction costs remain, it does not seem worth the effort of including them explicitly in order to add a touch of realism. The alternative adopted in Section 5.1 of treating the market structure as exogenous is brutally simple but it allows a consistent story to be told. In Chapter 6 it will be seen that even with a complete set of markets the absence of trust generates a sequential structure and hence a demand for money, in the economy. This is an extreme case in which only assets with terminal demands are used and no forward markets are used. It is the limiting case of complete absence of trust. Nonetheless it is possible to see in this limiting case the more complex story which could be told in a complete model, where competing assets could, at some cost, be substituted for money. Money would then be just one end of a spectrum of assets but its function would not have changed.

Notes

1. This does not explain why some government debt is not money, however. The reason why Treasury bills are not money, for example, has something to do with indivisibilities, price uncertainty, etc.

CHAPTER 5—PART 2

Sequences of budget constraints

5.6 The classical theorems of welfare economics

Although it may seem an odd place to start, the Arrow–Debreu economy provides an extremely useful benchmark for the analysis of economies with incomplete markets. The Arrow–Debreu model is the home of efficiency. By contrasting other types of economies with it, we can see why they are less successful in achieving allocative efficiency. This insight paves the way for the study of money in general equilibrium and its effect on welfare.

The Arrow–Debreu model assumes the existence of a finite number l of *commodities*. Commodities are defined in a very special way. They are distinguished not only by physical characteristics but also by the date and location at which they are to be delivered. If there is uncertainty, *contingent commodities* are introduced. These are contracts which promise the delivery of a good if and only if a particular event occurs. Thus, wheat for immediate delivery is a different commodity from wheat to be delivered in six months' time and an insurance policy which promises a certain sum of money in the event of death is obviously different from one which promises the same sum if the house burns down. When agents trade in commodities they must specify not only the physical good but when and where it is to be delivered and the event (if any) on which its delivery is contingent. The theory assumes that there exist markets for all these commodities, that is, they can all be traded at a single date. In the jargon of the theory, there is a *complete* set of markets at the first trading date. This horrendous assumption, which accounts for the efficiency properties of the Arrow–Debreu model as well as much of its elegance, is clearly not satisfied by actual economies. The incompleteness of markets turns out to be an important cause of inefficiency in more realistic models. For the purpose of this discussion it will be sufficient to consider a pure exchange economy. Producers could be added without changing the efficiency-story in any of its essential points.

The economy is assumed to consist of a finite number of consumers $i = 1, \ldots, n$. A consumer is represented by an ordered triple $(X, \prec, e)$ called his *characteristic*. X is his *consumption set*, that is, the set of consumption bundles which are physically sustainable for him. X is a subset of the commodity space $\mathbb{R}^l$. $\prec$ is a binary relation on X called a *preference relation*. Formally, it is a subset of $X \times X$ and $(x, x') \in \prec$ means x' is preferred to x (usually written $x' \succ x$). The relation $\prec$ is *transitive* if $(x, x') \in \prec$ and $(x', x'') \in \prec$ imply that $(x, x'') \in \prec$. e is a vector in X called the *endowment* of the agent. It is a bundle of commodities representing his initial resources. An economy can be described by an n-tuple of characteristics, one for each consumer. This motivates the following definition.

5.6.1 Definition *An exchange economy* $\mathscr{E}$ *is an n-tuple of characteristics* $\{(X_1, \prec_1, e_1), \ldots, (X_n, \prec_n, e_n)\}$ *such that for* $i = 1, \ldots, n$:

(i) $e_i \in X_i \subset \mathbb{R}^l$
(ii) $\prec_i \subset X_i \times X_i$ *is a transitive, binary relation.*

Let $\mathscr{E}$ be an exchange economy. An *allocation* for $\mathscr{E}$ is an n-tuple $x = (x_1, \ldots, x_n)$ such that $x_i \in X_i$, for each $i = 1, \ldots, n$. An allocation x is *attainable* for $\mathscr{E}$ if $\sum_i x_i = \sum_i e_i$. Let x and x' be allocations for $\mathscr{E}$; x' *strongly Pareto-dominates* x (is Pareto-superior to x, is Pareto-preferred to x) if x' is attainable and $x'_i \succ_i x_i$ for $i = 1, \ldots, n$. An allocation x is said to be *weakly Pareto-efficient* if it is not strongly Pareto-dominated by any allocation.

A *price system* for $\mathscr{E}$ is a non-zero vector $p = (p_1, \ldots, p_l)$ in $\mathbb{R}^l$ with the interpretation that p_h is the price of commodity h. A *Walrasian equilibrium* for $\mathscr{E}$ is an ordered pair (x, p), where x is an attainable allocation and p a price system, such that for $i = 1, \ldots, n$, x_i is maximal for $\prec_i$ in the budget set $\{x'_i \in X_i \mid p.x'_i \leq p.e_i\}$. (To say that "$x_i$ is maximal for $\prec_i$" means there is no x'_i in the budget set such that $x'_i \succ_i x_i$). An allocation x is a *Walras allocation* if there is a p such that (x, p) is a Walrasian equilibrium.

5.6.2 Proposition *If* $\mathscr{E}$ *is an exchange economy and x is a Walras allocation for* $\mathscr{E}$ *then x is weakly Pareto-efficient.*

Proof Suppose that x is strongly Pareto-dominated by x'. Then for $i = 1, \ldots, n$, $x'_i \succ_i x_i$ so $p.x'_i > p.e_i$. But $\sum_i x'_i = \sum_i e_i$ so

$$0 < \sum_i (p.x'_i - p.e_i) = p.\sum_i (x'_i - e_i) = 0$$

a contradiction. □

If an allocation x is weakly Pareto-efficient then it is not possible to make everyone better off. But it may be possible to make some agents better off without, in some as yet unspecified sense, making any agent worse off. Define a binary relation $\succsim_i$ on X by the condition that $(x_i, x_i') \in \succsim_i$ if and only if $x_i, x_i' \in X_i$ and $(x_i, x_i') \notin \prec_i$ for $i = 1, \ldots, n$. Let x and x' be allocations for $\mathscr{E}$. x' *weakly Pareto-dominates* x if x' is attainable, $x_i' \succsim x_i$ for every $i = 1, \ldots, n$ and $x_i' \succ_i x_i$ for some $i = 1, \ldots, n$. An allocation x is *strongly Pareto-efficient* if it is not weakly Pareto-dominated by any allocation.

A preference relation $\prec_i$ is said to be *negatively transitive* if $(x', x'') \in \prec_i$ and $(x', x) \in \succsim_i$ imply $(x, x'') \in \prec_i$.[1] The relation $\prec_i$ is *locally non-satiable* if, for any $x \in X$, there exists $x' \in X$ arbitrarily close to x (in the usual sense) such that $(x, x') \in \prec_i$.

5.6.3 Theorem *Let $\mathscr{E}$ be an exchange economy such that $\prec_i$ is negatively transitive and locally non-satiable for $i = 1, \ldots, n$. Then every Walras allocation for $\mathscr{E}$ is strongly Pareto-efficient.*

Proof Suppose that x is a Walras allocation and x' weakly Pareto-dominates it. If $x_i' \succ_i x_i$ then $p.x_i' > p.e_i$. If $x_i' \succsim_i x_i$ and $p.x_i' < p.e_i$ then by local non-satiability there is $x_i'' \succ_i x_i'$ such that $p.x_i'' \leq p.e_i$. By negative transitivity, $x_i'' \succ_i x_i$, a contradiction of the hypothesis that x is a Walras allocation. Thus, $p.x_i' \geq p.e_i$ for every $i = 1, \ldots, n$ and $p.x_i' > p.e_i$ for some $i = 1, \ldots, n$. But $\sum_i x_i' = \sum_i e_i$ implies

$$0 < \sum_i p.(x_i' - e_i) = p.\sum_i (x_i' - e_i) = 0.$$

a contradiction. □

These results show that under very weak conditions the Walrasian equilibrium is efficient; in fact, weak Pareto-efficiency follows almost by definition. To prove some sort of converse requires stronger conditions, however. Specifically, a preference relation $\prec_i$ is said to be *convex* if, for every x_i in X_i, the set $\{x_i' \mid (x_i, x_i') \in \prec_i\}$ is convex. With this assumption and a "connectedness" assumption, it is possible to show that every efficient allocation is competitive in a certain sense. It is convenient to break the proof into two parts, showing first that an efficient allocation is a "pseudo-equilibrium" and then considering conditions under which a "pseudo-equilibrium" is competitive. A *pseudo-equilibrium* is an ordered pair (x, p), where x is an attainable allocation for $\mathscr{E}$ and p a price system, such that for $i = 1, \ldots, n$, $(x_i, x_i') \in \prec_i$ implies $p.x_i' \geq p.x_i$.

5.6.4 Theorem *Let $\mathscr{E}$ be an exchange economy such that $\prec_i$ is convex and locally non-satiable for $i = 1, \ldots, n$. If x is a weakly Pareto-efficient allocation for $\mathscr{E}$ then for some p, (x, p) is a pseudo-equilibrium.*

The proof requires the following well-known lemma (Supporting Hyperplane Theorem):

> *if C is a convex subset of $\mathbb{R}^l$ and x a vector in $\mathbb{R}^l$ such that $x \notin C$, then there exists a vector $p \neq 0$ in $\mathbb{R}^l$ such that $p.x \leq p.z$ for any $z \in C$.*

Proof of 5.6.4 Let x be a weakly Pareto-efficient allocation for $\mathscr{E}$ and, for every $i = 1, \ldots, n$, define

$$Z_i := \{z \in \mathbb{R}^l \mid (x_i, x_i + z) \in \prec_i\}$$

and put $Z := \sum_i Z_i$. It is easy to see that every Z_i is convex and therefore Z is convex. Also, $0 \notin Z$ because x is not weakly dominated by any allocation. Hence, there is a price system $p \neq 0$ such that for any $z \in Z$, $p.z \geq p.0 = 0$. I now claim that $(x_i, x_i') \in \prec_i$ implies $p.x_i' \geq p.x_i$ for any i. If not, there is some $i = 1, \ldots, n$ and $(x_i, x_i') \in \prec_i$ such that $p.x_i' \leq p.x_i - \varepsilon$ for some $\varepsilon > 0$. For $j \neq i$, choose $(x_j, x_j') \in \prec_j$ so that $p.x_i' \leq p.x_i + \varepsilon/M$, where $M > 0$ is a large number. This is always possible by local non-satiability. Then putting $z_j := x_j' - x_j$, for $j = 1, \ldots, n$, and $z := \sum_j z_j$ it is clear that $z \in Z$ and, for M sufficiently large, $p.z < 0$. This contradiction establishes the theorem. □

An *income distribution* is an n-tuple $w = (w_1, \ldots, w_n)$ of real numbers; w_i is interpreted as agent i's wealth or income expressed in units of account. An allocation x is said to be *competitive at the price system p and income distribution w* if x is attainable and, for $i = 1, \ldots, n$, x_i is maximal for $\prec_i$ in the budget set $\{x_i' \in X_i \mid p.x_i' \leq w_i\}$. A preference relation $\prec_i$ is called *continuous* if $\prec_i$ is an open subset of $X \times X$.

5.6.5 Theorem *Let $\mathscr{E}$* be an exchange economy and assume *$\prec_i$ is continuous and X_i is convex for $i = 1, \ldots, n$. Let (x, p) be a pseudo-equilibrium such that*

$$p.x_i > \inf p.X_i \qquad (i = 1, \ldots, n).$$

Then for some w, x is competitive at p and w.

Proof Set $w_i := p.x_i$ for $i = 1, \ldots, n$. It remains to prove that x_i is maximal for $\prec_i$ in the budget set $\{x_i' \in X_i \mid p.x_i' \leq w_i\}$. Suppose not. Then there exists $x_i' \succ_i x_i$ and $p.x_i' \leq p.x_i = w_i$. By hypothesis there exists $\bar{x}_i \in X_i$ such that $p.\bar{x}_i < p.x_i$. Let $x_i^t = tx_i' + (1-t)\bar{x}_i$. By convexity, $x_i^t \in X_i$ for $0 \leq t \leq 1$ and by construction, $p.x_i^t < p.x_i$ for $0 < t < 1$. By continuity, $(x_i, x_i^t) \in \prec_i$ for t close to 1, contradicting the definition of a pseudo-equilibrium. □

In order to show that $p.x_i > \inf p.X_i$ for $i = 1, \ldots, n$, a connectedness assumption is needed.[2] Two agents i and j are said to be *resource related* at some given allocation x if there is a vector z such that $(x_i, x_i + z) \in \prec_i$ and $(x_j - z) \in X_j$. Two agents i and j are said to be *indirectly resource related* at x if there exists a finite sequence $\{i_k : k = 1, \ldots, K\}$, satisfying $i_1 = i$, $i_K = j$, such that i_k and i_{k+1} are resource related for all $k = 1, \ldots, K-1$.

5.6.6 Theorem *Let $\mathscr{E}$ be an exchange economy such that $\sum_i e_i$ belongs to the interior of $\sum_i X_i$. If (x, p) is a pseudo-equilibrium and i and j are indirectly resource related at x for every $i, j = 1, \ldots, n$ and $i \neq j$, then*

$$p.x_i > \inf p.X_i \qquad (i = 1, \ldots, n).$$

Proof There must be some i such that $p.x_i > \inf p.X_i$. Otherwise it would be true that $p.\sum_i e_i = p.\sum_i x_i = \inf p.\sum_i X_i$ which contradicts $p \neq 0$ and $\sum_i e_i \in \operatorname{Int} \sum_i X_i$. Let I be the set of agents for whom $p.x_i > \inf p.X_i$ and suppose $I \neq \{1, \ldots, n\}$. Since I is non-empty and all agents are indirectly resource related there must be an $i \in I$ and $j \notin I$ such that i and j are resource related. There exists a vector z such that $(x_i, x_i + z) \in \prec_i$ and $(x_j - z) \in X_j$. Since $i \in I$, $p.(x_i + z) > p.x_i$, that is, $p.z > 0$. Then $p.x_j > p.(x_j - z) \geq \inf p.X_j$, contradicting $j \notin I$. Thus $I = \{1, \ldots, n\}$. □

5.6.7 Remarks It is worth noting how weak the assumptions needed for the various results are. Proposition 5.6.2 needs nothing beyond the definitions, not even the transitivity of $\prec_i$ which is included in Definition 5.6.1. Theorem 5.6.3 needs slightly more to ensure strong instead of weak Pareto-efficiency. Going the other way, the results all apply to weakly (and hence strongly) Pareto-efficient allocations. It is interesting that Theorem 5.6.4, which shows that weakly Pareto-efficient allocations can be supported as pseudo-equilibria, requires convexity of preferences but otherwise its assumptions are as weak as Theorem 5.6.3. The really strong assumptions (and lots of them) are required to show that a pseudo-equilibrium is actually competitive (Theorems 5.6.5 and 6). This suggests that a more elegant way to proceed would be to investigate the correspondence between pseudo-equilibria and efficient allocations first, leaving the relationships between pseudo-equilibria and Walrasian equilibria (or, more generally, the competitive allocations) on one side for later study. I have chosen to put the efficiency of the Walrasian equilibrium (as exemplified by Proposition 5.6.2 and Theorem 5.6.3) first because it is this fact that is of central importance for what comes later.

In proving these results, the budget constraints play a crucial role. This is a theme which runs through every discussion of efficiency in sequence economies.

5.7 Economies with incomplete markets

In the Arrow–Debreu model all commodities can be traded at a single date. In the definition of the Walrasian equilibrium it is implicitly assumed that all trades are arranged at this first date. From then on the course of the economy is completely determined. In reality, of course, nothing like this happens. At any particular date agents can trade in only a few of the vast number of commodities defined by the Arrow–Debreu model. Most traded commodities are available for immediate delivery. There is a restricted set of markets on which forward trades are arranged (tin, cocoa, foreign currency, etc.). Some insurance contracts are available, promising cash payments if the event specified in the contract should occur. But there is nothing like the complete set of markets envisaged by Arrow–Debreu. By itself this fact does not constitute a criticism of the Arrow–Debreu model because, as pointed out above, the model's usefulness derives from its role as a benchmark.

The first task is to describe the market structure of the economy, that is, to specify the markets available at each date and in each event. The framework introduced now is based on Radner's model of equilibrium in a sequence of markets. In the Arrow–Debreu model the dimensions of time, space and uncertainty are hidden in the definition of commodities. Here they must be made explicit in the description of the economy. There is assumed to be a finite number T of *dates* indexed by $t = 1, \ldots, T$ and a finite set S of *states of nature*. The dates represent elementary time intervals in which trading takes place. A state of nature is a complete description of the environment of the economy throughout its whole history, from date 1 to date T. The environment can be thought of as all those exogenous variables which determine the needs, tastes and resources of the agents. At any date t, however, agents will not know the true state of nature. In particular, they do not know the future values of the exogenous variables. Their knowledge at t is represented by a partition $\mathscr{F}_t$ of the set S. At t the agents "observe" one of the sets in $\mathscr{F}_t$; then they know that the true state belongs to that set but they cannot discriminate among the states in the set. A *date-event pair* is any ordered pair (t, F) where $t = 1, \ldots, T$ and F belongs to $\mathscr{F}_t$. The sequence $\{\mathscr{F}_t : t = 1, \ldots, T\}$ of partitions is non-decreasing in fineness, i.e. if F is in $\mathscr{F}_t$ and F' in $\mathscr{F}_{t+1}$ then either $F \cap F' = \phi$ or $F' \subset F$. This simply means that agents do not lose information as time passes. If the partitions are non-decreasing in fineness there is a natural partial ordering on the set of date-event pairs. A date-event pair (t, F) has a unique *predecessor* $(t - 1, F')$, defined by the condition $F \subset F'$, if $t > 1$. The pair (t, F) has a set of *successors*, that is, pairs of the form $(t + 1, F')$ such that $F' \subset F$, if $t < T$. Write $(t, F) < (t + 1, F')$ if (t, F) is the predecessor of $(t + 1, F')$. $<$ can be extended easily: write $(t, F) < (t', F')$ if there is a finite sequence $\{(t + k, F^{(k)}) : k = 0, \ldots, t' - t\}$ such that $F^{(0)} = F$, $F^{(t'-t)} = F'$ and for every $k = 0, \ldots, t' - t - 1$, $(t + k, F^{(k)}) < (t + k + 1, F^{(k+1)})$ in the sense defined above. Then $<$ is a transitive, irreflexive binary relation on the set of date-event pairs. It defines in a precise way the sequential structure of the economy.

A concrete example will make these abstract notions somewhat clearer. Suppose that the only exogenous factor to affect the economy is the weather. The weather at date t is a random variable W_t which takes on one of two values: *Rain* or *Shine*. A complete history of the environment must specify the weather at each date. More precisely, it is a T-tuple $W = (W_1, \ldots, W_T)$ where each W_t says either *Rain* or *Shine*. The set of states of nature is the set of all possible T-tuples like W. Formally, $S := \{Rain, Shine\}^T$, the T-fold Cartesian production of $\{Rain, Shine\}$. At date t, agents know the history of the weather up to and including that date. Let $(\bar{W}_1, \ldots, \bar{W}_t)$ be the partial history of the weather. Then the event observed at t is $\{W \in S \mid W_\tau = \bar{W}_\tau \text{ for } \tau = 1, \ldots, t\}$, i.e. the set of states having the observed partial history. The partition $\mathscr{F}_t$ consists of those subsets of S which have the form $\{W \in S \mid W_\tau = \bar{W}_\tau \text{ for } \tau = 1, \ldots, t\}$ for *some* partial history $(\bar{W}_1, \ldots, \bar{W}_t)$ in $\{Rain, Shine\}^t$. In this very simple example it is possible to identify the subsets belonging to $\mathscr{F}_t$ with the partial histories $(W_1, \ldots, W_t)$. A date-event pair is then a $(t + 1)$-tuple $(t, W_1, \ldots, W_t)$. Also, $(t, W_1, \ldots, W_t) < (t', W'_1, \ldots, W'_{t'})$ if and only if $t < t'$ and $W_\tau = W'_\tau$ for $\tau = 1, \ldots, t$. In other words, one date-event pair precedes another if the partial history of the first agrees with the second over the relevant period.

Returning to the general framework, let U denote the set of date-event pairs with generic elements u and v. Write $u \leq v$ if $u < v$ or u

$= v$, where $<$ is the partial ordering defined above. At each u in U there is a finite number l_u of commodities available for delivery. Let $l := \sum_{u \in U} l_u$ be the total number of commodities. The set of markets which open at some point in the history of the economy is described by a set M of ordered triples of the form (u, v, h) where $u \leq v$ and $h = 1, \ldots, l_v$. If (u, v, h) belongs to M then at the date-event pair u in U it is possible to arrange trades in good h for delivery at the date-event pair v in U. An *admissible trade plan* is an array (z^h_{uv}) of numbers, one for each (u, v, h) in M. The set of all admissible trade plans is called the *trade set* and is denoted by Z. At the first date agents now choose a trade plan z in Z which specifies the amount of each tradeable commodity they wish to trade at each date-event pair. The resulting final consumption is a vector x defined by the condition:

$$x^h_v = e^h_v + \sum_{\{u:(u,v,h) \in M\}} z^h_{uv}$$

for every v in U and $h = 1, \ldots, l_v$. The interpretation is fairly clear: x^h_v and e^h_v are respectively the quantity consumed and initial endowment of good h at the date-event pair v and z^h_{uv} is the quantity of this commodity traded at u, where (u, v, h) belongs to M.

It is probably worth summarizing this formalism. To begin with, there is a finite number of dates and a finite set of states. Then there is a sequence $\{\mathcal{F}_t\}$ of information structures (partitions of S) which are non-decreasing in fineness and represent the information available at each date. From these concepts it is possible to derive the set of date-event pairs and order them in a natural way. To specify the set of available markets it only remains to list the goods which can be delivered at each date-event pair and then to specify which commodities can be traded at each date-event pair. Given the set M of available markets, a trade plan for an agent is a specification of how much he intends to trade in each market (u, v, h) in M.

Now, this formalism has developed quite naturally and is easy to interpret; but it has several disadvantages, not least of which is its complexity. Besides being rather cumbersome, much of the detail is unnecessary. A much simpler and more general framework is outlined below. The motivation for this framework comes from the concepts introduced above but it is logically quite independent. Unless explicitly stated, the notation and concepts introduced above are not used in the sequel.

There is a finite number l of *commodities*, indexed by $h = 1, \ldots, l$. The *commodity space* is $\mathbb{R}^l$. There is a finite set D of date-event pairs or *events* for short. The *market structure* is a family $\{Z^d : d \in D\}$ of linear subspaces Z^d of $\mathbb{R}^l$. Z^d represents the markets available at the event d. There is a partial ordering $<$ on D which has the following properties:

(1) $<$ is transitive and irreflexive;
(2) there is a unique *initial element*, denoted 0, such that $d \leq 0$ implies $d = 0$;
(3) for any $0 < d$, there is a unique *predecessor* d' defined by the conditions $d' < d$ and $d'' < d$ implies $d'' \leq d'$.

A *trade plan* is a function z from the set D of date-event pairs to the commodity space $\mathbb{R}^l$. A trade plan z is *admissible* if, for every d in D, $z(d) \in Z^d$. The set of admissible trade plans is called the *trade set* and is denoted by Z. It is assumed that

$$\mathbb{R}^l \subset \sum_{d \in D} Z^d.$$

That is, every commodity is traded at *some* date-event pair. The market structure defined above includes Radner's framework but it is much more general. In particular, it admits markets on which *bundles* of commodities (sometimes called "securities") must be traded.

Now consider an exchange economy $\mathscr{E} = \{(X_i, \prec_i, e_i) : i = 1, \ldots, n\}$ of the sort defined in Section 5.6. By specifying a partially ordered set $(D, <)$ and a family $\{Z^d\}$, an economy with a sequence of markets can be defined using the basic structure $\mathscr{E}$. The next problem is to find a concept of equilibrium for this economy. Suppose that (x, p) is a Walrasian equilibrium for $\mathscr{E}$. From the assumption that $\mathbb{R}^l \subset \sum_d Z^d$ it follows that for any excess demand $(x_i - e_i)$ there exists an admissible trade plan z_i such that $\sum_d z_i(d) = (x_i - e_i)$. This suggests a definition of equilibrium for an economy with a sequence of markets. A *trade plan allocation* is an n-tuple $z = (z_1, \ldots, z_n)$ such that, for every $i = 1, \ldots, n$, $z_i \in Z$ and $(e_i + \sum z_i(d)) \in X_i$. A trade plan allocation is *attainable* if $\sum_i z_i = 0$ (i.e. every *market* clears). A Walrasian sequence equilibrium for an economy with a sequence of markets is an ordered pair (z, p), where z is an attainable trade plan allocation and p a price system (in $\mathbb{R}^l$), such that, for $i = 1, \ldots, n$, $x_i \equiv e_i + (\sum_d z_i(d))$ is maximial in the budget set $\{x'_i \in X_i \mid p . x'_i \leq p . e_i\}$. If (z, p) is a Walrasian sequence equilibrium, there is a corresponding Walrasian equilibrium (x, p) for $\mathscr{E}$ and the final consumption of agent i is x_i in both. Thus, the equilibrium defined above has the same efficiency properties as a Walrasian equilibrium for $\mathscr{E}$.

This definition of equilibrium is not of much interest in its own right. This is partly because it is essentially the same as the concept of Walrasian equilibrium for $\mathscr{E}$ and hence adds nothing to our repertoire of equilibrium theories. It is also intrinsically uninteresting because there is no reason to suppose (a) that agents face a single budget constraint covering the whole sequence of markets and (b) that a single system p, known from the beginning, rules throughout the whole sequence of markets. But the idea of a Walrasian sequence equilibrium for an economy with a sequence of markets contains an important lesson. Incomplete markets do not by themselves lead to inefficiency. If there is a single budget constraint and (consequently) a single price system which clears markets throughout the sequence, the resulting equilibrium will be Pareto-efficient under very weak conditions.

The hallmark of equilibrium in an economy with sequence of markets is a sequence of budget constraints. But the notion of a Walrasian sequence equilibrium (with a single budget constraint) for a sequence of markets is not entirely irrelevant. It turns out to be a useful criterion of efficiency in economies with a sequence of markets.

5.8 Concepts of equilibrium in a sequence of markets

Let $\mathscr{E}$ be an exchange economy in the sense of Definition 5.6.1. When nothing more is said, $\mathscr{E}$ is understood to have a complete set of markets at the first date. In that case it is also natural to assume that there is a single budget constraint. To define an economy with a sequence of markets it is necessary to add a set of date-event pairs $(D, <)$ and a market structure $\{Z^d : d \in D\}$. A partially ordered set $(D, <)$ will be called a *tree* if $<$ satisfies conditions (1)–(3) listed in Section 5.7, i.e. $<$ is transitive and irreflexive, there is a unique initial element of D and every d in D, other than the initial element, has a unique predecessor.

Consider the following example. There are two dates $t = 0, 1$ and two states of nature $s = 1, 2$. At date 0, individuals have no information so $\mathscr{F}_0 = \{S\}$ and at date 1, the true state is revealed so $\mathscr{F}_1 = \{\{1\}, \{2\}\}$. There are three date-event pairs in Radner's sense, namely, $(0, \{1, 2\})$, $(1, \{1\})$ and $(1, \{2\})$. Let

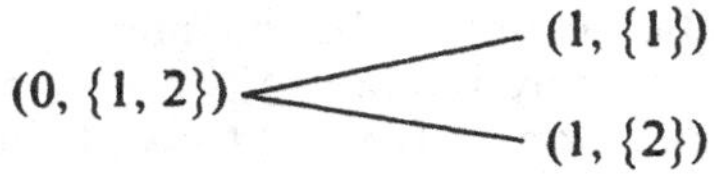

Figure 5.8.1

these events be denoted by d_0, d_1 and d_2 respectively. The tree $(D, <)$ is in this case defined by putting

(i) $D = \{d_0, d_1, d_2\}$
(ii) $d_0 < d_1$ and $d_0 < d_2$.

Suppose there are two goods available for delivery at each date in each event. Then $l = 6$. The commodities will be indexed as follows: $h = 1, 2$ are delivered at d_0, $h = 3, 4$ are delivered at d_1 and $h = 5, 6$ are delivered at d_1. At the second date, when the true state of nature is known, agents will only want to exchange goods for delivery at that date and in that event, i.e. commodities 3 and 4 if $s = 1$ and commodities 5 and 6 if $s = 2$. Then

$$Z^{d_1} = \{z \in \mathbb{R}^6 \mid z = (0, 0, z_3, z_4, 0, 0)\}$$

$$Z^{d_2} = \{z \in \mathbb{R}^6 | z = (0, 0, 0, 0, z_5, z_6)\}.$$

Now consider the event d_0. There must be spot markets for goods 1 and 2 since this is the only time they can be traded. There may also be forward markets, however. Suppose that agents can trade both goods for future delivery *independently of the state of nature*. That is, if they buy one unit of a good for delivery at date 1, they get the one unit regardless of the state which is observed. This assumption is expressed by saying that agents can only trade in bundles which contain the same amounts of goods 3 and 5 and 4 and 6 respectively. More precisely,

$$Z^{d_0} = \{z \in \mathbb{R}^6 | z = (z_1, z_2, z_3, z_4, z_5, z_6), z_3 = z_5 \text{ and } z_4 = z_6\}.$$

5.8.1 Definition *An economy with a sequence of markets is defined by an exchange economy $\mathscr{E}$, a tree $(D, <)$ and a family $\{Z^d : d \in D\}$ of linear subspaces of $\mathbb{R}^l$ such that $\sum_{d \in D} Z^d = \mathbb{R}^l$.*

It will be convenient to denote an economy with a sequence of markets by $\mathscr{E}$ alone when the set of date-event pairs $(D, <)$ and the market structure $\{Z^d : d \in D\}$ are understood and there is no risk of confusion. As in Section 5.7, Z denotes the set of admissible trade plans. A trade plan allocation for $\mathscr{E}$ is defined to be an n-tuple $z = (z_1, \ldots, z_n)$ such that, for $i = 1, \ldots, n$, $z_i \in Z$ and $(\sum_{d \in D} z_i(d) + e_i) \in X_i$. A trade plan allocation z is attainable for $\mathscr{E}$ if $\sum_{i=1}^n z_i = 0$. Note that this is stronger than the corresponding attainability condition for a static economy. In the present notation, attainability for a static economy requires $\sum_{i=1}^n \sum_{d \in D} z_i(d) = 0$. A *price sequence* for $\mathscr{E}$ is a function p^* from D to $\mathbb{R}^l$; for every d in D, the vector $p^*(d)$ in $\mathbb{R}^l$ represents the price system ruling at d.

To return to the example, an admissible trade plan specifies, for each of the date-event pairs d_0, d_1 and d_2, a vector of net trades in $\mathbb{R}^6$. These vectors must be contained in the corresponding subspace, e.g. $z_i(d_1) = (0, 0, z_{i3}(d_1), z_{i4}(d_1), 0, 0)$ and so on. The amount of a commodity an agent finally consumes is simply the sum of his initial endowment and the net trades in that commodity which are arranged at each date-event pair. For example, consumption of commodity 3 is equal to $e_{i3} + z_{i3}(d_0) + z_{i3}(d_1)$ since there is no trade in commodity 3 at d_2. An allocation is simply a description of each agent i's trade plan z_i and it is attainable if every agent's final consumption bundle belongs to the consumption set and the sum of excess demands is zero, *at each date-event pair*. If each agent's consumption set is $\mathbb{R}^6_+$, for example, attainability requires $e_{i3} + z_{i3}(d_0) + z_{i3}(d_1) \geq 0$ and $\sum_{i=1}^{n} z_{i3}(d_0) = \sum_{i=1}^{n} z_{i3}(d_1) = 0$.

5.8.2 Definition *An equilibrium of plans, prices and price expectations for an economy $\mathscr{E}$ with a sequence of markets is an ordered pair (z, p^*), where z is an attainable trade plan allocation and p^* a price sequence such that for $i = 1, \ldots, n$, z_i is maximal for $\prec_i$ in the set of trade plans z_i' satisfying:*

(i) $z_i' \in Z$;
(ii) $(\sum_{d \in D} z_i'(d) + e_i) \in X_i$;
(iii) $p^* \otimes z_i' \leq 0$.

The reference to expectations requires some explanation. Strictly speaking, this equilibrium describes only the *plans* that agents make at the first date. These plans are optimal with respect to their preferences at the first date. If preferences were to change between the first date and the second, say, agents might wish to revise their plans. The result would be a different equilibrium allocation. Thus, the definition describes an allocation of plans which are expected to be in equilibrium but may not be. Likewise with prices. In the example described above, agents actually observe the price vector $p^*(d_0)$ at the first date. The vectors $p^*(d_1)$ and $p^*(d_2)$ are only the prices agents *expect* to rule in d_1 and d_2. Of course, if agents are intertemporally consistent, i.e., do not wish to revise their plans, then $p^*(d_1)$ and $p^*(d_2)$ will actually be equilibrium price vectors in d_1 and d_2 respectively. The consumers have quasi-rational expectations. For example, they all expect $p^*(d_1)$ to rule in d_1 but they may differ widely in the probability they assign to the occurrence of d_1.

An equilibrium of plans, prices and price expectations is the concept used by Radner in his theory of equilibrium in a sequence of markets. This and related notions of equilibrium have come to be known as *sequence equilibria* for short. I shall use the expression sequence equilibrium only when referring to an equilibrium in the sense of Definition 5.8.2.

In a sequence equilibrium, the i-th agent chooses a trade plan z_i in Z, which results in a consumption x_i in X_i, subject to the constraints $p^* \otimes z_i \leq 0$, i.e., $p^*(d).z_i(d) \leq 0$ for every d in D. z_i is chosen maximally with respect to $\prec_i$, of course.

It is clear that the essential difference between a sequence equilibrium and the Walrasian equilibrium (of the static economy) lies in the form of the budget constraints. Instead of a single constraint, the sequence equilibrium imposes a sequence of constraints, one for each d in D. Whatever differences arise between the efficiency properties of the two types of equilibria are attributable to the form of the budget constraints. This suggests that they deserve a closer look.

At the event d in D, the i-th agent faces a budget constraint of the form $p(d).z_i(d) \leq 0$. The vector $z_i(d)$ describes the trades *arranged* at d but the commodities are delivered not just at d but also at future events $d' \geq d$. In words, the constraint requires that the value of the trades arranged at d be less than or equal to zero, regardless of when the commodities are delivered. In less precise but more suggestive language, goods bought today must be paid for today, regardless of their delivery date. To see how appropriate this is, consider a few examples. Insurance policies are the closest analogue in actual economies to the contingent commodities in a sequence economy. A contingent commodity is a "promise" to deliver a unit of some good at a particular date-event pair d' in D. An insurance policy (e.g. a policy insuring a house against fire) is a promise to pay a sum if a specified event (in this case the house catching fire) occurs. Typically, the policy holder pays the insurer a stream of premiums throughout the life of the policy. Each premium is a payment for the continuation of the policy over some future period of time. So if we think of the policy as consisting of subpolicies, each covering a single time period and paid for with a single premium, it is clear that the subpolicy is paid for when the transaction is "arranged", not when the goods are delivered. This agrees with the budget constraints in the definition of a sequence equilibrium. But there are other cases which do not agree with the definition.

The most important class of organized forward markets for goods is the commodities futures market. A futures contract in cocoa, for example, is a promise to deliver a unit of cocoa at a price specified when the contract is made. Almost by definition, the payment for the contract is made at the time of delivery. A buyer of a futures contract is promising to accept delivery of a unit of cocoa and to deliver the agreed amount of money at some date in the future, regardless of the state of nature. Of course, futures contracts are rarely realized in this way. The buyer "sells" the cocoa on the spot market instead and gives the difference between the spot and the agreed price to the seller. This makes no difference to the form of the budget constraint.

Another counterexample is provided by the purchase of investment goods. In terms of the value of transactions carried out, this must be one of the most important types of forward trading. An order for a ship, a factory, a blast furnace or even a hydro-electric dam is a purchase for future delivery. Yet in most cases the payment for the goods is made at the time of delivery or afterwards. This example, like many others one could think of, is complicated by the fact that there is likely to be borrowing and lending going on in the background. The contractor building a factory borrows from his banker against the security of his contract with the purchaser. It may be argued that the purchaser is implicitly borrowing the money (since the interest payments are included in the purchase price) so as to defer payment. In general it could be argued that "cash on delivery" is equivalent to payment at the moment the order is placed, together with an implicit loan. This is an issue which cannot be resolved until borrowing and lending are explicitly introduced into the model. In an exchange economy with no borrowing and lending, "cash on delivery" is plainly inconsistent with the definition of a sequence equilibrium.

In any actual economy a wide variety of payments schemes are used. The form of the budget constraint in the definition of a sequence equilibrium implies that payment is made at the time of purchase (payment is received at the time of sale) but this is only a limiting case. "Cash on delivery" or payment at the time of delivery is another limiting case. Rather than try to accommodate all the possible payments arrangements in a single definition of equilibrium, I shall consider the other limiting case (cash on delivery) as an alternative or complement to the sequence equilibrium. The alternative equilibrium concept will be called a "futures equilibrium" because payment is made in the same way as in a commodity futures market.

For each d in D, let l_d denote the number of commodities available for delivery at d. Of course, $l = \sum_{d \in D} l_d$. Now let X^d denote the l_d-dimensional linear subspace of $\mathbb{R}^l$ spanned by the commodities delivered at d, for every d in D. From the definition of commodities it is clear that $\mathbb{R}^l$ is the direct sum of the family $\{X^d : d \in D\}$. Any trade plan z_i is a function from D to $\mathbb{R}^l$ and $z_i(d)$ is therefore a vector in $\mathbb{R}^l$. Let $z_i^d(d')$ denote the projection of $z_i(d')$ into X^d for any d, d' in D and let z_i^d be the corresponding trade plan. z_i^d is the part of the trade plan consisting of goods delivered at d and $\sum_d z_i^d = z_i$.

An illustration may help. In the example used earlier,

$$X^{d_0} = \{x \in \mathbb{R}^6 \mid x = (x_1, x_2, 0, 0, 0, 0)\}$$
$$X^{d_1} = \{x \in \mathbb{R}^6 \mid x = (0, 0, x_3, x_4, 0, 0)\}$$
$$X^{d_2} = \{x \in \mathbb{R}^6 \mid x = (0, 0, 0, 0, x_5, x_6)\}.$$

A trade plan z_i associates a vector $z_i(d)$ in $\mathbb{R}^6$ with every event d in D. There is a *unique* way to express $z_i(d)$ as the sum of vectors in the subspaces X^d $(d \in D)$. For example, if $z_i(d_0) = (4, -10, 0, 3, 0, 3) \in Z^{d_0}$, the unique way of writing this as a sum of vectors in X^d $(d \in D)$ is

$$(4, -10, 0, 0, 0, 0) + (0, 0, 0, 3, 0, 0) + (0, 0, 0, 0, 0, 3).$$

Each of these vectors is the projection of $(4, -10, 0, 3, 0, 3)$ into the corresponding subspace X^d and represents the trades, arranged at d_0, for delivery at d. For example, $(0, 0, 0, 3, 0, 0)$ represents the purchase at date 0 of three units of commodity 4 for delivery at date 1 if state 1 occurs. Just as the vector $z_i(d')$ can be uniquely decomposed into vectors $z_i^d(d')$ of goods delivered at d in D, so the trade plan z_i can be uniquely decomposed into trade plans z_i^d. The trade plan z_i^d describes trades arranged at different events d' in D for delivery at d. For example, if $z_i(d_0) = (4, -10, 0, 3, 0, 3)$ and $z_i(d_1) = (0, 0, -6, 2, 0, 0)$ then, for $d = d_1$, z_i^d is defined by

$$z_i^d(d_0) = (0, 0, 0, 3, 0, 0)$$
$$z_i^d(d_1) = (0, 0, -6, 2, 0, 0)$$

and

$$z_i^d(d_2) = (0, 0, 0, 0, 0, 0).$$

When discussing price sequences p^* for futures equilibria it is always assumed that $p^*(d)$ belongs to Z^d. This restriction, which makes no difference to the definition of a sequence equilibrium, is substantive here. This point is discussed below.

5.8.3 *Definition* *A futures equilibrium for an economy $\mathscr{E}$ with a sequence of markets is an ordered pair (z, p^*), where z is an* *attainable trade plan allocation and p^* a price sequence, such that for $i = 1, \ldots, n$, z_i is maximal for $\prec_i$ in the set of trade plans satisfying:*

(i) $z_i' \in Z_i := \{z_i' \in Z \mid e_i + \sum_d z_i'(d) \in X_i\}$;
(ii) $\sum_{d' \in D} p^*(d').z_i^d(d') \leq 0$ for $d \in D$.

Comparison with Definition 5.8.2 indicates that only the budget constraints have changed. The value of trades in goods delivered at d must sum to zero, regardless of the event at which the trades were arranged. In other words, "cash on delivery". A normal futures contract involves the delivery of goods at a certain date independently of the state of nature. The restriction $p^*(d) \in Z^d$ then says that the price specified in the contract is also independent of the state in which delivery takes place (though not, of course, independent of d).

5.9 Efficiency properties of sequence equilibria

Let $\{x_1, \ldots, x_n\}$ be an allocation for $\mathscr{E}$ and let V be a subset of $\mathbb{R}^l$. Then $(x_1, \ldots, x_n)$ can be *weakly* (resp. *strongly*) *V-dominated* if there is an attainable allocation $(x_1', \ldots, x_n')$ such that:

$$(x_i' - x_i) \in V \qquad \text{for } i = 1, \ldots, n$$

and $(x_1', \ldots, x_n')$ weakly (resp. strongly) Pareto-dominates $(x_1, \ldots, x_n)$. V-domination is like Pareto-domination except that allocations can only be varied in certain directions, not others. An attainable allocation is said to be *weakly* (resp. *strongly*) *V-efficient* if it cannot be strongly (resp. weakly) V-dominated. The concept of V-efficiency is of no intrinsic interest. It should be treated as an artifact for the moment. The usefulness of the concept of V-efficiency is that it allows us to *characterize* concepts of equilibrium according to their efficiency. For each of the two types of equilibria encountered so far, there is a set V such that every V-efficient allocation is an equilibrium (with lump sum transfers) and every equilibrium is V-efficient. The set V sums up what is known about the efficiency of the equilibrium which it characterizes. The payoff comes in Section 5.11 where it is shown that, although the futures equilibrium is, in some sense, "less efficient" than the sequence equilibrium, the introduction of money renders them "equally efficient".

One specification of V that is of special interest is $V = \cup\{Z^d : d \in D\}$.

5.9.1 Theorem *Let $\mathscr{E}$ be an economy with a sequence of markets* *and let* (z, p^*) *be a sequence equilibrium for* $\mathscr{E}$. *Then z is weakly V-efficient for any* $V \subset \cup Z^d$.

Proof It is convenient to prove the result for the case $Z = \cup Z^d$, from which the more general result, for $V \subset \cup Z^d$, immediately follows. Let $x = (x_1, \ldots, x_n)$ be the allocation associated with the trade plan allocation z. If it is not weakly V-efficient there exists another attainable allocation $(x'_1, \ldots, x'_n)$ such that $x'_i \succ_i x_i$ and $(x'_i - x_i) \in V$, for $i = 1, \ldots, n$. By hypothesis, for every $i = 1, \ldots, n$, there is an event d_i, say, such that $(x'_i - x_i) \in Z^{d_i}$. Then $p^*(d_i).(x'_i - x_i) > 0$, for $i = 1, \ldots, n$, since x'_i is preferred to x_i and x_i is most preferred in the budget set.

Now let D' be the set of events d in D such that $0 \neq (x'_i - x_i) \in Z^d$ for some $i = 1, \ldots, n$. Let Z' be the set of trade plans z' in Z such that $z'(d) = 0$ if $d \notin D'$. I claim that for any $z' \in Z'$ such that $\sum_{d \in D} z'(d) = 0$, if $p^* \otimes z' \geq 0$ then $p^* \otimes z' = 0$. Suppose the contrary, i.e. there exists $z' \in Z'$ such that $\sum_{d \in D} z'(d) = 0$ and $p^* \otimes z' > 0$. Suppose $p^*(d).z'(d) > 0$. For some $i = 1, \ldots, n$, $d = d_i$. If agent i were to choose the plan $z_i + \lambda z'$ $(\lambda < 0)$ he would receive the same final consumption, since $\sum_d z'(d) = 0$. But $p^*(d).[z_i(d) + \lambda z'(d)] \leq 0$, for all $d \in D$, and the inequality is strict for $d = d_i$. Thus, $z_i + \lambda z'$ belongs to the budget set. By choosing λ very large one can make $p^*(d_i).[z_i(d_i) + \lambda z'(d_i)]$ as large in absolute value as one likes. Then, for some λ, agent i could afford x'_i which he prefers to x_i. (Let him choose the plan z''_i where $z''_i(d) = z_i(d) + \lambda z'(d)$ if $d \neq d_i$ and $z''_i(d_i) = z_i(d_i) + \lambda z'(d_i) + x'_i - x_i$). This contradicts the optimality of x_i and establishes the claim.

For all d in D', let $I(d)$ be the set of agents i such that $(x'_i - x_i) \in Z^d$. Let $\bar{z}(d) := \sum_{I(d)} (x'_i - x_i)$, for all d in D'. For each d in D, either $\bar{z}(d) = 0$ or $p^*(d).\bar{z}(d) > 0$. But $\sum_d \bar{z}(d) = 0$, a contradiction. □

Remarks The comparative difficulty of the proof results from the following facts. In the usual way it is possible to show, that for each d,

$$\sum_{i \in I(d)} p^*(d).(x'_i - x_i) > 0$$

if $I(d)$, which is defined to be the set of agents i for whom $(x'_i - x_i) \in Z^d$, is non-empty. A contradiction would result immediately if it were true that

$$\sum_{i \in I(d)} (x'_i - x_i) = 0\,.$$

This need not be the case, however, and all we do know is

$$\sum_{i=1}^{n} (x_i' - x_i) = 0.$$

In equilibrium, the net trades made at each date must sum to zero, i.e. $\sum_i z_i(d) = 0$ for each d in D. A central planner, on the other hand, is only constrained to satisfy $\sum_i x_i = \sum_i e_i$.

The argument contained in the second paragraph of the proof is essentially an arbitrage argument. In equilibrium, it should be impossible to make a profit by buying goods at one date-event pair and reselling them at another.

A preference relation $\prec_i$ is called *locally non-satiable in* Z^d if, for every x_i in X_i, there is an x_i' in X_i such that $(x_i' - x_i) \in Z^d$, $x_i \prec_i x_i'$ and $x_i' - x_i$ is arbitrarily small.

5.9.2 Theorem *Let $\mathscr{E}$ be an economy with a sequence of markets and let (z, p^*) be a sequence equilibrium for $\mathscr{E}$. Suppose that, for $i = 1, \ldots, n$, $\prec_i$ is negatively transitive and locally non-satiable at every event in D. Then z is strongly V-efficient for any $V \subset \cup Z^d$.*

Proof Suppose that x' weakly dominates x, which is the allocation corresponding to the trade plan allocation z. If $(x_i' - x_i) \in Z^d$ and $x_i' \succ_i x_i$, for some $i = 1, \ldots, n$ and some d in D, then clearly $p^*(d).(x_i' - x_i) > 0$. If $(x_i' - x_i) \in Z^d$ and $x_i' \nprec_i x_i$ then $p^*(d)\,(x_i' - x_i) \geq 0$. Otherwise there exists $x_i'' \in X_i$ such that $x_i'' \succ_i x_i'$, $(x_i'' - x_i') \in Z^d$ and $p^*(d).(x_i'' - x_i) \leq 0$ by local non-satiability at d. By negative transitivity, $x_i'' \succ_i x_i$, contradicting the optimality of x_i. If d_i is defined, for $i = 1, \ldots, n$, by the condition that $(x_i' - x_i) \in Z^{d_i}$, then

$$\sum_i p^*(d_i).(x_i' - x_i) > 0.$$

In order to obtain a contradiction of this inequality and complete the proof, it suffices to follow the arbitrage argument used in Theorem 5.9.1. The argument differs at one point only. Let Z_0' be defined as in the proof of Theorem 5.9.1. Suppose that for $z' \in Z_0'$, $p^* \otimes z' > 0$. Then for some $d' \in D'$, any agent can increase his wealth at d' without decreasing it at any event in D. But this contradicts the optimality of x_i $(i = 1, \ldots, n)$ because of the local non-satiability of $\prec_i$ in $Z^{d'}$. This contradiction establishes that $z' \in Z_0'$ and $p^* \otimes z' \geq 0$ imply $p^* \otimes z' = 0$. □

To establish any sort of converse to these results is much more difficult than in the static case. Up to a certain point one simply applies the static results to Z^d, for each event d in D. The trouble begins when an attempt is made to link up these results to provide a converse to Theorem 5.9.1. A *pseudo-sequence equilibrium* is an ordered pair (z, p^*), where z is an attainable trade plan allocation and p^* a price sequence, such that for $i = 1, \ldots, n$, if $x_i' \succ_i x_i$ and $(x_i' - x_i) \in Z^d$ then $p^*(d).(x_i' - x_i) \geq 0$.

5.9.3 Theorem *Let $\mathscr{E}$ be an exchange economy with a sequence of markets such that $\prec_i$ is convex and locally non-satiable in every Z^d for $i = 1, \ldots, n$. If z is a weakly V-efficient trade plan allocation then (z, p^*) is a pseudo-sequence equilibrium for some $p^* \in Z^d$ such that $p^*(d) \neq 0$ for $d \in D$, for any $V \supset \cup\{Z^d : d \in D\}$.*

Proof The proof follows easily on application of Theorem 5.6.4. For some fixed d in D, consider the static exchange economy with commodity space Z^d, with consumption sets $\{\xi \in Z^d \mid (x_i + \xi) \in X_i\}$, preferences $\prec_i^d$ defined by $(\xi, \xi') \in \prec_i^d$ if $(x_i + \xi, x_i + \xi') \in \prec_i$ and $(\xi, \xi') \in Z^d \times Z^d$, and endowments 0, for $i = 1, \ldots, n$. This economy satisfies the conditions of Theorem 5.6.4 by hypothesis, so there exists a price vector $p^*(d)$ in Z^d $(\neq 0)$ such that, for any $i = 1, \ldots, n$, $\xi' \succ_i^d \xi$ implies $p^*(d).(\xi' - \xi) \geq 0$.

Defining $p^*(d)$ in this way for all d in D, a price sequence p^* is constructed. It is obvious that (z, p^*) is a pseudo-sequence equilibrium. □

Remark The proof uses an idea which, though very simple, is extremely useful. Hold the net trades at every date-event pair $d' \neq d$ constant. There is a one-one relation now between net trades at d and final consumption bundles. This allows us to define a set of feasible net trades at d (i.e. those which correspond to feasible consumption bundles) and preferences over that set. The result is a "subeconomy" which looks just like an ordinary exchange economy whose commodity space is Z^d. Theorems about exchange economies can be applied to the "subeconomies" defined at each event d in D.

A *transfer system* for an economy with a sequence of markets is an n-tuple $t = (t_1, \ldots, t_n)$ of real-valued functions on D. For each d in D, $t_i(d)$ is interpreted as a lump sum transfer to i (or from i if negative) at the event d. A trade plan allocation z is said to be *partially competitive at* (p^*, t), where p^* is a price sequence and t a transfer system, if z is attainable and, for $i = 1, \ldots, n$, $z_i(d)$ is maximal for $\prec_i^d$ in the budget set $\{\xi \in Z_i^d \mid p^*(d).\xi \leq t_i(d)\}$ for every d in D, where $Z_i^d := \{\xi \in Z^d \mid x_i - z_i(d) + \xi \in X_i\}$.

5.9.4 Theorem *Let $\mathscr{E}$ be an economy with a sequence of markets and suppose $\prec_i$ is continuous and X_i convex for $i = 1, \ldots, n$. Let (z, p^*) be a pseudo-sequence equilibrium such that:*

$$p^*(d).z_i(d) > \inf p^*(d).Z_i^d$$

for $i = 1, \ldots, n$ and $d \in D$. Then for some t, z is partially competitive at (p^*, t).

Proof Define t by putting $t_i = p^* \otimes z_i$ for $i = 1, \ldots, n$. To show that z is partially competitive at (p^*, t) it is sufficient to show that for any i and d, z_i is maximal for $\prec_i^d$ in the budget set $\{\xi \in Z_i^d \mid p^*(d).\xi \leq t_i(d)\}$. But this follows from the assumptions and Theorem 5.6.5. □

The inequality in Theorem 5.9.4 can be derived from a connectedness assumption analogous to the one used in Theorem 5.6.6. Say that two agents i and j are *directly resource related in* Z^d at the allocation x if there exists $\xi \in Z^d$ such that $(x_i, x_i + \xi) \in \prec_i$ and $(x_j - \xi) \in X_j$. Two agents i and j are indirectly resource related in Z^d if there exists a finite sequence $\{i_k : k = 1, \ldots, K\}$ such that $i_1 = i$, $i_K = j$ and i_k and i_{k+1} are directly resource related in Z^d for $k = 1, \ldots, K - 1$.

5.9.5 Theorem *Let $\mathscr{E}$ be an economy with a sequence of markets such that, for any $i, j = 1, \ldots, n$ $(i \neq j)$ and d in D, i and j are indirectly resource related in Z^d and $\sum_i e_i$ belongs to the interior of $\sum_i X_i$. If (z, p^*) is a pseudo-sequence equilibrium for $\mathscr{E}$, $p^* \in Z$ and $p^*(d) \neq 0$ for $d \in D$, then*

$$p^*(d).z_i(d) > \inf p^*(d).Z_i^d.$$

Proof Simply apply Theorem 5.6.6 in the obvious way. □

This sequence of theorems has shown that if z is weakly V-efficient $(V \supset \cup Z^d)$ then under conditions analogous to those used in Section 5.6, (z, p^*) is partially competitive for some price sequence p^*. But partial competitiveness does not provide much of a converse to the V-efficiency of the sequence equilibrium. What is needed is full competitiveness, i.e. z_i is maximal for $\prec_i$ in the budget set $\{z'_i \in Z_i | p^* \otimes z'_i \leq t_i\}$ where $Z_i := \{z \in Z | \sum_d z_i(d) + e_i \in X_i\}$. There are two obstacles to the transition from partial to full competitiveness. Consider the diagram below:

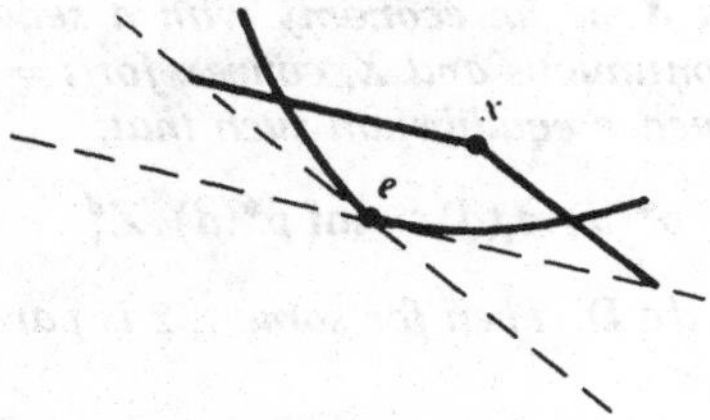

Figure 5.9.1

The solid curve represents an indifference surface which is kinked at the point e. The two dashed lines represent the budget constraints for two different events d and d', say. Both support the agent's endowment of the two goods in question. For concreteness, suppose that the steeper line is the budget constraint in forward markets at d and the other line is the budget constraint in spot markets at d'. If there are no other markets or commodities it is clear that e is partially competitive at these prices, for the agent cannot make himself better off by trade at one of the events alone. It is equally clear that by trading at d and d' together a point such as x could be reached which is preferred to e. The problem is that there are too many supporting hyperplanes. By selecting a price vector $p^*(d)$ for each Z^d independently one may end up with a price sequence which allows profitable arbitrage between events. To rule this out in the example illustrated by Figure 5.9.1 requires that $p^*(d)$ and $p^*(d')$ be proportional. This condition is satisfied if, for example, preferences are represented by a differentiable utility function.

Another sort of problem arises when an agent is on the boundary of his consumption set. Consider two events d and d' and suppose that there is a single commodity h, say, which can be traded at d for delivery at d'. Now suppose there is some agent i who is indifferent to the amount of h he consumes. If h is also desired by some agent j then V-efficiency requires that i's consumption of h be zero. However, at the price sequence p^* agent i may wish to buy h forward at d' and sell it spot at d in order to increase his income at d. This could not happen if h were desired by i and consumed in positive amounts for in that case V-efficiency would ensure that the "marginal utility of income" is the same at d and d'.

These problems are of rather different kinds. The first is a problem of choosing the correct price sequence from among the several available. The second is more intractable, suggesting that the definition of V-efficiency is not strong enough to characterize the competitive allocations. It is fairly easy to show that if the two possibilities mentioned above are ruled out then a partially competitive allocation is fully competitive. An attainable trade plan allocation z is said to be a *fully competitive sequence allocation at* (p^*, t) if, for $i = 1, \ldots, n$ and any $z'_i \in Z_i$ if $x'_i \succ_i x_i$ then $p^*(d).z'_i(d) > t_i(d)$ for some $d \in D$. Say that preferences $\prec_i$ *are smooth at* x_i if there is a vector a_i in $\mathbb{R}^l$ such that for any ξ in $X_i - \{x_i\}$, $a_i.\xi > 0$ if and only if $(x_i + \lambda\xi) \succ_i x_i$ for some $\lambda > 0$. When preferences can be represented by a differentiable function u_i, the vector a_i can be chosen equal to the gradient vector $\partial u_i(x_i)/\partial x_i$.

5.9.6 Theorem *Let $\mathscr{E}$ be an economy with a sequence of markets and let z be partially competitive at (p^*, t). If x is the corresponding allocation then z is fully competitive at (p^*, t) if, for $i = 1, \ldots, n$,*

(i) $\prec_i$ *is smooth at* x_i;
(ii) $x_i \in \text{Int } X_i$.

Proof Suppose that z is not fully competitive. For some $i = 1, \ldots, n$, there is a $z'_i \in Z$ such that $p^* \otimes z'_i \leq t_i$, $x'_i \in X_i$ and $x'_i \succ_i x_i$, where $e_i + \sum_d z'_i(d) = x'_i$. Since $a_i.(x'_i - x_i) > 0$ there is some d for which $a_i(z'_i(d) - z_i(d)) > 0$. Since $x_i \in \text{Int } X_i$, for some small $\lambda > 0$, $x_i + \lambda(z'_i(d) - z_i(d)) \in X_i$. But $p^* \otimes z_i \leq t_i$ and $p^* \otimes z'_i \leq t_i$, so $p^*(d).(\lambda z'_i(d) + (1 - \lambda)z_i(d) \leq t_i(d)$. This contradicts the partial competitiveness of z. $\square$

It does not appear that these conditions can be weakened in an economically interesting way. Of the two assumptions in the theorem, the requirement that x_i be in the interior of X_i seems the more restrictive and also the more indispensable. If x_i is on the boundary of X_i then it is always possible that agent i will wish to reallocate wealth between two events even though a planner restricted to choosing a variation in V would not. Nor is this economically unimportant. The connectedness of events, i.e. the ability to reallocate wealth between events when there is a sequence of budget constraints, is the crucial problem in a sequence economy. It cannot be assumed away.

The notion of V-efficiency is not entirely satisfactory as a characterization of sequence equilibrium; but the exercise of studying the relationship between the two is nonetheless useful. It demonstrates graphically the importance of the budget constraints in obstructing the attainment of Pareto-efficiency. It must be emphasized that the use of the concept of V-efficiency is not intended to suggest that a sequence equilibrium is in any sense efficient. It simply characterizes the extent to which a sequence equilibrium falls short of the objective of full Pareto-efficiency.

5.10 Efficiency properties of the futures equilibrium

The budget constraints in the definition of the futures equilibrium are much more complicated than those in the definition of sequence equilibrium. If p^* and z_i are an equilibrium price sequence and trade plan respectively then for every event d in d:

$$\sum_{d \in D} p^*(d').z_i^d(d') \leq 0.$$

Recall that $\mathbb{R}^l$ is taken to be the direct sum of the linear subspaces X^d spanned by commodities delivered at d in D and that $z_i^d(d')$ denotes the canonical projection of $z_i(d')$ into X^d. In contrast to the budget constraints in the sequence equilibrium the futures equilibrium constraints include price vectors $p^*(d')$ and trade vectors $z_i(d')$ from several different events. It is not clear what concept of V-efficiency, if any, would serve to characterize a futures equilibrium. $V = \cup Z^d$ will not do here because the budget constraints are wrong and $V = \cup X^d$ is clearly too weak. Rather than tackle this problem in its full generality I shall look at a special case which provides a good deal of insight at relatively little cost.

Suppose that there are only two dates. The initial event is denoted by 0 and the terminal events at the second date (which can be identified with the states of nature) are denoted by s in S. There are l_0 commodities available for delivery at each event so the commodity space is $\mathbb{R}^l$, where $l := l_0.|S \cup \{0\}|$. Let $\mathscr{E}$ be an exchange economy with this commodity space and with a sequence of markets defined as follows. At 0 agents can trade in all commodities for immediate delivery and for future delivery independently of the state of nature. Then $Z^0 := \{z \in \mathbb{R}^l | z^s = z^{s'}, \text{all } s, s' \in S\}$, where z^s denotes the projection of z into X^s. Z^0 can be regarded as the direct sum of X^0 and some subspace $\tilde{Z}$ say. At every event s in S there are spot markets only, i.e. $Z^s = X^s$. Every agent can be thought of as choosing a consumption bundle x_i and a vector $y_i \in \tilde{Z}$ of futures contracts. It is easy to see that under the definition of Z given above there is a unique trade plan z_i in Z corresponding to each choice of (x_i, y_i) in $X_i \times \mathbb{R}^{l_0}$. Let (z, p^*) be a futures equilibrium for $\mathscr{E}$. For each $i = 1, \ldots, n$, the following budget constraints must be satisfied:

$$p^*(0) . z_i(0) \leq 0$$

$$p^*(0) . z_i^s(0) + p^*(s) . z_i^s(s) \leq 0$$

Now $z_i^0(0) \equiv (x_i^0 - e_i^0)$, where x_i^0 and e_i^0 are the projections of x_i and e_i respectively into X^0, so identifying $p^*(0)$ with $(p^0, q) \in Z^0$, the first constraint can be rewritten as:

(1) $$p^0 . (x_i^0 - e_i^0) \leq 0 .$$

Similarly, noting that $z_i^s(0) \equiv y_i^s$ and $(x_i^s - e_i^s) \equiv z_i^s(0) + z_i^s(s)$ the second constraint can be rewritten as:

(2) $$p^s . (x_i^s - e_i^s) + (q - p^s) . y_i^s \leq 0 \qquad (s \in S)$$

where p^s is the projection of $p^*(s)$ into X^s. There is a one to one correspondence between pairs (x_i, y_i) satisfying the second pair of constraints and trade plans z_i satisfying the first. This leads to a convenient reformulation of the definition of a futures equilibrium. A *futures allocation* is an ordered pair (x, y) where x is a consumption allocation and $y = (y_1, \ldots, y_n)$. It is *attainable* if x is attainable and $\sum_{i=1}^n y_i = 0$. A *price system* is an ordered pair $(p, q) \in \mathbb{R}^l \times \tilde{Z}$. A *futures equilibrium* can now be defined as a four-tuple (x, y, p, q), where (x, y) is an attainable future allocation and (p, q) a price system, such that for $i = 1, \ldots, n$, (x_i, y_i) is maximal for $\prec_i$ in the budget set $\{(x_i, y_i) \in X_i \times \tilde{Z} \mid (1) \text{ and } (2) \text{ are satisfied}\}$.

5.10.1 Theorem *Let $\mathscr{E}$ be an exchange economy with a sequence of markets. Suppose $\mathscr{E}$ has two dates, with spot markets at the second date and spot and uncontingent forward markets at the first, i.e. the market structure described above. If (z, p^*) is a futures equilibrium for $\mathscr{E}$ then x is weakly V-efficient for any $V \subset (\cup X^s) \cup X^0 \cup \tilde{Z}$.*

Proof Suppose x is not weakly V-efficient, where $V = (\cup X^s) \cup X^0 \cup \tilde{Z}$. Then there exists an attainable x' such that $(x_i' - x_i) \in V$ and $x_i' \succ_i x_i$ for $i = 1, \ldots, n$. Let I_0 be the set of agents for whom $(x_i' - x_i) \in X^0$, let I_s be the set of agents for whom $(x_i' - x_i) \in X^s$ and let I_z be the set of agents for whom $(x_i' - x_i) \in \tilde{Z}$. For each $i = 1, \ldots, n$, the trade plan z_i has a corresponding ordered pair (x_i, y_i) which satisfies the budget constraints:

$$p^0 . (x_i - e_i) \leq 0$$

$$p^s . (x_i^s - e_i^s) + (q - p^s) . y_i^s \leq 0 \qquad (s \in S).$$

For every $i \in I_0$, $p^0.(x_i^{0'} - x_i^0) > 0$. Otherwise the preferred pair (x_i', y_i) would satisfy the budget constraints. Similarly, $i \in I_s$ implies that $p^s.(x_i^{s'} - x_i^s) > 0$ and $i \in I_z$ implies $q.(y_i^{s'} - y_i^s) > 0$, where $(y_i^{s'} - y_i^s) \equiv (x^{s'} - x_i^s)$ for all $s \in S$. Now attainability implies that

$$\sum_{i \in I_0} (x_i^{0'} - x_i^0) = 0$$

so $p^0.(x_i^{0'} - x_i^0) > 0$ for $i \in I_0$ implies $I_0 = \phi$. Thus,

$$\sum_{i \in I_z} (q - p^s).(y_i^{s'} - y_i^s) + \sum_{i \in I_s} p^s.(x_i^{s'} - x_i^s) > 0$$

for some $s \in S$. But attainability requires that

$$\sum_{i \in I_z} (y_i^{s'} - y_i^s) + \sum_{i \in I_s} (x_i^{s'} - x_i^s) = 0$$

for all $s \in S$ and this contradiction establishes the theorem. □

The strong version of this theorem is easily proved with the aid of an appropriate non-satiability assumption. Say that the preference relation $\prec_i$ is *locally non-satiable in* X^0 (resp. X^s, $\mathcal{Z}$) if, for every $x_i \in X_i$ there is x_i' arbitrarily close to x_i, such that $x_i' \succ_i x_i$ and $(x_i' - x_i) \in X^0$ (resp. X^s or $\mathcal{Z}$).

5.10.2 Theorem *Let $\mathscr{E}$ be an economy as described in* 5.10.1 *and suppose that for $i = 1, \ldots, n$, $\prec_i$ is locally non-satiable in X^0, X^s (for $s \in S$) and $\mathcal{Z}$. If (z, p^*) is a futures equilibrium then x, the corresponding consumption allocation, is strongly V-efficient for any $V \subset (\cup X^s) \cup X^0 \cup \mathcal{Z}$.*

The proof is left to the reader; it follows lines which should be now be familiar.

To establish the converse is also quite easy, once it is realized that a futures equilibrium is formally equivalent in the simple two-period economy to a special kind of sequence equilibrium. The result then follows from an application of Theorems 5.9.3–5.9.6. Let z be an attainable trade plan allocation for an economy $\mathscr{E}$ with a sequence of markets. In the usual way z can be identified with a consumption allocation and an allocation of futures contracts $y = (y_1, \ldots, y_n)$. Corresponding to $\mathscr{E}$ there is another, artificial economy $\mathscr{E}_a$ with a sequence of markets defined as follows. The market structure is assumed to be $Z_a^0 := X^0$, $Z_a^s := X^s$, for every s in S, and $Z_a^+ := \mathcal{Z}$ where "+" represents a fictional date-event pair at which futures trading takes place. A trade plan allocation for $\mathscr{E}_a$ can be derived uniquely from each allocation (x, y) for $\mathscr{E}$. Put $z_i^a(0) := (x_i^0 - e_i^0)$, $z_i^a(s) := (x_i^s - e_i^s - y_i)$, for s in S, and $z_i^a(+) = y_i$.

This defines a trade plan z_i^a, for each $i = 1, \ldots, n$, and hence a trade plan allocation z^a for $\mathscr{E}_a$. It is also clear that to each price sequence p^* for $\mathscr{E}$ there corresponds a unique price sequence p^a for $\mathscr{E}_a$ represented by the price vectors p^0, p^s $(s \in S)$ and q. Let z be an attainable trade plan allocation for $\mathscr{E}$, p^* a price sequence for $\mathscr{E}$, z^a the corresponding trade plan allocation for $\mathscr{E}_a$ and p^a the corresponding price sequence. Define (z, p^*) to be a *pseudo-futures equilibrium* for $\mathscr{E}$ if and only if (z^a, p^a) is a pseudo-sequence equilibrium, in the sense of Section 5.9, for the artificial economy $\mathscr{E}_a$.

5.10.3 Theorem *Let $\mathscr{E}$ be a two-period exchange economy with a sequence of markets such that $\prec_i$ is convex and locally non-satiable in X^0, $\hat{Z}$ and X^s, for every s in S, for $i = 1, \ldots, n$. If z is a weakly V-efficient trade plan allocation then (z, p^*) is a pseudo-futures equilibrium for some $p^* \in Z$ such that $p^*(d) \neq 0$ for $d \in D$, for any $V \supset (\cup X^s) \cup X^0 \cup \hat{Z}$.*

Proof z^a is also V-efficient and satisfies the conditions of Theorem 5.9.3. Therefore (z^a, p^a) is a pseudo-sequence equilibrium for the artificial economy $\mathscr{E}_a$ for some p^a. Let p^* be some price sequence for $\mathscr{E}$ such that p^a corresponds, in the manner described above, to p^*. Then, by definition, (z, p^*) is a pseudo-sequence equilibrium. □

Let (z, p^*) and (z^a, p^a) be corresponding pseudo-equilibria as before and let t be a transfer system for $\mathscr{E}$. Derive the corresponding transfer system for $\mathscr{E}_a$ by putting $t_i^a(0) = t_i(0)$, $t_i^a(s) = t_i(s) - q \, . \, y_i^s$ $(s \in S)$ and $t_i^a(+) = q \, . \, y_i$. Define z to be partially competitive for $\mathscr{E}$ at (p^*, t) if and only if z^a is partially competitive for $\mathscr{E}_a$ at (p^a, t^a), in the sense of Section 5.9.

5.10.4 Theorem *Let $\mathscr{E}$ be a two-period economy with a sequence of markets and suppose $\prec_i$ is continuous and X_i convex for $i = 1, \ldots, n$. Let (z, p^*) be a pseudo-futures equilibrium such that the corresponding (z^a, p^a) satisfies the inequality:*

$$p^a(d) \, . \, z_i^a(d) > \inf p^a(d) \, . \, Z_{ia}^d \qquad (i = 1, \ldots, n)$$

for every date-event pair d in D_a. Then z is partially competitive at (p^*, t) for some t.

Proof From Theorem 5.9.4, z^a is partially competitive at (p^a, t^a) for some transfer system t^a. If t is a transfer system to which t^a corresponds then by definition, z is partially competitive at (p^*, t). □

Theorem 5.9.5 provides sufficient conditions for (z^a, p^a) to satisfy the inequality in 5.10.4. The analogous theorem will therefore not be repeated here.

In Theorems 5.10.3 and 5.10.4 the proofs rely on the fact that the pseudo-futures equilibrium is defined in terms of the corresponding pseudo-sequence equilibrium of the artificial economy. Similarly the notion of partial competitiveness of a pseudo-futures equilibrium is defined in terms of partial competitiveness of the corresponding pseudo-sequence equilibrium. The justification for this approach comes from the following definition and theorem. Let z be an attainable trade plan allocation for the two period economy $\mathscr{E}$. z is a *fully competitive futures allocation at* (p^*, t) if, for $i = 1, \ldots, n$, z^i is maximal for $\prec_i$ in the budget set:

$$\{z_i' \in Z_i \mid \sum_{d'} p^*(d') . z_i^d(d') \leq t_i(d), d \in D\}.$$

5.10.5 Theorem *Let $\mathscr{E}$ be a two-period economy with a sequence of markets and let z be partially competitive for $\mathscr{E}$ at (p^*, t). If x is the resulting consumption allocation and, for $i = 1, \ldots, n$,*

(i) *$\prec_i$ is smooth at x_i*
(ii) $x_i \in \operatorname{Int} X_i$;
then z is a fully competitive futures equilibrium at (p^*, t).

Proof Let (z^a, p^a) be the corresponding pseudo-sequence equilibrium for the artificial economy. By hypothesis z^a is partially competitive at (p^a, t^a). Then Theorem 5.9.6 implies that z^a is a fully competitive sequence allocation at (p^a, t^a). Now suppose that z is not a fully competitive futures allocation at (p^*, t). For some $i = 1, \ldots, n$, z_i is not maximal in the budget set. There is therefore some z_i' in the budget set such that $x_i \prec_i x_i' = e_i + \sum_d z_i'(d)$. Define $z_i^{a\prime}$ by putting $z_i^{a\prime}(0) := (x_i^{0\prime} - e_i^0)$, $z_i^{a\prime}(s) := (x_i^{s\prime} - e_i^s - y_i^{s\prime})$ $(s \in S)$ and $z_i^{a\prime}(+) := y_i$, where z_i' is identified with the pair (x_i', y_i') of course. Since (x_i', y_i') lies in the budget set for the pseudo-futures equilibrium (z, p^*) it follows that:

$$p^a(0) . z_i^{a\prime}(0) \leq t_i^a(0)$$
$$\begin{aligned} p^a(s) . z_i^{a\prime}(s) &= p^s . (x_i^{s\prime} - e_i^s - y_i^{s\prime}) \\ &= p^s . (x_i^{s\prime} - e_i^s) + (q - p^s) . y_i^{s\prime} - q . y_i^{s\prime} \\ &\leq t_i(s) - q . y_i^{s\prime} = t_i^a(s) \end{aligned}$$

and

$$p^a(+) . z_i^{a\prime}(+) = q . y_i' \leq t_i^a(+).$$

This contradicts the fact that z^a is a fully competitive sequence equilibrium for $\mathscr{E}_a$ at (p^a, t^a). □
This completes the formal analysis of the futures equilibrium's efficiency properties. Although the two-period economy is a very special case it manages to convey the character of the futures equilibrium. Futures contracts allow reallocation of goods among states of nature at a given date. In other words, it allows "hedging" against risks but it does not allow transfer of resources between dates. The futures equilibrium is less efficient, in a special sense, than the sequence equilibrium. For the two-period economy with the specified market structure, the sequence equilibrium is V-efficient with $V \subset \cup Z^d = Z^0 \cup \{\cup X^s\}$. The futures equilibrium is V-efficient with $V \subset X^0 \cup Z \cup \{\cup X^s\}$. Since $Z^0 \supset X^0 \cup Z$, the notion of efficiency characterizing the sequence equilibrium is unambiguously *stronger* than that characterizing the futures equilibrium. The comparison is slightly artificial however. The difference between the two definitions lies in the form of the budget constraints. In practice, one would expect different payments arrangements to be associated with different kinds of markets, for reasons which have yet to be investigated. In general, one cannot choose the equilibrium concept independently of the market structure. Nonetheless, the comparison does demonstrate the importance of choosing the right equilibrium concept. If the sequence equilibrium were used for the two-period economy when the futures equilibrium was more appropriate it might suggest that the inefficiency of an economy with a sequence of markets is less serious than it is.
Extreme care has to be exercised in drawing conclusions from these characterizations, however. The fact that the sequence equilibrium is characterized by a stronger type of V-efficiency does not imply that in a *particular* instance the sequence equilibrium is "more efficient" than the futures equilibrium. Indeed the latter might Pareto-dominate the former. Consider a two-period economy with no uncertainty and no forward markets. The two equilibrium concepts coincide here. It is well known that an economy of this sort may have two equilibria, one of which is strictly Pareto-preferred to the other. This example is trivial but it illustrates quite well the limitations of characterizations of equilibria as a way of describing their efficiency properties.

5.11 Introducing money

The results of the last five sections make very clear the importance of the precise form of the budget constraints. At the same time they clarify the role of money and other assets. For money and other assets serve to consolidate the sequence of budget constraints by allowing the transfer of wealth between dates or date-event pairs. This does not mean that money necessarily increases efficiency, however. Adding money to an economy is like opening new markets. It is well known that opening a new market can make everyone worse off. For the moment it will be sufficient to introduce money in the simplest possible way and see how it alters the equilibrium.

The economy used for the discussion will be of the simple, two-period type described in Section 5.10. There are two dates with spot and futures markets at the first and spot markets only at the second. Formally, the set D of events consists of an initial event 0 at which agents have no information and a set of terminal events at which the true state is revealed. These last events can be identified with the states s in S so D is identified with $S \cup \{0\}$. The market structure $\{Z^d: d \in D\}$ is defined by putting $Z^0 = X^0 \oplus \tilde{Z}$ and $Z^s = X^s$ for $s \in S$, where $\tilde{Z}$ is a linear subspace with the property that $z \in \tilde{Z}$ implies $z^s = z^{s'}$ for all $s, s' \in S$.

There is assumed to be a government or monetary authority whose only function is to issue *fiat* money (i.e. paper money) to consumers at the beginning of the first date and collect it at the end of the second. This rather arbitrary set up is largely a matter of expediency, designed to avoid the following "terminal problem". In the second period, agents want to spend all their money since it has no intrinsic utility and must be spent then or never. If everyone feels like this the value of money must fall to zero, i.e. it will purchase nothing. If agents have rational expectations they will not wish to hold any money at the end of the first period either, since it will purchase nothing in the second. Thus the value of money in the first period falls to zero as well. An economy in which the value of money is zero is essentially a non-monetary economy since there is no function money can perform which does not require it to have a positive exchange value. It follows that the terminal problem cannot be solved by assigning money some other useful function such as medium of exchange. The terminal problem can be solved only by introducing an infinite horizon, dropping the rational expectations assumption or adopting an expedient such as having the money returned to the government. The first solution is technically very difficult and the second makes any discussion of efficiency impossible. In the circumstances the expedient solution does not appear unreasonable.

With the convention that each agent has an initial endowment of one unit of money, which must be returned to the government at the end of the second period, any exchange economy $\mathscr{E}$ can be turned into a monetary economy. I shall use the symbol $\mathscr{E}$ to denote both and use the phrases "exchange economy" and "monetary economy" to indicate which interpretation is required.

5.11.1 Definition *A (two-period) monetary economy is an exchange economy $\mathscr{E}$, a set of events $D \equiv S \cup \{0\}$ and a market structure $\{Z^d : d \in D\}$ defined by:*

$$Z^0 = X^0 \oplus \tilde{Z}$$

$$Z^s = X^s \ (s \in S)$$

where $\tilde{Z}$ has the property that $z \in \tilde{Z}$ implies $z^s = z^{s'}$ for all $s, s' \in S$. Each agent has one unit of paper money at the beginning of date 0 which is returned to the "government" at the end of date 1.

An agent's demand for money at date 1 is simply the one unit he needs to give to the government. To determine his trades in money it is sufficient to specify the amount he holds at the end of date 0 and carries forward to date 1. Let m_i denote this amount for the i-th agent. A *money allocation* is the n-tuple $m = (m_1, \ldots, m_n)$ in $\mathbb{R}^n_+$ which describes each agent's money balance at the end of date 0. A money allocation is *attainable* if $\sum_{i=1}^n (m_i - 1) = 0$. An allocation for the (two-period) monetary economy $\mathscr{E}$ is an ordered pair (z, m), where z is a trade plan allocation and m a money allocation, and it is *attainable* if z and m are.

All prices in a monetary economy are expressed in terms of money. A price sequence, as before is a function p^* from D to the commodity space $\mathbb{R}^l$ such that $p^*(d) \in Z^d$ for all $d \in D$. Recall that $Z^0 = X^0 \oplus \tilde{Z}$. Let p^0 and q represent the projections of $p^*(0)$ into X^0 and $\tilde{Z}$ respectively. This is not quite the same usage as in the last section, but the difference is innocuous. Similarly, let p^s denote the vector $p^*(s)$ belonging to X^s. A price sequence is represented interchangeably by p^* and by p^0, q and p^s $(s \in S)$.

5.11.2 Definition *An equilibrium for the two-period monetary economy $\mathscr{E}$ is an ordered triple (z, m, p^*) comprising an attainable allocation (z, m) and a price sequence p^* such that, for $i = 1, \ldots, n$, (z_i, m_i) is maximal for $\prec_i$ in the budget set defined by the conditions:*

(i) $z_i' \in Z_i$ and $m_i' \geq 0$;
(ii) $p^0 . z_i^{0\prime}(0) + (m_i' - 1) \leq 0$;
(iii) $p^s . z_i^{s\prime}(s) + q . z_i^{s\prime}(0) + (1 - m_i') \leq 0$, $(s \in S)$.

The budget constraints may look slightly unfamiliar but they are simply the constraints used in Section 5.10 with money added. $p^0 . z_i^{0\prime}(0)$ is equal to $p^0 . (x_i^{0\prime} - e_i^0)$ and $p^s . z_i^{s\prime}(s)$ is equal to $p^s . (x_i^{s\prime} - e_i^s - y_i^{s\prime})$. As before the trade plan allocation z can be represented interchangeably by $(x_1, \ldots, x_n)$ and $(y_1, \ldots, y_n)$ as well.

5.11.3 Theorem *Let (z, m, p^*) be an equilibrium for a two-period monetary economy $\mathscr{E}$. If $\prec_i$ is continuous and $m_i > 0$ for $i = 1, \ldots, n$ then x is weakly V-efficient for any $V \subset \cup Z^d$.*

Proof From continuity and the assumption that $m_i > 0$, it follows easily that z_i is maximal for $\prec_i$ subject to the budget constraints:

$$p^0 . (x_i^0 - e_i^0) + q . y_i^s + p^s . (x_i^s - e_i^s - y_i^s) \leq 0 .$$

Since it is already known that x is V-efficient for $V \subset X^0 \cup \tilde{Z} \cup (\cup X^s)$ it is sufficient to look at variations in Z^0. Suppose that x' is an attainable allocation such that $x_i' \succ_i x_i$ and $(x_i' - x_i) \in Z^0$ for $i = 1, \ldots, n$. Let z' be a trade plan allocation such that $z_i'(s) = z_i(s)$ for all $s \in S$ and $\sum_d z_i'(d) = (x_i' - e_i)$. Clearly, for each i there is an $s \in S$ such that:

$$p^0 . z_i^{0\prime}(0) + q . y_i^{s\prime} > p^0 . z_i^0(0) + q . y_i^s .$$

This leads to a contradiction of attainability in the usual way since $q . y_i^{s\prime}$ and $q . y_i^s$ are independent of $s \in S$. □

5.11.4 Theorem *Let (z, m, p^*) be an equilibrium for the two-period monetary economy $\mathscr{E}$. If $\prec_i$ is continuous and is locally non-satiable in Z^d $(d \in D)$ and $m_i > 0$, for $i = 1, \ldots, n$, then z is strongly V-efficient for $V \subset \cup Z^d$.*

The proof should be obvious. These two theorems show money to be a link between the concepts of futures equilibrium and sequence equilibrium. It is crucial to this result that the futures contract be state-independent, that is, y_i is delivered in each state at the second date. From the earlier discussion it is clear that forward contracts for goods generally satisfy this condition. Note that it is also implicit that the futures prices are also state-independent. Since $q \in \tilde{Z}$, $q^{s'}$ is the "same" as q^s for all s', $s \in S$. This would not be the case, for example, with a cost plus contract. Other state-dependent contracts, mainly insurance policies, require payment in advance, i.e. they are of the sequence equilibrium type. What these theorems suggest, therefore, is that as long as there is enough money in the system, "cash on delivery" is not an obstacle to efficiency. A futures equilibrium is as efficient as the comparable sequence equilibrium.

The rub of course is that each agent must want to hold $m_i > 0$ at the equilibrium prices. Here money is simply handed out to individuals. When there is a cost to acquiring cash balances, there is no guarantee that the economy will possess the optimum quantity of money.

To establish a converse to Theorems 5.11.3 and 5.11.4 is quite easy. We have already seen under what conditions V-efficiency implies that an attainable trade plan allocation can be sustained as a fully competitive sequence allocation. The following theorem shows that a fully competitive sequence allocation can be sustained as a fully competitive futures allocation with money.

5.11.5 Theorem *Let $\mathscr{E}$ be a two-period exchange economy and suppose that z is a fully competitive sequence allocation at (p^*, t^*). Then for some money allocation m, (z, m) can be sustained as a fully competitive futures allocation if $p^*(0).\tilde{Z} \neq \{0\}$, i.e. if it is possible to make forward trades which have non-zero value.*

Proof The budget constraints of the sequence allocation have the form:

$$p^*(0).z_i^*(0) = t_i^*(0)$$

$$p^*(s).z_i^*(s) = t_i^*(s) \qquad (s \in S).$$

Let p^0 (resp. p^s) be the projection of $p^*(0)$ (resp. $p^*(s)$) into X^0 (resp. X^s) and choose $q \in \tilde{Z}$ so that $q.\xi = p^*(0).\xi$ for any $\xi \in \tilde{Z}$. This is possible because of the definition of $\tilde{Z}$. Then define t_i by putting:

$$p^0.z_i^0(0) = t_i(0)$$

$$p^s.z_i(s) + q.z_i^s(0) = t_i(s)$$

and put $m_i = 1$ for all $i = 1, \ldots, m$. It is clear that (z_i, m_i) satisfies the budget constraints appropriate to a futures allocation at the prices p^0, p^s and q and the lump sum transfers t_i. To see that (z_i, m_i) is maximal for $\prec_i$ subject to these budget constraints it is sufficient to show that any trade plan z_i' which satisfies these constraints for some m_i', also satisfies the budget constraints for the sequence allocation. This is left as an exercise for the reader. □

Notice that, although there are no trades in money ($m_i = 1$), the role of money is not trivial. The possibility of trading in money makes the equilibrium conditions stronger than they would be otherwise. It is clear that a different definition of t_i would allow trades in money without altering the story in any other respect.

Notes

1. Suppose that the relation $\prec$ is defined by the condition: $(x, x') \in \precsim$ if and only if $x_h < x'_h$ for $h = 1, \ldots, l$. Then $\prec$ is transitive and irreflexive. But the weaker "preferred-or-indifferent to" relation, defined by putting $(x, x') \in \precsim$ if and only if $(x', x) \notin \prec$, is not transitive. Let $l = 2$ and let $a > b > c$ be real numbers. Then $(b, c) \precsim (c, a)$ and $(c, a) \precsim (a, b)$ but $(a, b) \succ (b, c)$. (The reader may find it helpful to draw a picture.) The relation $\prec$ is not negatively transitive either. For $(a, b) \succ (b, c)$ and $(b, c) \succsim (c, a)$ but it is not true that $(a, b) \succ (c, a)$.

2. This is not the only possible approach. An alternative is to assume local non-satiation and that (roughly speaking) every consumer has a positive endowment of every good.

CHAPTER 6

Monetary equilibrium: a cooperative approach

In general equilibrium theory money has one function. It is a store of value. There is no useful distinction to be made between its role as an asset and its role as a "medium of exchange". Because of the information costs of trading named commodities, in particular the named commodities which are close substitutes for money, we observe a market structure which reflects Clower's maxim: *money buys goods and goods buy money; but goods do not buy goods.* This is a statement about the set of markets available, not about some special function performed by money. At least, this is the way it looks through the lens of general equilibrium theory. It is the sequence of budget constraints, however, that provide a role for money and other assets. The incompleteness of markets is neither a necessary nor a sufficient condition for the existence of a demand for money whereas a sequence of constraints is both. To make this point very clear, in this chapter I deal only with economies in which the set of *goods* markets is complete at every date.

What remains is the task of explaining first, why there should be a sequence of budget constraints rather than a single constraint and second, why money can be used to consolidate these constraints when other assets (verbal I.O.U.s, for example) cannot. In the last chapter a rudimentary, general equilibrium model of exchange was studied. In that context, it was argued, there is no reason not to have a single budget constraint if agents are trustworthy. This suggests that the absence of trust will be part of the explanation of why there is a sequence of constraints. But so far there has been no precise statement of what is meant by the absence of trust. Neither has it been explained why the absence of trust should create a demand for money and not for personal bonds, say. These questions are logically prior to any other questions about money in general equilibrium because a sequence of budget constraints and the consequent role of money as a store of value are the *sine qua non* of any general equilibrium theory of money.

In order to explain why there is a sequence of budget constraints it is necessary to provide a rationale for a particular definition of monetary equilibrium, in the same way that the theory of the core provides a rationale for the concept of the Walrasian equilibrium. One way to do this would be by extending the classical theory of the core to deal with monetary economies. The starting point is a reconsideration of the Arrow–Debreu model.

6.1 The classical theory

Let $\mathscr{E}$ be an exchange economy with a complete set of markets. A *Walrasian equilibrium* for $\mathscr{E}$ is an ordered pair (x, p), comprising an attainable allocation x and a price system p, such that for every $i = 1, \ldots, n$, x_i is maximal for $\prec_i$ in the budget set $\{x'_i \in X_i \mid p.x'_i \leq p.e_i\}$. An allocation x is called a *Walras allocation* if, for some p, (x, p) is a Walrasian equilibrium. The Walrasian equilibrium formalizes the notion of competition in an exchange economy. For some people the definition is sufficient in itself, but others want to know what lies behind the definition; they want a *rationale* for the definition of Walrasian equilibrium. The problem is this: if you only know the definition then you will always know a Walrasian equilibrium when you see one; but you will not know where to find one, i.e. in what circumstances the Walrasian equilibrium is the appropriate equilibrium concept. What is needed is a theory to tell us when an economy is competitive and when it is not.

The classical theory of the core of an economy is one idealization of the competitive process. It gives an account of the circumstances in which perfectly competitive behaviour is to be expected, *viz.* when every agent is infinitesimally small relative to the economy as a whole. The core itself is simply a solution concept for a cooperative game. In the background is some notion of coalitions of players forming to exchange goods or bargain with other players but this is not part of the formal theory. The core itself is defined in terms of a simple criterion of stability. A *coalition* is any non-empty subset of the set $\{1, \ldots, n\}$ of agents or *players*. If x is an allocation for $\mathscr{E}$, the coalition T can *improve on* x if and only if there is an attainable allocation x' such that $x'_i \succ_i x_i$ for all $i \in T$ and $\sum_{i \in T} x'_i = \sum_{i \in T} e_i$. In other words, T can improve on x if, by reallocating its own resources, it can make each of its members better off. The *core* of $\mathscr{E}$, which is denoted by $C(\mathscr{E})$, is defined to be the set of attainable allocations which cannot be improved on by any coalition. The core does not describe the process by which an allocation is chosen; it merely sets up a criterion of what is a reasonable outcome of the game, *viz*. an allocation belonging to the core. Coalitions never "form"; the existence of an improving coalition, in the mathematical sense, is sufficient to rule out an allocation as being "unstable" or "unreasonable". Nonetheless, the motivation for the core comes from the idea that competition somehow consists of people getting together in coalitions and working out deals to their mutual advantage. Freedom of entry, for example, corresponds here to the freedom of coalitions to work out more advantageous terms of trade than the *status quo* allows, if it is feasible to do so.

The simplified picture of competition presented by the core provides a rationale for the concept of Walrasian equilibrium because, under certain circumstances the core is precisely the set of Walras allocations. Let $W(\mathscr{E})$ denote the set of Walras allocations.

6.1.1 Theorem $W(\mathscr{E}) \subset C(\mathscr{E})$.

Proof Suppose that x is a Walras allocation for the exchange economy $\mathscr{E}$, that is, for some price system p the ordered pair (x, p) is a Walrasian equilibrium. If x does not belong to the core of $\mathscr{E}$ then there is a coalition T and an attainable allocation x' such that:

$$x'_i \succ_i x_i \qquad \text{for } i \in T$$

and

$$\sum_{i \in T} x'_i = \sum_{i \in T} e_i .$$

From the first condition it follows that $p.x'_i > p.e_i$ for $i \in T$, which contradicts the second since T is non-empty. □

To prove, conversely, that $C(\mathscr{E}) \subset W(\mathscr{E})$ requires a strong assumption, that each agent is "small" relative to the whole, and it requires a fairly sophisticated model to describe this sort of economy precisely. For the time being it is sufficient to know that such a result exists. These two results (i.e. Theorem 6.1.1 and its partial converse) show that, if competition is identified with the process of coalition formation that notionally lies behind the definition of the core, the Walrasian equilibrium is an appropriate equilibrium concept when every agent is negligible relative to the whole economy. In this way the core simultaneously provides a rationale for the Walrasian equilibrium concept and tells us when to use it.

The core-theory begs many questions. Indeed, its power as an analytical tool is largely the product of this question-begging. The core does not specify what strategies the players can adopt, what information they have or how great their ability to communicate with one another is. Furthermore, there is no account of how coalitions form or of the process by which a specific allocation in the core is "chosen". In particular, there are many reasons for thinking an improving coalition would not actually "form", in which case the exact significance of the improving coalition in the definition is not clear. Whatever its faults, the core does provide some insights into the underpinnings of the Walrasian theory. It remains the best foundation so far discovered for the theory and some foundation is surely needed.[1] For it is not obvious in particular circumstances that the Walrasian theory is the right one. Without embedding the theory in a game which allows other forms of behaviour, it is impossible even to discuss the question of its appropriateness.

I have dwelt at some length on the way in which the core provides a rationale for the Walrasian equilibrium because it is important to know why the exercise is necessary and what it accomplishes. Equilibrium theory does not stand on its own two feet; it must be supported by something else. In the last chapter two plausible but quite different definitions of equilibrium for an economy with a sequence of markets were offered. An extension of the Walrasian definition for a sequence of markets was mentioned in passing and other possibilities could easily be invented. Some theory is required to discriminate among them. The need for a theory to rationalize the definition of equilibrium is even more important when money is introduced. For it is the form of the budget constraints and in particular, the way in which money appears in those constraints, which determines the role money plays in the economy. To explain all this it is necessary, at the very least, to develop a model of a monetary economy (as a game) and show how the concept of monetary equilibrium arises from the application of a sensible solution concept. This programme is the subject of the remainder of this chapter.

6.2 The problem of trust

One of the crucial assumptions of the Arrow–Debreu model is the existence of a complete set of markets. Commodities are distinguished by the date and location at which they are to be delivered and also by the event, if any, on whose occurrence their delivery is conditional. Everyone of the commodities so defined can be traded at the first date.

There is another aspect of the model which has received less attention and which hides an implicit assumption quite as important as the assumption of complete markets. In the Arrow–Debreu model the description of the trading process runs in terms of the exchange of commodities. In an economy in which there is no uncertainty and all goods are delivered at the same place on the same date, it is possible to imagine economic agents actually handing goods back and forth. When commodities by definition have different delivery dates etc. agents are really writing contracts at the first date, the terms of which are to be fulfilled later. To retain the language of exchange, imagine that at the first date agents actually exchange pieces of paper bearing the words "I promise to give the bearer one unit of X if Y" where X denotes some physical good and Y denotes a place, time and event. If one thinks of the pieces of paper as "commodities", there is nothing inconsistent in saying that all "commodities" are exchanged at the first date. This much is trivial and makes no difference to the formal theory. In terms of interpretation it is quite important because it is only permissible to identify commodities with pieces of paper if it is assumed that the contracts will be carried out. The Arrow–Debreu model concerns itself with trading at the first date only, because it implicitly assumes that a promise to deliver a commodity is as good as the thing itself. For want of a better expression I shall describe this state of affairs by saying that in an Arrow–Debreu model agents *trust* each other (to keep their promises). In an equilibrium characterized by trust there is no reason to distinguish between contracts, agreements, etc. and their execution. The fact that contracts are fulfilled through time and contingent on uncertain events is irrelevant when there is complete trust, but not otherwise. So, like the assumption of complete markets, the assumption that agents trust one another is necessary if the Arrow–Debreu treatment of time and uncertainty is to make sense.

This little observation is not very interesting in itself but it suggests an interesting question. What happens in the absence of trust? To fix ideas consider the following simple example of an exchange economy. There are two agents, a and b. There are two dates and one state of nature (i.e. no uncertainty). At each date there is one commodity available, a consumption good. Each agent's preferences are described by a Cobb–Douglas utility function with equal weights. Suppose that agent a's endowment is represented by the vector $(1 - \varepsilon, \varepsilon)$ where ε is a small, positive number, and agent b's endowment is represented by $(\varepsilon, 1 - \varepsilon)$. To reach any allocation on the contract curve of this economy agent a must give agent b a positive amount of the consumption good at the first date and agent b must give agent a a positive amount of the consumption good at the second date. Suppose the two agents agree, at the first date, on an allocation lying on the contract curve. Then at the second date, agent b, having already consumed part of a's endowment, will have an incentive to break the agreement he made at the first date, i.e. he will be better off if he breaks his promise and keeps his entire endowment of the consumption good at the second date.

In the absence of trust the fact that commodities are delivered sequentially becomes all-important. The problem is simply this: If I exchange a unit of consumption today for a unit of consumption tomorrow, I am giving up an actual unit of consumption goods and receiving the mere promise of one in return. There is no reason for me to expect an agent who is only interested in maximizing utility to keep his promise. For this reason I may be unwilling to use forward markets even when these markets exist and are costless. The real problem though is to give a formal account of how agents behave in the absence of trust and this is more difficult than making critical remarks about the conventional theory.

The same point can be made in the language of game theory. Nash defined a cooperative game to be one in which there is unlimited communication before play begins and the players are able to make self-binding commitments. The classical core describes a cooperative game in this sense. The absence of trust, as described above, implies that agents are unable to make binding agreements. If they were, everything could be settled at the first date. A game characterized by lack of trust is therefore only quasi-cooperative. This quasi-cooperativeness of the game has an important implication for the appropriate definition of the solution concept. Recall the classical definition of the core given above. An improving coalition was required to be self-sufficient *at every date*:

$$\sum_{i\in T} x_i' = \sum_{i\in T} e_i .$$

If $\mathscr{E}$ were a two-period economy, for example, this rules out the possibility of a coalition "forming" at the second date, having already traded with the rest of the economy at date 1 and consumed its first-period allocation. The following notation is helpful: if x_i and x_i' are consumption bundles for the i-th agent, let $(x_i|x_i^{s\prime})$ denote the consumption bundle obtained by replacing the consumption x_i^s at the event s with the consumption $x_i^{s\prime}$. A coalition T *can improve on the allocation* x *at the event* $s\in S$ if there is an attainable allocation x' such that:

$$(x_i | x_i^{s\prime}) \succ_i x_i \quad \text{for} \quad i \in T$$

and

$$\sum_{i \in T} x_i^{s\prime} = \sum_{i \in T} e_i^s.$$

The second condition says that if a coalition is improving at the second date it is only required to be self-sufficient at the event at which it forms. The *sequential core* of $\mathscr{E}$ is denoted by $C^s(\mathscr{E})$ and it is defined to be the set of attainable allocations which cannot be improved on by any allocation either in the classical sense, at date 0, or in the above sense at some event $s \in S$ at date 1. If an allocation does not belong to the sequential core then even if all agents agree to it at the outset some coalition has an incentive to break the agreement later on. In the absence of trust it would seem that such an allocation is unstable, just as a non-core allocation is unstable in the classical theory. In the same way, a reasonable outcome should belong to the sequential core. The sequential core gives a precise, though tentative, picture of what might happen in an economy without trust.

Implicit in the discussion of the sequential core above is the idea that the "same" solution concept should be applied at date 0 and at each event $s \in S$ at date 1. This idea can be made precise using the concept of a "subeconomy". Suppose that the allocation x has been chosen at date 0 and the i-th agent consumes x_i^0. At the second date an event $s \in S$ is observed. The i-th agent now finds himself with an endowment e_i^s, with a consumption set $X_i^s := \{\xi | (x_i | \xi) \in X_i\}$ and with a preference relation defined on X_i^s by the condition that:

$$\xi \textit{ is preferred to } \xi' \textit{ if and only if } (x_i | \xi) \succ_i (x_i | \xi').$$

The "subeconomy" defined by these characteristics, i.e. the new endowments, consumption sets and preferences, is an exchange economy in its own right. If the classical core is the appropriate solution concept for the original economy at date 0 then it should also be the appropriate solution concept for each of the subeconomies defined at date 1. The only difference between $\mathscr{E}$ and the subeconomies is the dimensionality of the commodity space—which obviously should not influence the choice of a solution concept—and the fact that at date 1 there exist the agreements reached at date 0. But these agreements are not binding on the agents; in fact, this is precisely what is meant by the absence of trust. If the classical core is the appropriate solution concept for an exchange economy with trust (binding commitments) then in the absence of trust an allocation must, if it is stable, belong both to the (classical) core of the economy at date 0 and to the (classical) core of each of the subeconomies defined at date 1. This is exactly the definition of the sequential core. In this precise sense, therefore, the sequential core is the natural generalization of the classical core to deal with the absence of trust.

Of course, there remain objections to the sequential core as a solution concept. In the first place, most objections to the classical core would apply equally well to the sequential core. For example, the core can be interpreted rather literally as implying that if a non-core allocation is proposed then an improving coalition actually forms to "block" it. In this case, the definition of an improving coalition seems unreasonable. The fact that there exists an allocation which is attainable for the coalition, and makes its members better off, does not guarantee that they will achieve that allocation. Indeed, some of the members of the coalition may be worse off at a core allocation.[2] For this reason, potential members of an improving coalition may prefer the *status quo*. This criticism applies *a fortiori* to the sequential core. In the absence of trust an improving coalition ought to take into account the fact that a sub-coalition may be improving at a later date.

In defence of the core it can be argued that it should not be taken literally as a description of the allocation process. Instead, it should be treated as a *criterion* of stability. But this simply begs the question of how a core allocation is chosen. A better argument would be that the core is an interesting concept because it characterizes the Walrasian equilibrium in a large economy.[3] The competitive model is a useful vehicle for studying many problems, not because of its realism, but because of its simplicity and attractive normative properties. In other words, it serves as a "benchmark". By extension, the core may be a useful starting point for the study of trust, despite its flaws as a descriptive model. The problems mentioned should be the subject of future research. In the present chapter they will be overlooked.

An immediate problem which cannot be avoided is the possibility that the sequential core may be empty. This is certainly the case in the two-person example mentioned earlier. The coalition consisting of agent *b* alone can improve at date 1 on any allocation in the classical core. Since the sequential core is always contained in the classical core, it must be empty in this example. If the sequential core is so easily shown to be empty it may be doubted whether it is a useful solution concept. This view is unduly pessimistic, however.

If trust disappeared overnight and if it were not replaced by another institution, one would not be surprised if the allocation process broke down. In practice, however, institutions do develop to meet such needs and it can be shown that the institution of money can act as a substitute for trust.

For example, consider the two-person example given above. This economy can be turned into a monetary economy by issuing each of the agents with one unit of fiat money at the beginning of the first date and demanding it back at the end of the second. The two agents are eventually required by the tax constraint to return to the government the amount of money they started with, but in the interim they can exchange it among themselves. An allocation must specify not only the consumption of each agent at each date but also his money holdings at the end of the first date. Thus, in the example, if agent b gives part of his money endowment to agent a at the first date he must somehow retrieve it at the second date. The sequential core as previously defined was empty because agent a, having given some of his endowment to agent b, had no way of persuading agent b to keep his promise. In particular, he could not retaliate if agent b broke their agreement. But if, in exchange for consumption at date 0, agent b gives agent a some money, this provides agent b with an incentive to co-operate with agent a at date 1, i.e. to deliver the consumption goods as promised. Otherwise he will not receive the money he needs to pay his taxes. It is not obvious what will happen at date 1; agent a may use his newfound power to extort more than the agreed amount of consumption from agent b at date 1. This is a complex bargaining problem. But there is a fairly natural way of extending the definition of the sequential core to a monetary economy. An improving coalition is allowed to form only if its current money endowment is sufficient to cover the second period taxes of all its members. The introduction of money thus reduces the number of coalitions that can form and hence enlarges the sequential core. The sequential core in this example is now non-empty.[4]

6.3 Introducing money

For the purposes of illustration, assume that there is no uncertainty (S contains a single element) and that there are only two dates. Let $\mathscr{E}$ be an exchange economy, as defined at the beginning of Section 5.1. Let σ_i (resp. τ_i) denote the number of units of fiat money given to (resp. demanded from) the i-th agent by the government, at the beginning of date 0 (resp. end of date 1). σ_i is simply an initial endowment of money and τ_i is the terminal tax demand required to keep money from falling out of the system. Let $\sigma = (\sigma_1, \ldots, \sigma_n)$ and $\tau = (\tau_1, \ldots, \tau_n)$. The ordered triple $(\mathscr{E}, \sigma, \tau)$ is called a *monetary economy* when $\sigma \geq 0$, $\tau \geq 0$ and $\sum_i \sigma_i = \sum_i \tau_i$.

In a monetary economy, agents are allowed to trade money back and forth so an allocation must specify the amount of money they hold at the end of the first date, after trade has taken place. Let m_i denote the i-th agent's cash balance at the end of date 0. This amount is carried forward and becomes his initial endowment of money at the beginning of date 1. An *allocation* for this economy is now an ordered pair $(x, m) = (x_1, \ldots, x_n, m_1, \ldots, m_n)$ such that x_i belongs to X_i and $m_i \geq 0$ for every $i = 1, \ldots, n$. The allocation is *attainable* if $\sum_i x_i = \sum_i e_i$ and $\sum_i m_i = \sum_i \sigma_i$.

Let (x, m) be an attainable allocation. The coalition T is admissible at a given date if and only if its members have enough money to meet their collective tax demand. Thus, T is *admissible at date* 0 if and only if[5]

$$\sum_{i \in T} \sigma_i \geq \sum_{i \in T} \tau_i .$$

Similarly, T is *admissible at date* 1 (given m) if and only if

$$\sum_{i \in T} m_i \geq \sum_{i \in T} \tau_i .$$

We have already encountered the notion of coalitions which can improve on a commodity allocation at date 1 or at date 0, the latter being the classical notion of an improving coalition. Both concepts apply here without alteration and can be used to define the sequential core of a monetary economy. If $(\mathscr{E}, \sigma, \tau)$ is a monetary economy, let the *sequential core* of $(\mathscr{E}, \sigma, \tau)$ to be the set of attainable allocations (x, m) such that x cannot be improved on by any admissible coalition at date 0 or at date 1, where admissibility at date 1 is defined relative to m, of course. The essential difference from the definition of the sequential core of the exchange economy $\mathscr{E}$ is that only coalitions which are self-sufficient in money are allowed to form. The sequential core thus defined is denoted by $C^s(\mathscr{E}, \sigma, \tau)$.

There is a natural concept of equilibrium for a monetary economy. Define the budget set of the i-th agent at the price system $p = (p^0, p^1)$ to be the set of ordered pairs (x_i, m_i) in $X_i \times \mathbb{R}_+$ such that

$$p^0 . x_i^0 + m_i \leq p^0 . e_i^0 + \sigma_i$$

and

$$p^1 . x_i^1 + \tau_i \leq p^1 . e_i^1 + m_i .$$

This budget set is denoted by $\beta_i(p)$. Now the natural way to define an equilibrium is as follows: it consists of a price system p and an attainable allocation (x, m) such that, for every $i = 1, \ldots, n$, (x_i, m_i) is maximal with respect to the preference relation $\prec_i$ in the budget set $\beta_i(p)$. In other words, agents are maximizing utility subject to a sequence of budget constraints and they use money to transfer wealth between the two dates. Call (x, m) an *equilibrium allocation* if (p, x, m) is an equilibrium for some p. One would like to show that every equilibrium allocation belonged to the sequential core of $(\mathscr{E}, \sigma, \tau)$ but unfortunately this is not the case. The reason is that core-allocations must be Pareto-efficient; otherwise the coalition consisting of all the agents, which is certainly admissible, could improve on x at the first date. An equilibrium allocation will not be Pareto-efficient, however, unless $m_i > 0$ for all $i = 1, \ldots, n$. When $m_i > 0$ the i-th agent can exchange a little bit more consumption tomorrow for a little bit less today or *vice versa* and this ensures that the marginal utility of money is the same at both dates. If $m_i = 0$ the marginal utility of money at date 0 might be higher but the i-th agent can do nothing about it. The outcome will be inefficient since for *some* agents $m_i > 0$ and for them the marginal utility of money at both dates will be the same. In general, a stronger concept of equilibrium is required and this is explored in the sequel (Chapter 5, Part 2). For the present it suffices to assume $m_i > 0$.

6.3.1 Theorem *Let (x, m) be an equilibrium allocation for $(\mathscr{E}, \sigma, \tau)$. If $m \gg 0$ and $\prec_i$ is convex then (x, m) belongs to $C^s(\mathscr{E}, \sigma, \tau)$.*

Proof The proof breaks naturally into two parts.

(a) For every $i = 1, \ldots, n$, x_i is maximal in the budget set $\{x_i \in X_i \mid p . x_i + \tau_i \leq p . e_i + \sigma_i\}$. To see this assume the contrary, i.e. that y belongs to this set and $x \prec_i y$. From the convexity of $\prec_i$ it follows that y can be chosen arbitrarily close to x, without loss of generality. Let

$$m_i' = p^1 . y^1 + \tau_i - p^1 . e_i^1 .$$

From the definition of equilibrium and monotonicity

$$0 < m_i = p^1 . x_i^1 + \tau_i - p^1 . e_i^1 .$$

Since y is arbitrarily close to x_i, it follows that $m_i' \geq 0$. The ordered pair (y, m') satisfies the budget constraints

$$p^1 . y^1 + \tau_i \leq p^1 . e_i^1 + m'$$

and

$$\begin{aligned} p^0 . y^0 + m_i' &= p^0 . y^0 + p^1 . y^1 + \tau_i - p^1 . e_i^1 \\ &= p . y + \tau_i - p^1 . e_i^1 \\ &\leq p . e_i + \sigma_i - \tau_i + \tau_i - p^1 . e_i^1 \\ &= p^0 . e_i^0 + \sigma_i \end{aligned}$$

by construction. This contradicts the optimality of (x_i, m_i) in $\beta_i(p)$ and establishes the claim.

(b) Suppose that (x, m) does not belong to $C^s(\mathscr{E}, \sigma, \tau)$. Then there must exist an admissible improving coalition. Suppose that T is an admissible, improving coalition at date 0. Then $\sum_i \sigma_i \geq \sum_i \tau_i$ and there exists a consumption allocation $(y_1, \ldots, y_n)$ such that $\sum_{i \in T} y_i = \sum_{i \in T} e_i$ and $x_i \prec_i y_i$ for every $i \in T$. From (a) it follows that, for every $i \in T$,

$$p . y_i > p . e_i + \sigma_i - \tau_i$$

or, summing over T and rearranging terms,

$$p . \sum_{i \in T} (y_i - e_i) > \sum_{i \in T} (\sigma_i - \tau_i)$$

contradicting the twin assumptions that $\sum_{i \in T} (\sigma_i - \tau_i) \geq 0$ and $\sum_{i \in T} (y_i - e_i) = 0$. A similar argument produces a contradiction if we assume that T is an admissible, improving coalition at date 1. □

This theorem accomplishes two things. First of all, it introduces money into the theory of the core in a non-trivial way. Second, it shows how money replaces trust. Without money, the fact that coalitions can form at any date would often render the sequential core empty. When improving coalitions are required to be self-sufficient in money, the number of improving coalitions is reduced just enough to ensure the core is always non-empty. Even with perfect information, a complete set of markets at the first date and no transactions costs, the theorem provides a *rationale* for using money: if agents do not behave in this way some coalition will be able to improve and the rest will find their plans frustrated.

In equilibrium, money is assumed to be used in a very special way. Agents exchange money and goods so as to satisfy a budget constraint, taking market prices as given. There is no compulsion on individuals to exchange money in this way so a complete theory must account for the fact that everyone satisfies a budget constraint and faces the same terms of trade. It is not true in general that money replaces trust only if agents exchange money and goods "as if" they were in equilibrium. For example, in a small economy a disequilibrium allocation may belong to the sequential core. A partial converse to Theorem 6.3.1 is available in the case of a large economy. What we should like to prove is that in a large economy, that is, when every agent is negligible relative to the whole, only equilibrium allocations belong to the sequential core of a monetary economy. This is indeed the case, but only if the definition of the equilibrium is weakened slightly to allow for the possibility that, in certain pathological cases, the price of money must be zero. These cases are pathological because they arise only when it is possible to reconcile Pareto-efficiency with a sequence of budget constraints without the use of money. This possibility can be safely ignored and, with that qualification, it can be said that the sequential core of a large, monetary economy is precisely the set of equilibrium allocations. In other words, money can perform its function of replacing trust only if the terms of trade between money and goods are taken as given and are the same for everyone. If agents do not behave "as if" they were in a monetary equilibrium some improving coalition will have an incentive to form and the rest will have their plans frustrated.

The results have a formal resemblance to the classical equivalence of the core and set of Walras allocations of a large exchange economy. Under the surface, however, something rather different is going on. The classical results can be explained in terms of what has come to be called the "no surplus" principle. Suppose that x belongs to the classical core of an exchange economy $\mathscr{E}$. Then x must be Pareto-efficient. Otherwise the coalition of the whole would improve on x. Under the usual assumptions (convexity, etc.) efficiency entails the existence of a price vector p such that, for every $i = 1, \ldots, n$,

$$x_i \prec_i y \quad \text{implies} \quad p.x_i < p.y.$$

To show that x is a Walras allocation it is sufficient to show that $p.x_i = p.e_i$ for every i. Suppose that, for some $i = j$, $p.x_j > p.e_j$. Let T be a coalition consisting of all agents except j and let

$$y_i = x_i + \frac{1}{n-1}(x_j - e_j).$$

Clearly, $\sum_{i \in T} y_i = \sum_{i \in T} e_i$ so T is self-sufficient. Now suppose that every agent has smooth preferences. As indicated in the figure below, for any vector z, $p.z > 0$ if and only if

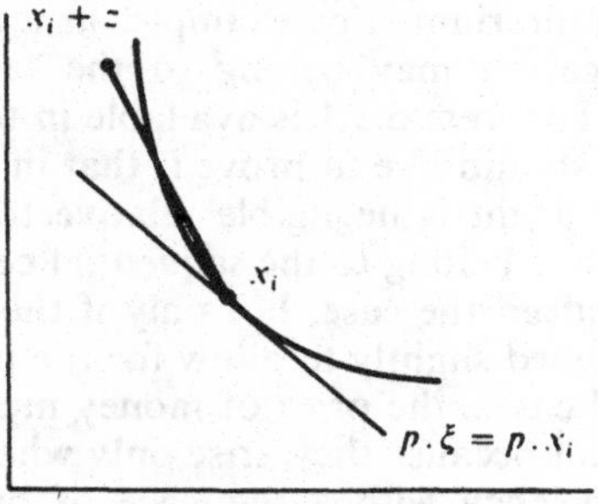

Figure 6.3.1

$x_i \prec_i (x_i + tz)$ for all $t > 0$ sufficiently small. Clearly T is an improving coalition if n is sufficiently large, contradicting the hypothesis that x belongs to the core. Thus, where n is large enough, $p.x_i \leq p.e_i$ for every $i = 1, \ldots, n$. Then attainability implies that $p.x_i = p.e_i$. When an agent is very small the rest of the economy can use the efficiency prices to measure their gains from trade with him. Since every agent takes a very small fraction of this trade, he can treat his utility function as approximately linear. They will continue to trade with the first agent only if he makes a non-positive surplus from trading with them.[6] This very simple idea is what lies behind the powerful classical results. Equally clearly, it does nothing to explain the new results. Applying the same argument to the core of a monetary economy, one could show that

$$p.(x_j - e_j) \leq 0 \quad \text{unless} \quad \sigma_j > \tau_j$$

(for $\sigma_j > \tau_j$ would imply that T was inadmissible) but this is not enough to show that $p.(x_j - e_j) = \sigma_j - \tau_j$. For that one needs a considerably more sophisticated argument involving a continuum of agents.

Another oddity of the sequential core of a large monetary economy is that it typically contains an infinite number of allocations, unlike the classical core which is almost always finite. The reason is quite simple. In a Walrasian equilibrium multiplying all prices by a positive scalar has no real effect. When agents have nominal debts and credits $(\sigma_i - \tau_i)$, a change in the price level has real distribution effects. Within a range determined by the need to avoid bankruptcies, there is an equilibrium corresponding to every price level. What is interesting is that in a monetary economy the "power" or advantage possessed by an individual who has an endowment of money in excess of his needs seems to be largely indeterminate. The indeterminacy only disappears in the case $\sigma = \tau$. Real balance effects are commonplace in equilibrium theory, of course, but there is nothing in the traditional theory of the core to explain their presence here.

The case in which $\sigma = \tau$ is also of special interest because in this case the government does not need any information about individuals or the transactions they undertake. It simply hands out an amount of securities to each individual and demands it back at the end of date 1. It may even choose σ_i = constant for all $i = 1, \ldots, n$. In that case the government does not even need to be able to distinguish agents. This clearly has advantages if information gathering, storage and retrieval are costly. There are several other points that should be noted.

First, it is not the invention of paper money which restores trustworthiness. The Walras allocations are trustworthy in the monetary economy only because there is, in the background, a government which can enforce, evidently at no cost, the payment of taxes. Thus, we have introduced not just a new commodity (money) but a new social institution. In reality this institution would probably be costly, in which case there is a real loss of utility when trust disappears and has to be replaced.

Second, the role of money may seem rather artificial since it can be argued that the government, which enforces the payment of taxes, could just as easily have enforced the original commodity contracts, i.e. intervened directly in the market to make sure that agents kept their promises without introducing "the social contrivance of money". But money has a number of advantages in the general case. First of all, there may be many goods, many dates and many states of nature. Since there are correspondingly many transactions the use of money (or securities) reduces the number of obligations the government has to enforce. Second, by using money the government avoids the need to gather information about the transactions carried out in the economy. It merely sets taxes equal to endowments of money, thus economizing on information costs. In short, the advantage of money is that it allows transactions to be made trustworthy in a *decentralized* way.

A third point is that the model is based on the extreme assumption that agents *never* renege on tax obligations. If the penalties are sufficiently gruesome this may seem reasonable but it would be better to tell a less fanciful story. Of course, the assumption that agents *never* keep their promises unless it is in their interest to do so is also extreme. These assumptions are adopted here for lack of better ones, but they obviously require further, critical study.

To sum up, the monetary arrangement described in the theorem works because it is a social institution, i.e. it is backed up by the power of government to enforce taxes. This may be costly but it does economize on the cost of enforcing transactions because money decentralizes enforcement.

The theory developed so far has achieved to some extent the three objectives set out at the beginning of this chapter. It has provided a role for money (paper assets) in a cooperative trading game. It has provided a rationale for a sequence of budget constraints in the definition of equilibrium.[7] And it shows how these assets can replace trust, ensuring that the sequential core is non-empty. In short, it provides some sort of foundation for a theory of monetary equilibrium.

6.4 The sequential core with an incomplete set of assets

The theory outlined in Section 6.3 is a worthwhile beginning. It can be generalized substantially to allow for many dates and states of nature, as long as it is also assumed that in each case the set of assets is complete. Specifically, there must be a separate paper asset for each state of nature. The need to assume the existence of so many paper assets is rather embarrassing, since only one of them can be identified with money. In any case, it is highly unlikely that the set of assets will be complete in practice and this makes the assumption doubly unattractive.

When the set of assets is incomplete the sequential core can still be characterized by an appropriate equilibrium concept but the characterization is likely to be vacuous. More precisely, it is possible to show that the sequential core is contained in a set of equilibrium allocations, suitably defined, but this set is almost certain to be empty. The reason why is of some importance. Because the coalition of the whole is always admissible, an allocation belonging to the sequential core must be Pareto-efficient; otherwise the coalition consisting of all the agents would improve at the first date. When there is a sequence of budget constraints an equilibrium allocation is almost always Pareto-inefficient unless there is a complete set of assets. Of course, one can define an equilibrium so that it must be efficient—and this is essentially what is done in Part 2 of this Chapter—but in that case, when the set of assets is incomplete, an equilibrium simply will not exist.

The trouble with an incomplete set of assets lies not in characterizing an allocation in the sequential core as an equilibrium, but rather in showing that the sequential core is non-empty. The source of the problem is clarified by an example. Suppose there are two agents, a and b, who have identical preferences but different endowments. There are two dates, $t = 0, 1$, and two states of nature, $s = 0, 1$, which are revealed only at the second date. No consumption takes place at the first date. At the second date, agent a (resp. b) has one unit of consumption goods in state 0 (resp. state 1) and nothing in state 1 (resp. state 0). I shall assume that the agents' preferences are symmetric between consumption in state 0 and consumption in state 1. If preferences are also strictly quasi-concave, it follows easily that in any Pareto-efficient allocation an agent must consume the same amount in each state.

Suppose that both agents have an initial endowment of one unit of money at the beginning of date 0 which they must surrender to the government, in either state, at the end of date 1. In this case, it is easy to show that the sequential core must be empty. First of all, Pareto-efficiency requires that both agents receive the same amount of consumption in each state. Furthermore, each agent must be at least as well off as he would be if he consumed his initial endowment of goods (individual rationality). If preferences are monotonic, this implies that each agent has positive consumption in each state. Attainability then implies that agent a (resp. b) consumes less than his endowment in state 0 (resp. state 1) at the second date. Clearly, agent a (resp. b) can improve on any core allocation at the second date if state 0 (resp. state 1) occurs. If the sequential core is non-empty it must be because the coalitions $\{a\}$ and $\{b\}$ are both inadmissible at the beginning of the second date. Clearly, this is impossible since attainability implies that at least one of the agents has at least one unit of money. Therefore, the sequential core is empty.

The behaviour of the agents in this example is at best myopic and at worst irrational. At the first date the two agents insist on a Pareto-efficient allocation. Any inefficient allocation is improved on by the coalition $\{a, b\}$. Yet both agents know that any Pareto-efficient and individually rational allocation can be improved on at the second date by some admissible coalition, either $\{a\}$ or $\{b\}$, in one of the two states. By demanding Pareto-efficiency they are asking for something which their own behaviour renders unattainable. This sort of behaviour is irrational and ought to be ruled out. Any coalition which seeks to improve on the status quo at date 0 must do so by choosing an allocation which cannot be improved on at date 1. In the present example, the sequential core is non-empty when the definition is amended in this way. In fact, it contains a unique element, the no-trade allocation, which is what one would expect. In general, however, the picture is not so pretty. It is difficult to explore the problem very deeply without embarking on a rather technical discussion, so I shall restrict myself to a brief sketch, leaving a fuller treatment to Part 2. In a large economy, with an incomplete set of assets, the sequential core is normally empty, even if we rule out the sort of irrational behaviour described in the example above. Money is a very flexible means of replacing trust; too flexible as it turns out. In a large economy, agents must exchange money and goods "as if" they were trading in a sequential equilibrium, if money is to serve the function of replacing trust. Thus, a unit of money today corresponds to a bundle of commodities tomorrow, depending on the terms of trade between money and goods in each state of nature. When there is an incomplete set of assets, agents have different marginal rates of substitution between consumption in different states and this means that they value differently changes in the bundle corresponding to a unit of money. In fact, coalitions will form with the express purpose of changing the composition of this bundle since by doing so, with appropriate side payments, they can all make themselves better off.

Notes

1. Other solution concepts can be used to characterize the competitive equilibrium of a large economy. For example, the Shapley value and the bargaining set both give the competitive outcome but they both require the notion of transferable utility, which limits their applicability.

2. Consider, for example, the two-person, two-good economy represented by the Edgeworth Box in the figure below.

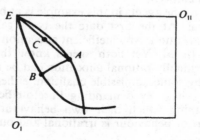

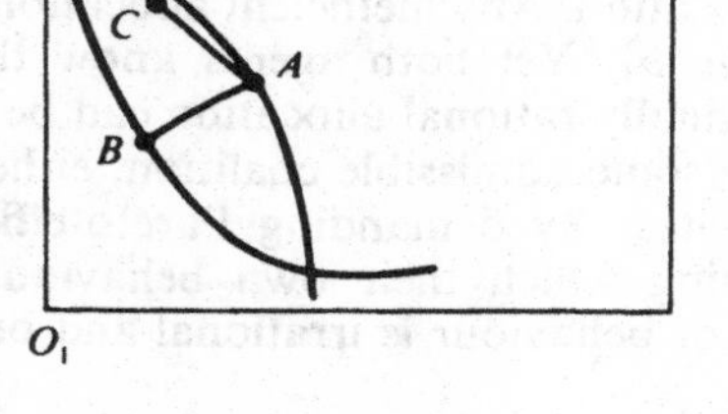

The core of this economy is the familiar contract curve AB. If the economy were replicated so that there were two agents of each type, the core would shrink. In particular, the point A would no longer belong to the core. To see this let C be the midpoint of the line segment AE (E is the endowment point). A coalition consisting of two agents of type II and one agent of type I can improve on A as follows. Give the type I agent his consumption at A and the type II agents their consumption at C. The coalition is self-sufficient because EA is twice EC. The type II agents are better off and the type I agent no worse off. (A small redistribution of goods will ensure they are all better off than at A.) Thus point A is eliminated from the core of the 2-fold replica economy. But note: (a) the type I individual is worse off at any core allocation than he is at A since the core of the 2-fold replica is contained in the core of the original economy; (b) any coalition which can improve on A must contain a type I agent. A can only be eliminated by coalitions which are attempting to realize illusory gains.

3. By "large" I mean, of course, an economy with a large number of individually insignificant agents.

4. I want to emphasize that I am not claiming that money is the only institution which will ensure that agreements are not broken. The law is an obvious alternative. Money can perform this function, however, and in some cases it will be the most economical means of replacing trust. For example, the fact that there are fixed costs involved in going to law suggests that money will be used in making small transactions. This is what we actually observe. Moreover, the central theme of the analysis in the sequel is not merely to point out that money can replace trust but to show that, in a large economy, it can only do so if there is a "monetary equilibrium".

5. Tax obligations rest on individuals but it is clear that the coalition can distribute its collective holdings of money among its members in a way which gives each member enough to meet his personal obligation, if and only if this inequality is satisfied.

6. If z is the first agent's net trade, the rest of the agents can be thought of as trading $-z/(n-1)$ with him. If n is very large, the gain from trading with this agent is

$$u_i(x_i) - u_i(x_i + z/(n-1)) \approx -\frac{\partial u}{\partial x_i}\cdot\frac{z}{n-1}$$

$$= -\frac{\lambda_i p . z}{n-1}$$

which is non-negative only if $p . z \leq 0$.

7. In a large economy, every agent's trades must satisfy a sequence of budget constraints; otherwise some coalition will upset the allocation.

CHAPTER 6—PART 2

Monetary equilibrium: a cooperative approach

6.5 Large economies

In discussing large economies, measure-theoretic concepts are often unavoidable. The reader who is unfamiliar with these is referred to the Mathematical Appendix. Apart from various technicalities, the description of a large economy requires two conceptual innovations: the idea of the set of agents as a measure space and the idea of an economy as a measurable function on that space. Let A denote the set of agents. A might be finite, for example the set $\{1, \ldots, n\}$ used previously, or it might be infinite. In this chapter A will always be a separable metric space. The set of possible coalitions is represented by a family $\mathscr{A}$ of subsets of A. $\mathscr{A}$ is usually required to be a σ-field and in this chapter it will be assumed to be the σ-field generated by the metric topology on A (i.e. the Borel sets of A). The ordered pair $(A, \mathscr{A})$ is a measurable space, of course, so it is possible to define a probability measure ν say, on $(A, \mathscr{A})$. For any coalition T in $\mathscr{A}$, $\nu(T)$ is interpreted as the mass or weight of the coalition. It is also the proportion of agents belonging to T since $\nu(A) = 1$. Because $\mathscr{A}$ is assumed to be a σ-field the empty set ϕ is now a possible coalition and so are other sets of measure zero. To exclude these sets, in the definition of an improving coalition, for example, the explicit requirement that $\nu(T) > 0$ must be added. Having specified a set of agents A and the set of possible coalitions $\mathscr{A}$ and a measure ν which gives the weight of each coalition, we have a probability measure space $(A, \mathscr{A}, \nu)$ which represents a *measure space of agents*.

To illustrate the concept of a measure space of agents consider the finite economies used until now. The set of agents A is $\{1, \ldots, n\}$. The set of possible coalitions $\mathscr{A}$ is the set of all subsets (including ϕ) of A. The measure ν is defined by the equation:

$$\nu(T) = \nu \# T / \# A$$

for all T in $\mathscr{A}$.[1] Notice that $v(T)$ does not measure the number of agents in T but the weight; nonetheless, the weight is used in exactly the same way as the number would be if it were finite. In particular this is true when it comes to adding up quantities of goods. If each member of a coalition T consumes one unit of some commodity, the total consumed is $v(T)$ units.

In order to describe an economy it is necessary to give a rather formal description of the agents' characteristics. As before an agent can be completely described by an ordered triple comprising his consumption set, preference relation and endowment of goods. The consumption set of agent a is denoted by X_a. It is assumed to be a closed, non-empty subset of $\mathbb{R}^l$. His preference relation $\prec_a$ is an open subset of $X_a \times X_a$ and it is assumed, as usual, to be a transitive and irreflexive binary relation on X_a. Let $\mathscr{P}'$ denote the set of ordered pairs $(X_a, \prec_a)$ satisfying these conditions. $\mathscr{P}'$ can be endowed with a topology known as the topology of closed convergence. With this topology it becomes a separable, metrizable space. There is a corresponding σ-field generated by the topology and $\mathscr{P}'$ taken together with this σ-field thus becomes a measurable space.

In what follows, a subset of $\mathscr{P}'$ is of particular interest. Let $\mathscr{P}$ denote the set of ordered pairs $(X_a, \prec_a)$ in $\mathscr{P}'$ such that $X_a = \mathbb{R}^l_+$ and $\prec_a$ is monotonic, i.e. for any x, x' in $\mathbb{R}^l_+$, $x > x'$ implies $x \succ_a x'$.

To complete the description of agents' characteristics it is necessary to specify each agent's endowment of goods, which is denoted in the usual way by e_a. To describe the whole economy it is only necessary to define a function from A to $\mathscr{P}' \times \mathbb{R}^l$ that associates with each agent a his characteristic $(X_a, \prec_a, e_a)$ in $\mathscr{P}' \times \mathbb{R}^l$. Formally, an *exchange economy* is a measurable function $\mathscr{E}$ from $(A, \mathscr{A}, v)$ to $\mathscr{P} \times \mathbb{R}^l_+$. Since $\mathscr{P}$ has not yet been described as a measurable space, $\mathscr{E}$ is taken to be measurable when regarded as a function from $(A, \mathscr{A}, v)$ to $\mathscr{P}' \times \mathbb{R}^l$. To illustrate the concept of exchange economy used here, consider once again the familiar, finite economy. An exchange economy was identified with the n-tuple of characteristics $\{(X_1, \prec_1, e_1) \ldots, (X_n, \prec_n, e_n)\}$. Now it is identified with the function $\mathscr{E}$ from $\{1, \ldots, n\}$ to $\mathscr{P}' \times \mathbb{R}^l$ defined by:

$$\mathscr{E}(i) := (X_i, \prec_i, e_i)$$

for every $i = 1, \ldots, n$. In the finite case the measurability requirement is vacuous. These ideas are summarized in the following formal definition.

6.5.1 Definition *A measure space of agents is an ordered triple $(A, \mathscr{A}, \nu)$ consisting of a separable metric space A, the σ-field $\mathscr{A}$ generated by the topology of A and a probability measure ν defined on $(A, \mathscr{A})$. The characteristics space is the product $\mathscr{P}' \times \mathbb{R}^l$ of the set of ordered pairs $(X, \succ)$ such that X is closed and non-empty and $\prec \subset X \times X$ is a continuous, transitive and irreflexive binary relation. The subset $\mathscr{P} \subset \mathscr{P}'$ comprises the ordered pairs $(X, \prec)$ such that $X = \mathbb{R}^l_+$ and $\prec$ is monotonic. An exchange economy is a measurable function*

$$\mathscr{E}: (A, \mathscr{A}, \nu) \to (\mathscr{P} \times \mathbb{R}^l_+, \mathscr{B}(\mathscr{P} \times \mathbb{R}^l))$$

where $\mathscr{B}(\mathscr{P} \times \mathbb{R}^l)$ denotes the Borel σ-field of $\mathscr{P} \times \mathbb{R}^l_+$ and $\mathscr{P} \times \mathbb{R}^l_+$ is endowed with the product of the usual topologies.

To capture the idea of largeness, the measure space of agents is assumed to be *non-atomic*. This means that for any coalition $T \in \mathscr{A}$, if $\nu(T) > 0$ then there exists a sub-coalition $T' \subset T$ such that $0 < \nu(T') < \nu(T)$, i.e. coalitions are divisible. In particular, every singleton set has measure zero: $\nu(\{a\}) = 0$. This is a precise statement of the hypothesis that every agent is negligible relative to the whole economy. Clearly, this could not be true in a finite economy.

6.6 Some classical equivalence theorems

With the aid of the definitions introduced in the preceding section it is possible to state precisely theorems which establish the equivalence between the core and set of Walras allocations of a large economy. The definitions of allocations, improving coalitions and the core of an exchange economy must first be suitably generalized, of course.

A *consumption allocation* for the economy $\mathscr{E}$ is a measurable function f from $(A, \mathscr{A}, \nu)$ to $\mathbb{R}^l_+$, where $\mathbb{R}^l$ is regarded as a measure space with the usual σ-field. That is, f associates with each agent a in A a consumption bundle $f(a)$ in $\mathbb{R}^l_+$. The consumption allocation f is *attainable* for $\mathscr{E}$ if:

$$\int_A f \, d\nu = \int_A e \, d\nu .$$

(If $\mathbf{e}$ is the projection of $\mathscr{P} \times \mathbb{R}^l_+$ into $\mathbb{R}^l_+$ then $e := \mathbf{e} \circ \mathscr{E}$). An allocation f *can be improved on* by a coalition $T \in \mathscr{A}$ if $\nu(T) > 0$ and there is an attainable allocation g such that $f(a) \prec_a g(a)$ for every $a \in T$ and

$$\int_T g \, dv = \int_T e \, dv.$$

The (classical) *core* of $\mathscr{E}$ is the set of attainable allocations which cannot be improved on by any coalition. It is denoted, as before, by $C(\mathscr{E})$.

A *Walrasian equilibrium* for $\mathscr{E}$ is an ordered pair (f, p), where f is an attainable allocation and p a price system in $\mathbb{R}^l$, such that a.e. in A, $f(a)$ is maximal for $\prec_a$ in the budget set $\{x \in \mathbb{R}^l_+ \mid p.x \leq p.e_a\}$. An allocation f is called a *Walras allocation* for $\mathscr{E}$ if there is a price system p such that (f, p) is a Walrasian equilibrium. The set of Walras allocations for an exchange economy $\mathscr{E}$ is denoted by $W(\mathscr{E})$. The following theorem can be proved using essentially the same argument used for Theorem 6.1.1.

6.6.1 Theorem *$W(\mathscr{E}) \subset C(\mathscr{E})$ for any exchange economy $\mathscr{E}$.*

The partial converse, which will not be proved here, is a special case of results to be proved later.

6.6.2 Theorem *Let $\mathscr{E}:(A, \mathscr{A}, v) \to \mathscr{P} \times \mathbb{R}^l_+$ be an exchange economy such that $\int e \, dv \gg 0$. If $(A, \mathscr{A}, v)$ is atomless, then $C(\mathscr{E}) \subset W(\mathscr{E})$.*

A Walras allocation always belongs to the core and, if each agent is negligible, a core allocation is also a Walras allocation. The theory suggests the proper idealization of a competitive economy, and the appropriate place to use the concept of Walrasian equilibrium, is a large economy composed of individually insignificant agents.

6.7 Monetary economies

Returning to the subject of trust and money, two problems remain. First, in order to introduce money into the cooperative game represented by the core it has to be given some kind of role in the process of coalition-formation. Second, an appropriate definition of monetary equilibrium has to be found before the question of its equivalence with the core-concept can even be raised. Consider first of all the problem of introducing money. Since the ultimate objective is to work our way back to the kind of theory represented by the futures equilibrium, say, it seems sensible to begin in the same way. That is, to assume that agents are given pieces of paper by the monetary authority and required to surrender them at the end of the last period. This convention does not by itself provide money with a role; for that the definition of improving coalitions must be changed. The convention does suggest a definition of a monetary economy, however. For reasons that will only too soon become apparent, it is convenient to generalize the earlier notion somewhat by assuming first, that there are several assets and second, that agents are not necessarily required to hand back the same amount of each asset that they started with.

There is a finite number k of paper assets (different kinds of pieces of paper). The initial endowment of *securities*, as these will be called, is described by an integrable function σ from $(A, \mathscr{A}, \nu)$ to $\mathbb{R}^k_+$. That is, $\sigma(a)$ is the bundle of securities initially held by agent a. The terminal constraints are represented by an integrable function τ from $(A, \mathscr{A}, \nu)$ to $\mathbb{R}^k_+$. $\tau(a)$ is interpreted as the "tax obligation" of agent a, i.e. the bundle of securities he is obliged to give the government at the end of the last period. A *monetary economy* is a triple $(\mathscr{E}, \sigma, \tau)$, where $\mathscr{E}$ is an exchange economy and $\int \sigma \, d\nu = \int \tau \, d\nu$, i.e. the total endowment of securities equals the total tax bill. More formally:

6.7.1 Definition *A monetary economy is an ordered triple* $(\mathscr{E}, \sigma, \tau)$ *where* $\mathscr{E}:(A, \mathscr{A}, \nu) \to \mathscr{P} \times \mathbb{R}^l_+$ *is an exchange economy,* σ *and* τ *are integrable functions from* $(A, \mathscr{A}, \nu)$ *to* $\mathbb{R}^k_+$ *and* $\int \sigma \, d\nu = \int \tau \, d\nu$.

In order for the introduction of securities to have any effect on the definition of the core there has to be some change in the definition of improving coalitions. Precisely, there ought to be a change in the self-sufficiency condition. Call a coalition T *admissible* if $T \in \mathscr{A}$ and $\int_T \sigma \, d\nu \geq \int_T \tau \, d\nu$. In other words, a coalition is admissible if it has enough securities to meet its collective tax bill, without depending on the rest of the economy. Now define an *improving coalition* to be an admissible coalition $T \in \mathscr{A}$ such that $\nu(T) > 0$ and for some attainable consumption allocation g:

(i) $g(a) \succ_a f(a) \qquad (a \in T)$
(ii) $\int_T g \, d\nu = \int_T e \, d\nu$.

The *core* of the monetary economy $(\mathscr{E}, \sigma, \tau)$ is denoted by $C(\mathscr{E}, \sigma, \tau)$ and defined to be the set of attainable consumption allocations that cannot be improved on in the above sense. This definition of the core clearly generalizes the classical definition. The two concepts coincide when $\sigma = \tau$. There is therefore no harm in using the same name for both.

Similarly, one can generalize the concept of Walrasian equilibrium to deal with monetary economies. A *price system* for the monetary economy $(\mathscr{E}, \sigma, \tau)$ is an ordered pair of vectors $(p, q) \in \mathbb{R}^l_+ \times \mathbb{R}^k_+$, where p represents the prices of consumption goods and q the prices of securities. A *Walrasian equilibrium* for the monetary economy $(\mathscr{E}, \sigma, \tau)$ is the ordered triple (f, p, q) consisting of an attainable consumption allocation (f) and a price system (p, q) such that, a.e. in A,

> $f(a)$ *is maximal with respect to* $\prec_a$ *in the budget set* $\{x \in \mathbb{R}_+ \mid p.x + q.\tau(a) \leq p.e(a) + q.\sigma(a)\}$.

f is called a *Walras allocation* for $(\mathscr{E}, \sigma, \tau)$ if (f, p, q) is a Walrasian equilibrium for some (p, q). The set of Walras allocations is denoted $W(\mathscr{E}, \sigma, \tau)$. It is clear that this definition of the Walras allocation generalizes the previous one. The two concepts coincide when $\sigma = \tau$.

6.7.2 Theorem *Let* $(\mathscr{E}, \sigma, \tau)$ *be any monetary economy. Then* $W(\mathscr{E}, \sigma, \tau) \subset C(\mathscr{E}, \sigma, \tau)$.

Proof Suppose that f is a Walras allocation for $(\mathscr{E}, \sigma, \tau)$. Then for some price system $(p, q) \in \mathbb{R}^l_+ \times \mathbb{R}^k_+$, (f, p, q) is a Walrasian equilibrium. If f can be improved on, there exists a coalition $T \in \mathscr{A}$ and an attainable allocation q such that:

(i) $v(T) > 0$, $\int_T \sigma \, dv \geq \int_T \tau \, dv$;

(ii) $\int_T g \, dv = \int_T e \, dv$.

and

(iii) $g(a) \succ_a f(a)$ for every $a \in T$.

The definition of the Walrasian equilibrium implies that for every $a \in T$,

$$p.g(a) > p.e(a) + q.(\sigma(a) - \tau(a)).$$

Since $\int_T g \, dv = \int_T e \, dv$, this implies that

$$q.\int_T (\sigma - \tau) \, dv < 0.$$

Since $q \geq 0$ and $\int_T \sigma \, dv \geq \int_T \tau \, dv$, there is a contradiction here. So f cannot be improved on. □

The converse requires stronger assumptions, in particular that $\mathscr{E}$ be a large economy.

6.7.3 Theorem *Let $\mathscr{E}:(A, \mathscr{A}, \nu) \to \mathscr{P} \times \mathbb{R}^l_+$ be a non-atomic economy such that $\int e \, d\nu \gg 0$ and let σ, τ be integrable functions from $(A, \mathscr{A}, \nu)$ to $\mathbb{R}^k_+$ such that $\int \sigma \, d\nu = \int \tau \, d\nu$. Then*

$$C(\mathscr{E}, \sigma, \tau) \subset W(\mathscr{E}, \sigma, \tau).$$

Proof For every $a \in A$ define

$$\prec_a(f) := \{x \in \mathbb{R}^l_+ \mid x \succ_a f(a)\}$$

and

$$\chi(a) := \prec_a(f) - \{e_a\}.$$

For every agent $a \in A$ define

$$\zeta(a) := \{w \in \mathbb{R}^k \mid w \geq \tau(a) - \sigma(a)\}.$$

For every $a \in A$, put $\psi(a) := (\chi(a) \times \zeta(a)) \cup \{0\}$. I claim that

$$0 \notin \text{int} \int \psi \, d\nu.$$

Suppose the contrary. Then there exist a pair of integrable functions h^1 and h^2 from A to $\mathbb{R}^l$ and $\mathbb{R}^k$ respectively such that

$$\int (h^1, h^2) \, d\nu \ll 0.$$

Let $T := \{a \in A \mid (h^1(a), h^2(a)) \neq 0\}$. Then $\nu(T) > 0$,

$$\int_T \sigma \, d\nu \geq \int_T \tau \, d\nu$$

and $h^1(a) \in \chi(a)$ for every $a \in T$. There is an attainable consumption allocation g such that

$$g(a) := e(a) + h^1(a) - \int h^1 \, d\nu / \nu(T)$$

for every $a \in T$. Then $\int_T g \, d\nu = \int_T e \, d\nu$ and $g(a) \succ_a f(a)$ for every $a \in T$. Thus, T is an improving coalition, contradicting the hypothesis that $f \in C(\mathscr{E}, \sigma, \tau)$.

Since $(A, \mathscr{A}, \nu)$ is a non-atomic measure space, $\int \psi \, d\nu$ is a convex set (for a proof, see the appendix). Thus the Minkowski Theorem tells us that there exists a non-zero vector $(p, q) \in \mathbb{R}^l \times \mathbb{R}^k$ such that

$$0 \leq \inf (p, q) \cdot \int \psi \, d\nu.$$

It can be shown that the correspondence ψ has a measurable graph (for a definition and proof see the appendix) and this implies (by a theorem; see the appendix) that:

$$\inf(p, q) . \int \psi \, \mathrm{d}\nu = \int \inf(p, q) . \psi \, \mathrm{d}\nu .$$

By definition, $0 \in \psi(a)$ for every $a \in A$ so $0 \geq \inf(p, q) . \psi(a)$ for every $a \in A$. Then, combining these results:

$$0 \leq \inf(p, q) . \int \psi \, \mathrm{d}\nu = \int \inf(p, q) . \psi \, \mathrm{d}\nu \leq 0 .$$

From this it easily follows that

$$0 = \inf(p, q) . \psi(a)$$

a.e. in A. Then, a.e. in A, $x \succ_a f(a)$ implies that

$$p . x + q . \tau_a \geq p . e_a + q . \sigma_a .$$

By continuity it follows that a.e. in A,

$$p . f(a) + q . \tau(a) \geq p . e(a) + q . \sigma(a) .$$

Suppose that the inequality were strict for a set of agents of positive measure. Then $p . \int f \, \mathrm{d}\nu + q . \int \tau \, \mathrm{d}\nu > p . \int e \, \mathrm{d}\nu + q . \int \tau \, \mathrm{d}\nu$. This contradicts the attainability of f and the assumption that $\int \sigma \, \mathrm{d}\nu = \int \tau \, \mathrm{d}\nu$. Thus, a.e. in A, $p . f(a) + q . \tau(a) = p . e(a) + q . \sigma(a)$.

From the monotonicity of preferences and the definition of ψ it is fairly clear that $(p, q) \geq 0$. There are two cases to be considered, the one where $p > 0$ and the one where $p = 0$. Suppose first that $p > 0$. Since $\int e \, \mathrm{d}\nu \gg 0$ there is a set of agents of positive measure for whom $p . e(a) + q . \sigma(a) - q . \tau(a) > 0$. Suppose that for one of these agents $x \succ_a f(a)$ and $p . x + q . \tau_a = p . e_a + q . \sigma_a$. By continuity of preferences there is a number $0 < \lambda < 1$ such that $\lambda x \succ_a f(a)$ and $\lambda p . x + q . \tau_a < p . e_a + q . \sigma_a$. This is a contradiction and it establishes that if $p . e_a + q . (\sigma_a - \tau_a) > 0$ then $f(a)$ is maximal for $\prec_a$ in the budget set $\{x \in \mathbb{R}^l_+ \mid p . x + q . \tau_a \leq p . e_a + q . \sigma_a\}$. The monotonicity of $\prec_a$ then implies that $p \gg 0$ by an easy argument. Now for any $a \in A$, either $p . e_a + q . (\sigma_a - \tau_a) > 0$ or the budget set is $\{0\}$. Then a.e. in A, $f(a)$ is maximal for $\prec_a$ in the budget set. This completes the proof under the assumption that $p > 0$.

Suppose now that $p = 0$ and hence $q > 0$. Since it has already been proved that $p . f(a) + q . \tau(a) = p . e(a) + q . \sigma(a)$, a.e. in A, the assumption $p = 0$ implies that $q . \tau(a) = q . \sigma(a)$, a.e. in A. There may be several vectors with this property. Let $Q := \{q > 0 \mid q . \tau(a)$

$= q.\sigma(a)$, a.e. in $A\}$. Let K' be the set of securities $j = 1, \ldots, k$ such that $q_j > 0$ for some $q \in Q$ and let J be the complementary set of securities $j = 1, \ldots, k$ such that $q_j = 0$ for any $q \in Q$. Suppose that $T \in \mathscr{A}$ is an admissible coalition, i.e. $v(T) > 0$ and $\int_T \sigma \geq \int_T \tau$. By construction for any $j \in K'$ there exists $q \in Q$ such that $q \geq 0$, $q_j > 0$ and $q.\int_T \sigma = q.\int_T \tau$. Hence $\int_T \sigma_j = \int_T \tau_j$ since $\int_T \sigma_j > \int_T \tau_j$ would imply $q.\int_T \sigma > q.\int_T \tau$, a contradiction.

For any non-empty set $J \subset \{1, \ldots, k\}$ let $\mathbb{R}^J$ be the linear subspace of $\mathbb{R}^k$ carrying the securities $j \in J$. Let π_J be the canonical projection from $\mathbb{R}^k$ to $\mathbb{R}^J$. For any vector $w \in \mathbb{R}^k$ let $w_J := \pi_J(w)$ and for any function σ: $(A, \mathscr{A}, v) \neq \mathbb{R}^k$ let $\sigma_J := \pi_J \circ \sigma$. The preceding discussion has shown that $T \in \mathscr{A}$ is admissible if and only if $v(T) > 0$, $\int_T \sigma_J \geq \int_T \tau_J$ and $\int_T \sigma_{K'} = \int_T \tau_{K'}$. It is clear that, as far as the determination of admissibility is concerned, some of the securities in K' are superfluous. Suppose for example that $\int_T \sigma_j = \int_T \tau_j$ for all $j \in K' \backslash \{j_0\}$. Then $\int_T \sigma_j = \int_T \tau_j$ for all $j \in K'$ since $q.\int_T \sigma = q.\int_T \tau$ for some $q \in Q$ such that $q_{j_0} > 0$. Therefore the admissibility of T is determined by the set of securities $J \cup K' \backslash \{j_0\}$. A set $K \subset K'$ is said to be a *sufficient* set if, for any T such that $v(T) > 0$, $\int_T \sigma_K = \int_K \tau_K$ if and only if $\int_T \sigma_{K'} = \int_T \tau_{K'}$. A sufficient set is said to be *minimal* if it does not contain a sufficient, proper subset. Let K be a minimal sufficient set and let $L = K' \backslash K$. Then the set $\{1, \ldots, k\}$ of securities is partitioned by J, K and L and the functions σ and τ are "partitioned" accordingly: $\sigma = \sigma_J + \sigma_K + \sigma_L$ and $\tau = \tau_J + \tau_K + \tau_L$.

The securities in L effectively drop out of the analysis. As far as the definition of the core is concerned they might as well not exist. Let the correspondence χ be defined as before, let

$$\zeta(a) := \{w \in \mathbb{R}^{J \cup K} | w_J \geq \tau_J(a) - \sigma_J(a) \quad \text{and} \quad w_K = \tau_K(a) - \sigma_K(a)\}$$

for every a in A and let ψ be defined as before. It follows that

$$0 \notin r \operatorname{int} \textstyle\int \psi \, dv$$

where "r int" stands for the interior relative to $\mathbb{R}^l \times \mathbb{R}^{J \cup K}$. This fact is proved using the same argument as in the earlier case, except that the criterion of admissibility has changed. Instead of $\int_T \sigma \geq \int_T \tau$ I now need $\int_T \sigma_J \geq \int_T \tau_J$ and $\int_T \sigma_K = \int_T \tau_K$. From this point one can proceed as before to establish the existence of an ordered pair $(p, q) \in \mathbb{R}^l \times \mathbb{R}^{J \cup K}$ such that $(p, q) \neq 0$ and, a.e. in A, $x \succ_a f(a)$ implies that

$$\begin{aligned} p.x + q.\tau(a) &\geq p.f(a) + q.\tau(a) \\ &= p.e(a) + q.\sigma(a). \end{aligned}$$

From the monotonicity of preferences and the definition of ψ it is clear that $p \geq 0$ and $q_J \geq 0$. Suppose that $p = 0$. Then as before, a.e. in A, $q.\sigma(a) = q.\tau(a)$. If $q_J = 0$ then $q_K \neq 0$ and $q_K.\sigma_K(a) = q_K.\tau_K(a)$, a.e. in A, contradicting the assumption that K is a minimal sufficient set of securities. Thus $q_J > 0$. For each $j \in K \cup L$ there exists $q^{(j)} \in Q$ such $q_j^{(j)} > 0$. Let $\bar{q} = \sum_{j \in K \cup L} q^{(j)}$. Then $\bar{q} \in Q$ and $\bar{q}_j > 0$ for all $j \in K \cup L$. For some $\lambda > 0$ sufficiently large, $\hat{q} = q + \lambda \bar{q}_j > 0$ and $\hat{q}.\sigma(a) = \hat{q}.\tau(a)$, a.e. in A. Hence $\hat{q} \in Q$. Since $\hat{q}$ and $\bar{q}$ belong to Q, $\hat{q}_J = 0 = \bar{q}_J$. This in turn implies that $q_J = 0$, a contradiction. Hence $p > 0$.

It has now been established that there exists a price system $(p, \hat{q})$ in $\mathbb{R}^l_+ \times \mathbb{R}^k_+$ such that $p > 0$ and a.e. in A, $x \succ_a f(a)$ implies $p.x + q.\tau_a \geq p.f(a) + q.\tau_a = p.e_a + q.\sigma_a$. The rest of the proof is exactly the same as in the first case. □

These two theorems provide a generalization of the classical theorems which demonstrate the equivalence of the core and the set of Walras allocations of a large exchange economy. The most interesting thing about these results is the way in which they provide a role for money—strictly speaking, for paper assets. The following story provides a concrete interpretation of these results. Suppose that goods are allocated within a large economy by a competitive process which, for present purposes, may be identified with "coalition-formation". Then the outcome will be a consumption allocation lying in the (classical) core of the economy. This allocation will be efficient but the distribution of income may leave something to be desired. If the government wanted to implement some other (efficient) allocation it could hand out paper assets to the agents and demand them back in different amounts from each one. The agents could then be left to arrange their own trades competitively as before. The result will be an allocation corresponding to an equilibrium with lump sum transfers. If the government has planned carefully, i.e. chosen the lump sum transfers correctly, the allocation will be the one it wanted.

There is a fly in this otherwise attractive ointment however. Corresponding to any particular distribution of securities (σ) and tax obligations (τ) there is a large, in fact infinite, number of Walras allocations. Suppose there were only one asset and one consumption good and normalize prices by putting $q = 1$. Let (σ, τ) be given. For any number $p > 0$ such that no agent is bankrupt, i.e. $p.e_a + (\sigma_a - \tau_a) \geq 0$, the allocation f defined by putting

$$f(a) := p.e_a + (\sigma_a - \tau_a)/p \qquad (a \in A)$$

is a Walras allocation. To see this note that $\int f = \int e + \int (\sigma - \tau)/p = \int e$ and that $f(a)$ maximizes x subject to the constraint $p.x$

$\leq p.e_a + (\sigma_a - \tau_a)$. Since there is only one good, maximizing x is equivalent to maximizing utility so $f(a)$ is maximal for $\prec_a$ in the budget set $\{x \geq 0 | p.x \leq p.e_a + (\sigma_a - \tau_a)\}$, a.e. in A. There is evidently a large number of equilibrium prices: if p is an equilibrium price so is any $p' \geq p$ since an agent who is not bankrupt at p cannot be bankrupt at p'. Furthermore, the allocations corresponding to each p are different unless $\sigma = \tau$. Every Walras allocation belongs to the core so, even in a large economy, the core is infinite when $\sigma \neq \tau$.

The size of the core is rather interesting in its own right. The classical core of a large economy without money, say, an Arrow–Debreu economy, is equal to the set of Walras allocations. Under mild regularity conditions the set of Walras allocations, and hence the core, is finite. It seems odd that the introduction of a single asset should increase the size of the core so much. It is easy to see why the introduction of money should increase the set of equilibria. Each agent's excess demand for money is $\tau_a - \sigma_a$, independently of prices. Since $\int \sigma = \int \tau$, the "money market" clears automatically, independently of prices. The vector of asset prices can therefore be chosen more or less arbitrarily and if the price system (p, q) has been normalized in the usual way, changes in q must have real distribution effects. It is not at all clear what the analogous explanation of the size of the core would be, however. It appears that the change in an agent's bargaining power induced by the imposition of a net tax is indeterminate. The core only imposes the condition that equals, including coalitions, be treated equally.

This indeterminacy does not apply, however, to the case $\sigma = \tau$, which is of special interest in what follows. The case $\sigma \neq \tau$ is dealt with here because it is a necessary part of the analysis of the sequential game. The same holds for the case $k > 1$, which is essentially the same as the case $k = 1$ when there is only a single time period. These remarks will become clearer in the next section.

6.8 The sequential core

The definitions of the sequential core and the set of Walras allocations for a *monetary* economy allow paper assets to play a role in the cooperative market game, even though they have no intrinsic utility and even though trade can be carried on perfectly well without them. The really important function of these assets is revealed only in an economy without trust, however; for there the role of assets is not simply to effect lump sum transfers but also to act as a substitute for trust.

So far $\mathscr{E}$ has been treated like an ordinary, Arrow–Debreu economy but in the background there is a set D of date-event pairs reflecting the presence of time, uncertainty and information structures. It is implicitly assumed that assets can be handed back and forth quite freely and that the bundle of securities with which an agent begins a period is precisely what he held at the end of the preceding period. An allocation of securities thus needs to specify the holdings of assets of each agent at the end of each event d in D. Define a *security allocation* for $(\mathscr{E}, \sigma, \tau)$ to be a measurable function (f^m) from $(A, \mathscr{A}, \nu) \times D$ to $\mathbb{R}^k_+$ such that for every $d \in \bar{D}$, the set of terminal events, $f^m(a, d) \geq \tau(a)$ for every $a \in A$. In other words, every agent ends up with enough securities to honour his terminal tax obligation. A security allocation f^m is *attainable* for $(\mathscr{E}, \sigma, \tau)$ if, for every $d \in D$,

$$\int f^m(a, d)\nu(da) = \int \sigma \, d\nu .$$

$f^m(a, d)$ is agent a's holdings of securities at the *end* of the event $d \in D$. An *allocation* for $(\mathscr{E}, \sigma, \tau)$ is an ordered pair (f, f^m) consisting of a consumption allocation f and a security allocation f^m for $(\mathscr{E}, \sigma, \tau)$. The pair (f, f^m) will, for convenience, be denoted by $\hat{f}$. $\hat{f}$ is *attainable* if both f and f^m are attainable.

Suppose that an attainable allocation $\hat{f}$ has been chosen somehow and consider the situation which arises at some event d in D. Agent a has the characteristic $(X_a, \prec_a, e_a)$ and has been allocated the bundle $f(a)$ of goods and the sequence of security holdings $f^m(a, .)$. The only choices which are relevant at d are those which can affect consumption or security holdings at events $d' \geq d$. The past cannot be changed and decisions relating to events which are impossible (have probability zero) at d are irrelevant. Let $F = \{d' \in D \mid d' \geq d\}$. F represents the present and future at d. At d the commodity space is $X^F := \oplus\{X^{d'} : d' \in F\}$. The consumption set X^F_a is the projection of $\mathbb{R}^l_+$ into X^F. Agent a has an endowment of goods e^F_a which is the projection of e_a into X^F. He has an initial endowment of securities $f^m(a, d^-)$, where d^- is the predecessor of d. And, of course his tax obligation is $\tau(a)$ as usual. His preferences over consumption bundles in X^F_a are defined as follows. Let $\tilde{X}^F_a := \{x \in X_a \mid x^{d'} = f^{d'}(a)$ for $d' \notin F\}$ and let $\tilde{\prec}^F_a := \prec_a \cap \tilde{X}^F_a \times \tilde{X}^F_a$. Then define $\prec^F_a$ to be the projection of $\tilde{\prec}^F_a$ into X^F. In other words, $x^F \succ^F_a \bar{x}^F$ if $x \succ_a \bar{x}$, where x^F and $\bar{x}^F$ are bundles in X^F and x and $\bar{x}$ are the unique bundles in X_a which agree with x^F and $\bar{x}^F$, respectively, on F and agree with $f(a)$ elsewhere.

Thus, in a quite natural sense, agent a has a new characteristic at d, defined relative to $\hat{f}(a)$, namely the ordered triple $(X^F_a, \prec^F_a, e^F_a)$. This leads to the concept of the *exchange sub-economy* at d, $(\mathscr{E}^d | \hat{f})$ defined relative to $\hat{f}$. When there is no risk of confusion this subeconomy will be referred to simply as $\mathscr{E}^d$. $\mathscr{E}^d$ is defined by the relation:

$$\mathscr{E}^d(a) := (X^F_a, \prec^F_a, e^F_a)$$

for every $a \in A$, where $F := \{d' \in D | d' \geq d\}$. It is easy to see that $\mathscr{E}^d$ is an exchange economy in its own right, i.e. satisfies the conditions of Definition 6.8.1. Similarly, it is possible to define a monetary economy at d relative to $\hat{f}$, namely the ordered triple $(\mathscr{E}^d, f^m(., d^-), \tau)$. This is a monetary economy in the sense of Definition 6.7.1 if $\hat{f}$ is attainable.

6.8.1 *Definition* *Let $\hat{f}$ be an attainable allocation for the monetary economy $(\mathscr{E}, \sigma, \tau)$. The exchange subeconomy at d defined relative to f is an exchange economy $(\mathscr{E}^d | f)$ or $\mathscr{E}^d$ defined by the relation*

$$\mathscr{E}^d(a) := (X^d_a, \prec^F_a, e^F_a)$$

for every $a \in A$. The monetary subeconomy at d defined relative to $\hat{f}$ is the monetary economy $(\mathscr{E}^d, f^m(., d^-), \tau)$.

The notion of a subeconomy at d models economic activity at the event d, taking as given everything pertaining to other events. It represents in a natural way the options open to agents who have chosen $\hat{f}$ but have the opportunity to revise their plans at d. One point should be noted. As defined above the preference relation $\prec^F_a$ apparently depends on consumption in the same period at events other than d. This may seem unreasonable since the consumption planned for other events at date 1 is only notional once d is observed. To resolve the difficulty it is sufficient to adopt a separability assumption, for example the expected utility hypothesis. Another way out is to interpret $\prec^F_a$ not as agent a's actual preferences at d but as his anticipated preferences. The theory of the sequential core (defined below) is then a theory about anticipated rather than actual consumption.

Since the economy $(\mathscr{E}^d, f^m(., d^-), \tau)$ is a monetary economy in its own right it has a core and set of Walras allocations, denoted by $C(\mathscr{E}^d, f^m(., d^-), \tau)$ and $W(\mathscr{E}^d, f^m(., d^-), \tau)$ respectively. If f is a consumption allocation for $\mathscr{E}$ then let f^F be the consumption allocation for $\mathscr{E}^F$ defined by putting $f^F(a)$ equal to the projection of $f(a)$ into X^F for every $a \in A$. Define attainability of f^F in the obvious way.

The *sequential core* of $(\mathscr{E}, \sigma, \tau)$ is the set of attainable allocations $\hat{f}$ such that for every $d \in D$:

$$f^F \in C(\mathscr{E}^d, f^m(.,d^-), \tau) \quad \text{where} \quad F := \{d' \in D \mid d' \geq d\}.$$

The sequential core is denoted by $C^s(\mathscr{E}, \sigma, \tau)$. The idea behind the sequential core is that in the absence of trust coalitions may improve at any date-event pair. Thus, a "trustworthy" allocation $\hat{f}$ must be one such that f^F belongs to the core of the subeconomy $(\mathscr{E}^d, f^m(.., d^-), \tau)$ for every $d \in D$ and $F := \{d' \in D | d' \geq d\}$. An allocation in the sequential core is trustworthy since it cannot be improved on at any date-event pair. Indeed the concept of the sequential core can be taken to characterize trustworthiness in a monetary economy since an allocation not in the sequential core can be improved on at some date. The concept of an "improvement at the event d" is not explicitly defined in the foregoing but it is clear what must be meant. A coalition $T \in \mathscr{A}$ can improve on f at d if there is an attainable consumption allocation g^F at d such that:

(i) $g^F(a) \succ_a^F f^F(a)$ for every $a \in T$ and
(ii) $\int_T g^F \, dv = \int_T e^F \, dv$

and if T is admissible at d, i.e. $v(T) > 0$ and

(iii) $\int_T f^m(., d^-) v(da) \geq \int_T \tau \, dv$.

In a similar way, one can define a *sequential allocation* to be an attainable allocation $\hat{f}$ such that for every $d \in D$:

$$f^F \in W(\mathscr{E}^d, f^m(.,d^-), \tau).$$

and $F := \{d' \in D | d' \geq d\}$. The set of sequential allocations for the monetary economy $(\mathscr{E}, \sigma, \tau)$ is denoted by $W^s(\mathscr{E}, \sigma, \tau)$. The following results follow immediately from the definitions and Theorems 6.7.2 and 6.7.3.

6.8.2 Theorem *Let $(\mathscr{E}, \sigma, \tau)$ be a monetary economy. Then $W^s(\mathscr{E}, \sigma, \tau) \subset C^s(\mathscr{E}, \sigma, \tau)$.*

6.8.3 Theorem *Let $\mathscr{E} = (A, \mathscr{A}, v) \to \mathscr{P} \times \mathbb{R}^l_+$ be a non-atomic economy such that $\int e \, dv \gg 0$ and let σ, τ be integrable functions from $(A, \mathscr{A}, v)$ to $\mathbb{R}^k_+$ such that $\int \sigma \, dv = \int \tau \, dv$. Then $C^s(\mathscr{E}, \sigma, \tau) \subset W^s(\mathscr{E}, \sigma, \tau)$.*

These theorems show how the absence of trust imposes a sequence of budget constraints. In the absence of trust it would be unreasonable of agents to agree to an allocation that could be improved on at a later date-event pair. So the allocation one would expect to observe must belong to the sequential core. But this means that in a large economy the allocation satisfies the constraints:

$$p^F.f^F(a) + q.\tau(a) = p^F.e^F(a) + q.f^m(a, d^-)$$

a.e. in A for every $d \in D$. The necessity of a sequence of constraints suggests that the absence of trust has put us on the right track. But the definition of the sequential equilibrium is quite unlike any equilibrium concept encountered so far. The relationship between the sequential equilibrium and other concepts such as the futures equilibrium deserves closer inspection.

6.9 Concepts of equilibrium in a sequence of markets

The monetary economy $(\mathscr{E}, \sigma, \tau)$ is not an economy with a sequence of markets in the strict sense because no market structure has been defined for it. However, since markets are evidently complete at every date event pair, $\mathscr{E}$ can be regarded as a special case, albeit a trivial one, of an economy with a sequence of markets. Suppose that $\mathscr{E}$ were a two-period economy, i.e. $D \equiv \{0\} \cup S$, and that $\sigma = \tau$. These assumptions will be retained in the remainder of this chapter so it is worth taking advantage of them to simplify the notation slightly. Almost every agent ends up holding precisely the bundle of securities needed to meet his tax obligations. So a security allocation really only needs to specify the bundle held by each agent at the end of the first period and carried forward by him to the second period. A security allocation for the two period economy is therefore treated as a measurable function f^m from $(\mathscr{A}, A, \nu)$ to $\mathbb{R}^k_+$. $f^m(a)$ is agent a's security holdings at the end of date 0. f^m is attainable if $\int f^m \, d\nu = \int \sigma \, d\nu$, of course. The other definitions hold as before except to the extent that they are affected by this change.

Suppose the definition of a futures equilibrium were extended in the natural way to cover a monetary economy with a complete set of markets at each event. It should be clear that in equilibrium there will be no need for any forward markets at the first date. Because the future equilibrium has a "cash on delivery" constraint, futures trading allows wealth to be reallocated among the various states at date 1 but it does not allow the transfer of wealth between dates. A futures contract is a gamble on prices; but if there is a complete set of contingent markets then there is perfect arbitrage. Consequently, the futures price at date 0 equals the spot price at date 1. Any purchases or sales of futures contracts have no effect on the distribution of wealth across states at date 1. There is no loss of generality, therefore, in assuming that no futures trading takes place.[2] Equivalently, there are only spot markets at each event $d \in D$.

A futures equilibrium for a two-period, monetary economy with complete markets can thus be defined to be an attainable allocation $\hat{f}$ together with a pair of price sequences (p^*, q^*) such that, a.e. in A,

> *$\hat{f}(a)$ is maximal for $\prec_a$ in the budget set consisting of ordered pairs $(x, w) \in \mathbb{R}^l_+ \times \mathbb{R}^k_+$ satisfying:*

$$p^0 . (x^0 - e^0_a) + q^0 . (w - \tau_a) \leq 0$$

$$p^s . (x^s - e^s_a) + q^s . (\tau_a - w) \leq 0 \qquad (s \in S).$$

Here p^0 and p^s are the spot price vectors for consumption goods at the events 0 and s respectively. q^0 and q^s are the spot price vectors for securities at the events 0 and s respectively. Now suppose that $\hat{f} \in W^s(\mathscr{E}, \sigma, \sigma)$. Then $f \in W(\mathscr{E}, \sigma, \sigma)$ so, a.e. in $A, f(a)$ is maximal for $\prec_a$ in the budget set $\{x \in \mathbb{R}^l_+ \mid p . x \leq p . e_a\}$ for some price system $p \in \mathbb{R}^l$. Similarly, $f^s \in W(\mathscr{E}^s, f^m, \sigma)$ implies that for some price system $(p^s, q^s) \in \mathbb{R}^l \times \mathbb{R}^k$, a.e. in $A, f^s(a)$ is maximal for $\prec^s_a$ in the budget set $\{x^s \in X^s_a \mid p^s . x^s + q^s . \tau_a \leq p^s . e^s_a + q^s . f^m(a)\}$. Elsewhere the notation p, p^s etc. has been used to indicate that p^s is the projection of p into X^s etc. This is not necessarily the case here. Under certain conditions, however, *for some normalization of prices*, p^s is the projection of p into X^s for every s in S. For example, if there is a non-null set of agents for whom the preferences $\prec_a$ are smooth at $f(a)$ and $f(a) \gg 0$, then p and p^s are uniquely determined up to a scalar multiple. But much weaker conditions will do as well. Rather than pursue these details here I shall simply define a sequential allocation to be *regular* if there are equilibrium prices p, p^s etc. such that for some normalization p^s is the projection of p for every $s \in S$. And in what follows only regular sequential allocations are considered.

Summing the second-period budget constraints over $s \in S$,

$$\sum_{s \in S} [p^s . f^s(a) + q^s . \sigma_a] = \sum_{s \in S} [p^s . e^s_a + q^s . f^m(a)]. \tag{1}$$

The first-period constraint is

$$p . f(a) = p . e_a. \tag{2}$$

Subtracting (1) from (2) and defining $p^0 := p - \sum_{s \in S} p^s$ and $q^0 := \sum_{s \in S} q^s$, yields:

$$p^0 . f^0(a) + q^0 . f^m(a) = p^0 . e^0_a + q^0 . \sigma_a$$

since $\sigma = \tau$ and $f^0(a) = f(a) - \sum_{s \in S} f^s(a)$ etc. Thus the regular sequential allocation $\hat{f}$ satisfies the budget constraints appropriate to the futures equilibrium with complete markets at the prices p^0, p^s etc. Now suppose there is an ordered pair $(\bar{x}, \bar{w}) \in \mathbb{R}^l_+ \times \mathbb{R}^k_+$ which satisfies the constraints:

$$p^0 . \bar{x}^0 + q^0 . \bar{w}^0 \leq p^0 . e^0_a + q^0 . \sigma_a$$

$$p^s . \bar{x}^s + w^s . \sigma_a \leq p^s . e^s + q^s . \bar{w}^0 \qquad (s \in S).$$

Summing these constraints shows that $p . \bar{x} \leq p . e_a$ since $q^0 = \sum_{s \in S} q^s$. If $f(a)$ is maximal for $\prec_a$ in the set $\{x \in \mathbb{R}^l_+ | p . x \leq p . e_a\}$ it follows that $f(a) \succsim_a \bar{x}$. Thus, a.e. in A, $\hat{f}(a)$ is maximal for $\prec_a$ in the futures equilibrium budget set. This proves:

6.9.1 Theorem *Let $(\mathscr{E}, \sigma, \tau)$ be a two-period monetary economy with the property that $\sigma = \tau$. A regular sequential allocation $\hat{f}$ for $(\mathscr{E}, \sigma, \tau)$ is also a futures allocation for $(\mathscr{E}, \sigma, \tau)$ regarded as an economy with a sequence of complete markets.*

The converse, of course, is false.

An inspection of the definition of the futures equilibrium for an economy with complete markets shows that it is the same as the natural definition of the sequence equilibrium for a monetary economy, *under the assumption that there are spot markets only.* Thus, Theorem 6.9.1 has an obvious analogue for sequence equilibria. However, the *assumption* that there are spot markets only is unacceptable here. The economy is clearly one in which trading is costless and information is perfect so there is no reason why markets should not be complete. In fact, the assumption is needed here only to make sure that the budget constraints have the right form. Since there is no inherent relationship between the completeness or incompleteness of markets and the form of the budget constraints this "backdoor" method of getting the desired result seems quite arbitrary. The desired result comes quite naturally from the futures equilibrium because the budget constraints there are the right ones to start with. When the absence of trust is used to provide a rationale for a sequence of budget constraints, the "right" equilibrium concept would appear to be the futures equilibrium, not the sequence equilibrium.

Another point to note is that unlike the Walrasian equilibrium, the sequential equilibrium provides a role for assets without introducing the indeterminacy of the former. As noted earlier, $W(\mathscr{E}, \sigma, \tau)$ contains an infinite number of allocations unless $\sigma = \tau$, in which case assets are irrelevant. In $W^s(\mathscr{E}, \sigma, \tau)$, however, assets are relevant even when $\sigma = \tau$ because the second-period constraints in general require some trade in assets ($f^m \neq \sigma$) to ensure that $\hat{f}$ be trustworthy. Yet with $\sigma = \tau$ there is no indeterminacy because there are no distribution effects. Of course, $W(\mathscr{E}^s, f^m, \tau)$ will contain an infinite number of equilibria if $f^m \neq \tau = \sigma$, but this does not matter if $W(\mathscr{E}, \sigma, \sigma)$ is finite.

So far, using a variety of concepts—the "monetary economy", the "core" of a monetary economy, the "sequential core" etc.—it has been possible to suggest a role for money (paper assets) and a rationalization of a sequence of budget constraints, all based on the absence of trust. But the foregoing results do not imply that paper assets are necessary in the sort of economy described. For example, the theorems and definitions all apply to the special case $k = 0$. But the discussion at the beginning of this Chapter suggests that in that case the sequential core may be empty. This observation leads to the study of the conditions under which the sequential core is non-empty and this in turn shows the necessity of having paper assets to overcome the absence of trust.

The usual way to show that the core is non-empty is to prove the existence of an equilibrium under certain conditions and then appeal to the fact that an equilibrium allocation belongs to the core. A slightly easier approach is available here. Once again $\mathscr{E}$ is assumed to be a two period economy. Recall that an *atom* of the measure space $(A, \mathscr{A}, \nu)$ is any singleton $\{a\}$ say, such that $\nu(\{a\}) > 0$. An exchange economy $\mathscr{E}: (A, \mathscr{A}, \nu) \to \mathscr{P} \times \mathbb{R}^l_+$ is called *convex* if every atom has convex preferences, i.e. $\nu(\{a\}) > 0$ implies $\prec_a$ is convex. *Notice the implicit assumption that $k = |S|$ in the next theorem; it is crucial.*

6.9.2 Theorem *Let $\mathscr{E}: (A, \mathscr{A}, \nu) \to \mathscr{P} \times \mathbb{R}^l_+$ be a convex exchange economy such that $\int e \, d\nu \gg 0$ and let f be a weakly Pareto-efficient consumption allocation for $\mathscr{E}$. Then there exist integrable functions σ, $\tau: (A, \mathscr{A}, \nu) \to \mathbb{R}^S_+$ and a security allocation $f^m: (A, \mathscr{A}, \nu) \to \mathbb{R}^S_+$ such that:*

(i) *$(\mathscr{E}, \sigma, \tau)$ is a monetary economy;*
(ii) *$\hat{f} \in W^s(\mathscr{E}, \sigma, \tau) \subset C^s(\mathscr{E}, \sigma, \tau)$.*

Proof For every $a \in A$ define:

$$\prec_a(f) := \{x \in \mathbb{R}^l_+ \mid x \succ_a f(a)\}$$

and

$$\chi(a) := \prec_a(f) - \{e(a)\}.$$

Since the economy is convex it follows that $\int \chi \, dv$ is convex. (A proof is given in the appendix). Since f is efficient and the preferences are monotonic:

$$\int \chi \, dv \cap \Omega = \phi$$

where $\Omega := \{x \in \mathbb{R}^l \mid x \ll 0\}$. The Minkowski Theorem says that these two sets can be separated by a hyperplane; there exists $p \neq 0$ such that

$$0 \leq \inf p . \int \chi \, dv .$$

Under the assumptions of the theorem, χ has a measurable graph (the reader is referred to the appendix). But since χ has a measurable graph it follows (again from a theorem in the appendix) that:

$$\inf p . \int \chi \, dv = \int \inf p . \chi \, dv .$$

Then $0 \leq \int \inf p . \chi \, dv$. Because of the monotonicity of preferences $[f(a) - e(a)]$ belongs to the closure of $\chi(a)$ for every $a \in A$. Therefore, a.e. in A,

$$p . (f(a) - e(a)) \geq \inf p . \chi(a) .$$

Suppose the inequality were strict for a set of agents of positive measure. Then, because $\int f \, dv = \int e \, dv$,

$$0 = p . \int (f - e) \, dv > \int \inf p . \chi \, dv \geq 0 ,$$

a contradiction. So, a.e. in A, $p . [f(a) - e(a)] = \inf p . \chi(a)$. Thus, a.e. in A, $x \succ_a f(a)$ implies that $p . x \geq p . f(a)$.

The monotonicity and continuity of preferences together with the assumption that $\int e \, dv \gg 0$ imply that $p \gg 0$. The argument is standard and will not be given here (Cf. Theorem 6.7.3). For any $a \in A$, either $p . f(a) > 0$ or $f(a) = 0$. Suppose that for some $a \in A$, $x \succ_a f(a)$ and $p . x = p . f(a)$. Clearly, $f(a) \neq 0$. By continuity there exists $\bar{x} < x$ such that $\bar{x} \succ_a f(a)$. Then $p . \bar{x} < p . f(a)$, a contradiction. Hence, $x \succ_a f(a)$ implies $p . x > p . f(a)$.

Define a consumption price sequence p^* by putting $p^*(d) = p^d$, the projection of p into X^d, for every $d \in D$. It is immediate that $x^s \succ_a^s f^s(a)$ implies $p^s . x^s > p^s . f^s(a)$ for every $s \in S$.

Because $k = |S|$ there is a one to one correspondence between securities and states. Label both securities and states by the index $j = 1, \ldots, k$. Define q^* by putting

$$q_j^*(s) = 1 \quad \text{if} \quad s = j$$
$$= 0 \text{ otherwise}$$

for all $s \in S$, $j = 1, \ldots, k$. Put $q^*(0) := \sum_{s \in S} q^*(s)$. Now let τ be an integrable function from $(A, \mathscr{A}, \nu)$ to $\mathbb{R}^S_+$. Define the function f^m by the condition:

$$p.(f^s(a) - e^s(a)) + q^s.(\tau(a) - f^m(a)) = 0,$$

for every $a \in A$ and $s \in S$. f^m is uniquely determined by these equations and is integrable since τ is integrable. Now let σ be an integrable function such that $\int \sigma \, d\nu = \int \tau \, d\nu$ and

$$p.(f(a) - e(a)) + q^*(0).(\tau(a) - \sigma(a)) = 0.$$

There are many such functions. Now σ and f^m may not be non-negative. Let σ^- and $(f^m)^-$ be the negative parts of σ and f^m respectively. Replace σ, f^m and τ by $(\sigma + \sigma^- + (f^m)^-)$, $(f^m + \sigma^- + (f^m)^-)$ and $(\tau + \sigma^- + (f^m)^-)$, respectively if these are different. Then σ and τ, redefined, are integrable functions from $(A, \mathscr{A}, \nu)$ to $\mathbb{R}^S_+$. This means that $(\mathscr{E}, \sigma, \tau)$ is a monetary economy. f^m is an integrable function from $(A, \mathscr{A}, \nu)$ to $\mathbb{R}^S_+$ and $\int f^m \, d\nu = \int \sigma \, d\nu$ (this follows from $\int \sigma = \int \tau$, $\int f = \int e$ and the definition of f^m) so $\hat{f} = (f, f^m)$ is an attainable allocation. It is clear from the construction of f^m, σ, τ and the supporting property of p that $f \in W(\mathscr{E}, \sigma, \tau)$ and $f^s \in W(\mathscr{E}^s, f^m, \tau)$. Thus, $\hat{f} \in W^s(\mathscr{E}, \sigma, \tau)$. □

Theorem 6.9.2 is the analogue of the second Fundamental Theorem of Welfare Economics. Here the *net* tax obligations $(\tau - \sigma)$ act like lump sum transfers. Any weakly Pareto-efficient allocation can be made "trustworthy" by an appropriate choice of σ and τ. And if f is a Walras allocation of $\mathscr{E}$ then we can choose $\sigma = \tau$. In this way money (paper assets) replaces trust. But there must be a lot of securities; one for each state of nature.

6.10 Characterization of strongly improving conditions

The results in the preceding sections provide a benchmark theory of a monetary economy, by showing that the efficient commodity allocations of a large economy can be made trustworthy if and only if sufficient assets are introduced and then exchanged as if the economy were in equilibrium with a sequence of budget constraints. In a descriptive theory, on the other hand, the need to assume a complete set of assets is rather unsatisfactory. In the first place, there is unlikely to be a complete set of assets in practice. In the second, even if there are several assets they cannot all claim to be "money". This suggests the need for a separate analysis of what goes on in an economy with an incomplete set of assets. As a vehicle for this analysis I shall use a very simple model of a monetary economy. Let $\mathscr{E}$ be an exchange economy. Then $\hat{\mathscr{E}} = (\mathscr{E}, \sigma, \tau)$ will denote the corresponding monetary economy in which:

(1) there are two dates $t = 0, 1$ and the set of date-event pairs is $D = \{0\} \cup S$;
(2) there is a single asset, called money;
(3) for every a in A, $\sigma(a) = \tau(a) = 1$;
(4) there is a single consumption good available for delivery at each date-event pair, i.e. $l = |D|$.

These assumptions allow certain further simplifications to be made to the notation and definitions already used in Section 6.9. For each s belonging to $\{0\} \cup S$, f^s and e^s are functions from $(A, \mathscr{A}, \nu)$ to $\mathbb{R}_+$. Once the event s in S has occurred at date 1 the only way an agent can be made better off is by receiving more of the single consumption good. If the coalition T can improve on $\hat{f}$ once s has occurred it must be the case that $\int_T e^s \, d\nu > \int_T f^s \, d\nu$. This fact suggests the simpler definition of an improving coalition as follows: T can *improve on* $\hat{f}$ *at* s in S if and only if $\int_T e^s \, d\nu > \int_T f^s \, d\nu$. Clearly, this definition implies that $\nu(T) > 0$.

The allocations $\hat{f}$ which cannot be improved on at the second date are easily characterized. In what follows assume that $\int e \gg 0$ and that $(A, \mathscr{A}, \nu)$ is atomless and let $\hat{f}$ be an attainable allocation for $\hat{\mathscr{E}}$. A subeconomy at s in S will be denoted by $(\mathscr{E}^s, \sigma, \tau)$ and may be defined by putting

$$(5) \quad \begin{cases} \mathscr{E}^s(a) := (\mathbb{R}_+, <, e^s(a)) \\ \sigma(a) := f^m(a) \\ \tau(a) := 1 \end{cases}$$

for every a in A. The interpretation is the same as for the subeconomies introduced in Section 6.8. I have simply taken advantage of the assumptions (1) to (4) to simplify the definition. Because there is only one good traded at s the consumption set is effectively $\mathbb{R}_+$. Everyone prefers more consumption to less so the common preference relation is the linear ordering $<$. Finally, agent a's initial endowment of goods is just his endowment of the consumption good delivered at s. His initial endowment of money is just what was carried forward from date 0 so $\sigma(a) = f^m(a)$ and his tax demand is unchanged at one unit of money.

The artificial economy $(\mathscr{E}^s, \sigma, \tau)$ is easily seen to be a monetary economy in the sense of Definition 6.7.1. $\mathscr{E}^s$ is measurable if $\mathscr{E}$ is measurable (in fact, since every agent has the same preference relation at s, $\mathscr{E}^s$ is measurable if and only if e^s is measurable). The preference relation $(\mathbb{R}_+, <)$ obviously belongs to $\mathscr{P}$ and e^s is non-negative since e is non-negative. Hence, $\mathscr{E}^s$ is a measurable function from $(A, \mathscr{A}, \nu)$ to $\mathscr{P} \times \mathbb{R}_+$. Also, σ and τ map $(A, \mathscr{A}, \nu)$ to $\mathbb{R}_+$ and since $\hat{f}$ is attainable, $\int \sigma = 1 = \int \tau$.

If $(\mathscr{E}^s, \sigma, \tau)$ is a monetary economy we can define the core in the usual way (cf. Section 6.7). Suppose f^s belongs to $C(\mathscr{E}^s, \sigma, \tau)$. Then there exists no coalition T such that $\nu(T) > 0$, $\int_T \sigma \geq \int_T \tau$ and, for some allocation g^s at s, $\int_T g^s = \int_T e^s$ and $g^s(a) > f^s(a)$, for every a in T. This immediately implies there is no coalition T such that T is admissible at the second date given $\hat{f}$ and $\int_T e^s > \int_T f^s$. In other words, no admissible coalition can improve on $\hat{f}$ at s. Conversely, it is straightforward to show that if $\hat{f}$ is an attainable allocation for $\hat{\mathscr{E}}$ and no coalition can improve on $\hat{f}$ at s then f^s belongs to the core of the artificial monetary economy $(\mathscr{E}^s, \sigma, \tau)$. Hence

(6) *if $\hat{f}$ is attainable for the SME $\hat{\mathscr{E}}$ and cannot be improved on by any coalition at $s = 1, \ldots, S$, then f^s belongs to $C(\mathscr{E}^s, \sigma, \tau)$ for every $s = 1, \ldots, S$, where $(\mathscr{E}^s, \sigma, \tau)$ is defined by* (5). *Similarly, if f^s belongs to $C(\mathscr{E}^s, \sigma, \tau)$ then $\hat{f}$ cannot be improved on by any coalition at s, for $s = 1, \ldots, S$.*

It has been assumed that $(A, \mathscr{A}, \nu)$ is atomless and $\int e \gg 0$ and so it follows that $(\mathscr{E}^s, \sigma, \tau)$ satisfies the conditions of Theorem 6.7.3. The allocation f^s belongs to $C(\mathscr{E}^s, \sigma, \tau)$ if and only if it belongs to $W(\mathscr{E}^s, \sigma, \tau)$, i.e. if and only if there exist numbers (p^s, q^s) in $\mathbb{R}^2_+$ such that

(7) *a.e. in A, $f^s(a)$ is maximal for $<$ in the budget set* $\{x^s \in \mathbb{R}_+ | p^s.x^s + q^s.1 \leq p^s.e^s(a) + q^s.f^m(a)\}$.

The monotonicity of preferences implies that $p^s > 0$ and, by definition, $q^s \geq 0$. Since there is only one commodity at s, (7) is satisfied if and only if, for some number $z^s \geq 0$,

(8) *a.e. in* $A, f^s(a) = e^s(a) + (f^m(a) - 1)z^s \geq 0$.

For (7) immediately implies (8) if we put $z^s = q^s/p^s$ and if (8) is satisfied for some $z^s \geq 0$ it is possible to find p^s and q^s in $\mathbb{R}_+$ so that (7) is satisfied. Consequently, putting (6)–(8) together:

(9) *an attainable allocation $\hat{f}$ for $\hat{\mathscr{E}}$ cannot be improved on by any admissible coalition $s = 1, \ldots, S$ if and only if* (9) *is satisfied for some $z^s \geq 0$, $s = 1, \ldots, S$.*

This "representation theorem" is quite handy for analysing the sequential core, as will become apparent in the next section. It also suggests how to break down the analysis into more tractable parts, first looking at the determinants of f^0 and f^m and then at the determinants of $z = (z^1, \ldots, z^S)$. If $\hat{f}$ is an allocation for $\hat{\mathscr{E}}$ and it has the form

$$f^s(a) = e^s(a) + (f^m(a) - 1)z^s, \qquad \text{a.e. in } A,$$

for every $s = 1, \ldots, S$ and some vector $z = (z^1, \ldots, z^S)$ in $\mathbb{R}^S_+$, then I use the notation $\hat{f} = (f^0, f^m, z)$ to indicate the fact. Similarly, given the triple (f^0, f^m, z), if f^0 and f^m are measurable functions from $(A, \mathscr{A}, \nu)$ to $\mathbb{R}_+$ and z belongs to $\mathbb{R}^S_+$, we can define an allocation $\hat{f}$ *via* the equation (8) as long as

$$e^s(a) + (f^m(a) - 1)z^s \geq 0, \qquad \text{a.e. in } A.$$

The triple (f^0, f^m, z) is called an *allocation* if it satisfies these conditions and it is called *attainable* if $\int (f^0, f^m) = \int (e^0, 1)$. It is clear that an attainable allocation (f^0, f^m, z) uniquely defines $\hat{f}$ *via* (8).

As a first application of this characterization, consider the question of what should count as an improving coalition at date 0. In one sense, the position of a coalition at date 0 is the same as in a monetary economy. Recall that a coalition T can improve on f in $(\mathscr{E}, \sigma, \tau)$ if $\nu(T) > 0$, $\int_T \sigma \geq \int_T \tau$ and there is a commodity allocation g such that $\int_T g = \int_T e$ and $f(a) \prec_a g(a)$ for every a in T. In $\hat{\mathscr{E}}$, every coalition is admissible at date 0 since $\sigma(a) = \tau(a) = 1$ a.e. in A. If the coalition forms at date 0, it will have to be self-sufficient in all commodities at both dates so it is tempting to say that T can improve if and only if there is an allocation $\hat{g}$ such that $\int_T \hat{g} = \int_T (e, 1)$ and $f(a) \prec_a g(a)$ for all a in T. But this is far too liberal a definition, for reasons explained in Section 6.4. In a sequential economy, coalitions are allowed to improve at date 1 and any allocation which can be improved on at the second date will be deemed "unstable", i.e. it should not belong to the sequential core, however defined. As was shown in Section 6.4, if improving coalitions are allowed to insist on allocations which can be improved on (by some sub-coalition) at the second date, the sequential core may be empty. More important, the behaviour of such coalitions is *irrational.* If coalition T knows that $\hat{g}$ can be improved on at s, say, by some subcoalition $T' \subset T$, then it cannot believe that it is improving on $\hat{f}$ by insisting on $\hat{g}$; for $\hat{g}$ is, in a very real sense "unattainable". In fact, the only allocations which are "attainable" in this sense are the ones that cannot be improved on, at any $s = 1, \ldots, S$, by any subcoalition.

This argument leads to a more involved definition of an improving coalition. A coalition T can *improve strongly on* $\hat{f}$ *at the first date* if $v(T) > 0$ and there exists an allocation $\hat{g}$ such that $\int_T \hat{g} = \int_T (e, 1)$, $f(a) \prec_a g(a)$, for every a in T, and no coalition $T' \subset T$ can improve on $\hat{g}$ at any $s = 1, \ldots, S$. Only the possibility of subcoalitions $T' \subset T$ improving on $\hat{g}$ is considered because the behaviour of the counter-coalition and hence of coalitions T' not contained in T is immaterial if T really wants to be self-sufficient. In fact, it makes no difference to the subsequent analysis whether T' is contained in T or not.

Using the argument encapsulated in (6)–(9) it can be shown that $\hat{g}$ cannot be improved on by any coalition $T' \subset T$ at $s = 1, \ldots, S$, if and only if

$$g^s(a) = e^s(a) + (g^m(a) - 1)z^s, \tag{10}$$

a.e. in T, for some $z^s \geq 0$. Since the value of g at a not in T is irrelevant, there is no loss of generality in assuming (10) to hold a.e. in A. This means that $\hat{g} = (g^0, g^m, z)$ for some $z \geq 0$. An equivalent definition of a strongly improving coalition at date 0 would be the following. The coalition T can *improve strongly on* $\hat{f}$ *at the first date* if $v(T) > 0$ and there exists an allocation $\hat{g} = (g^0, g^m, z)$ such that $\int_T \hat{g} = \int_T (e, 1)$ and $f(a) \prec_a g(a)$ for every a in T.

Summary
In a sequential economy, where coalitions can form at the second date, the only allocations which are really "attainable" are those which cannot be improved on at date 1 in any event s. Thus the "attainable" allocations have the form (f^0, f^m, z). These are the only allocations which are candidates for membership in the sequential core and the only ones that should be chosen by improving coalitions at date 0.

6.11 Formal results

If a coalition can improve at the second date, in a sequential economy it will do so. This is the principle on which the theory of the sequential core is based. Any allocation which can be improved on at the second date is considered to be unstable. Therefore, a necessary condition for an allocation to belong to the sequential core, however we choose to define it, must be that no coalition can improve on it at the second date. The characterization given in the last section shows that a necessary condition for an allocation $\hat{f}$ to belong to the sequential core of a large economy is that it have the form $\hat{f} = (f^0, f^m, z)$.

The examples in Part 1 of this Chapter made it clear that there might be no "stable" allocations if coalitions were allowed to improve at date 1 as well as in the usual way at date 0. The reason is simple. The coalition of the whole will insist on a Pareto-efficient allocation at date 0 but Pareto-efficiency is unattainable if coalitions can form at date 1 and the set of assets is incomplete. The agents in this case are being irrational in demanding something at date 0 which their own behaviour at date 1 will render unattainable. Their behaviour at the two dates is clearly inconsistent. The way round this inconsistency is to make coalitions which form at date 0 choose from the set of allocations which cannot be improved on at date 1. This observation leads to the notion of a *strongly* improving coalition, that is, one which can improve at date 0 by choosing an allocation of the form $\hat{g} = (g^0, g^m, z)$.

Now we are ready to consider the central question of what should be the appropriate definition of the sequential core. The "natural" definition and the only one which is really in the spirit of the classical theory is the following. Define the weak sequential core to be the set of attainable allocations which cannot be strongly improved on at date 0 or improved on at date 1. The solution concept is called "weak" to distinguish it from the "stronger" concept used in Section 6.8. The criterion for an improvement at date 0 is "stronger" here, i.e. more restrictive; hence the criterion for membership in the solution set is "weaker", i.e. less restrictive. Assume in what follows that $\mathscr{E}$ is a large economy and $\int e \gg 0$. An attainable allocation $\hat{f}$ belongs to the *weak sequential core* of $\hat{\mathscr{E}}$ if and only if the following conditions are satisfied:

(i) $\hat{f} = (f^0, f^m, z)$ for some $z \geq 0$
(ii) There exists no coalition T and allocation $\hat{g} = (g^0, g^m, y)$ such that $v(T) > 0$, $\int_T \hat{g} = \hat{e}$ and $f(a) \prec_a g(a)$ for every a in T.

(i) is the necessary and sufficient condition for $\hat{f}$ not to be improved on by any coalition, in any state, at the second date. (ii) is the definition of an allocation which cannot be strongly improved on by any coalition at the first date. Let $C^*(\hat{\mathscr{E}})$ denote the weak sequential core of $\hat{\mathscr{E}}$.

Although the weak sequential core is the "natural" solution concept it is not, as will become apparent presently, very well behaved. There is another possible definition, though it is not an obvious one. Suppose that a coalition T wishing to improve on an allocation $\hat{f} = (f^0, f^m, z)$ must choose an allocation $\hat{g} = (g^0, g^m, z)$. In other words, the improving coalition treats z as a parameter rather than an object of choice. Say that an attainable allocation $\hat{f}$

belongs to the *pseudo-core* of $\hat{\mathscr{E}}$ if and only if the following conditions are satisfied:

(iii) $\hat{f} = (f^0, f^m, z)$ for some $z \geq 0$
(iv) There exists no coalition T and allocation $\hat{g} = (g^0, g^m, z)$ such that $\nu(T) > 0$, $\int_T \hat{g} = \int_T \hat{e}$ and $f(a) \prec_a g(a)$, for every a in T.

Let $P(\hat{\mathscr{E}})$ denote the pseudo-core of $\hat{\mathscr{E}}$. The only difference between (i)–(ii) and (iii)–(iv) is that $y = z$ in (iv) but the difference turns out to be crucial. The pseudo-core has no very obvious justification as a solution concept but it occupies a distinguished place in the theory by virtue of the next theorem.

First, a definition of equilibrium. *A weak sequential equilibrium* (WSE) *allocation* for $\hat{\mathscr{E}}$ is an attainable allocation $\hat{f}$ such that for some price system (p, q) in $\mathbb{R}^l_+ \times \mathbb{R}^l_+$, a.e. in A, $\hat{f}(a)$ is maximal for $\prec_a$ among the set of pairs (x, m) such that:

(a) $(x, m) \in \mathbb{R}^l_+ \times \mathbb{R}_+$
(b) $p^0 . x^0 + q^0 . m \leq p^0 . e^0_a + q^0 . 1$
(c) $p^s . x^s + q^s . 1 \leq p^s . e^s_a + q^s . m \qquad (s \in S)$.

The set of weak sequential allocations of $\hat{\mathscr{E}}$ is denoted by $W^*(\hat{\mathscr{E}})$. The ordered triple $(\hat{f}, p, q)$ is called a *weak sequential equilibrium*. What is required in the weak sequential equilibrium is that almost every agent should choose a consumption bundle x and a cash balance m to maximize his preferences subject to the budget constraints (b) and (c). Implicitly, only spot trades of money and goods are allowed and the agent's initial endowment (resp. tax demand) of one unit of money at date 0 (resp. date 1) is treated as his supply of (resp. demand for) money at that date.

6.11.1 Theorem *Let* $\mathscr{E}: (A, \mathscr{A}, \nu) \to \mathscr{P} \times \mathbb{R}^l_+$ *be an atomless, monetary economy such that* $\int e \, d\nu \gg 0$. *Then* $W^*(\varepsilon) \subset P(\hat{\mathscr{E}})$.

6.11.2 Theorem *If* $\hat{\mathscr{E}}$ *satisfies the conditions of Theorem* 6.11.1 *then* $P(\hat{\mathscr{E}}) \subset W^*(\hat{\mathscr{E}})$.

The proofs will be left until Section 6.12.

In a large economy the weak sequential allocations are pretty much the ones in the pseudo-core, so if we are interested in providing a rationale for a particular notion of monetary equilibrium which seems rather natural in the circumstances, then the pseudo-core seems to have some relevance. The intuition behind the equivalence theorem is easy enough. Suppose that agent a has a preference relation $\prec_a$ which can be represented by the utility function u_a. If z belongs to $\mathbb{R}^s_{++}$, (x^0, m) belongs to $\mathbb{R}_+ \times \mathbb{R}_+$ and $e^s_a + (m-1)z^s \geq 0$ for $s = 1, \ldots, S$, then the triple (x^0, m, z) defines a unique consumption bundle x in $\mathbb{R}_+$ *via* the equation $x^s = e^s_a + (m-1)z^s$ for $s = 1, \ldots, S$. If z is given, then for every a in A it is possible to define an *indirect utility function* u^*_a by putting $u^*_a(x^0, m) = u_a(x^0, m, z)$ where (x^0, m, z) denotes the unique consumption bundle defined above in terms of x^0, m and z. Of course, u^*_a is only defined for ordered pairs (x^0, m) satisfying the inequalities above. Using the indirect utility functions u^*_a it is possible to define an artificial economy in which there are two commodities, the consumption good and money, and in which every agent a has an initial endowment $(e^0_a, 1)$ of goods and money, a consumption set consisting of pairs (x^0, m) for which u^*_a is defined and, of course, preferences on this set given by u^*_a. An allocation (f^0, f^m) belongs to the classical core of this artificial economy if and only if (f^0, f^m, z) belongs to the pseudo-core of $\hat{\mathscr{E}}$. Similarly, (f^0, f^m) is a Walras allocation for the artificial economy if and only if (f^0, f^m, z) is a weak sequential allocation for $\hat{\mathscr{E}}$. By Theorems 6.6. 1–2, the classical equivalence theorem, the core of the artificial economy is the set of Walras allocations (since the agents form a continuum). Then the pseudo-core of $\hat{\mathscr{E}}$ must be the set of WSE allocations.

The trouble with the pseudo-core is the requirement that improving coalitions at date 0 should treat z as a parameter. Some justification is required for this assumption but none is provided by the theory. It is an *ad hoc* restriction, delivering the formal results but in an arbitrary manner. The obvious question to raise is whether a weaker condition will suffice. The short answer is—usually not. That is the central result of this section. It will be used to show both that the weak sequential core, the "natural" solution concept, is not equal to the task of providing a foundation for the theory of sequential equilibrium and that the assumption that z be parametric is almost necessary. The explanation and significance of these results are discussed in Section 6.13. The remainder of the present section is devoted to setting up a formal framework in which the above claims can be analysed, and to the statement of the main results.

To carry out this exercise two special pieces of equipment are needed. The first is a more general definition of the sequential core, which contains the weak sequential core and pseudo-core as special cases. In the former, the choice of z by an improving coalition at date 0 is unrestricted; in the latter it is required to be the same as in the allocation which is improved on. To generalize this notion, one only has to specify a set of possible variations in z. Let Z be a linear subspace of $\mathbb{R}^S$. An attainable allocation $\hat{f}$ is said to belong to the z-core if and only if the following conditions are satisfied:

(v) $\hat{f} = (f^0, f^m, z)$ where $z \geq 0$.
(vi) There exists no coalition T and allocation $\hat{g} = (g^0, g^m, y)$ such that $(y - z) \in Z$, $v(T) > 0$, $\int_T \hat{g} = \int_T \hat{e}$ and $f(a) \prec_a g(a)$ for every a in T.

The definition differs from (i)–(ii) and (iii)–(iv) only in the requirement that $(y - z)$ belong to Z. The z-core coincides with the weak sequential core when $Z = \mathbb{R}^l$, for then y can take any value in $\mathbb{R}^S$ as in (ii). The z-core coincides with the pseudo-core when $Z = \{0\}$, for then $y = z$ as in (iii). There is a continuum of possibilities in between.

The second piece of equipment is an economy with a finite number of *types* of consumers. A type $i = 1, \ldots, n$ is represented by a characteristic $(\mathbb{R}^l_+, \prec_i, e_i)$ where $\prec_i$ is the preference relation of agents of that type and e_i the endowment of goods. An exchange economy with a finite number of types is completely characterized by an n-tuple $\mathbf{t} = (t_1, \ldots, t_n)$ of positive numbers, with the interpretation that t_i is the measure of the set of agents of type $i = 1, \ldots, n$. An economy with a finite number of types will be called *regular* if, for every $i = 1, \ldots, n$, the following conditions are satisfied:

(a) $e_i \gg 0$;
(b) $\prec_i$ is representable by a C^1, strictly concave, utility function $u_i\colon \mathbb{R}^l_+ \to \mathbb{R}$;
(c) $x \nprec_i e_i \Rightarrow x \gg 0$ for any x in $\mathbb{R}^l_+$.

These assumptions are made to avoid mathematical complications which are irrelevant to the problem at hand. They are somewhat restrictive but economists often make the same assumptions when they wish to use differential arguments in the analysis of finite economies.

Finally, in what follows I assume $z \gg 0$.

Now consider a regular, atomless exchange economy with a finite number of types. The measure space $(A, \mathscr{A}, v)$ is identified with the n-vector $\mathbf{t}^* = (t_1^*, \ldots, t_n^*)$ and the function $\mathscr{E}$ is identified with the n-tuple $\{(\mathbb{R}^{S+1}_+, u_i, e_i) \colon i = 1, \ldots, n\}$. If $\hat{f} \in P(\hat{\mathscr{E}})$ then, as Theorem 6.11.2 shows, $\hat{f}$ is a WSE allocation. It follows from strict concavity of the functions u_i that agents of the same type choose the same consumption bundles. Then the allocation $\hat{f}$ can be identified with the n-tuple $\{(x_i^*, m_i^*) \colon i = 1, \ldots, n\}$ where x_i^* is the i-th type's consumption bundle and m_i^* the i-th type's money balance at the end of date 0. It is also clear that if (x_i^*, m_i^*) is chosen in equilibrium then $x_i^* \gg 0$ for $i = 1, \ldots, n$. Since u_i is monotonic and C^1, it is meaningful to define

$$\mu_i^s := \left(\frac{\partial u_i}{\partial x^0}\right)^{-1}\left(\frac{\partial u_i}{\partial x^s}\right)\Bigg|_{x=x_i^*}$$

for all $s \in S$ and $i = 1, \ldots, n$ and put $\mu_i := \{\mu_i^s : s \in S\}$ for $i = 1, \ldots, n$. Let a_0 be the n-vector $\{(x_1^{0*} - e_1^0), \ldots, (x_n^{0*} - e_n^0)\}$ where x_i^{0*} denotes first-period (equilibrium) consumption of the i-th type and let a_s be the n-vector $\{(m_1^* - 1)\mu_1^s, \ldots, (m_n^* - 1)\mu_n^s\}$ for each s in S. Let $\langle a_0, a_s : s \in S\rangle$ denote the linear hull of the set $\{a_0, a_s : s \in S\}$ in $\mathbb{R}^n$.

Lemma *Let $\mathscr{E} : (A, \mathscr{A}, \nu) \to \mathscr{P} \times \mathbb{R}_+^l$ be a regular, atomless, monetary economy with a finite number of types. If $\hat{f}$ belongs to the z-core of $\hat{\mathscr{E}}$ then*

$$\dim Z + \dim\langle a_0, a_s : s \in S\rangle \leq S + 1\,.$$

(For any linear vector space L, $\dim L$ denotes the dimension of L.)

μ_i^s is the marginal rate of substitution between consumption at date 0 and consumption at date 1 in state s, for the i-th type of agent. If the prevailing allocation has the form $\hat{f} = (f^0, f^m, z)$ then $(m_i^* - 1)\mu_i^s$ measures the effect of a change in z^s, on the utility of the i-th type of consumer, in terms of consumption at date 0. If the change in z^s is dz^s, the corresponding change in consumption at date 1 in state s is $dx_i^s = (m_i^* - 1)dz^s$. The change in first-period consumption required to cause an equivalent change in utility is $dx_i^0 = (m_i^* - 1)\mu_i^s dz^s$. Thus, a_s is (approximately) the vector of equivalent variations in first-period consumption, for each type of agent, when z^s increases by one unit. a_0 is just the vector of net trades in consumption at the first date.

If f belongs to the z-core of $\hat{\mathscr{E}}$ then $\hat{f}$ belongs to the pseudo-core. To see this, note that the pseudo-core is identical to the z-core when $Z = \{0\}$. Since any linear space Z contains 0 and the difference between the z-core and the pseudo-core is the specification of Z, the z-core is at least as strong as the pseudo-core, however Z is specified. Therefore, $\hat{f}$ is a WSE allocation if it belongs to the z-core, for any specification of Z. Suppose that $\hat{f}$ is a WSE allocation. From the first order conditions for a consumer optimum it is easy to see that, in a WSE, for every $i = 1, \ldots, n$,

$$\frac{\partial u_i}{\partial x^0}\bigg|_{x=x_i^*} = \lambda_i p^0$$

and

$$\sum_{s \in S} \left(\frac{\partial u_i}{\partial x^s} \frac{q^s}{p^s} \right) \bigg|_{x = x_i^*} = \lambda_i q^0$$

for some λ_i, where p^0 is the equilibrium price of consumption at 0. It easily follows that $\mu_i . z = q^0/p^0$, for every $i = 1, \ldots, n$. Apart from this restriction, however, there is nothing to limit the dimension of $\langle a_0, a_s : s \in S \rangle$. It is difficult to say precisely what the dimension of this space will be but familiarity with the arguments used in proving "generic" theorems suggests that, for *almost all* economies $\langle a_0, a_s : s \in S \rangle$ will have the largest possible dimension i.e. $\min(S, n)$. An allocation $\hat{f}$ in the z-core will be said to have *full dimension* if $\dim\langle a_0, a_s : s \in S \rangle = \min(S, n)$.

6.11.3 Theorem *Let $\mathscr{E}$ satisfy all the conditions of the Lemma. If $\hat{f}$ belongs to the z-core of $\hat{\mathscr{E}}$, has full dimension and $n \geq S$ then* $\dim Z = 1$.

In other words, if $\hat{f}$ has full dimension (the "usual" case) and there are at least as many types as there are states of nature then the z-core is non-empty only if it is *by definition* the same as the p-core. This does not simply mean that the z-core equals the pseudo core; it means the improving coalitions are, in each case, the same. In this sense, the p-core is the strongest concept that preserves equivalence.

It is idle to speculate whether the number of types is actually greater than the number of states. What Theorem 6.11.3 makes fairly clear, however, is that if we want a simple definition which guarantees the core is non-empty in general, something like the p-core is necessary. Anything stronger will not work for a large class of well-behaved economies like those described in Theorem 6.11.3. Anything weaker will not be contained in the set of WSE allocations (Theorem 6.11.2).

As a corollary of the Lemma it can be shown that an attainable allocation belongs to the weak sequential core if and only if it is Pareto-efficient. In that case, the weak sequential core coincides with the strong sequential core (the concept used in Section 6.8). More importantly, the weak sequential core will usually be empty since Pareto-efficiency is incompatible with a sequence of budget constraints. If $\hat{f}$ belongs to the weak sequential core it also belongs to the pseudo-core. By Theorem 6.11.2 it must be a WSE allocation so every agent of a given type i has the same consumption bundle (x_i^*, m_i^*). In an obvious notation we can write: $\hat{f} = \{(x_1^*, m_1^*), \ldots, (x_n^*, m_n^*)\}$.

6.11.4 Theorem *Let $\mathscr{E}: (A, \mathscr{A}, \nu) \to \mathscr{P} \times \mathbb{R}^l_+$ be a regular atomless exchange economy with a finite number of types. If $\hat{f} = \{(x_1^*, m_1^*), \ldots, (x_n^*, m_n^*)\}$ belongs to the weak sequential core of $\mathscr{E}$ and $m_i^* \neq 1$, for $i = 1, \ldots, n$, then $f = (x_1^*, \ldots, x_n^*)$ is Pareto-efficient.*

6.12 Proofs

6.11.1 Theorem *Let $\mathscr{E}: (A, \mathscr{A}, \nu) \to \mathscr{P} \times \mathbb{R}^l_+$ be an atomless exchange economy such that $\int e \, d\nu \gg 0$. Then $W^*(\hat{\mathscr{E}}) \subset P(\hat{\mathscr{E}})$.*

Proof Suppose, to the contrary, that $\hat{f}$ is a WSE allocation which does not belong to the pseudo-core of $\hat{\mathscr{E}}$. Since $\hat{f}$ is a WSE allocation there exists a price system $(p, q) \in \mathbb{R}^l_+ \times \mathbb{R}^l_+$ such that, a.e. in A, $\hat{f}(a)$ is maximal for $\prec_a$ in the budget set of ordered pairs $(x, m) \in \mathbb{R}^l_+ \times \mathbb{R}_+$ satisfying:

$$p^0 . x^0 + q^0 . m \leq p^0 . e^0(a) + q^0 . 1$$
$$p^s . x^s + q^s . 1 \leq p^s . e^s(a) + q^s . m \qquad (s = 1, \ldots, S).$$

The monotonicity of preferences implies that $p^s > 0$, for all s, and that, a.e. in A,

$$p^s . f^s(a) + q^s . 1 = p^s . e^s(a) + q^s . f^m(a) .$$

In other words, $\hat{f} = (f^0, f^m, z)$ for some $z \in \mathbb{R}^S_+$. As was shown in Section 6.10, an allocation of the form (f^0, f^m, z) cannot be improved on by any coalition at the second date. Therefore if $\hat{f}$ does not belong to the pseudo-core it must be because there exists a strongly improving coalition at the first date. From the definition of the pseudo-core there exists a coalition T and an allocation $\hat{g} = (g^0, g^m, z)$ such that $\nu(T) > 0$, $\int_T \hat{g} = \int_T \hat{e}$ and $f(a) \prec_a g(a)$ for every $a \in T$. I claim that, a.e. in T, $p^0 . g^0(a) + q^0 . g^m(a) > p^0 . e^0(a) + q^0 . 1$. To prove this claim, suppose to the contrary that for a non-null subset of T, $p^0 . g^0(a) + q^0 . g^m(a) \leq p^0 . e^0(a) + q^0 . 1$. For any such a,

$$g^s(a) = e^s(a) + (g^m(a) - 1)z^s$$
$$= e^s(a) + (g^m(a) - 1)q^s/p^s$$

so

$$p^s . g^s(a) + q^s . 1 \leq p^s . e^s(a) + q^s . g^m(a) .$$

Therefore, the bundle $(g(a), g^m(a))$ belongs to the budget set of agent a. Since $f(a) \prec_a g(a)$ for every a in T, this contradicts the hypothesis that $\hat{f}$ is a WSE allocation. This contradiction proves that, a.e. in T,

$$p^0 . g^0(a) + q^0 . g^m(a) > p^0 . e^0(a) + q^0 . 1 .$$

Integrating over T yields

$$(p^0, q^0) \cdot \int_T (g^0, g^m) > (p^0, q^0) \cdot \int_T (e, 1)$$

which contradicts the assumption that $\int_T \hat{g} = \int_T \hat{e}$. □

6.11.2 Theorem *Let* $\mathscr{E}: (A, \mathscr{A}, \nu) \to \mathscr{P} \times \mathbb{R}^l_+$ *be an atomless exchange economy such that* $\int e \, \mathrm{d}\nu \gg 0$. *Then* $P(\hat{\mathscr{E}}) \subset W^*(\hat{\mathscr{E}})$.

Proof From the definition of the pseudo-core, if $\hat{f}$ belongs to $P(\hat{\mathscr{E}})$ then $\hat{f} = (f^0, f^m, z)$ and $z \geq 0$. Then, for each $s = 1, \ldots, S$, there exist numbers p^s and q^s such that $p^s > 0$, $q^s \geq 0$ and $z^s = q^s/p^s$. Let these be the prices of the consumption good and money respectively at date 1 in state s.

For every a in A, let $\xi(a, m)$ be the unique vector defined by putting $\xi^s(a, m) = (m - 1)z^s + e^s(a)$ for $s = 1, \ldots, S$. If $\hat{g}$ is an attainable allocation then $\hat{g} = (g^0, g^m, z)$ if and only if $g^s(a) = \xi^s(a, m)$, a.e. in A, for $s = 1, \ldots, S$. Now define an artificial economy $\mathscr{E}^0$ in terms of $\mathscr{E}$ by putting

$$\mathscr{E}^0(a) = (X^0_a, \prec^0_a, (e^0_a, 1)) \qquad (a \in A)$$

where

$$X^0_a = \{(x^0, m) \in \mathbb{R}^2_+ \mid \xi(a, m) \geq 0\}$$

$$\prec^0_a = \{(x^0, m, \hat{x}^0, \hat{m}) \in X^0_a \times X^0_a \mid (x^0, \xi(a, m), \hat{x}^0, \xi(a, \hat{m})) \in \prec_a\}$$

and e^0_a has the usual interpretation. It is fairly straightforward to show that $\mathscr{E}^0$ is an exchange economy in the sense of Definition 6.5.1. There are two commodities and a single time-period. Money is treated like an ordinary good and in particular there is no tax demand. $\mathscr{E}^0$ is measurable and, for every a in A, $\prec_a$ is monotonic and continuous. Clearly, (f^0, f^m) is an attainable allocation for $\mathscr{E}^0$ since $\hat{f}$ is an attainable allocation for $\hat{\mathscr{E}}$. If (f^0, f^m) does not belong to the classical core of $\mathscr{E}^0$ there exists a coalition T and an attainable allocation (g^0, g^m) for $\mathscr{E}^0$ such that $\nu(T) > 0$, $\int_T (g^0, g^m) = \int_T (e^0, 1)$ and $(f^0(a), f^m(a)) \prec^0_a (g^0(a), g^m(a))$ for every a in T. Let $\hat{g} = (g^0, g^m, z)$. By the construction of $\mathscr{E}^0$, $\hat{g}$ is an attainable allocation for $\hat{\mathscr{E}}$ if (g^0, g^m) is attainable for $\mathscr{E}^0$; $\int_T \hat{g} = \int_T \hat{e}$ if $\int_T (g^0, g^m) = \int_T (e^0, 1)$; and $f(a) \prec_a g(a)$ for every a in T if $(f^0(a), f^m(a)) \prec^0_a (g^0(a), g^m(a))$ for every a in T. Then the coalition T can strongly improve on $\hat{f}$ in $\hat{\mathscr{E}}$ at date 0, using $\hat{g} = (g^0, g^m, z)$. This contradicts the hypothesis that $\hat{f}$ belongs to $P(\hat{\mathscr{E}})$. Thus (f^0, f^m) must belong to $C(\mathscr{E}^0)$ if $\hat{f}$ belongs to $P(\hat{\mathscr{E}})$.

Theorem 6.6.2 now implies that (f^0, f^m) belongs to $W(\mathscr{E}^0)$. There exists a price system $\pi = (\pi^0, \pi^m)$ in $\mathbb{R}^2_+$ such that, a.e. in A,

(1) $(f^0(a), f^m(a))$ is maximal for $\prec_a^0$ in the budget set $\{(x^0, m) \in X_a^0 | \pi^0 . x^0 + \pi^0 . m \le \pi^0 . e^0(a) + \pi^m . 1\}$.

Put $p^0 = \pi^0$ and $q^0 = \pi^m$. Then, a.e. in A,

(2) $f(a)$ is maximal for $\prec_a$ in the set of ordered pairs $(x, m) \in \mathbb{R}^l_+ \times \mathbb{R}_+$ such that

$$p^0 . x^0 + q^0 . m \le p^0 . e^0(a) + q^0 . 1$$

$$p^s . x^s + q^s . 1 \le p^s . e^s(a) + q^s . m \qquad (s = 1, \ldots, S).$$

For, without loss of generality, it can be assumed that the second inequality in the budget set holds as an equality for every $s = 1, \ldots, S$, i.e. $x^s = \xi(a, m)$ for $s = 1, \ldots, S$. In that case (1) and (2) are equivalent by the definition of X_a^0 and $\prec_a^0$. (2) states that $\hat{f} \in W^*(\hat{\mathscr{E}})$ as required. □

Recall that when an economy has a finite number of types the measure space of agents $(A, \mathscr{A}, \nu)$ can be replaced by the n-vector $\mathbf{t}^* = (t_1^*, \ldots, t_n^*)$ where t_i^* denotes the number or proportion of agents of type i. Similarly any coalition $T \in \mathscr{A}$ can be represented by the n-vector $\mathbf{t} = (t_1, \ldots, t_n) > 0$. As was noted in Section 6.11 any allocation $\hat{f}$ which belongs to the z-core of $\hat{\mathscr{E}}$ can be replaced by the n-tuple $\{(x_i^*, m_i^*) \in \mathbb{R}^l_+ \times \mathbb{R}_+ : i = 1, \ldots, n\}$ where $\mathscr{E}$ is a large economy. If $\hat{f} = (f^0, f^m, z^*)$ then $x_i^s = e_i^s + (m_i^* - 1)z^{s*}$, for every $s = 1, \ldots, S$ and $i = 1, \ldots, n$, so $\hat{f}$ can equally well be represented by the $(n + 1)$-tuple $\{(x_1^{0*}, m_1^*), \ldots, (x_n^{0*}, m_n^*), z^*\}$. In the proof of the Lemma, only allocations of this form are needed.

Lemma *Let $\mathscr{E} : (A, \mathscr{A}, \nu) \to \mathscr{P} \times \mathbb{R}^l_+$ be a regular, atomless exchange economy with a finite number of types of consumers. If $\hat{f}$ belongs to the z-core of $\hat{\mathscr{E}}$ then*

$$\dim Z + \dim \langle a_0, a_s : s = 1, \ldots, S \rangle \le S + 1 .$$

Proof From regularity and $\hat{f} \in W^*(\hat{\mathscr{E}})$ it follows that $x_i^* \gg 0$. By assumption $z^* \gg 0$. Without loss of generality $\mathbf{t} \gg 0$. The strategy is to find sufficient conditions for the existence of a coalition which can improve on $\hat{f}$ and use these to obtain the inequality in the Lemma. In the proof, only coalitions $\mathbf{t}$ such that $d\mathbf{t} = \mathbf{t} - \mathbf{t}^*$ is small are considered. These coalitions will be assumed to choose $\mathbf{x}^0 = (x_1^0, \ldots, x_n^0)$ and $z \in Z + z^*$ so that $d\mathbf{x}^0 = d\mathbf{x}^0 - \mathbf{x}^{0*}$ and $dz = z - z^*$ are all small. Since $x_i^* \gg 0$ and $\mathbf{t}^* \gg 0$, the non-negativity constraints $\mathbf{t} \geq 0$ can be ignored if $\mathrm{d}\mathbf{t}$, $\mathrm{d}z$ and $\mathrm{d}\mathbf{x}^0$ are small. I am assuming here that x_i is given by the equation:

$$x_i = x_i^* + (\mathrm{d}x_i^0, (m_i^* - 1)\,\mathrm{d}z) \qquad (i = 1, \ldots, n).$$

In other words, the coalition $\mathbf{t}$ does not reallocate money balances. It only changes consumption at date 0 and the vector z at date 1. The problem now is to find conditions under which $(\mathrm{d}\mathbf{t}, \mathrm{d}\mathbf{x}^0, \mathrm{d}z)$ can be chosen so that $\mathbf{t}$ is improving on $\hat{f}$ at 0. From the definition of the z-core all that is required for the existence of an improving coalition at the first date is that $\mathrm{d}z \in Z$, that $u_i(x_i) > u_i(x_i^*)$ for $i = 1, \ldots, n$ and that the new allocation be feasible for the coalition, i.e. that $\mathbf{t}$ be self-sufficient.

For small values of $(\mathrm{d}x_i^0, \mathrm{d}z)$, $u_i(x_i) > u_i(x_i^*)$ if and only if $\mathrm{d}x_i^0 + (m^* - 1)\mu_i.\mathrm{d}z > 0$. Self-sufficiency requires

(a) $$\sum_{i=1}^{n} t_i(x_i^0 - e_i^0) = 0$$

(b) $$\sum_{i=1}^{n} t_i(m_i^* - 1) = 0$$

(c) $$\sum_{i=1}^{n} t_i(m_i^* - 1)z = 0$$

(b) implies (c). (b) is implied by the condition

(b)′ $$\sum_{i=1}^{n} \mathrm{d}t_i(x_i^{0*} - e_i^0) = 0$$

since

$$\sum_{i=1}^{n} t_i(m_i^* - 1) = \sum_{i=1}^{n} (\mathrm{d}t_i + t_i^*)(m_i^* - 1)$$

and $\sum t_i^*(m_i^* - 1) = 0$ if $\hat{f}$ is attainable and $\sum \mathrm{d}t_i(m_i^* - 1) = -\sum \mathrm{d}t_i p^\circ(x_i^{0*} - e_i^0)$ if $\hat{f} \in W^*(\hat{\mathscr{E}})$. Finally (a) is implied by (b)′ and the condition

(a)′ $$\sum_{i=1}^{n} t_i\,\mathrm{d}x_i^0 = 0.$$

Collecting these conditions together, a sufficient condition for the existence of a z-improving coalition is that for some $(\mathrm{d}\mathbf{t}, \mathrm{d}\mathbf{x}^0, \mathrm{d}z)$ sufficiently small, $\mathrm{d}z \in Z$, $\mathrm{d}x_i^0 + (m_i^* - 1)\mu_i.\mathrm{d}z > 0$, for all $i = 1, \ldots, n$, and (a)′, (b)′ are satisfied. Suppose that for some $(\mathrm{d}\mathbf{t}, \mathrm{d}z)$

sufficiently small, $dz \in Z$, (b)′ is satisfied and

(d) $$\sum_{i=1}^{n} t_i(m_i^* - 1)\mu_i . dz > 0$$

It is easy to see that there exists a small (dx^0) such that (dt, dx^0, dz) satisfies the sufficient conditions for the existence of an improving coalition. Thus, a sufficient condition for the existence of an improving coalition is that for some (dt, dz) sufficiently small, $dz \in Z$ and (b)′ and (d) are satisfied.

Let
$$a_0 := \{(x_1^{0*} - e_1^0), \ldots, (x_n^{0*} - e_n^0)\}$$
and
$$a_s := \{(m_1^* - 1)\mu_1^s, \ldots, (m_n^* - 1)\mu_n^s\} \qquad (s = 1, \ldots, S).$$

The vector a_0 defines a hyperplane $H(a_0)$ in $\mathbb{R}^n$, i.e.
$$H(a_0) = \{\xi \in \mathbb{R}^n \,|\, a_0 . \xi = 0\}.$$

The vectors $\{a_s : s = 1, \ldots, S\}$ define a linear transformation $\xi \mapsto A\xi$ from $\mathbb{R}^n$ to $\mathbb{R}^S$. The vector $A\xi$ is defined by the equation
$$(A\xi)^s \equiv a_s . \xi \qquad (s = 1, \ldots, S)$$
for every ξ in $\mathbb{R}^n$, where $(A\xi)^s$ denotes the s-component of the vector $A\xi$. Condition (b)′ is equivalent to $dt \in H(a_0)$ and (d) is equivalent to $A(dt + t^*) . dz > 0$.

Since $\hat{f}$ is in the z-core there cannot exist a strongly improving coalition at the first date. For any small (dt, dz) in $H \times Z$, $A(dt + \mathbf{t}^*) . dz \leq 0$ but since Z is a linear subspace this implies that

(e) $A(dt + \mathbf{t}^*) . dz = 0$.

If (e) holds for small values of dz then it obviously holds for all values and this implies that, for any small dt in H, $A(dt + \mathbf{t}^*) \in Z^\perp$, the annihilator of Z. $Z^\perp$ is a linear subspace so if it contains $A(dt + \mathbf{t}^*)$ and $A\mathbf{t}^*$ it must contain $A\,dt$ for any small dt in H. If $A\,dt$ belongs to $Z^\perp$ for all small dt in H then clearly
$$AH \subset Z^\perp$$
since A is linear.

Let A_H denote the restriction of A to H. Then
$$\dim \ker A_H + \dim \operatorname{Im} A_H = \dim H$$
where $\ker A_H$ and $\operatorname{Im} A_H$ denote the kernel and image of A_H respectively. Since $\dim \ker A_H = \dim[H \cap \ker A] = n -$

$\dim\langle a_0, a_s : s \in S\rangle = n - k$, say, it follows that

$$n - k + \dim \operatorname{Im} A_H = \dim H = n - 1,$$

so $\dim \operatorname{Im} A_H = k - 1$. But $AH = \operatorname{Im} A_H$ and $\dim Z^\perp + \dim Z = S$ so $AH \subset Z^\perp$ implies

$$(k - 1) + \dim Z \leq S. \quad \square$$

6.11.4 Theorem *Let $\mathscr{E}:(A, \mathscr{A}, \nu) \to \mathscr{P} \times \mathbb{R}^l_+$ be a regular, atomless exchange economy with a finite number of types of consumers. If $\hat{f}$ belongs to $C^*(\hat{\mathscr{E}})$ then there is no loss of generality in replacing $\hat{f}$ with $\{(x_i^*, m_i^*)\}$. If $m_i^* \neq 1$ for $i = 1, \ldots, n$ then $(x_1^*, \ldots, x_n^*)$ is Pareto-efficient.*

Proof Since $C^*(\hat{\mathscr{E}})$ coincides with the z-core when $Z = \mathbb{R}^l$ the Lemma implies that $k \leq 1$. Since $m_i^* \neq 1$, for $i = 1, \ldots, n$, by hypothesis, $\dim\langle \mu_1, \ldots, \mu_n\rangle = 1$. Then $(x_1^*. \ldots, x_n^*)$ is Pareto-efficient. In fact, it is a Walras allocation for $\mathscr{E}$. $\square$

6.13 Discussion of results

The results obtained have been largely negative in character. In seeking an appropriate cooperative solution concept it has become increasingly clear that only rather unnatural restrictions will guarantee a non-empty solution set.

From the game-theoretic point of view the main difference between an Arrow–Debreu economy and a sequential economy is that in the latter coalitions are allowed to form at any date. When the set of assets is complete the possibility of coalitions forming at any date does not lead to insuperable problems. It merely provides an interesting role for paper assets, namely, as a substitute for trust. In a sequential economy, on the other hand, there is only one asset (money) and possibly several states of nature. If coalitions are allowed to form in the usual way at the first date, a necessary condition for an allocation *not* to be improved on is that it be Pareto-efficient. But as was shown by example in Section 6.4, it is not possible in general to make a Pareto-efficient allocation trustworthy, i.e. to prevent coalitions from improving at the second date, when the set of assets is incomplete.

The problem can be posed another way. In a sequential economy, the "natural" or distinguished definition of equilibrium is provided by the WSE. There are no forward trades in goods and money serves as a store of value. It can do so because there is a sequence of budget constraints, one for each date-event pair, in which the value of net trades of goods is balanced by net trades of money. With an incomplete set of assets a sequence of budget constraints is incompatible with efficiency. An agent who increases his holdings of money at the first date increases his consumption of goods in every state at the second. This sort of adjustment cannot guarantee that the marginal rate of substitution between consumption at date 0 and consumption at date 1 in state s will be equalized for all consumers. So a WSE allocation is normally Pareto-inefficient. Therefore, a cooperative solution concept which characterizes the WSE allocations, in the sense that the solution set (for a large economy) is equal to the set of WSE allocations, must allow for Pareto-inefficient outcomes. Inevitably some restrictions must be placed on the improving coalitions at date 0.

The first step in the analysis seems quite straightforward. There is an unambiguous definition of an improving coalition at date 1 in state s. When the second date arrives and the true state of nature is revealed, agents are essentially dealing with a single-period problem. One only has to adapt the definition of improving coalition from a single-period economy. Also, it is pretty obvious that an allocation can be stable for a SME only if no coalition can improve on it at date 1 in any state. As shown in Section 6.10, this means that in a large economy an allocation $\hat{f}$ is stable only if it has the form (f^0, f^m, z) for some $z \geq 0$. So the definition of the sequential core begins with the requirement that core-allocations have the form (f^0, f^m, z). It is less clear where one should go from here. As pointed out above, the ordinary definition of an improving coalition at date 0 leads to problems. The reason is that improving coalitions at date 0 will insist on a Pareto-efficient allocation at date 0 and this is usually incompatible with the requirement that the allocation have the form (f^0, f^m, z). However, the agents in these coalitions are behaving irrationally to the extent that they demand something (Pareto-efficiency) at date 0 which their behaviour at date 1 renders "unattainable". If they were consistent they would only choose an allocation if it had the form (f^0, f^m, z).

This observation leads to the notion of a *strongly improving coalition*, i.e. one which can improve on $\hat{f}$ at date 0 by choosing an allocation of the form (g^0, g^m, y). The *weak sequential core* is defined to be the set of attainable allocations f which cannot be improved on at the second date, i.e. $\hat{f} = (f^0, f^m, z)$, and cannot be strongly improved on at the first. The weak sequential core is the "natural" definition and certainly seems to be the most reasonable one available. But as Theorem 6.11.4 shows, it is rather badly behaved. When the number of types of agents is greater than the number of states we should expect the weak sequential core to be empty. The *pseudo-core*, on the other hand, does give the required characterization of the WSE allocations (Theorems 6.11.1 and 2). An allocation $\hat{f}$ belongs to the pseudo-core if and only if it has the form (f^0, f^m, z) for some $z \geq 0$ and no coalition can improve strongly on $\hat{f}$ by choosing an allocation of the form (g^0, g^m, z). Unfortunately the pseudo-core lacks any theoretical justification; in particular, there is no justification for the assumption that improving coalitions take z as given. The really unfortunate thing is that the assumption appears inescapable.

The weak sequential core requires an improving coalition at date 0 to choose an allocation of the form (f^0, f^m, y); but agents are free to choose any $y \geq 0$ they wish. The pseudo-core requires an improving coalition to choose $y = z$, if $\hat{f} = (f^0, f^m, z)$ is the allocation to be improved on. Between these two extremes lies a continuum of possible restrictions which are represented by specifying a set Z in $\mathbb{R}^S$ and requiring that $y - z \in Z$. Z is the set of possible directions in which z may be varied and it generates the weak sequential core when $Z = \mathbb{R}^S$ and the pseudo-core when $Z = \{0\}$. Theorem 6.11.3 shows that in order to guarantee the existence of an allocation in the z-core, Z must be chosen so that $\dim Z \leq 1$. (Obviously, y proportional to z is, for all intents and purposes, the same as $y = z$). Thus the pseudo-core appears to be the only solution concept, in this family, that characterizes the WSE allocations.

These results can be reinterpreted using Lancaster's idea of representing a commodity as a bundle of *characteristics*. In a WSE, an agent who purchases one unit of money at the first date is really purchasing a bundle of commodities at the second. A unit of money will purchase (q^s/p^s) units of the consumption good at date 1 in state s. This unit of money can be *identified* with the bundle $z = (z^1, \ldots, z^S)$ of commodities, where $z^s = (q^s/p^s)$ for $s = 1, \ldots, S$. The vector z represents the real characteristics of money. Unlike Lancastrian commodities, however, the characteristics of money are not fixed since the characteristics vector z is endogenous to the system. The agents choose not only the quantities of goods and money to trade at date 0 but also the bundle of characteristics corresponding to money. The pseudo-core requires agents to take the characteristics of money as given or "parametric". Roughly paraphrased, the theorems in Section 6.11 show that when agents do not treat the characteristics vector z as a parameter, the model explodes and the sequential core is empty. In a competitive economy it seems reasonable that individual agents should take the real characteristics as given, though the apparent reasonableness of the assumption is perhaps only a hangover from equilibrium habits of thought. The theorist's problem is to justify the parametric assumption, using cooperative game theory or some other kind of analysis. The failure to find some justification is worrying. If one takes the theory of the sequential core seriously, one is led to the conclusion that the WSE allocations of a monetary economy are inherently unstable.

The assumption that z is a parameter for coalitions is like a *competitive conjecture*. Coalitions which take z as given are, in effect, assuming that in each state of nature at date 1 they can exchange cash balances for consumption at fixed terms of trade (q^s/p^s). The objective of core-theory is to explain how trades come to take place at market-clearing prices but here parametric prices are being smuggled in by the back door. It cannot be claimed that the core provides any foundation for the theory of monetary equilibrium if it is necessary to impose competitive conjectures on agents.

It may be that the theory of cooperative games and the core in particular are ill-suited to provide a foundation for the theory of monetary equilibrium. If so, we face the prospect of having one kind of foundation for the theory of equilibrium in a non-monetary economy and another kind for a monetary economy.

Part of the reason why sequence economies are hard to analyse as cooperative games is that their sequential nature is itself incompatible with a purely cooperative theory. Nash defined a cooperative game as one in which players were allowed unlimited pre-play communication and could make self-binding commitments. But it is precisely the inability to make self-binding commitments in certain cases which distinguishes sequential from non-sequential games. From the outset the sequential core is a hybrid. It is a mainly cooperative but partly non-cooperative game. Conjectures (about the behaviour of other players) arise naturally in non-cooperative games. Perhaps it is only by recognizing explicitly the non-cooperative aspects of the problem that a rationale for competitive conjectures will be found.

Notes

1. For any set X, $\neq X$ denotes the number of elements in X.

2. In a futures equilibrium individuals can arrange trades at date 0 and pay for the goods when they arrive at date 1. Suppose that the futures price of corn for delivery in state s at date 1 were greater than the spot price in state s at date 1. Any individual could make an unboundedly large profit by selling futures at date 1 and buying an equivalent amount on the spot market in state s at date 1. Thus, the futures price must be less than or equal to the future spot price. A similar argument establishes the reverse inequality. If the two prices are the same, however, there is no advantage to trading in futures. Since goods are paid for on delivery one might as well arrange all trades on the spot market.

CHAPTER 7

Monetary equilibrium: a non-cooperative approach

In the last chapter I attempted to explain the positive value of money in general equilibrium using the tools of cooperative game theory. One line of argument applies to the strong sequential core. An allocation in the strong sequential core is, almost by definition, Pareto-efficient. The equivalence theorem shows that the allocation must satisfy a sequence of budget constraints; in fact it is an equilibrium allocation. Now Pareto-efficiency and a sequence of budget constraints are incompatible unless there is some way of transferring wealth between events, so that the sequence of constraints is consolidated into a single constraint. One implication is that, in equilibrium, the paper assets must have positive value. This is a useful insight: an efficiency property together with a sequence of budget constraints implies assets have a positive value.

The concept of the strong sequential core has limited application, because it is normally empty unless there is a large number of assets. To cope with the incompleteness of the set of assets new solution concepts must be introduced, concepts which, among other things, have weaker efficiency properties than the strong sequential core. The pseudo-core is one such concept. It characterizes a reasonable notion of equilibrium, the weak sequential equilibrium, but it does not guarantee a positive value of money. Consider a two-period, one-good exchange economy. If the price of money were zero and the price of consumption goods positive at every event, then there would be an equilibrium in which every agent chose not to trade. The no-trade allocation belongs to the pseudo-core, of course, because of the equivalence theorem. The problem here is that elements of the pseudo-core do not satisfy sufficiently strong efficiency properties to rule out those in which there is no trade in money.

A better way of looking at the problem is from the point of view of the equilibrium concept. Any monetary economy contains within it a non-monetary economy, namely, the one obtained by putting the price of money identically equal to zero. For fiat money functions only if it has a positive exchange value. The motive which led people to hold money disappears when the price is zero (and is expected to remain so). Suppose the non-monetary economy possesses an equilibrium. Then this is also an equilibrium for the monetary economy since with the price of money equal to zero there will be no demand for it (more precisely, agents are indifferent to the quantity they hold). This is exactly what happens in the one-good example mentioned above. If the price of money is zero at every date-event pair then there is no possibility of transferring wealth from date 0 to date 1. Since this transfer of wealth is the only reason for trading money, all agents will be indifferent to the quantity held at the end of date 0. The pseudo-core's only failing is to be equal to the set of *all* equilibrium allocations, including this rather odd one. If there were some sort of efficiency-criterion for membership in the pseudo-core, then it might be possible to exclude the "non-monetary" allocations. In the one-good case, for example, the no-trade allocation will typically be dominated (in the Pareto sense) by another pseudo-core allocation. This is a pretty strong reason for excluding it, but in more general cases things are unlikely to be so simple.

The problem discussed in the context of the one-good economy is quite a general one. It was first studied by F. Hahn in his seminal paper *On Some Problems of Proving the Existence of a Monetary Equilibrium*. Hahn laid the problem out in all its simplicity and intractability. When the value of money is zero (and is expected to remain so) the demand for real balances is also zero. Whether money is required as an asset or as a "medium of exchange", whether it is a cash constraint or some sort of transaction technology or a liquidity premium which leads to the demand for money, *money is only desired for what it will purchase*. When it will purchase *nothing*, these sources of demand dry up. What Hahn showed so lucidly is that, if an economy satisfies the usual conditions for the existence of equilibrium and also the condition that demand for real balances is zero when the price of money is zero, then there always exists a non-monetary equilibrium. Hahn also showed that under certain conditions there also exists a monetary equilibrium, i.e. one in which the value of money is positive; but this leaves open the possibility that the economy may fall into the wrong equilibrium. As in the case of the one-good economy there are grounds for expecting a cooperative game to reject certain equilibria on efficiency grounds. It is not inconceivable, however, that in certain circumstances the introduction of an asset (money) might make everyone worse off. A certain amount of delicacy is required and it is not clear how this is to be achieved using the core. Does one simply add an *ad hoc* "efficiency test" to the definition of the core? If so, what is it? There are independent reasons for wishing to complement, if not replace, the core theory with some other approach. Some are mentioned in Chapter 6.

The core leaves a great deal unsaid. This silence is both its strength and its weakness. It is a strength because it allows many questions—some of which are surely unanswerable in the present state of our knowledge—to be laid on one side while we attend to the more pressing business of characterizing a solution. The core gives some indication of the outcome of a market game without ever specifying, for example, what the process of coalition formation looks like.

This lack of detail is a serious weakness from a purely game-theoretic point of view. In the first place, the more incomplete a story is, the less convincing it will be, other things being equal. Second, when one asks questions like those raised in Chapter 6 it is difficult to say what will or ought to happen if the game being analysed is only very incompletely specified. For example, it seemed clear that an improving coalition should take into account the existence and possible reactions of the counter-coalition. At that point it would have been helpful to know whether an improving coalition actually forms in this game or whether it is merely a proposal in some kind of coalitional *tâtonnement*. What, in any case, are the strategy sets and what is the order of play? Is the counter-coalition simply a passive set of players excluded from the improving coalition or does it have a strategy of its own? These and dozens of similar questions are simply ignored by the theory. By ignoring these questions we can say something about the solution set, but this can never be a satisfactory state in which to leave the theory.

7.1 A non-cooperative approach

It is easier to point out shortcomings than to rectify them. In this chapter I intend to treat the essentially cooperative process of trading goods and assets in a non-cooperative way. The idea is to treat every sort of interaction which occurs between players before the game is actually "played" as a game in its own right and analyse this as a non-cooperative game. The business of negotiating and forming coalitions and entering into binding agreements must be described so precisely that the result is a formal game which accommodates all possible negotiations, agreements etc. A strategy in this game must specify how a player will conduct negotiations in every eventuality. Once a joint strategy has been chosen, the outcome of negotiations is completely determined and in turn determines how the cooperative game will be played.

Nash first proposed the idea of embedding every cooperative game in a non-cooperative one. The strategy has thus come to be known as the Nash Programme. Nash regarded the *contest* as the most basic type of game. A contest is a *one-shot* game in which there is no communication among players before the game commences and for this reason no possibility of binding agreements or indeed any agreements at all. The only thing a player can do is choose his strategy and hope for the best. Threats and revision of strategies play no part. In this situation, where players choose strategies simultaneously and there is no other kind of interaction, the appropriate solution concept is the *Nash equilibrium*. At a Nash equilibrium, no agent will later regret his action. Once the strategy is chosen it is too late for other players to change theirs. In a one-shot game, this is a very cogent argument for taking the Nash equilibrium as the correct solution concept.

In a contest, everything is quite well defined (if one overlooks the existence of multiple equilibria and the question of how players actually discover the equilibrium strategies). The game itself is defined in terms of strategy sets and payoff functions. There is perfect information and there is no communication before play. The players choose their strategies simultaneously and the result is a Nash equilibrium. There are no loose ends in *this* story!

Now consider a cooperative game of the sort studied in Chapter 6, the classical core for example. The core pretends to be a description of the outcome of a game in which there is unlimited pre-play communication and in which players can enter into self-binding commitments of all sorts. But what actually goes on before an allocation in the core is selected is never specified. That there is some embarrassment about this gap is reflected in the way that game theorists have dropped the "blocking coalition" and ambiguously renamed it the "improving coalition". Though it may never be known what an improving coalition actually does, one presumes there is a great deal of negotiating going on. Proposals, counterproposals and compromises float about and players enter into self-binding commitments which may be contingent on other players executing or entering into commitments of their own. There is virtually no limit to the complexity of these negotiations but, supposing they can be represented as a formal game, several points follow more or less from our conception of a "negotiation game".

First of all, since the negotiation game is intended to be comprehensive, i.e. to be a complete model of the negotiations preceding the playing of the cooperative game, it cannot itself be preceded by any negotiations. Thus, there is no communication among players before the negotiation game is played. As a further consequence, there can be no self-binding commitments about how the "negotiation game" is to be played. Once the negotiations are completed, the play of the original cooperative game is determined. This too follows from the conception of the "negotiation game" as a complete description of what goes on before the play of the cooperative game. The "negotiation game" is therefore a one-shot game. A strategy for any player in the negotiation game tells him how to conduct his negotiations in every eventuality. The strategy must be chosen before the actual negotiations commence so the players may be thought of as choosing their strategies simultaneously, though this is not the only way to proceed. The "negotiation game" is clearly a contest, almost by definition, and it should be analysed as such. This, in a nutshell, is the logic of Nash's argument. Every cooperative game must be embedded in a non-cooperative "negotiation game" which is analysed as a contest. A Nash equilibrium of the "negotiation game" will determine the correct outcome of the original cooperative game.

To construct a game which accurately describes the negotiation procedure appropriate to any particular cooperative game will be very difficult. It is not necessary to adopt a constructive approach, however; an alternative is to study classes of abstract games representing a wide range of possible negotiation procedures. If it is possible to characterize the Nash equilibria of a class of abstract, non-cooperative games, then the question of which negotiation game is appropriate for a given cooperative game can be ignored. As long as the negotiation game belongs to this particular class, the characterization applies.

Without some structure on the class of games considered it is highly unlikely that an interesting characterization can be found. In particular, something in the structure of these games must reflect the fact that the negotiation contest represents the prelude to a cooperative game. Otherwise the class of contests could simply be any set of abstract, non-cooperative games. The most important characteristic of cooperative games is that their outcomes are expected to be efficient in some degree. The assumption that there is unlimited pre-play communication and that players may enter into any form of self-binding commitment removes any obstacle to a Pareto-improving move. This suggests that attention should be restricted to non-cooperative games whose outcomes are Pareto-efficient allocations for some sort of economy. It is possible to show, by adding a little more structure to the games, that the Nash equilibria of large Pareto-efficient market games (i.e. games with a continuum of players, the outcomes of which are efficient allocations in some underlying economy) can be characterized as equilibria of the economy in question. In this way the Nash Programme is carried out without specifying the actual negotiation procedure to be followed. For since any "negotiation game" belongs to this class of large, efficient market games by hypothesis, the outcome must be a market equilibrium, whichever negotiation procedure is followed.

To sum up, the cooperative market game whose outcomes are normally represented by the core, say, is embedded in a non-cooperative negotiation game. Rather than model the negotiation game explicitly, it is enough to look at a large class of games, which contains all the candidates from which the correct "negotiation game" might be chosen. The Nash equilibria of these games can be precisely characterized so it is possible to analyse these cooperative games non-cooperatively (i.e. carry through the Nash Programme) without being forced to construct the negotiation contest at all.

7.2 Abstract market games

The first task is to construct a family of games which will include all the negotiation contests of interest. The approach is of necessity an abstract one. The games in this family will be called *abstract market games*; "abstract" because they are described only in very general terms and "market" games because their outcomes are allocations in an exchange economy. Underlying these games is a family of economies. To begin with I shall consider a class of games defined for pure exchange economies only. The description of these economies differs somewhat from the description in Chapter 6. Some of these differences are merely notational but others are substantive.

An agent will be described by a *net trade set* and a *preference relation* on this set. An agent was previously described by a consumption set, an ordering on that set and an endowment. The new practice implicitly assumes that if two agents have the same net trade set and the same preference relation on that set, then they must be treated in the same way, even if they have different endowments, for example. The assumption is not unrestrictive. A *characteristic* is now an ordered pair $(X, \prec)$ say, where $X \subset \mathbb{R}^l$ is the set of possible *net trades* the agent can make and $\prec$ the preference relation on this set. The *characteristics space* is thus a collection of ordered pairs of this form. A more restrictive representation will be adopted in the sequel, however. It will be assumed that the characteristics space, or at least the relevant part of it, can be parametricized in a particular way. Let Θ denote the open interval of the real line between 0 and 1. This is the parameter set. $(\Theta, \mathscr{S})$ is a measurable space, where $\mathscr{S}$ denotes the family of Lebesgue sets in (0, 1). The characteristics themselves are represented by a pair of functions (X, U). X is a function from Θ to the family of closed, non-empty subsets of $\mathbb{R}^l$. For every θ in Θ, $X(\theta)$ represents the net trade set associated with θ. U is a real-valued function defined on the graph of X. For every θ in Θ, $U(.,\theta)$ is a utility function defined on $X(\theta)$. Since the ordered pair $\{X(\theta), U(., \theta)\}$ is a characteristic for each θ in Θ, it seems natural to refer to θ as a "characteristic" too. It is a harmless abuse of language anyway and proves convenient below. The reason for introducing a parametricization in the first place is to allow some further restrictions to be put on the characteristics. To be precise, it provides a convenient way of describing a *regular family of characteristics*. This notion is formalized in the following definition.

7.2.1 Definition *A regular family of characteristics is an ordered pair (X, U) of functions satisfying these conditions:*

(1) *$X(\theta)$ is a closed, convex subset of $\mathbb{R}^l$. It is bounded below, $X(\theta) + \mathbb{R}^l_+ \subset X(\theta)$ and $0 \in \operatorname{int} X(\theta)$.*
(2) *$U(., \theta)$ is a strictly quasi-concave, monotonic, real-valued function on $X(\theta)$.*
(3) *U is a continuously differentiable function.*
(4) *The indirect utility function $v(p, w, \theta)$ (which is well-defined here) has a partial derivative $\partial v/\partial w$ which is positive and bounded away from 0.*

An exchange economy would normally be described by a function $\mathscr{E}$ from a measure space $(A, \mathscr{A}, v)$ of agents to the characteristics space Θ. It can also be described by the *distribution* of $\mathscr{E}$, that is, by the measure μ on $(\Theta, \mathscr{S})$, which is defined by putting

$$\mu(S) = v\{a \in A | \mathscr{E}(a) \in S\}$$

for every measurable set S in $\mathscr{S}$. Every function $\mathscr{E}$ defines a unique distribution μ but the converse is false. The information which is lost by looking at μ rather than $\mathscr{E}$ is small, however. In the games which are of most interest to economists, it is an agent's characteristic θ and not his name "a" that matters. When the economy is large, i.e. ν is non-atomic, the distribution μ contains all the information needed to determine the Walrasian equilibrium prices etc. In any case, in the sequel only symmetric games are studied, that is games where characteristics and not names matter. Let $M(\Theta)$ denote the set of measures μ on $(\Theta, \mathscr{S})$ such that $\mu(\Theta) = 1$. For any μ in $M(\Theta)$ the ordered triple $(\Theta, \mathscr{S}, \mu)$ represents an *exchange economy* and for convenience I shall often simply refer to the exchange economy μ, when $(\Theta, \mathscr{S})$ is understood. For any economy μ there is a measure space of agents $(A, \mathscr{A}, \nu)$ and a function $\mathscr{E}$ such that μ is the distribution of $\mathscr{E}$. But $\mathscr{E}$ and $(A, \mathscr{A}, \nu)$ do not matter except in one respect. The exchange economy μ is called *large* if ν is non-atomic. The significance of this assumption lies entirely in the fact that the strategy choice of a single agent on his own does not affect the payoff of any other player. This will become clearer shortly.

Let $(\Theta, \mathscr{S}, \mu)$ be an exchange economy as described above. An abstract market game *based* on this economy will be a game whose outcomes are allocations of net trades for this economy. Players choose strategies from a common strategy set Σ called the *message or signal space*. Σ is arbitrary except to the extent that it must be possible to define a σ-field on Σ, in order that Σ can be regarded as a measurable space. This is unrestrictive. A *joint strategy* is a measurable function $\boldsymbol{\sigma}$ from Θ to Σ. This definition implies that two agents with the same characteristic θ will choose the same strategy $\boldsymbol{\sigma}(\theta)$. This need not be true but it will always be assumed in the sequel. Players can be thought of as simultaneously announcing how they will negotiate. The joint strategy $\boldsymbol{\sigma}$ is a long list of negotiating postures, one for each player (characteristic). Once the lawyers have unscrambled the implications of these threats, commitments, proposals etc. a unique outcome of the cooperative game embedded in the "negotiation game" is determined. An *abstract market game* is defined to be an ordered pair (g, Σ), where g is a function from $\Sigma \times M(\Sigma)$ to $\mathbb{R}^l$ such that:

for any $\boldsymbol{\sigma}$, $g(.,\mu_{\boldsymbol{\sigma}})$ *is* $\mu_{\boldsymbol{\sigma}}$*-measurable and* $\int g(.,\mu_{\boldsymbol{\sigma}})\, \mathrm{d}\mu_{\boldsymbol{\sigma}} = 0$, *where* $\mu_{\boldsymbol{\sigma}}$ *is the distribution of* $\boldsymbol{\sigma}$.

Each player is assigned a net trade vector $g(\boldsymbol{\sigma}(\theta), \mu_{\boldsymbol{\sigma}})$ in $\mathbb{R}^l$ which depends only on the message he sends (and this in turn depends only on his characteristic θ) and on the distribution $\mu_{\boldsymbol{\sigma}}$ of messages sent (which is independent of the message sent by the agent himself when the economy is large). Market games of this sort have a *symmetry* or *anonymity property* analogous to those of competitive market processes.

Let (g, Σ) be an abstract market game based on a large, exchange economy μ. A *Nash equilibrium* for (g, Σ) is a joint strategy $\boldsymbol{\sigma}$ such that, for every θ in ⊕,

$$\boldsymbol{\sigma}(\theta) \textit{ is maximal for } U(.,\theta) \textit{ in the set } \{\sigma \in \Sigma | g(\sigma, \mu_{\boldsymbol{\sigma}}) \in X(\theta)\}.$$

The Nash equilibria of these games can be reduced to solutions of a simpler game. It is analytically helpful, and involves no loss of generality, to simplify them as follows. A *revelation game* is an abstract market game (g, Σ) such that $\Sigma = ⊕$. In other words, the messages players send are simply their own characteristics. The intuition behind this is simple. If all the players have attended the Nash School of Game Theory, then instead of announcing a negotiating strategy the player might as well announce the sort of person he is. Everyone will know what this implies about the way he intends to play the negotiation game. Of course, he may commit himself to behaving like a different sort of person if this is to his advantage. A Nash equilibrium $\boldsymbol{\sigma}$ for the revelation game $(g, ⊕)$ is called *truthful* if $\boldsymbol{\sigma}(\theta) = \theta$ for all θ in ⊕.

7.2.2 Proposition *Let $\boldsymbol{\sigma}$ be a Nash equilibrium for the abstract market game (g, Σ). There exists a revelation game $(\hat{g}, ⊕)$ which has a truthful Nash equilibrium $\boldsymbol{\sigma}$ such that, for every θ in ⊕,*

$$g(\boldsymbol{\sigma}(\theta), \mu_{\boldsymbol{\sigma}}) = \hat{g}(\theta, \mu).$$

Proof Simply use the equation in the Proposition as a definition of $\hat{g}$ for that value of μ. □

The proposition shows that if we are interested in characterizing the trades that result from the Nash equilibrium messages sent by the players in an abstract market game, then there is no loss of generality in restricting attention to the truthful equilibria of revelation games. In what follows, therefore, I shall only consider these games and their truthful equilibria. Henceforth, it will be assumed that μ is fixed in $M(⊕)$ and a market game is a measurable function g (or g_μ if the dependence on μ needs to be emphasized) such that $\int g \, \mathrm{d}\mu = 0$. There is a slight abuse of notation here since g should be defined for all possible distributions of joint strategies $\boldsymbol{\sigma}$. The symbol μ is doing double duty as both the true distribution of characteristics and the distribution of $\boldsymbol{\sigma}$. There is no real harm in this, however, since only Nash equilibrium distributions are of interest and these are taken as given by agents in large economies. *A market game g will be said to have a Nash equilibrium if and only if, for every θ in* ⊕, *θ is maximal for U*(., θ) *in the set*

$$\{\eta \in \Theta \mid g(\eta) \in X(\theta)\}.$$

7.3 The Walrasian case

As an application of the non-cooperative approach described in the preceding section I shall give a characterization of the Nash equilibrium allocations of the abstract market games defined above. Let (⊕, μ, X, U) be fixed, where (X, U) is a regular family of characteristics and μ is some probability measure on ⊕. A *net trade* is simply a vector $x \in \mathbb{R}^l$. A *trade allocation* is a measurable function e from ⊕ to $\mathbb{R}^l$ such that $e(\theta) \in X(\theta)$, for every θ in ⊕. The trade allocation e is *attainable* for the economy μ if $\int e \, d\mu = 0$. A *price system* is a non-zero vector p in $\mathbb{R}^l$. An allocation e is called a *Walras allocation* for the economy μ if e is μ-attainable and there is a price system p such that, for every θ in ⊕,

> $e(\theta)$ *is maximal for* $U(., \theta)$ *in the budget set* $\{x \in X(\theta) \mid p.x \leq 0\}$.

The market game g is called *Walrasian* if the function e defined by $e := g_\mu(.)$ is a Walras allocation.

An allocation e for μ is called *Pareto-efficient* (for μ) if e is μ-attainable and there is no μ-attainable allocation $\hat{e}$ such that $\hat{e}(\theta)$ is preferred by θ to $e(\theta)$, for every θ in ⊕. A market game g is said to be *efficient* if the function e defined by $e := g_\mu(.)$ is an efficient allocation. Note that there is no reason *a priori* to expect $e = g_\mu$ to be an allocation at all, still less an attainable one. However, if g has a Nash equilibrium then it follows that both are true.

7.3.1 Theorem *If g is a Walrasian market game then it is efficient and has a Nash equilibrium.*

7.3.2 Theorem *Suppose that μ is a large, regular exchange economy, i.e.* (X, U) *represents a regular family of characteristics. If* g_μ *is an efficient market game and has a Nash equilibrium and if*

$$g_\mu(\theta) \in \operatorname{int} X(\theta) \quad \textit{for every} \quad \theta \in \Theta$$

then g_μ *is Walrasian.*

Proof of Theorem 7.3.1 The efficiency of the Walrasian market game follows from standard arguments which will not be repeated here. To show that g has the equilibrium property suppose the contrary. For some $\mu \in M(\Theta)$ and $\theta \in \Theta$,

$$(1) \qquad e(\eta) \in X(\theta) \quad \text{and} \quad U(e(\eta), \theta) > U(e(\theta), \theta).$$

Since g is Walrasian there is a price system p such that $p.e(\eta) \leq 0$ and $e(\theta)$ is maximal in the budget set $\{x \in X(\theta) \mid p.x \leq 0\}$. This contradicts (1) and thus proves the theorem. □

Proof of Theorem 7.3.2 Let μ be a fixed, arbitrary measure in $M(\Theta)$ and let $e = g(.,\mu)$. Since e is Pareto-efficient by hypothesis there exists a price vector $p \neq 0$ such that, a.e. in Θ, if $x \in X(\theta)$ and $U(x, \theta) > U(e(\theta), \theta)$ then $p.x \geq p.e(\theta)$. This follows, for example, from an application of the argument in Chapter 6. Because of the differentiability of U this statement can be extended to all $\theta \in \Theta$, i.e. for *any* $\theta \in \Theta$, $U(x, \theta) > U(e(\theta), \theta)$ implies $p.x \geq p.e(\theta)$. Now a standard argument shows that since $p \neq 0$ and $e(\theta) \in \operatorname{int} X(\theta)$, i.e. $p.e(\theta) > \inf p.X(\theta)$, $e(\theta)$ is maximal in the budget set $\{x \in X(\theta) \mid p.x \leq p.e(\theta)\}$.

Let (θ^r) be a sequence in Θ converging to θ. If

$$\limsup_r p.[e(\theta^r) - e(\theta)] > 0$$

then

$$\limsup_r [U(e(\theta^r), \theta^r) - U(e(\theta), \theta^r)] > 0$$

From the continuity of U:

$$\limsup_r [U(e(\theta^r), \theta) - U(e(\theta), \theta)] > 0$$

contradicting the equilibrium property of g. Hence,

$$\limsup_r p.[e(\theta^r) - e(\theta)] \leq 0.$$

By a similar argument one shows that

$$\liminf_r p.[e(\theta^r) - e(\theta)] \geq 0.$$

This establishes that the function $p.e(.)$ is continuous. It is straightforward to prove that $e(.)$ is continuous now.

From the definition of the equilibrium property, the continuity of

$\mathbf{w} = p.e(.)$ and the differentiability of U,

$$0 \geq U(e(\theta'), \theta) - U(e(\theta), \theta)$$
$$= \frac{\partial v(p, \mathbf{w}(\theta), \theta)}{\partial w}(\mathbf{w}(\theta') - \mathbf{w}(\theta)) + o(\theta' - \theta)$$

which implies that

$$\text{(2)} \qquad \mathbf{w}(\theta') - \mathbf{w}(\theta) \leq o(\theta' - \theta).$$

From the same considerations, plus the fact that $\partial v(p, \mathbf{w}(\theta'), \theta')/\partial m$ is positive and bounded away from zero, it follows that

$$\text{(3)} \qquad \mathbf{w}(\theta') - \mathbf{w}(\theta) \geq o(\theta' - \theta).$$

The inequalities (2) and (3) imply that $\mathbf{w}$ is differentiable and that the derivative is 0. Since $\int \mathbf{w}\, d\mu = 0$ it follows that $\mathbf{w}(\theta) = 0$ for all $\theta \in \Theta$. □

So far so good: the representation of the negotiation procedure as a market game has shown that if the outcome is efficient then in a large economy, the outcome must be a Walras allocation. This result is independent of the exact nature of the negotiation procedure. Indeed, the advantage of looking at *abstract* market games is precisely that it makes this point so clear. Apart from regularity, the only assumptions needed are that the solution be a Nash equilibrium (which follows from game-theoretic considerations) and that it be efficient (a reflection of the "cooperative" nature of the underlying game).

As an illustration of the theory outlined consider the following simple example. There are two goods, that is, $l = 2$ and an agent with characteristic θ in (0, 1) has a consumption set $\mathbb{R}^2_+$, an endowment vector $(\theta, 1 - \theta)$ and a Cobb–Douglas utility function with equal weights for the two goods. Suppose that characteristics are uniformly distributed, that is, μ is the ordinary Lebesgue measure on (0, 1). There is no loss of generality in assuming endowments are known because in this case there is a one to one correspondence between endowments and trade sets.

Under the above assumption the economy has a unique Walrasian equilibrium with a price system (proportional to) $p = (1, 1)$ and a consumption bundle $(\frac{1}{2}, \frac{1}{2})$ for every agent. In terms of the earlier notation, if g is efficient and has a Nash equilibrium then

$$g(\mu, \theta) = (\tfrac{1}{2}, \tfrac{1}{2}) - (\theta, 1 - \theta)$$
$$= (\tfrac{1}{2} - \theta, \theta - \tfrac{1}{2}).$$

for each θ in (0, 1).

It is easy to see why Theorem 7.3.1 must hold. Suppose the agent's true characteristic is η and he reports θ. Then his consumption is $(\frac{1}{2} + \eta - \theta, \frac{1}{2} + \theta - \eta)$ and his utility is $\log(\frac{1}{2} + \eta - \theta) + \log(\frac{1}{2} + \theta - \eta)$. This expression is maximized with respect to θ if $\eta - \theta = \theta - \eta$, i.e. $\eta = \theta$.

Similarly, an efficient game must give every agent a consumption with the form (λ, λ), that is, the agent must consume the same quantity of each good. Then the only thing that remains to be determined is the size of the scalar $\lambda > 0$ for each characteristic θ. Each agent will choose his strategy to maximize $\lambda(\theta)$ so Nash equilibrium requires that $\lambda(\theta)$ be a constant. Attainability now implies that $\lambda(\theta) = \frac{1}{2}$ for all θ in (0, 1). This establishes Theorem 7.3.2 for this special case.

7.4 Sequential market games

There is no room for money in the market game discussed above, so it has little to reveal about the workings of a monetary economy; however the experience of Chapter 6 suggests how this gap can be filled. The market game defined above was analyzed as a *contest*, that is, a one-shot game in which there is no pre-play communication. The imposition of these properties is justified by the conception of a negotiation procedure as a *comprehensive* method of deciding how the underlying game is to be played. This seems appropriate if communication is costless (compare Nash's definition of cooperative games), if there is unbounded rationality on the part of all players and if there are no restrictions on the self-binding commitments the players can make. It is not hard to imagine circumstances in which one or more of these conditions fails, however. In such cases, negotiations might proceed in stages. There might, for example, be a family of independent "negotiation games", each one concerned with deciding a different aspect of the play of the underlying game. To illustrate these ideas consider the earlier example. Suppose the example is interpreted as a model of a two-period economy with a single good available for delivery at each date. At the first date agents negotiate only about how to redistribute goods at the first date. At the second they negotiate about how to reallocate goods at the second date. These negotiation contests are independent in the sense that each player is allowed to choose a signal θ in (0, 1) in each contest and his choice in one contest is not constrained by his choice in the other. This is what is meant by "conducting negotiations in stages" or having "separate negotiating sessions" etc.

In the first period, each agent reports a characteristic. Suppose a particular agent reports the characteristic θ_1. Then, assuming every other agent also reports his true characteristic, an efficient game which has a Nash equilibrium will assign the agent a net trade $(\frac{1}{2} - \theta_1)$. At the second date it will assign him $(\theta_2 - \frac{1}{2})$ where θ_2 is the reported characteristic. But in each case the agent is choosing his message to maximize utility, that is, he chooses $(\theta_1, \theta_2) \in \Theta \times \Theta$ to maximize

$$\log(\tfrac{1}{2} + \theta_1 - \theta) + \log(\tfrac{1}{2} + \theta - \theta_2)$$

and it is clear that this will not lead him to choose $\theta_1 = \theta_2 = \theta$. Pareto-efficiency is evidently incompatible with Nash equilibrium, when agents can choose independent strategies at different dates.

This is rather sad, but it is not the end of the story. By introducing money in an appropriate way it is possible to ensure the game has a Nash equilibrium. Suppose, in the simple example, that each agent begins life with an endowment of one unit of money, where money is understood to be some sort of paper currency which has no inherent utility. Suppose also that this money can be exchanged as part of the underlying cooperative game. Consider the game which assigns the net trades $(\frac{1}{2} - \theta, \theta - \frac{1}{2})$ to any agent reporting the characteristic θ, and the net trades of money in each period are $(\theta - \frac{1}{2}, \frac{1}{2} - \theta)$. Notice that if money is treated as a numeraire and goods prices are given by $p = (1, 1)$ then the net trades of money and goods satisfy a budget constraint in each period, i.e. the value of net trades of goods and money sum to zero at each date. For example, in the first period the value of goods traded is $(\theta - \frac{1}{2})$, and of money $(\frac{1}{2} - \theta)$. Suppose that agents are required to give their endowment of money to the government at the end of period 2, i.e. every agent has to pay a tax of one unit of money. Then it turns out that the game described above is Pareto-efficient and has a Nash equilibrium. Efficiency is obvious. Now suppose the agent reports characteristics θ_1 and θ_2 in the first and second periods respectively, and his true characteristic is θ. He must end up with one unit of money at the end of period 2, and this means that

$$(\theta_1 - \tfrac{1}{2}) + (\tfrac{1}{2} - \theta_2) \geq 0$$

or $\theta_1 \geq \theta_2$. His net trades in goods are $(\frac{1}{2} - \theta_1, \ \theta_2 - \frac{1}{2})$ so optimality obviously requires $\theta_1 = \theta_2$. But if he is constrained to report the same characteristic in each period he is effectively in the static (one-period) situation again so he will report his characteristic truthfully (in each period).

This case is particularly interesting because it corresponds to a notion of sequential equilibrium. At each date an agent chooses net trades in money and goods, subject to a budget constraint, to maximize utility. Specifically, he chooses a pair (x, m) to maximize $U(x, \theta)$ subject to the constraints:

$$x \in X(\theta), \quad 1 + m^1 \geq 0, \quad 1 + m^1 + m^2 \geq 1,$$
$$p^1x^1 + m^1 \leq 0, \quad p^2x^2 + m^2 \leq 0$$

where $x \equiv (x^1, x^2)$ and $m \equiv (m^1, m^2)$ are excess demands for goods and money respectively. (The superscript refers to the time-period $t = 1, 2$). This suggests an analogue to Theorem 7.3.1: a sequence equilibrium in a monetary economy is an efficient, Nash equilibrium for an appropriately defined market game. In fact, this is only true if the equilibrium is an inessential sequence equilibrium, a sufficient condition for which is $1 + m^1 > 0$ for every agent. The converse, which would provide an analogue to Theorem 7.3.2 is false. As a counter-example, suppose that the game gives an agent with characteristic θ the following net trades of money in the two periods $t = 1, 2$:

$$m^1 := \sqrt{\theta} - \tfrac{1}{2}, \quad m^2 := \tfrac{1}{2} - \sqrt{\theta},$$

and the same net trades of goods as before. It is easy to check that this game has a Nash equilibrium but there is no price system at which the budget of every agent balances at both dates. This example suggests that there is an embarrassingly large number of games with Nash equilibria. In order to eliminate some of them it is necessary to enlarge the strategy set somewhat. Rather than do this formally I shall depart very slightly from the methodology of the Nash Programme and allow cooperation between pairs of agents. Precisely, they are allowed to make side payments in money and/or goods in order to improve on the strategies they might have chosen individually; but *not* to coordinate their choice of strategies in different negotiating sessions, i.e. there is no intertemporal cooperation. This innovation is justified by the argument that such a modest and foolproof type of cooperation would certainly be part of any cooperative game and could certainly be arranged during the negotiating session. In a Nash equilibrium such improvements ought therefore to be impossible. This requirement leads to the notion of a *strict* Nash equilibrium. To illustrate:

In the previous counter-example, an agent reporting the characteristic θ holds $(\tfrac{1}{2} + \sqrt{\theta})$ units of money at the end of the first period, because his initial endowment is one unit and his first-period net trade is $(\sqrt{\theta} - \frac{1}{2})$. Consider two agents a and b with true characteristics θ_a and θ_b respectively, where $\theta_a < \theta_b$. Suppose that for some small $\varepsilon > 0$, agent a reports $(\theta_a + \varepsilon)$ and agent b reports $(\theta_b - \varepsilon)$ in the first period. The pair of agents have the same combined net trade of goods in the first period as they would if they told the truth. Considering the graph of end-of-period money holdings as a function of θ, it is clear that their joint holdings at the end of period one have increased. Agent a's holdings increase by Δm_a and agent b's decrease by Δm_b, where $\Delta m_a > \Delta m_b$ because of the curvature of the graph. Thus, if we require *strict* Nash equilibrium this game has none, since agents a and b, by increasing their money holdings through collusion, are in a position to report higher values of θ in the second period than the true ones. This will increase their allocation of consumption in period two and hence their utility. In fact, only "linear" distributions of money, like the one in the first example, are compatible with Pareto-efficiency and strict Nash equilibrium.

To generalize these ideas some more notation will be helpful. Let μ be a *two-period economy*, that is, there is an underlying set D of date-event pairs having the form $\{0\} \cup S$. There are two dates. At the first date there is a single event 0 in which agents have no information about the true state of nature. At the second date, all agents discover the true state $s \in S$ so these events can be identified with the elements of S. The commodity space is $\mathbb{R}^l$ and there is assumed to be a single asset, "money".

7.4.1 Definition *A sequential market game for an exchange economy μ is an ordered pair (g^*, h^*), where g^* is a function from $\Theta \times D$ to $\mathbb{R}^l$ and h^* a function from $\Theta \times D$ to $\mathbb{R}$, such that for every d in D, $g^*(.., d)$ and $h^*(.., d)$ are μ-measurable and $\int g^*(\theta, d)\mu(d\theta) = 0 = \int h^*(\theta, d)\mu(d\theta)$.*

Remember that, strictly speaking, g^* and h^* depend on the distribution of *messages* and that this distribution need not equal μ, the true distribution of characteristics. However, since only Nash equilibria, in which agents can take the distribution as given and equal to μ, are of interest here, the abuse of language is quite innocuous. For each $d \in D$, the ordered pair $\{g^*(.., d), h^*(.., d)\}$ is like a market game in the sense of Section 7.3 except that there is now paper money to be traded as well. A sequential market game can be seen as a family of market games, one for each d in D. Because of bounded rationality or some other negotiation costs, the agents carry out their negotiations in a piecemeal fashion. Before each event they have a negotiating session in which they agree to reallocate goods and money. These reallocations are restricted, however; in general they affect some subset of goods, say, those for delivery at the corresponding date-event pair. For the moment there is no need to specify the subspace to which the negotiations are restricted, so the definition is quite general. Notice that although the different "negotiation games" are played independently they are linked by the fact that the outcome of one game affects the preferences of players in another.

In order to obtain the desired characterization of Nash equilibrium the definition must be strengthened in one respect and weakened in another. It is strengthened by the introduction of side trades, in goods or money, between pairs of players. These exchanges are used to tighten up the relationship between trades in money and goods derived from the definition of truthful Nash equilibrium. The additional condition is superfluous in the Walrasian case because of the assumption of Pareto-efficiency. In the sequential game, such a strong efficiency property is inappropriate and will not be required.

While pairs of players may coordinate their choice of strategies at a single date-event pair and make direct exchanges of goods and money, they are not allowed to coordinate their actions between date-event pairs. The rationale for this restriction is obvious: the negotiations undertaken at each date-event pair are carried out independently. Without this assumption there would be no point in having separate negotiating sessions.

A *signalling strategy*, or *signal* for short, is a function σ from D to Θ. For every d in D, $\sigma(d)$ indicates the message sent by the agent to the market during the corresponding "negotiation game". For any characteristic θ in Θ, the "truthful" strategy is the signal σ_θ defined by putting

$$\sigma_\theta(d) = \theta \quad \text{for all} \quad d \in D.$$

Let (g^*, h^*) be a fixed sequential game for the two-period economy μ and suppose that every player has chosen his "truthful" strategy. Let M be the set $\{m \in \mathbb{R}^D \mid m(0) + m(s) \geq 0 \text{ for all } s \in S\}$ and let Z be the set $\{z\colon D \to \mathbb{R}^l \mid z(d) \in Z^d \text{ for all } d \in D\}$ where Z^d is the smallest linear sub-space of $\mathbb{R}^l$ containing $\{g^*(\theta, d) \mid \theta \in (H)\}$. A pair of players θ_1, θ_2, can *improve at date* 0 *on the truthful strategies* $\sigma_{\theta_1}, \sigma_{\theta_2}$ respectively if there exist signals σ_i and trade plans $(z_i, m_i) \in Z \times M$ for $i = 1, 2$ such that:

(1) $z_i(s) = g^*(\sigma_i(s), s)$ and $m_i(s) = h(\sigma_i(s), s)$ for $i = 1, 2$ *and* $s \in S$;

(2) $\sum_{i=1}^{2} z_i(0) = \sum_{i=1}^{2} g^*(\sigma_i(0), 0)$ and $\sum_{i=1}^{2} m_i(0) = \sum_{i=1}^{2} h^*(\sigma_i(0), 0)$;

(3) $x_i \in X(\theta_i)$ and $U(x_i, \theta_i) > U(e(\theta_i))$, for $i = 1, 2$, *where*

$$x_i = \sum_{d \in D} z_i(d) \text{ and } e(\theta_i) = \sum_{d \in D} g^*(\theta_i, d) \text{ for } i = 1, 2.$$

Two players with characteristics θ_1 and θ_2 can improve at 0 on their truthful strategies if there are signals σ_1 and σ_2 which allow them to attain preferred consumption bundles x_1 and x_2, possibly by exchanging goods and money at 0. Note that the exchange of goods at 0 is constrained by Z^0. The family $\{Z^d: d \in D\}$ acts here as a market structure, although it is a characteristic of the market game and not the underlying economy. The family $\{Z^d: d \in D\}$ reflects the *scope* of the independent negotiating games. The two agents are only allowed to exchange goods at 0. To do otherwise would require them to to coordinate their actions in other negotiation games, which is ruled out by definition.

A pair (θ_1, θ_2) can improve on their truthful strategies at some event $s \in S$ if there exist signals σ_i and trade plans $(z_i, m_i) \in Z \times M$ such that:

(1) $z_i(d) = g^*(\theta_i, d)$ and $m_i(d) = h(\theta_i, d)$ for $i = 1, 2$ and $d \in D \backslash \{s\}$;

(2) $\sum_{i=1}^{2} z_i(s) = \sum_{i=1}^{2} g^*(\sigma_i(s), s)$ and $\sum_{i=1}^{2} m_i(s) = \sum_{i=1}^{2} h^*(\sigma_i(s), s)$;

(3) $x_i \in X(\theta_i)$ and $U(x_i, \theta_i) > U(e(\theta_i), \theta_i)$ for $i = 1, 2$, where

$$x_i = \sum_{d \in D} z_i(d) \text{ and } e(\theta_i) = \sum_{d \in D} g^*(\theta_i, d) \text{ for } i = 1, 2.$$

This definition is similar to the earlier one except that the agents can only alter their messages at s; it is too late to change their messages at other events.

7.4.2 Definition *A sequential market game* (g^*, h^*) *for the two-period economy* μ *has a strict Nash equilibrium if no pair of agents* θ_1, θ_2 *in* Θ *can improve on their "truthful" strategies at* 0 *or at any* s *in* S, *when all other agents choose their "truthful" strategies.*

In the definitions of improving pairs at events in D, there were already references to the sets Z and M which are concepts borrowed from equilibrium theory. Z is the set of commodity trade plans and M the set of money trade plans for an appropriate sequence of markets. Let $\{Z^d : d \in D\}$ be the "market structure" referred to above. A *commodity trade plan* is a function z from D to $\mathbb{R}^l$ such that $z(d) \in Z^d$ for every d in D. A *money trade plan* is a function m from D to $\mathbb{R}$. For any d in D, $z(d)$ (resp. $m(d)$) is the net trade in commodities (resp. money) transacted at d by the agent choosing the plan. Evidently only spot trades of money and trades of commodities in Z^d are allowed. This restriction reflects the limited scope of the negotiations at d. In the sequel I shall treat them as *defining* the scope of the negotiations and assume $\{Z^d : d \in D\}$ and M are given independently of the game.

A *trade plan* is an ordered pair (z, m) consisting of a commodity trade plan and money trade plan. A *commodity* (resp. money) *trade plan allocation* is a measurable function e^* (resp. f^*) from Θ to the set Z (resp. M) of commodity (resp. money) trade plans such that

$$\sum_{d \in D} e^*(\theta)(d) \in X(\theta)$$

for every $\theta \in \Theta$. There are two constraints to be satisfied by a trade plan allocation. The first is that the commodity trade plan assigned to an agent with characteristic θ results in a feasible consumption for θ. The second is implicit in the definition of the set of money trade plans M: if $m \in M$ then $m(0) + m(s) \geq 0$ for every $s \in S$. An agent planning to carry out these trades in money will end up with at least as much money as he started with. This is the usual convention required to keep money from falling out of the system. There is no requirement that money holdings should always be non-negative which would mean that $m(0) \geq -1$ since each agent initially holds one unit of money. The absence of this constraint is equivalent to allowing short sales of money or borrowing. If a non-negativity condition were to be included in the definition of M, the analysis would proceed as before *except* that it would be necessary to assume the constraint was not binding on any θ in Θ, i.e. $h^*(\theta, 0) > -1$ for all $\theta \in \Theta$.

A *trade plan allocation* is an ordered pair (e^*, f^*) comprising a commodity trade plan allocation e^* and a money trade plan allocation f^*. A commodity (resp. money) trade plan allocation e^* (resp. f^*) is called *attainable* (for μ) if

$$\int_{\Theta} e^* \, \mathrm{d}\mu = 0 \quad \left(\text{resp.} \int_{\Theta} f^* \, \mathrm{d}\mu = 0\right).$$

A trade plan allocation (e^*, f^*) is called *attainable* (for μ) if both e^* and f^* are. A *commodity* (resp. money) *price sequence* is a function

p^* (resp. q^*) from D to $\mathbb{R}^l$ (resp. $\mathbb{R}$). A *price sequence* is an ordered pair (p^*, q^*) consisting of a commodity price sequence p^* and a security price sequence q^*. At each event d in D, $p^*(d)$ represents the prices at which commodities in Z^d can be traded and $q^*(d)$ represents the spot price of money (possibly zero). For each θ in Θ let

$$Z_\theta := \left\{ z \in Z \mid \sum_{d \in D} z(d) \in X(\theta) \right\}$$

and define the *budget set of* θ *at the price sequence* (p^*, q^*) by putting:

$$B(p^*, q^*, \theta) := \{(z, m) \in Z_\theta \times M \mid p^*(d).z(d) + q^*(d).m(d) \le 0 \text{ for all } d \in D\},$$

for every θ in Θ and every price sequence (p^*, q^*). A *sequence equilibrium* for this economy μ is a four-tuple (p^*, q^*, e^*, f^*) consisting of a price sequence (p^*, q^*) and a μ-attainable trade plan allocation (e^*, f^*) such that, for every θ in Θ, the trade plan $(e^*(\theta), f^*(\theta))$ is maximal for $U(.,\theta)$ in $B(p^*, q^*, \theta)$. (e^*, f^*) is called a *sequence allocation* if for some (p^*, q^*), (p^*, q^*, e^*, f^*) is a sequence equilibrium.

Suppose that (g^*, h^*) is a sequential market game. Define (e^*, f^*) by putting:

$$e^*(\theta)(d) = g^*(\theta, d)$$

$$f^*(\theta)(d) = h^*(\theta, d)$$

for every θ in Θ and d in D. If $f^*(\theta) \in M$ and $e^*(\theta) \in Z_\theta$ for every θ in Θ then (e^*, f^*) is an attainable allocation for μ. There is a corresponding net trade allocation e defined by putting:

$$e(\theta) = \sum_{d \in D} e^*(\theta)(d) = \sum_{d \in D} g^*(\theta, d)$$

for every θ in Θ. The market game (g^*, h^*) is called *competitive* if the corresponding ordered pair (e^*, f^*) is a sequence allocation for μ. The market game (g^*, h^*) is called *V-efficient* if the corresponding function e is a V-efficient net trade allocation for μ.

The following theorem should come as no surprise.

7.4.3 Theorem *Let (g^*, h^*) be a competitive, sequential market game. Then (g^*, h^*) has a strict Nash equilibrium and is V-efficient for any $V \subset \cup Z^d$.*

Proof (a) *Nash equilibrium*: Suppose that some pair θ_1, θ_2 can improve on their truthful strategies at 0. Then there exist signals σ_1, $\sigma_2 \in \Sigma$ and trade plans (z_1, m_1), (z_2, m_2) such that, for $i = 1, 2$,

$$(z_i, m_i) \in Z_{\theta_i} \times M$$

$$z_i(s) = g^*(\sigma_i(s), s) \qquad (s \in S)$$

$$m_i(s) = h^*(\sigma_i(s), s) \qquad (s \in S)$$

$$\sum_{i=1}^{2} z_i(0) = \sum_{i=1}^{2} g^*(\sigma_i(0), 0)$$

$$\sum_{i=1}^{2} m_i(0) = \sum_{i=1}^{2} h^*(\sigma_i(0), 0)$$

and

$$U(x_i, \theta_i) > U(e(\theta_i), \theta_i)$$

where

$$x_i = \sum_{d \in D} z_i(d).$$

Since (g^*, h^*) is competitive it follows that, for $i = 1, 2$,

$$p^*(s).z_i(s) + q^*(s).m_i(s) \leq 0 \qquad \text{for all } s \in S$$

The fact that $(e^*(\theta), f^*(\theta))$ is maximal for $U(., \theta)$ in the budget set $B(p^*, q^*, \theta)$, for all θ, then implies

$$p^*(0).z_i(0) + q^*(0).m_i(0) > 0 \qquad \text{for } i = 1, 2.$$

Then

$$\sum_{i=1}^{2} \{p^*(0).g^*(\sigma_i(0), 0) + q^*(0).h^*(\sigma_i(0), 0)\} > 0$$

contradicting the competitiveness of (g^*, h^*), i.e. contradicting

$$p^*(0).g^*(\theta, 0) + q^*(0).h^*(\theta, 0) \leq 0$$

for all $\theta \in \Theta$. A similar argument shows that there can be no improving pair at any $s \in S$.

(b) *Efficiency*: It is clearly sufficient to prove that e is V-efficient for $V = \cup Z^d$. The argument is essentially the same as those used in Chapter 5. Suppose that e' is an attainable net trade allocation such that

$$U(e(\theta), \theta) < U(e'(\theta), \theta) \qquad (\theta \in \Theta)$$

and for each θ there is $d(\theta) \in D$ such that

$$e(\theta) - e'(\theta) \in Z^{d(\theta)}.$$

Let $\Theta^d = \{\theta \in \Theta \mid d = d(\theta)\}$ and define $z \in Z$ by putting:

$$z(d) = \int_{\Theta^d} [e(\theta) - e'(\theta)] \, \mathrm{d}\mu \qquad \text{for every } d \in D.$$

Θ^d is a measurable set since $Z^d \backslash \{0\}$ is a measurable set and $(e - e')$ is a measurable function. For every $\theta \in \Theta$,

$$p^*(d(\theta)).(e(\theta) - e'(\theta)) < 0$$

by competitiveness and this implies that, for all $d \in D$,

$$p^*(d).z(d) > 0 \qquad \text{unless } z(d) = 0.$$

There is thus a commodity trade plan $z \in Z$ with the property that

$$\sum_{d \in D} z(d) = 0$$

and $p^*(d).z(d) \geq 0$ for all $d \in D$, with strict inequality for some d. The existence of such a plan implies the possibility of arbitrage profits which is incompatible with the definition of equilibrium. □

To establish a converse requires much stronger conditions, though they are certainly weak enough to be interesting. To make the statement of the theorem easier I shall introduce a couple of preliminary definitions. Suppose the sequential market game (g^*, h^*) has a Nash equilibrium. This means, in particular, that

$$e(\theta) = \sum_{d \in D} g^*(\theta, d) \in X(\theta) \qquad (\theta \in \Theta).$$

The sequential market game (g^*, h^*) is called *smooth* if

$$e(\theta) \in \operatorname{int} X(\theta) \qquad (\theta \in \Theta)$$

and g^* and h^* are continually differentiable, i.e. for each d in D, the derivatives

$$\frac{\partial g^*(\theta, d)}{\partial \theta} \quad \text{and} \quad \frac{\partial h^*(\theta, d)}{\partial \theta}$$

exist and are continuous functions of θ at every $\theta \in \Theta$. A smooth sequential market game is called *regular* if the set of θ in Θ such that

$$\frac{\partial h^*(\theta, d)}{\partial \theta} = 0$$

for *some* $d \in D$, has an empty interior.

7.4.4 Theorem *Suppose that (g^*, h^*) is a smooth and regular sequential market game for the large exchange economy μ. If the game is V-efficient for any $V \supset \cup Z^d$ and has a strict Nash equilibrium, then it is competitive.*

The proof of this theorem is considerably more involved than the proof of Theorem 7.4.3 so I shall proceed by stages.

7.5 Proof of Theorem 7.4.4

In the course of the proof it is helpful to have a preliminary result about a simpler kind of market game. Let (e, f) be a pair of measurable functions from Θ to $\mathbb{R}^l$ and $\mathbb{R}$ respectively such that $\int e\, d\mu = 0 = \int f\, d\mu$. e is an attainable allocation of commodity net trades and f can be thought of as an attainable allocation of net trades in money. The ordered pair (e, f) is like the abstract market game, for a static economy, which was studied in Section 7.3. The pair (e, f) will be called an abstract market game for a *monetary* economy to distinguish it from its predecessor. The interpretation is simple. Each agent sends a signal $\sigma \in \Theta$ to the market and receives net trades of goods $e(\sigma)$ and money $f(\sigma)$. Of course, the net trades depend on the distribution of signals as well, but since I am only interested in Nash equilibria, where the distribution of signals is equal to μ, this dependence need not be made explicit.

The game (e, f) is called *smooth* if $e(\theta) \in \operatorname{int} X(\theta)$ for all $\theta \in \Theta$ and e and f are continually differentiable functions. The game is called *efficient* if e is an efficient trade plan allocation for μ. A pair of agents with characteristics θ_1, θ_2 in Θ *can improve on their truthful strategies* if there exist signals σ_1, σ_2 in Θ and net trades x_1, x_2 in $\mathbb{R}^l$ such that:

(i) $x_i \in X(\theta_i)$ and $U(x_i, \theta_i) > U(e(\theta_i), \theta_i)$ $(i = 1, 2)$;

(ii) $\sum_{i=1}^{2} x_i = \sum_{i=1}^{2} e(\sigma_i)$;

(iii) $\sum_{i=1}^{2} f(\sigma_i) \geq \sum_{i=1}^{2} f(\theta_i)$.

The agents send signals σ_1, σ_2 and share proceeds in such a way that each has greater utility and at least as much money as before. For the definition to be meaningful it must be the case that $e(\theta_i) \in X(\theta_i)$ for $i = 1, 2$. The game (e, f) is said to have a *strict* Nash equilibrium if $e(\theta) \in X(\theta)$ for every $\theta \in \Theta$ and no pair of agents can improve on their truthful strategies. One could add the condition $f(\theta) \geq -1$ for all $\theta \in \Theta$, but it makes no difference.

7.5.1 Lemma *Let (e, f) be a smooth market game for a monetary economy μ. If (e, f) is efficient and has a strict Nash equilibrium, then there exists a vector $(p, q) \in \mathbb{R}^l \times \mathbb{R}$ such that, for every $\theta \in \Theta$, $e(\theta)$ is maximal for $U(., \theta)$ in the budget set:*

$$\{x \in X(\theta) \mid p . x + q . f(\theta) \leq 0\}.$$

Proof By an argument which is quite familiar by now, the efficiency of e together with the assumption that $U(., \theta)$ is monotonic and $e(\theta) \in \text{int } X(\theta)$, for every $\theta \in \Theta$, implies that there is a vector $p \in \mathbb{R}^l$ such that:

$$x \in X(\theta) \quad \text{and} \quad U(x, \theta) > U(e(\theta), \theta) \quad \text{imply that} \quad p . x > p . e(\theta).$$

Define the continuously differentiable function $w: \Theta \to \mathbb{R}$ by putting $w(\theta) = p . e(\theta)$ for every $\theta \in \Theta$. Let $\partial w(\theta)$ and $\partial f(\theta)$ denote, respectively, the value of the derivatives of w and f at θ. Let $H := \langle (\partial w(\theta), \partial f(\theta)) : \theta \in \Theta \rangle$ be the smallest linear subspace spanned by the set of vectors $\{\partial w(\theta), \partial f(\theta) : \theta \in \Theta\}$ in $\mathbb{R}^2$. I claim that H is contained in a hyperplane. Suppose not; then H is all of $\mathbb{R}^2$ and this means that for some pair of characteristics θ_1 and θ_2 in Θ and some real numbers $d\theta_1$, $d\theta_2$ in $\mathbb{R}$

$$\sum_{i=1}^{2} \partial w(\theta_i) \, d\theta_i > 0$$

and

$$\sum_{i=1}^{2} \partial f(\theta_i) \, d\theta_i > 0$$

Clearly $(d\theta_1, d\theta_2)$ can be chosen as small as desired. Now suppose that a pair of agents with characteristics θ_1 and θ_2 choose signals $\sigma_1 = \theta_1 + d\theta_1$ and $\sigma_2 = \theta_2 + d\theta_2$. From the smoothness of (e, f) and the continuity of $X(.)$, it follows that for small values of $d\theta_i$:

$$e(\sigma_i) \in \text{int } X(\theta_i) \subset X(\theta_i)$$

and

$$\sum_{i=1}^{2} f(\sigma_i) = \sum_{i=1}^{2} \{\partial f(\theta_i) \, d\theta_i + o(\theta_i) + f(\theta_i)\} > \sum_{i=1}^{2} f(\theta_i)$$

To show that the pair is improving it suffices to find a pair of net trades $x_i \in X(\theta_i)$ such that $U(x_i, \theta_i) > U(e(\theta_i), \theta_i)$ for $i = 1, 2$.

Suppose that $x_i \in X(\theta_i)$ and $p . x_i > p . e(\theta_i)$. Then for $\varepsilon > 0$ sufficiently small,

$$U(e(\theta_i) + \varepsilon(x_i - e(\theta_i)), \theta_i) > U(e(\theta_i), \theta_i)$$

because $U(.,\theta_i)$ is smooth and strictly quasi-concave. Choose a pair (x_1, x_2) in $X(\theta_1) \times X(\theta_2)$ such that $p.x_i > p.e(\theta_i)$ and

$$\sum_{i=1}^{2} x_i \ll \sum_{i=1}^{2} (e(\theta_i) + \nabla e(\theta_i)\,\mathrm{d}\theta_i).$$

This is clearly possible if

$$\sum_{i=1}^{2} p.\nabla e(\theta_i)\,\mathrm{d}\theta_i \equiv \sum_{i=1}^{2} \partial w(\theta_i)\,\mathrm{d}\theta_i + o(\mathrm{d}\theta_i) > 0.$$

For ε sufficiently small it must be true that

$$e(\theta_i) + \varepsilon(x_i - e(\theta_i)) \in X(\theta_i)$$

and is preferred by θ_i to $e(\theta_i)$. A simple calculation shows that

$$\sum_{i=1}^{2} e(\theta_i) + \varepsilon(x_i - e(\theta_i)) \ll \sum_{i=1}^{2} e(\theta_i + \varepsilon\,\mathrm{d}\theta_i)$$

for ε sufficiently small. Since preferences are monotonic, it is obviously possible to find a pair $(\hat{x}_1, \hat{x}_2)$ such that $\hat{x}_i \in X(\theta_i)$ and

$$U(\hat{x}_i, \theta_i) \geq U(e(\theta_i) + \varepsilon(x_i - e(\theta_i), \theta_i) > U(e(\theta_i), \theta_i)$$

for $i = 1, 2$ *and*

$$\sum_{i=1}^{2} \hat{x}_i = \sum_{i=1}^{2} e(\theta_i + \varepsilon\,\mathrm{d}\theta_i).$$

This means that the agents can improve on their truthful strategies, contradicting the hypothesis that (e, f) has a strict Nash equilibrium.

If H is (contained in) a hyperplane there is a vector $a > 0$ in $\mathbb{R}^2$ such that, for all $\theta \in \Theta$,

$$a_1\,\partial w(\theta) + a_2\,\partial f(\theta) = 0.$$

Since w and f are continuously differentiable,

$$a_1 w(\theta) + a_2 f(\theta) = \text{constant} \qquad (\theta \in \Theta).$$

But the attainability of e and f and the definitional relation $w(\theta) = p.e(\theta)$ imply that

$$\begin{aligned} \text{constant} &= \int_{\Theta} (a_1 + a_2 f)\,\mathrm{d}\mu \\ &= 0. \end{aligned}$$

There is no loss of generality in assuming $a_1 = 1$. *If* $a_1 = 0$ then $a_2 \neq 0$ and this implies that $f = 0$. In that case Theorem 7.3.2 implies that $p.e(\theta) = 0$ for all $\theta \in \Theta$, which is equivalent to putting $a = (1, 0)$ above. Letting $a_1 = 1$ and $q = a_2$, it has been shown that, for all $\theta \in \Theta$,

$p.e(\theta) + q.f(\theta) = 0$, and $x \in X(\theta)$ and $U(x, \theta) > U(e(\theta), \theta)$ implies that $p.x + q.f(\theta) > 0$.

In other words, $e(\theta)$ is maximal in the budget set $\{x \in X(\theta) | p.x + q.f(\theta) \leq 0\}$. □

Consider, once again, the sequential market game (g^*, h^*) described in Theorem 7.4.4. For any $d \in D$, it is possible to define a regular family of characteristics (Θ, μ, X^d, U^d) by putting:

$$X^d(\theta) := \{\xi \in Z^d | e(\theta) - e^*(\theta)(d) + \xi \in X(\theta)\}$$

$$U^d(\xi, \theta) := U(e(\theta) - e^*(\theta)(d) + \xi, \theta) \quad \text{for} \quad \xi \in X^d(\theta),$$

for every $\theta \in \Theta$. It is easy to check that (X^d, U^d) has all the properties listed in Definition 7.2.1. One can also define a market game for a monetary economy, (e^d, f^d) say, by putting:

$$(e^d(\theta), f^d(\theta)) = (e^*(\theta)(d), f^*(\theta)(d))$$

for every $\theta \in \Theta$. It is clear that (e^d, f^d) is a smooth market game for the monetary economy (Θ, μ, X^d, U^d). The V-efficiency of (g^*, h^*) implies that (e^d, f^d) is efficient for the economy (Θ, μ, X^d, U^d). If a pair of agents could improve on their truthful strategies in (e^d, f^d) then they could also improve on their truthful strategies in (g^*, h^*) at d. To see this, note that the definition of an improving pair requires that there exist net trades ξ_1, ξ_2 and signals θ'_1, θ'_2 in Θ such that for some pair (θ_1, θ_2):

$$\xi_i \in X^d(\theta_i) \quad \text{and} \quad U^d(\xi_i, \theta_i) > U^d(e^*(\theta_i), (d), \theta_i);$$

$$\sum_{i=1}^{2} \xi_i = \sum_{i=1}^{2} e^d(\theta'_i); \quad \sum_{i=1}^{2} f^d(\theta'_i) \geq \sum_{i=1}^{2} f^d(\theta_i).$$

Define the signals σ_1, σ_2 by putting

$$\begin{aligned} \sigma_i(d') &= \theta_i & d' &\neq d \\ &= \theta' & d' &= d. \end{aligned}$$

Define x_1 and x_2 by putting

$$x_i = e(\theta_i) + \xi_i - e^*(\theta_i)(d)$$

and (z_1, m_1) and (z_2, m_2) by putting

$$z_i(d') = g^*(\theta_i, d') \quad \text{if} \quad d' \neq d$$
$$= \xi_i \quad \text{if} \quad d' = d$$

and

$$m_i(d') = h^*(\theta_i, d') \quad \text{if} \quad d' \neq d$$
$$\geq h^*(\theta_i, d') \quad \text{if} \quad d' = d\,.$$

Then $\xi_i \in X^d(\theta_i)$ implies $x_i \in X(\theta_i)$ and $U^d(\xi_i, \theta_i) > U^d(g^*(\theta_i, d), \theta_i)$ implies $U(x_i, \theta_i) > U(e(\theta_i), \theta_i)$. Checking the definitions given in Section 7.4, it is easy to see that the pair (θ_1, θ_2) can by choosing the signals σ_1 and σ_2 improve on their truthful strategies at d. The trade plans $(z_i, m_i) \in Z_{\theta_i} \times M$ differ from $(e^*(\theta_i), f^*(\theta_i))$ only at d and the resulting net trades x_i are preferred. Since (g^*, h^*) has a strict Nash equilibrium by hypothesis, the games (e^d, f^d) each have strict Nash equilibria, too. Otherwise, there would exist an improving pair for (e^d, f^d) which would also be an improving pair for (g^*, h^*), contradicting the assumption that (g^*, h^*) has a strict Nash equilibrium.

The games (e^d, f^d) satisfy all the conditions of the Lemma so, for every $d \in D$, there exists a vector $(p^*(d), q^*(d))$ such that, for every $\theta \in \Theta$,

$$p^*(d).g^*(\theta, d) + q^*(d).h^*(\theta, d) = 0$$

and if $x \in X(\theta)$, $U(x, \theta) > U(e(\theta), \theta)$ and $(x - e(\theta)) \in Z^d$, then $p^*(d).(x - e(\theta)) > 0$. The next step is to prove that $(e^*(\theta), f^*(\theta))$ is maximal in the budget set $B(p^*, q^*, \theta)$. It would be sufficient to find numbers $\{\lambda^d = d \in D\}$ such that

$$\lambda^0 q^*(0) = \sum_{s \in S} \lambda^s q^*(s)$$

and such that $x \in X(\theta)$ and $U(x, \theta) > U(e(\theta), \theta)$ imply

$$\sum_{d \in D} \lambda^d p^*(d).z(d) > \sum_{d \in D} \lambda^d p^*(d).g^*(\theta, d)\,.$$

To see this, suppose that there exist such numbers and that there is a trade plan $(z, m) \in B(p^*, q^*, \theta)$ such that $U(x, \theta) > U(e(\theta), \theta)$, where $x = \sum_{d \in D} z(d)$. Then

$$0 = \lambda^0 q^*(0) h^*(\theta, 0) - \sum_{s \in S} \lambda^s q^*(s) h^*(\theta, 0)$$

$$= \sum_{d \in D} \lambda^d q^*(d) h^*(\theta, d)$$

$$= -\sum_{d\in D} \lambda^d p^*(d).g^*(\theta, d)$$

$$> -\sum_{d\in D} \lambda^d p^*(d).z(d)$$

$$= \sum_{d\in D} \lambda^d q^*(d)m(d)$$

$$= \lambda^0 q^*(0)m(0) + \sum_{s\in S} \lambda^d q^*(s)m(s)$$

$$\geq 0,$$

a contradiction.

To show that numbers (λ^d) with this property exist, note first that for each d in D there exists a λ^d such that

$$(\lambda^d p^*(d) - a).Z^d = 0$$

where $a := \nabla U(e(\theta), \theta)$. Otherwise there is a $\xi \in Z^d$ such that $p^*(d).\xi \leq 0$ and $U(e(\theta) + \xi, \theta) > U(e(\theta), \theta)$, contrary to what has already been proved. For any $z \in Z_\theta$ and $x = \sum_{d\in D} z(d)$ such that $U(x, \theta) > U(e(\theta), \theta)$:

$$\sum_{d\in D} \lambda^d p^*(d).z(d) = a.\sum_{d\in D} z(d)$$

$$> a.\sum_{d\in D} g^*(\theta, d)$$

$$= \sum_{d\in D} \lambda^d p^*(d).g^*(\theta, d)$$

as required. It remains to show that $\sum_{s\in S} \lambda^s q^*(s) = \lambda^0 q^*(0)$.

If this condition is not satisfied then either $\lambda^0 q^*(0) < \sum_{s\in S} \lambda^s q^*(s)$ or $\lambda^0 q^*(0) > \sum_{s\in S} \lambda^s q^*(s)$. Suppose the latter is true. Assume also that θ satisfies $\partial h^*(\theta, d) \neq 0$ for all $d \in D$. As shown above,

$$p^*(d).\frac{\partial g^*(\theta, d)}{\partial \theta} = -q^*(d)\frac{\partial h^*(\theta, d)}{\partial \theta} \qquad (d \in D)$$

so

$$a.\frac{\partial g^*(\theta, d)}{\partial \theta} = -\lambda^d q^*(d)\frac{h^*(\theta, d)}{\partial \theta} \qquad (d \in D).$$

Choose numbers $\mathrm{d}\sigma(d)$ for every $d \in D$ so that

$$\partial h^*(\theta, s)\,\mathrm{d}\sigma(s) = -1 \quad \text{for} \quad s \in S$$

and $\partial h^*(\theta, 0)\, \mathrm{d}\sigma(0)$ is greater than but very close to 1. Then

$$a . \sum_{d \in D} \partial g^*(\theta, d)\, \mathrm{d}\sigma(d) > 0$$

and

$$\partial h^*(\theta, 0)\, \mathrm{d}\sigma(0) + \partial h^*(\theta, s)\, \mathrm{d}\sigma(s) > 0$$

for every $s \in S$. The smoothness of (g^*, h^*) implies that for sufficiently small $\varepsilon > 0$

$$U(x, \theta) > U(e(\theta), \theta)$$

$$h^*(\theta + \varepsilon\, \mathrm{d}\sigma(0), 0) + h^*(\theta + \mathrm{d}\sigma(s), s) \geq 0 \qquad (s \in S)$$

where

$$x = \sum_{d \in D} g^*(\theta + \varepsilon\, \mathrm{d}\sigma(d), d) \in X(\theta).$$

But this means that θ can do better than his truthful strategy contradicting the assumption that (g^*, h^*) has a strict Nash equilibrium. A similar argument produces a contradiction when $\lambda^0 q^*(0) < \sum_{s \in S} \lambda^s q^*(s)$.

What has been shown so far is that $(e^*(\theta), f^*(\theta))$ is maximal $U(.,\theta)$ in $B(p^*, q^*, \theta)$ if θ is one of those characteristics such that $\partial h^*(\theta, d) \neq 0$ for all $d \in D$. The set of characteristics with this property is dense in Θ and U and $B(p^*, q^*, .)$ are continuous (the continuity of $B(p^*, q^*, .)$ follows from standard arguments). It follows easily that $(e^*(\theta), f^*(\theta))$ is maximal in $B(p^*, q^*, \theta)$ for all θ in Θ.

This completes the proof of Theorem 7.4.4.

7.6 The value of money

Theorem 7.4.4 does not imply that the price of money is positive. Indeed, Theorem 7.4.3 says that a sequence equilibrium in which $q^*(d) = 0$ for all d in D corresponds to a sequential market game which has a strict Nash equilibrium and is V-efficient for any $V \subset \cup Z^d$. An equilibrium in which $q^* = 0$ is essentially the same as one in which there is no money. It does not follow that a "non-monetary" equilibrium exists. There is no general proof that a sequence equilibrium exists (even under standard convexity and continuity assumptions) let alone that there exists a "non-monetary" one. However, there is no presumption, when an equilibrium does exist, that it will be a "monetary" equilibrium. In this rather loose sense, a "non-monetary" equilibrium is as likely as a "monetary" one. In any case, Theorem 7.4.4 does not imply that $q^* \neq 0$. These arguments are not affected by the regularity assumption $\partial h^*(\theta, d) \neq 0$, for if the value of money is zero then the net trades in money are immaterial.

The first step towards discovering when money has positive value is to characterize (in terms of a concept of V-efficiency) those equilibria in which $q^* > 0$. Let (e^*, f^*, p^*, q^*) be a sequence equilibrium for a two-period economy μ. Define the subspace Z^m of $\mathbb{R}^l$ to be the set of net trades $x \in \mathbb{R}^l$ such that $x = \sum_{d \in D} z(d)$ for some commodity trade plan $z \in Z$ and

$$-q^*(s)p^*(0).z(0) = q^*(0)p^*(s).z(s)$$

for every $s \in S$. Let $V = Z^m + (\cup Z^d)$.

7.6.1 Proposition *If $e(\theta) \in \operatorname{int} X(\theta)$ for every $\theta \in \Theta$, where e is the net trade allocation corresponding to the equilibrium (e^*, f^*, p^*, q^*) and $q^*(d) > 0$ for all $d \in D$, then e is V-efficient for μ.*

Proof Suppose, to the contrary, that e is not V-efficient. For notational simplicity suppose that $q^*(d) = 1$ for each $d \in D$. There is a μ-attainable net trade allocation $\hat{e}$, say, such that

$$U(\hat{e}(\theta), \theta) > U(e(\theta), \theta)$$

$$\hat{e}(\theta) - e(\theta) \in Z^m + Z^{d(\theta)}$$

for every $\theta \in \Theta$. There exist measurable functions ξ_1 and ξ_2 on Θ such that, for every $\theta \in \Theta$, $\hat{e}(\theta) = e(\theta) + \xi_1(\theta) + \xi_2(\theta)$, $\xi_1(\theta) \in Z^m$ and $\xi_2(\theta) \in Z^{d(\theta)}$. Let $a(\theta) := \nabla\ U(e(\theta),\ \theta)$ for $\theta \in (H)$; then $a(\theta).(\xi_1(\theta) + \xi_2(\theta)) > 0$. Since $\xi_1(\theta) \in Z^m$ there exists a commodity trade plan $\hat{z} \in Z$ such that $\xi_1(\theta) = \Sigma\hat{z}(d)$.

$$p^*(0).\hat{z}(0) + p^*(s).\hat{z}(s) = 0 \qquad \text{(for every } s \in S\text{)}.$$

Since $(e^*(\theta), f^*(\theta))$ is maximal in $B(p^*, q^*, \theta)$ it follows that $a(\theta).\xi_1(\theta) \leq 0$ so $a(\theta).\xi_2(\theta) > 0$. This implies $p^*(d).\xi_2(\theta) > 0$ for $d = d(\theta)$. Let $\Theta^d := \{\theta \in \Theta | d = d(\theta)\}$ and, for every $d \in D$, put

$$\zeta(d) = \int_{\Theta^d} \xi_2 \, d\mu$$

$$\hat{\zeta}(d) = \int_{\Theta} \hat{z}(d) \, d\mu$$

where $\hat{z}$, regarded as a function of θ, is defined, for each θ, as the trade plan in Z such that $\xi_1(\theta) = \Sigma\hat{z}(d)$. It is non-trivial to show that $\hat{z}$ is measurable. I give a sketch here, drawing on results from the Mathematical Appendix. Let $\hat{Z}$ be a correspondence from Z^m to Z defined by the relation $\hat{Z}(\xi) = \{z \in Z \mid \xi = \Sigma z(d)$ and $p^*(0).\hat{z}(0) + p^*(s).\hat{z}(s) = 0$ for $s \in S\}$ for every $\xi \in Z^m$. It is not hard to show that $\hat{Z}$ has a measurable graph. Since ξ_1 is a measurable function the composition $\hat{Z} \circ \xi_1$ has a measurable graph. It follows that a measurable function $\hat{z}$ can be chosen as required.

For each $d \in D$,

$$p^*(d).(\zeta(d) + \hat{\zeta}(d)) \geq p^*(d).\zeta(d)$$

with strict inequality for some $d \in D$. For each $s \in S$,

$$\begin{aligned} 0 &= p^*(s).\zeta(s) + p^*(0).\zeta(0) \\ &\leq p^*(s).(\zeta(s) + \hat{\zeta}(s)) + p^*(0).(\zeta(0) + \hat{\zeta}(0)) \end{aligned}$$

with strict inequality for some $s \in S$. Then there exists a commodity trade plan $(\zeta + \hat{\zeta}) \in Z$ such that $\sum_{d \in D} (\zeta + \hat{\zeta})(d) = 0$ which allows pure arbitrage profits to be made at some $d \in D$. This contradicts the definition of equilibrium. □

It would be nice to have a converse to this result. Unfortunately it does not follow that if e is V-efficient, $q^* > 0$. For example, this would not be true if $Z^m \subset \cup Z^d$. In that case the money market is superfluous. Or it might happen by some fluke that a V-efficient allocation could be achieved without resorting to some of the existing markets. This last possibility should be regarded as pathological in the sense that it could only occur in a "negligible" class of economies. Call an economy μ an *essential sequence economy* if it does not possess a Pareto-efficient sequence equilibrium.

7.6.2 Theorem *Let μ be an essential sequence economy and let (e^*, f^*, p^*, q^*) be a sequence equilibrium for μ. If the equilibrium is V-efficient for some $V \supset Z^m + (\cup Z^d)$ then $q^*(0) > 0$.*

Proof First note that $q^*(d) \geq 0$ in equilibrium; otherwise an agent could, by purchasing money, increase his consumption at d by an unlimited amount. Also, $q^*(0) = 0$ implies that $q^*(s) = 0$ for all $s \in S$. Otherwise, by purchasing money at the first date an agent could increase consumption at some $s \in S$ without altering consumption at any other $d \in D$. Suppose, contrary to the assertion of the theorem, $q^*(0) = 0$. Then $Z^m = \mathbb{R}^l$ since $\Sigma_d Z^d = \mathbb{R}^l$. This means the equilibrium is Pareto-efficient, contrary to the hypothesis that μ is essential. □

These two results give a characterization of those equilibria in which the price of money at date 0—and consequently at some second-period events—is positive. To rationalize the positive value of money one must explain why the equilibria of a sequence economy i.e. the strict Nash equilibrium of a sequential market game, are V-efficient, where $V = Z^m + \cup Z^d$, but not Pareto-efficient. The linear space Z^d was originally defined to be the smallest sub-space of $\mathbb{R}^l$ containing the set

$$\{g^*(\theta, d): \theta \in \Theta\}.$$

The market structure $\{Z^d: d \in D\}$ so defined reflects the scope of the negotiating sessions at each $d \in D$ but their scope is not *restricted* to Z^d. The scope of negotiations undertaken at d must *at least* include the commodities in Z^d since Z^d is the space spanned by commodities actually traded at d. But the scope of the negotiations might extent to trading in other commodities as well, for example to commodities in Z^m. Whatever the scope of the negotiating session at d, the outcome ought to be efficient relative to the linear space spanned by commodities included in the scope of the discussions.

In the two-period economy there is a lot of natural structure which can usefully be imposed on the model. At any second-period event $s \in S$ it is clear that past trades cannot be reversed and trades of commodities for delivery at zero-probability events are irrelevant. There may be no loss of generality in assuming $Z^s = X^s$ for every $s \in S$. (This conclusion depends on the interpretation of the family of games as occurring in real time, rather than before actual play of the market game). Recall that X^s is defined to be the linear space spanned by commodities actually delivered at s. Now it is clear that if equilibrium is to be V-efficient, with $V \supset Z^m + (\cup Z^d)$, then the scope of negotiations at date 0 must include at least the commodities in $Z^0 + Z^m$.

The question which must be answered next is why the scope should be $Z^0 + Z^m$ rather than $\mathbb{R}^l$ (the static case) or X^0 (the "non-monetary" case) or something else. If negotiations cover commodities in $Z^0 + Z^m$ it means that agents want to "borrow" and "lend" at date 0, i.e. shift consumption between dates, but not to specify the final net trades they will make at date 1. The existence of separate negotiating sessions at second-period events means that agents are unable at the first date to negotiate about the whole range of commodities; but if they can include decisions at date 0 to consume more or less than their current endowments, the net trades arranged at 0 may well span a subspace like $Z^0 + Z^m$. The "cooperativeness" of the underlying game then ensures the appropriate degree of V-efficiency. The sequential market game has an outcome which is a monetary equilibrium because of three factors:

(i) the cooperativeness of the underlying game;
(ii) the existence of "borrowing and lending" at the first date;
(iii) the incompleteness of negotiations at the first date.

The analysis of conditions under which $q^*(0) > 0$ merely delineates the various factors on which an explanation of the positive value of money might be based. One must first accept the negotiations at each date are incomplete, that the game is cooperative in the sense that the outcome of each negotiating game is efficient relative to the scope of the negotiations and that the scope of the negotiations at date 0 is $Z^0 + Z^m$. If one accepts all this then a strict Nash equilibrium of the sequential market game is characterized by a positive value of money. As an "explanation" this line of reasoning may seem rather elliptical. It assumes the underlying game is cooperative whereas Hahn's problem arises from the non-cooperativeness of the competitive equilibrium. In equilibrium agents take all prices, including the price of money, as given or parametric. They try to maximize utility subject to the sequence of budget constraints defined by these prices but they never imagine that they could alter the value of money or any other commodity. If the value of money is zero then, from the agent's point of view, it is useless. By assuming the sequential market game is essentially cooperative, are we not begging the central question? The criticism is misconceived, however.

In the first place, it is not the case that the assumption of cooperativeness by itself implies that $q^*(0) > 0$. Consider the weak sequential core. It is a cooperative solution concept but there is no guarantee that core allocations are "monetary" ones. Another example is a sequential market game which is only V-efficient with $V \subset \cup X^d$ for $d \in D$. In both cases the value of money may have to be zero and the equilibrium allocation correspondingly inefficient. On the other hand, if $Z^0 = \mathbb{R}^l$ in the present game, then money is superfluous.

What provides a role for money is the existence of independent "negotiation games" which overlap, *but not too much*. The real substance of the characterization provided by Propositions 7.6.1 and 7.6.2 is the specification of the precise degree of incompleteness that ensures $q^*(0) > 0$.

Another crucial point is the assumption that there be no

cooperation *between* games. Each "negotiating game" is assumed to be cooperative (and hence efficient relative to its own scope) but, if agents were allowed to coordinate strategies between games, then cooperativeness would seem to imply Pareto-efficiency without the use of money. In other words, the sequential market game would collapse back to the static case. Of course, as I emphasized at the beginning of this chapter, the very idea of independent "negotiation games" requires that there be no inter-game cooperation. But it is nonetheless an important part of the explanation of the role of money in increasing efficiency (i.e. enlarging V) that there be no inter-game cooperation. Propositions 7.6.1 and 7.6.2 bring this out clearly.

7.7 Efficient market games

In the preceding sections it was simply assumed, wherever necessary, that the outcome of a cooperative game is efficient. This provided some intuitive justification for the assumption that the non-cooperative "negotiation games" were efficient. A more thorough treatment would have to reduce efficiency to more basic assumptions. This is the problem tackled by A. Mas-Colell in his paper *An Axiomatic Approach to the Efficiency of Non-cooperative Equilibrium in Economies with a Continuum of Traders*. Because it is so closely related to the present work, a brief discussion of his approach is appropriate here. Let Σ be the *signal space* and $e:\Sigma \times M(\Sigma) \rightarrow \mathbb{R}^l$ an *abstract market game*. A *joint strategy* is a measurable function $\boldsymbol{\sigma}$ from Θ to Σ. If $\mu_{\boldsymbol{\sigma}}$ is the distribution of the joint strategy $\boldsymbol{\sigma}$ on Σ, then a player with characteristic θ receives a net trade $e(\boldsymbol{\sigma}(\theta), \mu_{\boldsymbol{\sigma}})$. These ideas have already been introduced in Section 7.2. The set of net trades which can be obtained by a player when the distribution of the joint strategy is μ, is denoted by $B(\mu)$ and defined by putting $B(\mu) := e(\Sigma, \mu) \equiv \{e(\sigma, \mu) | \sigma \in \Sigma\}$. Of course, a player who has characteristic θ is restricted to the set of signals such that $e(\sigma, \mu) \in X(\theta)$. Thus, the set of net trades from which he effectively chooses his final net trade is $B(\mu) \cap X(\theta)$. A *Nash equilibrium for the game e* can be defined as a joint strategy $\boldsymbol{\sigma}$ such that, for every $\theta \in \Theta$,

> *$e(\boldsymbol{\sigma}(\theta), \mu)$ maximizes $U(x, \theta)$ on $B(\mu) \cap X(\theta)$ where μ is the distribution of $\boldsymbol{\sigma}$.*

Note that the underlying economy is assumed to be large so μ is independent of the signal sent by a single player.

A competitive market is anonymous in the sense that names do not affect the outcome. A somewhat stronger anonymity property is that an agent's identity is not known to the market, that is, to the other agents in the market. If a market were anonymous in this sense, there would be nothing to prevent an agent from entering the market several times, i.e. from sending several signals. This idea leads to the notion of a strict Nash equilibrium (in the sense of Mas-Colell). If a player can send as many signals as he likes then the set of net trades which can be achieved is at least $\bigcup_{n=1}^{\infty} nB(\mu)$ when the distribution of the joint strategy is μ. A *strict Nash equilibrium* (in the sense of Mas-Colell) is a joint strategy $\boldsymbol{\sigma}$ such that, for every $\theta \in \Theta$,

$$e(\boldsymbol{\sigma}(\theta), \mu) \text{ maximizes } U(x, \theta) \text{ on } X(\theta) \cap \bigcup_{n=1}^{\infty} nB(\mu).$$

There is an inconsistency in Mas-Colell's treatment at this point. If an agent may send several signals then $\boldsymbol{\sigma}$ should be a correspondence. But even a correspondence would not take account of repetitions of the same signal. Alternatively a strategy could be represented by an integer-valued measure on Σ but this would be rather awkward. It turns out that players only have to send a single signal (possibly several times) in order to generate the desired result, so I shall ignore the inconsistency in the interests of elegance.

An abstract market game e is said to be *interior* at the joint strategy $\boldsymbol{\sigma}$ if $0 \in B(\mu_{\sigma})$ and for some neighbourhood N of 0, $N \cap B(\mu_{\sigma})$ is a $(l-1)$-dimensional, C^1 manifold.

7.7.1 Theorem *Let $\boldsymbol{\sigma}$ be a strict Nash equilibrium of the abstract market game $e: \Sigma \times M(\Sigma) \to \mathbb{R}^l$. If e is interior at $\boldsymbol{\sigma}$ then there exists a price vector $p \neq 0$ such that, for every $\theta \in \Theta$,*

$$x \in X(\theta) \text{ and } U(x, \theta) > U(e(\boldsymbol{\sigma}(\theta), \mu), \theta) \text{ imply } p . x \geq 0.$$

Proof Let T be the tangent hyperplane to $B(\mu)$ at 0. This is well-defined by hypothesis. Any point $x \in T$ can be approximated arbitrarily closely by a point of the form nx' where n is a positive integer and $x' \in B(\mu)$. Because of the monotonicity of preferences, we can choose $p > 0$ such that $T = \{x \in \mathbb{R}^l \mid p . x = 0\}$. Suppose $p . \bar{x} < 0$ and $U(\bar{x}, \theta) > U(e(\boldsymbol{\sigma}(\theta), \mu), \theta)$. By monotonicity there exists $x \in T \cap \text{int } X(\theta)$ such that $U(x, \theta) > U(e(\boldsymbol{\sigma}(\theta), \mu), \theta)$. But then $nx' \in X(\theta)$ and $U(nx', \theta) > U(e(\boldsymbol{\sigma}(\theta), \mu), \theta)$ for some positive integer n and $x' \in B(\mu)$, contradicting the definition of equilibrium. □

Corollary *Suppose that each $X(\theta)$ has the form $\{x \in \mathbb{R}^l : x \geq \bar{x}(\theta)\}$ and $0 \in \text{int} \int X$. Then the game e is Pareto-efficient.*

Proof By a standard argument one shows that $x \in X(\theta)$ and $U(x, \theta) > U(e(\boldsymbol{\sigma}(\theta), \mu), \theta)$ imply $p.x > 0$. Efficiency follows immediately. □

It is crucial in the proof of Theorem 7.7.1 that $0 \in B(\mu)$. The possibility of inactivity (no trade) seems a reasonable requirement for a market game. By entering the market many times players can expand the part of $B(\mu)$ near the origin so that it approximates the hyperplane T. If everyone's choice set is the intersection of their consumption set with the hyperplane T it is clear that the outcome will be something like a Walrasian equilibrium. But it is the assumption that $0 \in B(\mu)$ together with the smoothness of $B(\mu)$ around 0 which make the theorem go and it is not so clear that the combination of these two assumptions is as reasonable as the no-trade condition on its own.

The reader might wonder whether the Mas-Colell approach could be used as an alternative to the one developed in the preceding sections. Up to a point it could but unfortunately the assumptions needed to obtain efficiency in each "negotiation game" (constrained efficiency) are strong enough to imply full Pareto-efficiency. More precisely, suppose that the interiority assumption held at each date-event pair $d \in D$ with respect to the linear subspace Z^d of $\mathbb{R}^l$. Then if $\Sigma Z^d = \mathbb{R}^l$ the interiority assumption is satisfied with respect to $\mathbb{R}^l$ for the whole game and Theorem 7.7.1 applies to the sequential market game regarded as an abstract market game in Mas-Colell's sense. Since full Pareto-efficiency is normally inconsistent with an incomplete set of assets the characterization would normally be vacuous.

7.8 Money, information and efficiency

In the sequential market game money acts as a store of information. This is best seen by analogy with a planning problem. Let (Θ, X, U, μ) be a large exchange economy and suppose it has a central planner who is responsible for allocating net trades of goods in a Pareto-efficient manner. To do this he needs to know the characteristics of the agents. If he only knows (Θ, X, U) to begin with, he might send out a questionnaire to discover μ. He could ask every agent to reveal his characteristic, compile the answers, determine a Pareto-efficient allocation for μ and then assign the appropriate net trade to each agent according to the agent's response. There is a snag, however. If agents know the use to which the central planner intends to put their information, they may have an incentive to lie.

Formally, the planner's problem is to choose a function e, called an *allocation mechanism*, which maps $\Theta \times M(\Theta)$ to $\mathbb{R}^l$ such that $e(\theta, \mu) \in X(\theta)$ for every $\theta \in \Theta$ and $\int e(\theta, \mu)\mu(d\theta) = 0$. The mechanism is called *incentive-compatible* if no agent has an incentive to reveal a characteristic other than his true one and *Pareto-efficient* if the resulting allocation is always Pareto-efficient. But the only Pareto-efficient and incentive-compatible allocation mechanism is the one that assigns a Walras allocation for every economy. The reason is obvious: *the allocation mechanism e is formally an abstract market game with an efficient Nash equilibrium.*

Now, if the planner's rationality were bounded he might find it impossible to achieve an efficient allocation in one go. This would transform his allocation problem into a sequential one. For example, if the planner can remember the distribution of characteristics revealed at the first date but not who said what, he may have to ask agents to repeat their signals at the second date. There is nothing to stop agents from reporting different signals at different dates. As the example with two goods and two dates showed, efficiency may be inconsistent with incentive-compatibility at each date. The introduction of money can help the planner here just as it helped restore efficient Nash equilibria to the sequential market game. Once again, the analogy between allocation mechanisms and market games is exact. A *sequential allocation mechanism* is a pair of functions (g^*, h^*) from $\Theta \times D \times M(\Theta)$ to $\mathbb{R}^l$ and $\mathbb{R}$ respectively such that

$$\sum_{d \in D} g^*(\theta, d, \mu) \in X(\theta)$$

$$\sum_{d \leq \bar{d}} h^*(\theta, d, \mu) \geq 0 \quad \text{for every} \quad \bar{d} \in \bar{D}$$

and

$$\int g^* \mu(d\theta) = 0 = \int h^* \mu(d\theta).$$

Formally, (g^*, h^*) is a sequential market game but the interpretation here is that at each date-event pair the agent is required to remind the planner of his characteristic. At each date-event pair the planner assigns a net trade in goods and money to the agent. If the agent is constrained to choose a net trade in his net trade set $X(\theta)$ and to end up with as much money as he started with, then the theorems on sequential market games, suitably translated, reveal that under appropriate conditions the planner can achieve V-efficiency (with $V \supset \cup Z^d$) using an incentive-compatible sequential mechanism. If money is actually used then $V \supset Z^m + (\cup Z^d)$.

Furthermore, if some collusion is allowed between pairs of players the only way the planner can achieve these results is to assign a competitive allocation. In particular, the trades in money must be arranged *as if* there were a uniform price for money and *as if* money were traded to balance the agents' budgets at each date-event pair.

It is clear from this interpretation in what sense money acts as a store of information. By arranging appropriate trades in money the planner can keep track of how much each agent has got out of the system in the past. Agents would like to pretend they were someone else but the terminal constraint on money holdings prevents them from doing this advantageously. Their money holdings provide just enough information to allow the planner to find out who they are; but the striking thing is that he can only do this if he treats money as if it had a uniform market price and uses it to "balance budgets". To put it more colourfully, money can perform its informational role effectively only in a competitive sequence equilibrium.

It is interesting to compare this function of money with its role in the sequential core. In the core theory, agents have complete information. The difficulty lies in trying to make them keep their promises. The existence of money provides a kind of collateral. To get goods today an agent has to give up money; to get his money back tomorrow he has to give up goods. The remarkable thing is that money must be exchanged as if it had a value. In the planning problem there is a lack of trust of a different sort. The planner would like to be in a position to require that an agent report the same characteristic in each date-event pair, but he cannot. Instead, by insisting on trades in money as well as goods he limits the ways in which the individual can misrepresent his characteristic. Again, only if money is exchanged *as if* it had a value does the agent have no incentive to cheat.

In the sequential market game, the problem is not lack of trust but something akin to it. Because of the lack of cooperation *between* the independent "negotiation games" the players have too many strategies available to achieve a very high degree of efficiency. It would be better for them if they could enter into self-binding agreements to choose the same "strategy" in every date-event pair. Then full Pareto-efficiency might be attainable as a Nash equilibrium of a sequential market game. But such agreements are for some reason impossible. The trades in money represent a sort of limited binding commitment. Because an agent must end up with the same amount of money he started with, he is committed, in spite of himself, to behave in a certain way in the future when he gives up money in the present. The sequential core is only a quasi-cooperative solution concept because the self-binding agreements into which players can enter are limited (the players are untrustworthy). Here is a link with sequential market games. In both cases money can be seen as allowing the extension of cooperation. But it only works if money is treated *as if* it had a value.

This chapter and the last have been devoted to providing *rationales* for several concepts of monetary equilibrium. They have provided a rationale in two senses. First, it has been shown that money has a role to play in certain kinds of cooperative market games and that it performs this role only if the outcome of the game can be described as a competitive equilibrium in a sequence of markets. Second, it has been shown that the use of money can increase efficiency in these games. This is in marked contrast to other attempts to rationalize the use of money in general equilibrium where the efficiency of monetary exchange is *assumed* (as in the transactions cost literature) or where monetary exchange actually *reduces* efficiency (as with Clower's cash constraint). These exercises help to provide some game theoretic foundations for a theory of money in general equilibrium; but if they are good foundations they ought to tell us something about the way money works in the world.

The principal lesson, I believe, is the simple, classical one. Both the cooperative and non-cooperative approaches require that there be a fixed stock of money in existence, which cannot be expanded. If private individuals were able to issue fiat money all the various models we have examined would collapse. Likewise if the government issued more money than was demanded in taxes. As long as the government maintains the equality of money supply and (terminal) money demand individuals will sort out an allocation which has at least some desirable efficiency properties. There is no telling what will happen otherwise.

Even if the government maintains equality between the supply of and (terminal) demand for money it may run into trouble if it tries to use the monetary system for the purpose of redistributing wealth. In the core theory it was observed (Chapter 6) that, by setting initial endowments of money and terminal taxes at the right level, the government could induce "lump sum transfers" in the core of a monetary economy. But the real value of these "lump sum transfers" is endogenous and unless their value is identically zero there will be an infinite number of allocations in the core of a monetary economy. This indeterminacy suggests very strongly that the core theory is not a plausible description of the behaviour of the economy when there are "lump sum transfers". At best the general price level (i.e. the value of money) is left unexplained; at worst the process of coalition-formation may break down altogether, resulting in a non-core allocation. Things are scarcely better in the sequential market games. In order to assign to different individuals different initial endowments of money and different tax liabilities it must first discover their characteristics. But as was shown for the static case, incentive-compatibility and efficiency require that there be no transfers.

In short, the government cannot have any real redistributive effect without upsetting the applecart. How seriously one wants to take this moral as applying to practical reality is a matter of taste. It should at least give pause for thought.

Mathematical Appendix

In Chapter 6 (Part 2) some concepts borrowed from Measure Theory are used to describe and analyse an exchange economy with a continuum of agents. This section is an extended glossary, explaining those terms which may be unfamiliar to a reader whose mathematical background is adequate for the rest of the book, and stating some technical facts which were omitted from the text. The standard reference for this material is W. Hildenbrand, *Core and Equilibria of a Large Economy*, of course.

Let A be an arbitrary set. A σ-field $\mathscr{A}$ of subsets of A is a family of subsets having the properties:

(i) $\phi \in \mathscr{A}$
(ii) $T \in \mathscr{A}$ implies $A \backslash T \in \mathscr{A}$
(iii) if $T_i \in \mathscr{A}$ for $i = 1, \ldots, \infty$ then $\bigcap_{i=1}^{\infty} T_i \in \mathscr{A}$.

The ordered pair $(A, \mathscr{A})$ is called a *measurable space* if A is a set and $\mathscr{A}$ a σ-field of subsets of A. A (probability) measure v on $\mathscr{A}$ is a function from $\mathscr{A}$ to $[0, 1]$ such that:

(i) $v(A) = 1$
(ii) if $T_i \in \mathscr{A}$ and $T_i \cap T_j = \phi$ for all $i, j = 1, \ldots, \infty$ $(i \neq j)$, then

$$v\left(\bigcup_{i=1}^{\infty} T_i\right) = \sum_{i=1}^{\infty} v(T_i).$$

A *measure space* $(A, \mathscr{A}, v)$ consists of a measurable space $(A, \mathscr{A})$ and a measure v on $\mathscr{A}$. A subset T of A is called an *atom* of the measure space $(A, \mathscr{A}, v)$ if $v(T) > 0$ and for any $T' \in \mathscr{A}$, $T' \subset T$ implies $v(T') = 0$ or $v(T') = v(T)$. The measure space $(A, \mathscr{A}, v)$ is called *atomless* or *non-atomic* if it has no atoms. In the same circumstances v may also be called atomless.

Suppose that A is a metric space. Then A may be given a special σ-field, called the *Borel σ-field* of A. It is sometimes denoted by $\mathscr{B}(A)$ and is defined to be the (unique) smallest σ-field containing all the open sets in A. That is, it is the σ-field "generated" by the open sets of A. If A is a metric space, $\mathscr{A}$ is the Borel σ-algebra of A and

$(A, \mathscr{A}, \nu)$ is an atomless measure space then every singleton set has measure zero, i.e. if $a \in A$ then $\{a\} \in \mathscr{A}$ and $\nu(\{a\}) = 0$. The Borel σ-fields make it particularly easy to deal with product spaces. Let A_1 and A_2 be separable, metric spaces (a metric space is called separable if it has a countable, dense subset) and let $A_1 \times A_2$ be the product space. Let $\mathscr{B}(A_1) \otimes \mathscr{B}(A_2)$ be the σ-field generated by $\mathscr{B}(A_1) \times \mathscr{B}(A_2)$. Then,

$$\mathscr{B}(A_1 \times A_2) = \mathscr{B}(A_1) \otimes \mathscr{B}(A_2).$$

In other words, the Borel σ-field of the product of the two spaces is generated by the product of the Borel σ-fields of the individual spaces. Measure-theoretic concepts for the product measure space can easily be defined in terms of the corresponding concepts for the individual spaces.

Let $(A_1, \mathscr{A}_1)$ and $(A_2, \mathscr{A}_2)$ be measurable spaces. A function f from A_1 to A_2 is called *measurable* if $f^{-1}(T) \in \mathscr{A}_1$ for every $T \in \mathscr{A}_2$, where $f^{-1}(T) := \{a \in A_1 \,|\, f(a) \in T\}$. In particular, if A_i is a metric space and $\mathscr{A}_i$ the Borel σ-field on A_i, $i = 1, 2$, then f is measurable if f is continuous.

In what follows, a metric space is always assumed to have the Borel σ-field and references to measurability, etc., should be interpreted in this way. Let $(A, \mathscr{A}, \nu)$ be a measure space and f a step-function from A to $\mathbb{R}$. There is a finite partition $\{T_1, \ldots, T_n\}$ of A such that, for $i = 1, \ldots, n$, $T_i \in \mathscr{A}$ and f is constant on T_i. The *integral* of f is denoted by $\int f \, d\nu$ or simply $\int f$ and is defined to be the number $\sum_i f(T_i)\nu(T_i)$. To define the integral of other measurable functions one uses the fact that any positive, measurable function f from A to $\mathbb{R}$ can be approximated by an increasing sequence (f_n) of measurable step-functions. For every such sequence, $\lim \int f_n \, d\nu$ exists (possibly infinite) and is independent of the particular sequence. If the limit is finite, f is said to be *integrable* and the integral is defined to be equal to this limit. An arbitrary measurable function is said to be integrable if it is the difference of two integrable functions. Its integral is defined to be the difference of the integrals of the two functions. Suppose that f is a function from A to $\mathbb{R}^n$, i.e. $f = (f^1, \ldots, f^n)$, where $f^i: A \to \mathbb{R}$ is the i-th coordinate function, for $i = 1, \ldots, n$. f is said to be *measurable*, *integrable*, etc., if every coordinate function f^i: $A \to \mathbb{R}$ is. The integral $\int f \, d\nu$ is defined to be the vector of integrals $(\int f^1 \, d\nu, \ldots, \int f^n \, d\nu)$.

Let ψ be a correspondence from A to $\mathbb{R}^n$. Let $\mathscr{L}_\psi$ denote the set of ν-*integrable selections* of ψ, that is, the set of ν-integrable functions $f: A \to \mathbb{R}^n$ with the property that $f(a) \in \psi(a)$, a.e. in A. The *integral* of ψ is defined to be the set of integrals of the integrable selections of ψ, i.e. $\int \psi := \{\int f \in \mathbb{R}^n | f \in \mathscr{L}_\psi\}$. It may be, of course, that $\int \psi = \phi$. It is important to know when the integral is non-empty. The answer to this question is provided by the following theorem.

Measurable Selection Theorem *Let ψ be a correspondence from a separable metric space A to $\mathbb{R}^n$ such that the graph of ψ belongs to $\mathscr{A} \otimes \mathscr{B}(\mathbb{R}^n)$. Then there exists a measurable function f from A to $\mathbb{R}^n$ such that $f(a) \in \psi(a)$, a.e. in A.*

The theorem is a special case of a more general result proved in Section D.II.2 of Hildenbrand, *op. cit.*

As an illustration of these ideas, consider the exchange economy discussed in Chapter 6, Part 2. Let $\mathscr{P}'$ denote the set of preference relations, i.e. the set of ordered pairs $(X, \prec)$ where X is a closed, non-empty subset of $\mathbb{R}^l$ (the consumption set) and $\prec$ is a transitive, continuous and irreflexive binary relation on X. Formally, $\prec$ is an open subset of $X \times X$ such that $(x, x) \notin \prec$ and if $(x, y) \in \prec$ and $(y, z) \in \prec$ then $(x, z) \in \prec$. The set $\mathscr{P}'$ can be endowed with a topology, called the *closed-convergence topology*, under which it becomes a separable metric space. Then $(\mathscr{P}', \mathscr{B}(\mathscr{P}'))$ is a measurable space with the nice properties, when forming products, mentioned above. The subspace $\mathscr{P}$ of $\mathscr{P}'$ containing the monotonic preference relations inherits its topology from $\mathscr{P}'$. T is open in $\mathscr{P}$ if $T = \mathscr{P} \cap T'$ and T' is open in $\mathscr{P}'$. The σ-field $\mathscr{B}(\mathscr{P})$ is, not surprisingly, the family $\{T \subset \mathscr{P} | T = \mathscr{P} \cap T' \text{ and } T' \in \mathscr{B}(\mathscr{P}')\}$. An *exchange economy* is defined to be a measurable function $\mathscr{E}$ from $(A, \mathscr{A}, \nu)$ to $\mathscr{P} \times \mathbb{R}^l_+$, i.e. for every set T in $\mathscr{B}(\mathscr{P}) \otimes \mathscr{B}(\mathbb{R}^l_+)$, $\mathscr{E}^{-1}(T) = \{a \in A | \mathscr{E}(a) \in T\}$ belongs to $\mathscr{A}$. Note that since $\mathscr{P}$ and $\mathbb{R}^l_+$ are separable metric spaces, $\mathscr{B}(\mathscr{P} \times \mathbb{R}^l_+) = \mathscr{B}(\mathscr{P}) \otimes \mathscr{B}(\mathbb{R}^l_+)$. A *monetary economy* is defined to be a triple $(\mathscr{E}, \sigma, \tau)$ consisting of the exchange economy $\mathscr{E}$ and a pair of measurable functions σ and τ from $(A, \mathscr{A}, \nu)$ to $\mathbb{R}^k_+$ such that $\int \sigma = \int \tau$. There is no ambiguity in this definition, for if $(\mathscr{E}, \sigma, \tau)$ were regarded as a single function from A to $\mathscr{P} \times \mathbb{R}^l_+ \times \mathbb{R}^k_+ \times \mathbb{R}^k_+$, the measurability condition would be the same since

$$\mathscr{B}(\mathscr{P} \times \mathbb{R}^l_+ \times \mathbb{R}^k_+ \times \mathbb{R}^k_+) = \mathscr{B}(\mathscr{P} \times \mathbb{R}^l_+) \otimes \mathscr{B}(\mathbb{R}^k_+) \otimes \mathscr{B}(\mathbb{R}^k_+).$$

For the same reason, if $\mathbf{e}$ denotes the projection of $\mathscr{P} \times \mathbb{R}^l_+$ into $\mathbb{R}^l_+$, the measurability of $\mathscr{E}$ implies that $e := \mathbf{e} \circ \mathscr{E}$ is a measurable function from $(A, \mathscr{A}, \nu)$ to $\mathbb{R}^l_+$.

Recall that as part of the proof of Theorem 6.7.3, it was necessary to define a correspondence ψ from $(A, \mathscr{A}, \nu)$ to $\mathbb{R}^l \times \mathbb{R}^k$ by putting

$$\psi(a) := \{(x, y) | x + e(a) \succ_a f(a), \quad y \geq \tau(a) - \sigma(a)\} \cup \{0\}$$

for all $a \in A$, where $f: A \to \mathbb{R}^l$ is a given measurable function. It was required to show that ψ had a measurable graph, i.e. that the set $\{(a, x, y) | (x, y) \in \psi(a)\}$ belongs to $\mathscr{A} \otimes \mathscr{B}(\mathbb{R}^l \times \mathbb{R}^k)$. The proof can be simplified by noting, first, that this set is the union of $\{0\} \times A$ and the set $\{(a, x, y) | (x, y) \in \psi(a) \backslash \{0\}\}$ and since the first is clearly measurable it is sufficient to prove that the second is. And note, second, that since $\{(a, x, y) | (x, y) \in \psi(a) \backslash \{0\}\}$ is the product of two sets it is sufficient to show that these sets are themselves measurable in the appropriate sense. Consider the set $\{(a, x) \| x + e(a) \succ_a f(a)\}$. It is a property of the topology of closed convergence on $\mathscr{P}$ that the set

$$G := (X, \prec, x, y) \in \mathscr{P} \times \mathbb{R}^l \times \mathbb{R}^l | x \succ y\}$$

is open in $\mathscr{P} \times \mathbb{R}^l_+ \times \mathbb{R}^l_+$ and hence it belongs to $\mathscr{B}(\mathscr{P} \times \mathbb{R}^l_+ \times \mathbb{R}^l_+)$. The function h from $A \times \mathbb{R}^l$ to $\mathscr{P} \times \mathbb{R}^l \times \mathbb{R}^l$, defined by

$$h(a, x) := (X_a, \prec_a, x + e(a), f(a))$$

for every $(a, x) \in A \times \mathbb{R}^l$ is measurable since the coordinate functions are measurable and $\mathscr{P}$ and $\mathbb{R}^l$ are separable, metric spaces. (The measurability of the function $a \to (X_a, \prec_a)$ follows from the measurability of $\mathscr{E}$ and the fact that $\mathscr{B}(\mathscr{P} \times \mathbb{R}^l_+) = \mathscr{B}(\mathscr{P}) \otimes \mathscr{B}(\mathbb{R}^l_+)$). Then $\{(a, x) \| x + e(a) \succ_a f(a)\} = h^{-1}(G)$ must be measurable. To prove that the other set $\{(a, y) \| y \geq \tau(a) - \sigma(a)\}$ belongs to $\mathscr{A} \otimes \mathscr{B}(\mathbb{R}^k)$ requires similar arguments. The details are left to the reader.

The fact that ψ has a measurable graph is needed to exploit the following proposition:

> *Let ψ be a correspondence from $(A, \mathscr{A}, \nu)$ to $\mathbb{R}^l \times \mathbb{R}^k$. If ψ has a measurable graph and $\int \psi \neq \phi$, then for any vector $(p, q) \in \mathbb{R}^l \times \mathbb{R}^k$,*
>
> $$\sup\,(p, q) . \int \psi = \int \sup\,(p, q) . \psi(.) .$$

Much more important is the following:

> *let ψ be a correspondence from an atomless measure space $(A, \mathscr{A}, \nu)$ to $\mathbb{R}^l \times \mathbb{R}^k$. Then the integral $\int \psi \, d\nu$ is a convex set in $\mathbb{R}^l \times \mathbb{R}^k$.*

The proof of this proposition is quite easy using the now-famous Liapunov's Theorem: *if ν_i $(i = 1, \ldots, m)$ are atomless measures on $(A, \mathscr{A})$ then the set $\{(\nu_1(T), \ldots, \nu_m(T)) | T \in \mathscr{A}\}$ is a closed, convex* *subset of* $\mathbb{R}^m$. Suppose that $z, z' \in \int \psi$ and $0 < \lambda < 1$. Then $z = \int f$, $z' = \int f'$ where $f, f' \in \mathcal{L}_\psi$. The set

$$\left\{\left(\int_T f, \int_T f'\right) \mid T \in \mathcal{A}\right\}$$

is convex by Liapunov's Theorem. It contains (0, 0) and (z, z') (simply put $T = \phi$ and A respectively) so it must contain $(\lambda z, \lambda z')$, i.e. for some set $T \in \mathcal{A}$,

$$\int_T (f', f') = (\lambda z, \lambda z').$$

Let f'' be the function defined by putting $f''(a) = f(a)$ if $a \in T$ and $f''(a) = f'(a)$ if $a \notin T$. It is easy to see that $f'' \in \mathcal{L}_\psi$ and $\int f'' = \lambda z + (1 - \lambda)z'$, which proves that $\int \psi$ is convex.

Bibliographical notes

Chapter 1

The standard reference for the material in the first part of the chapter is, of course, Patinkin, 1965; but the exposition and emphasis owe much to a characteristically limpid survey by Johnson, 1962. Much of the literature of the period now seems terribly tedious and dated. The only undoubted classics are Metzler, 1951, and Archibald and Lipsey, 1958. The reader who is interested in delving further will find extensive bibliographies in the Johnson survey and in the book of readings edited by Clower, 1969, now unfortunately out of print.

The discussion of homogeneity in the text is technically rather elementary. It ought to be emphasized that the conditions discussed are sufficient but not strictly necessary. For an up-to-date and very rigorous treatment the reader is referred to the more recent work by Kalman and Dusansky (see the paper by these authors in Kalman, 1978, and the references therein).

Standard references on the optimum quantity of money are Friedman, 1969, Johnson, 1970 and Samuelson, 1968. Early criticism is found in Hahn, 1971a, Perlman, 1971 and Feige and Parkin, 1971. The only really rigorous treatment along these lines is contained in Grandmont and Younès, 1973.

In the text I have taken a rather different approach, using the overlapping generations model to represent the efficiency loss of inflation as resulting from a distortion in rates of return on saving. The efficiency loss here is essentially the same as that discussed by Samuelson, 1958 and Cass and Yaari, 1966. A general treatment of the stationary case is contained in Grandmont and Laroque, 1973 and the non-stationary case is dealt with by Okuno and Zilcha, 1980.

The literature on rational expectations and monetary theory spawned during the 'seventies is both extensive and important. What follows can only attempt to be a representative sample. The idea that the non-neutrality of money is a short-term phenomenon, dependent on individuals making mistakes, is found in Friedman, 1968 and carried further in the collective volume edited by Phelps, 1970. From the point of view of pure theory, however, the seminal paper is Lucas, 1972, which provides a fully fledged conceptual framework for the theory of rational expectations equilibrium as well as providing a thorough analysis of the major issues.

The Lucas–Sargent Proposition is discussed in several places; perhaps the most accessible treatment is Sargent and Wallace, 1975. Criticism of the proposition has come from several directions but the dividing line between believers and non-believers seems to be the question of whether prices and wages are "flexible". Models in which non-neutrality arises from sticky prices are discussed in Phelps and Taylor, 1977 and Fischer, 1977. Non-neutrality can also arise from the so-called Tobin effect (Fischer, 1979) or during the transition to rational expectations equilibrium (Taylor, 1975). Hahn, 1980, attacks along a much broader front.

More recent research has focussed on more complicated models, attempting to give a more realistic picture of the impact of monetary policy (Lucas, 1975 and Barro, 1980), and also on the technical problems of deriving solutions to, mainly linear, models with rational expectations (e.g. Blanchard, 1978, Gourieroux, *et al.*, 1979, Schiller, 1978).

There are several good surveys of these topics (Barro, 1976, Barro and Fischer, 1976 and Gordon, 1976) as well as the recent textbook by Sargent, 1979.

Chapter 2

Lucas, 1972, provides a complete conceptual framework for the theory of rational expectations equilibrium. He also raises the major theoretical issues, such as existence, uniqueness, efficiency and informational efficiency. The paper is so densely written, however, that it makes a rather forbidding introduction to the subject. The question of existence is elegantly treated in Radner, 1979, where it is shown that for a rather large class of economies almost all economies possess a completely revealing rational expectations equilibrium. The paper is also notable for its very clear exposition of the central ideas. The results have been generalized in Allen, 1977. Non-existence is discussed by Green, 1977 and Jordan and Radner, 1979. The uniqueness of rational expectations equilibrium has become quite problematical in other contexts (see the notes to Chapter 4, below). In a Lucas-type model uniqueness depends on the assumption that equilibrium is stationary and that there is no extraneous uncertainty.

The question of efficiency, although in many ways the most vexed, has not been explored very much. Two exceptions are the papers by Polemarchakis and Weiss, 1977, and Muench, 1977. The second of these papers in particular provides a rich selection of efficiency concepts. The example given in the text of the inefficiency of equilibria in which all information is revealed is variously attributed to Alchian or Arrow. It may be a "folk theorem". A more sophisticated example is given by Green, 1973. But many authors persist in treating informational efficiency (i.e. complete revelation) as tantamount to economic efficiency. For an example, see Grossman, 1978.

Informational efficiency has, of course, been the most thoroughly studied question. In the non-monetary literature the emphasis has been on finding conditions in which prices reveal full information. Examples are Radner, 1979, Grossman, 1977, Bray, 1980 and Hellwig, 1980. Grossman and Stiglitz, 1980, by contrast provide arguments against full revelation. Monetary theorists have, from the first, been more interested in the possibility that prices are a noisy signal (cf. notes to Chapter 1, above).

The best single reference is the forthcoming survey by Radner, 1980.

Chapter 3

The starting point of this chapter, like the last but one, is a paper by Lucas, 1976, but unlike Lucas, 1972, this one does not seem to have produced any imitators. Nonetheless it is something of a watershed, representing as it does a mature statement of an important tendency in the development of the theory of policy. It is essential reading for anyone who wants to understand the issues raised in this chapter.

There is a dearth of good references on game theory and on the theory of repeated games in particular. The text by Friedman, 1971, provides a good deal of useful background material. The unpublished notes by Sorin, 1980, admirably survey the theory of (zero-sum) repeated games with incomplete information, but the overlap with the discussion in the text is small. The best general reference on repeated games is the unpublished notes of Aumann, 1977.

Chapter 4

The existence of "too many" rational expectations equilibria is a serious problem for the theory. The problem was first noted (in a purely monetary context) by Black, 1974. A solution has been suggested by Brock, 1974. In his model, individuals have infinite planning horizons and this imposes a transversality condition which rules out the possibility of prices tending to infinity. This piece of analysis has been used by many authors to justify the assumption of "stability", i.e., that prices tend to their steady-state values. Unfortunately it is not hard to show that there may be many paths with this property (Taylor, 1977 and Calvo, 1978). Also, the solution cannot be applied to models of overlapping generations in which each individual has a finite planning horizon. The most thorough treatment of the problem of multiple equilibria (in the context of a simple linear model) is the paper by Gourieroux, *et al.*, 1979.

Another problem, discovered by Taylor, 1977, is the possibility of extraneous uncertainty, that is, that equilibrium prices may depend in a non-trivial way on exogenous variables which have no effect on the structure of the economy—tastes, preferences, technology and resources. These "sunspots" as they are sometimes called have an effect because they are expected to have an effect, in the same way that, in a non-stochastic equilibrium, the price level is what it is today because of the price level expected tomorrow. This idea has been discussed as well in Shiller, 1978, Gourieroux, *et al.*, 1979 and Azariadis, 1980. The trouble with this idea is that it is not easy to see how one would ever get into an equilibrium with extraneous uncertainty.

The discussion of capital market imperfections which is the main concern of this chapter has few antecedents. A few authors have studied the impact of borrowing constraints but have done so in circumstances which preclude changes in the nominal rate from having any real effect. Heller and Starr, 1978, writing in the tradition of "Keynesian" disequilibrium theory use the fix-price assumption. Pissarides, 1978 and Jackman and Sutton, 1981, study the impact of borrowing constraints on consumption. However, the collateral constraint which is quite natural for consumers (they cannot borrow against future earnings) does not apply to firms who wish to invest the money they borrow in capital goods. In any case it is only real and not nominal values that matter in these models.

Chapter 5

A great deal of what constitutes the microfoundations of monetary theory is simply ignored in this chapter because it does not belong to general-equilibrium theory. This includes, in particular, inventory-theoretic approaches to the demand for money, whether in the tradition of Tobin and Baumol (Baumol, 1952) or of Miller and Orr, 1966, and work on exchange and money such as Brunner and Meltzer, 1971. Discussion of these topics is found in Hicks, 1965, Goodhart, 1975 and Niehans, 1978. A topic which might well have been included, but was not, is the theory of transaction costs in general equilibrium. An extensive though relatively informal discussion of the economics of transaction costs is found in Niehans, 1976. The beginning of the formal theory is found in Foley, 1970 and Hahn, 1971b. The link between money, efficiency and sequences of budget constraints was hinted at in Hahn, 1971, but was made precise in Starrett, 1973 and Hahn, 1973. More recent contributions are too numerous to mention. Further references as well as an interesting synthesis may be found in Ulph and Ulph, 1978.

The model of a sequence economy which is the precursor of the one used in the text first appeared in Radner, 1972. Radner had some difficulty proving existence and an example of non-existence was later provided by Hart, 1975. Most of Hart's paper was devoted to studying the efficiency properties of sequence equilibria, however. The idea of inventing an efficiency concept to characterize equilibrium first appeared in Grossman, 1977, and the programme was extended to general production economies in Grossman and Hart, 1979. The treatment in the text generalizes and simplifies earlier results on sequence equilibria; the work on futures equilibria is new.

Chapter 6

The first and definitive statement of the problem of demonstrating the positive value of money in general equilibrium is Hahn, 1965. He proved the existence of a monetary equilibrium under rather strong assumptions which were expressed directly in terms of properties of the demand functions. Later Grandmont, 1974, gave a complete description of a model of temporary equilibrium and proved the existence of a monetary equilibrium under the assumption that price expectations were bounded. This more or less settled the question as far as the existence of temporary monetary equilibrium was concerned.

The standard reference for anything concerning the core of an economy is Hildenbrand, 1974. Some of the results concerning the sequential core of an economy with a complete set of assets were published in Gale, 1978. Some of the later results are to be found in a somewhat different form in Gale, 1981.

Chapter 7

Many of the general remarks on game theory at the beginning of the chapter are borrowed from K. Binmore, though he should not be held responsible for my version of them or the use to which I put them. The model developed in the text is a sequential and monetary analogue of the one in Hammond, 1979. The more straightforward analysis of the case where the set of assets is complete can be found in Gale, 1980b.

Shubik, 1973, also models monetary equilibrium as a non-cooperative game though in an non-sequential model and without providing any rationale for the use of money (it serves essentially as a unit of account).

References

Allen, B. (1977). "Generic Existence of Completely Revealing Equilibria for Economies with Uncertainty when Prices Convey Information." Dept. of Economics, University of California, Berkeley (unpublished).

Archibald, G. and R. Lipsey (1958). "Monetary and Value Theory: a Critique of Lange and Patinkin." *Review of Economic Studies* **26**, pp. 1–22.

Aumann, R. (1976). "Lectures on Game Theory." Stanford University (unpublished).

Azariadis, C. (1980). "Self-Fulfilling Prophecies." CARESS Discussion Paper. University of Pennsylvania.

Barro, R. (1976). "Rational Expectations and the Role of Monetary Policy." *Journal of Monetary Economics* **2**, pp. 1–32.

Barro, R. (1980). "A Capital Market in an Equilibrium Business Cycle Model." *Econometrica* **48**, pp. 1393–418.

Barro, R. and S. Fischer (1976). "Recent Developments in Monetary Theory." *Journal of Monetary Economics* **2**, pp. 133–67.

Baumol, W. (1952). "The Transactions Demand for Cash: an Inventory Theoretic Approach." *Quarterly Journal of Economics* **66**.

Black, F. (1974). "Uniqueness of Price Level in Monetary Growth Models with Rational Expectations." *Journal of Economic Theory* **7**, pp. 53–65.

Blanchard, O. (1978). "The Non-Transition to Rational Expectations." M.I.T. (unpublished).

Blume, L. and D. Easley (1979). "Learning to Be Rational." CREST Working Paper C18, University of Michigan.

Bray, M. (1980). "Learning, Estimation and Stability of Rational Expectations." Graduate School of Business, Stanford University (unpublished).

Brock, W. (1974). "Money and Growth: the Case of Long-Run Perfect Foresight." *International Economic Review* **15**, pp. 750–77.

Calvo, G. (1978). "On the Indeterminacy of Interest Rates and Wages with Perfect Foresight." *Journal of Economic Theory* **19**, pp. 321–37.

Cass, D. and M. Yaari (1966). "A Re-examination of the Pure Consumption Loans Model." *Journal of Political Economy* **74**, pp. 353–67.

Clower, R. (1968). "A Reconsideration of the Microfoundations of Monetary Theory." *Western Economic Journal* **6**, pp. 1–9.

Clower, R. editor (1969). *Monetary Theory*. London: Penguin Books.

De Canio, S. (1979). "Rational Expectations and Learning From Experience." *Quarterly Journal of Economics* **92**, pp. 47–57.

Drèze, J. (1974). *Allocation and Uncertainty: Equilibrium and Optimality*. London: Macmillan.

Dusanky, R. and P. Kalman (1978). "Illusion-free Demand Behaviour in a Monetary Economy: The General Conditions." Chapter in Kalman, 1978, pp. 49–60.

Feige, E. and M. Parkin (1971). "The Optimal Quantity of Money, Bonds, Commodity Inventories and Capital." *American Economic Review* **61**, pp. 335–49.

Fischer, S. (1977). "Long Term Contracts, Rational Expectations and the Optimal Money Supply Rule." *Journal of Political Economy* **85**, pp. 191–205.

Fischer, S. (1979). "Anticipations and the Nonneutrality of Money." *Journal of Political Economy* **87**, pp. 225–52.

Friedman, J. (1977). *Oligopoly and the Theory of Games*. Amsterdam: North Holland.

Friedman, M. (1952). "Price, Income and Monetary Changes in Three Wartime Periods." *American Economic Review Proceedings* **42**, pp. 612–25.

Friedman, M., editor (1956). *Studies in the Quantity Theory of Money*. Chicago: Chicago University Press.

Friedman, M. (1957). *A Theory of the Consumption Function*. Princeton: Princeton University Press.

Friedman, M. (1960). *A Program for Monetary Stability*. New York: Fordham.

Friedman, M. (1968). "The Role of Monetary Policy." *American Economic Review* **58**, pp. 1–17.

Friedman, M. (1969). *The Optimum Quantity of Money*. Chicago: Aldine.

Gale, Douglas (1978). "The Core of a Monetary Economy without Trust." *Journal of Economic Theory* **19**, pp. 456–91.

Gale, Douglas (1980). "Money, Information and Equilibrium in Large Economies." *Journal of Economic Theory* **23**, pp. 28–65.

Gale, Douglas (1981). "Improving Coalitions in a Monetary Economy" *Review of Economic Studies* **48**, pp. 365–84.

Goodhart, C. (1975). *Money, Information and Uncertainty*. London: Macmillan.

Gordon, R. (1980). "Recent Developments in the Theory of Inflation and Unemployment." *Journal of Monetary Economics* **2**, pp. 185–219.

Gourieroux, C., J. Laffont and A. Montfort (1979). "Rational Expectations Models: Analysis of the Solutions." INSEE Working Paper. Institut National de la Statistique et des Etudes Economiques.

Grandmont, J.-M. (1974). "On the Short Run Equilibrium in a Monetary Economy." Chapter in Drèze, 1974.

Grandmont, J.-M. and G. Laroque (1973). "Money in the Pure Consumption Loan Model." *Journal of Economic Theory* **6**, pp. 382–95.

Grandmont, J.-M. and Y. Younès (1973). "On the Efficiency of a Monetary Equilibrium." *Review of Economic Studies* **40**, pp. 149–66.

Green, J. (1973). "Information, Efficiency and Equilibrium." HIER Discussion Paper 284. Harvard University (unpublished).
Green, J. (1977). "The Nonexistence of Informational Equilibria." *Review of Economic Studies* **44**, pp. 451–63.
Grossman, S. (1977). "A Characterization of the Optimality of Equilibrium in Incomplete Markets." *Journal of Economic Theory* **15**, pp. 1–15.
Grossman, S. (1978). "Further Results on the Informational Efficiency of Competitive Stock Markets." *Journal of Economic Theory* **18**, pp. 81–101.
Grossman, S. and O. Hart (1979). "A Theory of Competitive Equilibrium in Stock Market Economies." *Econometrica* **47**, pp. 293–330.
Grossman, S. and J. Stiglitz (1980). "On the Impossibility of Informationally Efficient Markets." *American Economic Review* **70**, pp. 393–408.
Gurley, J. and E. Shaw (1960). *Money in a Theory of Finance*. Washington: The Brookings Institution.
Hahn, F. (1965). "On Some Problems of Proving the Existence of an Equilibrium in a Monetary Economy." Chapter in Hahn and Brechling, editors, 1965, pp. 126–35.
Hahn, F. (1971a). "Professor Friedman's Views on Money." *Economica* **38**, pp. 61–80.
Hahn, F. (1971b). "Equilibrium with Transaction Costs." *Econometrica* **39**, pp. 417–39.
Hahn, F. (1973). "On Transaction Costs, Inessential Sequence Economies and Money." *Review of Economic Studies* **40**, pp. 449–61.
Hahn, F. (1978). "Keynesian Economics and General Equilibrium Theory: Reflections on Some Current Debates." Chapter in Harcourt, 1978, pp. 25–40.
Hahn, F. (1980). "Monetarism and Economic Theory." *Economica* **47**, pp. 1–18.
Hahn, F. and F. Brechling, editors (1965). *Theory of Interest Rates*. London: Macmillan.
Hammond, P. (1979). "Straightforward Individual Incentive Compatibility in Large Economies." *Review of Economic Studies* **46**, pp. 263–82.
Harcourt, G., editor (1978). *The Microeconomic Foundations of Macroeconomics*. London: Macmillan.
Hart, O. (1975). "On the Optimality of Equilibrium when Markets are Incomplete." *Journal of Economic Theory* **11**, pp. 418–43.
Heller, W. and R. Starr (1979). "Capital Market Imperfection, the Consumption Function and the Effectiveness of Fiscal Policy." *Quarterly Journal of Economics* **93**, pp. 455–63.
Hellwig, M. (1980). "On the Aggregation of Information in Competitive Markets." *Journal of Economic Theory* **22**, pp. 477–98.
Hicks, J. (1965). *Critical Essays in Monetary Theory*. Oxford: Oxford University Press.
Hildenbrand, W. (1974). *Core and Equilibria of a Large Economy*. Princeton: Princeton University Press.

Jackman, R. and J. Sutton (1981). "Imperfect Capital Markets and the Monetarist Black Box: Liquidity Constraints, Inflation and the Asymmetric Effects of Interest Rate Policy." ICERD Working Paper, London School of Economics.

Johnson, H. (1962). "Monetary Theory and Policy." *American Economic Review* **52**, pp. 335–84.

Johnson, H. (1969). "Inside Money, Outside Money, Income, Wealth and Welfare in Monetary Theory." *Journal of Money, Credit and Banking* **1**, pp. 30–45.

Johnson, H. (1970). "Is there an Optimum Money Supply." *Journal of Finance*, pp. 435–42.

Johnson, H. and J. Frenkel, editors (1977). *The Monetary Approach to the Balance of Payments*. London: Allen and Unwin.

Jordan, J. and R. Radner (1979). "The Nonexistence of Rational Expectations Equilibria: a Robust Example." Department of Economics, University of Minnesota (unpublished).

Kalman, P. (1978). *Some Aspects of the Foundations of General Equilibrium Theory*. New York: Springer Verlag.

Keynes, J. M. (1936). *The General Theory of Employment, Interest and Money*. London: Macmillan.

Kreps, D. (1978). "A Representation Theorem for 'Preference for Flexibility'." Graduate School of Business Research Paper No. 419, Stanford University.

Lipsey, R. (1960). "The Relation between Unemployment and the Rate of Change and Money Wage Rates in the United Kingdom, 1862–1952: a Further Analysis." *Economica* **27**, pp. 1–31.

Lucas, R. (1972). "Expectations and the Neutrality of Money." *Journal of Economic Theory* **4**, 103–24.

Lucas, R. (1975). "An Equilibrium Model of the Business Cycle." *Journal of Political Economy* **83**, pp. 1113–45.

Lucas, R. (1976). "Econometric Policy Evaluation: a Critique." *Journal of Monetary Economics* **2**, pp. 19–46.

Lucas, R. and L. Rapping (1969). "Real Wages, Employment and Inflation." *Journal of Political Economy* **77**, pp. 721–54.

Mas-Colell, A. (1978). "An Axiomatic Approach to the Efficiency of Non-Cooperative Equilibrium in Economies with a Continuum of Traders." IMSSS Technical Report 274. Stanford University.

Metzler, L. (1951). "Wealth, Saving and the Rate of Interest." *Journal of Political Economy* **59**, pp. 93–116.

Miller, M. and D. Orr (1966). "A Model of the Demand for Money by Firms." *Quarterly Journal of Economics* **80**, pp. 413–35.

Modigliani, F. (1944). "Liquidity Preference and the Theory of Interest and Money." *Econometrica* **12**, pp. 45–88.

Muench, T. (1977). "Optimality, the Interaction of Spot and Futures Markets and the Nonneutrality of Money in the Lucas Model." *Journal of Economic Theory* **15**, pp. 325–44.

Niehans, J. (1978). *The Theory of Money*. Baltimore: Johns Hopkins University Press.

Okuno, M. and I. Zilcha (1980). "On the Efficiency of a Competitive Equilibrium in Infinite Horizon Monetary Economies." *Review of Economic Studies* **47**, pp. 797–808.

Patinkin, D. (1965). *Money, Interest and Prices*. New York: Harper and Row.

Perlman, M. (1971). "The Roles of Money in an Economy and the Optimum Quantity of Money." *Economica* **38**, pp. 233–52.

Phelps, E. (1967). "Phillips Curves, Expectations of Inflation and Optimal Unemployment Over Time." *Economica* **34**, pp. 254–81.

Phelps, E. *et al.* (1970). *The Microeconomic Foundations of Employment and Inflation Theory*. New York: Norton.

Phelps, E. and J. Taylor (1977). "Stabilizing Powers of Monetary Policy under Rational Expectations." *Journal of Political Economy* **85**, pp. 163–90.

Phillips, A. (1958). "The Relation between Unemployment and the Rate of Change of Money Wage Rates in the United Kingdom, 1862–1957." *Economica* **25**, pp. 283–99.

Pissarides, C. (1978). "Liquidity Considerations in the Theory of Consumption." *Quarterly Journal of Economics* **92**, pp. 279–96.

Polemarchakis, H. and L. Weiss (1977). "On the Desirability of a 'Totally Random' Monetary Policy." *Journal of Economic Theory* **15**, pp. 345–50.

Radner, R. (1972). "Existence of Equilibrium of Plans, Prices and Price Expectations in a Sequence of Markets." *Econometrica* **40**, pp. 289–303.

Radner, R. (1979). "Rational Expectations Equilibrium: Generic Existence and the Information Revealed by Prices." *Econometrica* **47**, pp. 655–78.

Radner, R. (1980). "Equilibrium Under Uncertainty." Chapter in Arrow and Intriligator, editors, *Handbook of Mathematical Economics* Volume II. Amsterdam: North Holland (forthcoming).

Sargent, T. (1979). *Macroeconomic Theory*. New York: Academic Press.

Sargent, T. and N. Wallace (1975). "Rational Expectations, the Optimal Monetary Instrument and the Optimal Money Supply Rule." *Journal of Political Economy* **83**, pp. 241–57.

Samuelson, P. (1958). "An Exact Consumption Loan Model with or without the Social Contrivance of Money." *Journal of Political Economy* **66**, pp. 467–82.

Samuelson, P. (1968). "What Classical and Neo-Classical Monetary Theory Really Was." *Canadian Journal of Economics* **1**, pp. 1–15.

Schwödiauer, G., editor (1978). *Equilibrium and Disequilibrium in Economic Theory*. Boston: Reidel.

Shiller, S. (1978). "Rational Expectations and the Dynamic Structure of Macroeconomic Models—a Critical Review." *Journal of Monetary Economics* **4**, pp. 1–44.

Shubik, M. (1973). "Commodity Money, Oligopoly, Credit and

Bankruptcy in a General Equilibrium Model." *Western Economic Journal* **11**, pp. 24–8.

Shultze, C. (1959). *Recent Inflation in the U.S.*, Study Paper No. 1, Study of Employment, Growth and Price Levels. Washington: Joint Economic Committee, 86th Congress, 1st Session.

Sorin, S. (1980). "An Introduction to Two-Person Zero Sum Repeated Games with Incomplete Information." IMSSS Technical Report No. 312, Stanford University.

Starrett, D. (1973). "Inefficiency and the Demand for Money in a Sequence Economy." *Review of Economic Studies* **40**, pp. 437–48.

Taylor, J. (1975). "Monetary Policy during a Transition to Rational Expectations." *Journal of Political Economy* **83**, pp. 1009–21.

Taylor, J. (1977). "Conditions for Unique Solutions in Stochastic Macroeconomic Models with Rational Expectations." *Econometrica* **45**, pp. 1377–86.

Townsend, R. (1978). "Market Anticipations, Rational Expectations and Bayesian Analysis." *International Economic Review* **19**, pp. 481–94.

Ulph, A. and D. Ulph (1978). "Efficiency, Inessentiality and the Debreu Property of Prices." Chapter in Schwödiauer, 1978, pp. 337–62.

Index